OPPORTUNITIES FOR INDUSTRY

AND THE

SAFE INVESTMENT OF CAPITAL;

OR,

A Thousand Chances

TO MAKE MONEY.

BY E. T. FREEDLEY.

FOURTH THOUSAND.

PHILADELPHIA:
J. B. LIPPINCOTT & CO.
1859.

PHILADELPHIA:
STEREOTYPED BY GEORGE CHARLES.
PRINTED BY KING & BAIRD,
607 SANSOM STREET.

INDEX.

PAGE

ACID, for Preserving Meat, ... 86
Acorns, for Coffee, ... 328
Acre, what may be raised on one, ... 61
ADULTERATION of Liquors, frightful,... 340
" Profits of,.................. 341
Adventures, Commercial, ... 242
ADVERTISING, fortunes made by........43–48
AFRICA, trade with,......... 251
" exports of, ... 252
AGENCIES, Commercial, ... 283
Agents, chances for, ... 78
Ailanthus, the,.................................. 177
ALCHEMY and Astrology,................... 25
" Researches in,..................... 49
ALCOHOL, from what produced,.......... 346
" from Chinese Sugar Cane, ... 346
" new sources of,.................. 347
ALLIGATORS, uses for,........................ 335
ALLOYS, chance for a fortune in,......... 387
" principal kinds of,................ 388
" for Jewelry,........................ 310
Allspice, or Pimento,......................... 217
ALOES, cultivation and profits of,. 217
Alum, Ammoniacal,........................... 337
ALUMINUM, uses of,...... 303
" cost of preparing, ... 304
AMERICA, singular discovery of,......... 27
Americans, enterprise of,................... 223
Ants, how to drive away,.................. 349
APPLES, nineteen ways to preserve,.... 239
" Pell's method of shipping,..... 240
Amazon, riches in the Valley of,.. 258
Arizona, mines in, ... 000
Arrow-root, cultivation and profits of, 215
ARTIFICIAL SUBSTITUTES for various costly objects,................................ 306
ASBESTUS, uses of,............................ 299
" remarkable properties of,300–301
Asparagus, for Coffee, ... 328
Assumptions, (the author's),............... 82
Antigua, chances in,......................... 192
ASTOR, JOHN J., early history of,........ 39
" commercial operations, ... 40
" investments in real estate 40
" first thousand dollars,............ 55

BAKING, fortunes made in,................. 78
Balloons, future of,................ 379
BAMBOO, uses of in China.................. 138
Bananas, value of,........................... 208
BARNUM, P. T., on advertising,.......... 46
BARKS, valuable,..... 725–377

BARKS for Tanning,......................281–282
Bean Soup, how to make,.................. 62
BEEF AND PORK, how to pack,.......236–238
BEER Root, ... 388
" Spruce,...................................... 389
" excellent Table,....................... 389
BEET ROOT, for Sugar, ...127–130
Bene Plant, the,............................... 185
BEVERAGES,....................................... 340
BLACKING, how to make,. 389
" for Harness,..................... 389
Biche de Mar, or Sea-Slug,................ 80
Boils, cure for, ... 390
Bolivia, mines in,............................ . 261
BOOTS AND SHOES, how to preserve,..... 390
Boxwood tree, the 170
Brazil, Diamond mines in,............. . 261
BRANDY, cost of,.......................... ... 341
" profits in,............................ 341
" adulteration of, ... 341
BRICKS, to ship to Russia,.................. 254
Buffalo, value of domestic,................ 365
Bugs, how to destroy,....................... 349
BUILDINGS, new material for,....... 230
BURNING FLUIDS, substitutes for,........ 335
BUTTER, as an article of export,......... 230
" improvement in making,...... 320
" best mode of making,........... 231
" qualities of good,............231–232
" kind of firkins to be used for,. 232
" to restore rancid,................. 233
" Philadelphia,........................ 154

Cahoun Palm, the,............................ 215
Calcium, Oxy-sulphuret of,............... 181
CALIFORNIA, profits of farming in,..... 75
" of Quartz mining in,....... 370
" Water Companies in, ... 372
CAMEL, the, in the United States,....... 360
" best varieties of,..................... 361
Camphor Tree, the............................ 164
CANDLES, to improve tallow, ... 360
" from lard,......................... 361
Capital, how to get,,......................... 66
Cardamom Plant, the,........................ 176
Castor Oil Plant, the,........................ 175
CASSAREEP,....................................86–206
Cassava, or the Manioc, ... 206
" profits of growing,.............. 207
Cat, once a fortune,.......................... 28
CATTLE, South American,.................. 84
" in Venezuela,......... 85

PAGE
CATTLE, in Russia,........................... 256
Cedron, value of,............................ 276
CEMENTS, receipts for,...................320–325
" Portland, ... 320
" Hydraulic, ... 320
" for Marble,....................... 321
" Diamond,.......................... 321
" Wash, a great,.................... 323
" for Glass, China, etc.............. 324
CHINA, a great field for commerce,..... 262
" hints respecting,..................... 263
" what to ship to,...................... 266
China, cheap in Belgium,................. 273
" cements for mending,.................. 321
China Grass, value of the,............... 156
CHINESE, how they make money,....... 68
" SUGAR CANE,..................132–133
" " for Alcohol,...... 347
" quick-growing Rice,............ 157
" shrewdness of the,.............. 265
CHOCOLATE, how to make,.................. 391
" specific for low spirits,..... 391
CIDER, how to make good,....... 342
" receipt for improving,............ 343
Cigars, machine for making,.............. 340
CITIES, new plan of building,............ 368
CLOCKS AND WATCHES, for China,....... 266
" for Russia,...... 253
CLOTHING, revolution in manufacture of,.. 354
COAL, products from,........................ 337
" compared with wood,................ 353
" cheap substitute for,................ 314
" lands, fortunes in, ... 38
Coca Plant, the,............................. 163
COCOA, OR CACAO,.............................. 198
" profits of cultivating, ... 199
COCO-NUT Palm, cultivation and profits of,................................ 211–215
Cockroaches, to destroy,.................... 349
Colts, how to break,......................399–404
COFFEE, growing in W. Indies,......199–202
" consumption of,.................... 200
" substitutes for, ... 328
Columbus, error of,.......................... 27
COLZA Plant, for oil,........................ 183
Coolies in the Mauritius,................... 124
COOKERY, Schools,.................... 382
COMMERCE, origin of,........................ 20
" profitable openings in,......... 224
" chances in,...................223–288
" new fields for,.................. 241
CONTRACTS, fortunes in,....................31–71
CORDIALS, receipts for,...................... 392
CORN, King Philip or brown,............. 149
" large yield of,........................ 221
COSMETICS, best kinds,....................... 393
" receipts for,...................... 393
COTTON, trade with England,............. 79
" machine for spinning,........... 118
" industry, revolution in,......... 119
" yarns, profits of making, ... 120
" plantations, steam for,.......... 119
" profits of planting, ... 106
" prices of for 43 years,............ 107
" cost of raising one pound,..... 108
" price in Mobile for 14 years,.. 109
" operations in planting,.....110–113

PAGE
COTTON, improvements wanted,.......... 114
" best localities for planting,.... 115
" in Texas,............................... 116
" in Mexico,............................. 116
" plants, varieties of,............... 117
" best variety,.......................... 117
" the best opportunity for profit in,....................................... 118
" in linen, how to detect,......... 394
Cotton Seed, for oil,......................... 188
" cake, value of,............... 188
COVERLETS, prices of,........................ 21
Crœsus, wealth of, ... 23
Crocodiles, how captured in Siam,...... 335
Croton Oil,.. 187

Dandelion roots, for coffee,................ 329
Delirium Tremens, how to cure,........ 305
DEER, domestication of, ... 364
Dexter, and his Warming Pans,......... 29
Diamonds in Brazil,.......................... 261
Dinner, a cheap,.............................. 56
DITCHES, value of in California,......... 372
Drugs, manufacture of,..................... 169
DRUNKENNESS, cures for, ... 395
Dye-woods, new,..........................277–281

ECONOMY, aids in,...... 56
EDGE TOOLS, how to sharpen without whetting,.. 395
Eggs, quantity laid per year,............ 99
EGYPT, sources of fortunes in,........... 19
" trade with, ... 250
" fertility of land in,................ 20
Emeralds, how to make,.................... 308
Engravings, how to whiten,............... 396

FARMING, profits of,.......................... 220
" future of,.......................... 222
Fans, making of, ... 381
FEAR, power of,................................ 10
Figs, receipt for home-made,............. 396
FIRES, annihilator for,....................... 348
" how to extinguish,.................. 348
Fire Kindler, a cheap,....................... 396
FIRE PROOF, how to render dresses,... 396
" clothing from Asbestus,.. 300
FISH, for Russia,.............................. 253
" a valuable,........................ 374
FLAX AND HEMP, chances to make money in,.......................... 140–146
Flies, to keep from meats,.................. 350
FLORIDA, farming in,......................... 74
" Tobacco growing in, ... 140
Flying machines, a reality,................ 379
FLOWER FARMS, chance in,................ 181
Food, substances for,. 60
" waste of, in United States,......... 384
FORESTS, value of,............................ 179
FORTUNES in ancient times,................ 17
" of the old Romans,.............. 22
" in modern times,................. 28
" in Silver mines,................... 30
" in land,.............................. 37
Frankincense tree, the,...................... 180
FRANKLIN, rules of, for money getting,....................... 14
Franklinite, composition of,............... 295

PAGE
FRANCE, earnings of peasants in,........ 56
" salted meats in,.................... 234
FRUITS, growing near large cities,....... 86
" profit of shipping, ... 238
" how to preserve,.................. 239
Fuels, artificial, ... 314
FURS, profits of trade in,.................... 39
" prices of, in Russia,................... 253

GARDENS, in the South,..................... 77
Gas Burners, soapstone for............... 302
GERMANS, success of,.......................... 76
GERMAN SILVER, best kind of,............ 388
GINGER, the Plant,............ ....174, 217
" POP, receipt for,....................... 396
GINSENG, growth of,......................... 267
" value of, in China,.............. 268
GIRARD, STEPHEN,............................ 40
Glass Stopples, how to extract,.......... 397
GLYCERIN, for Tobacco,..................... 339
" " Boils,........................ 390
GOATS, value of,................................ 362
GOLD, artificial, how made,............... 309
" iron converted into,................. 310
" mining,....................................... 370
Graphite, (see *Plumbago*)................. 305
GRASS, new varieties of,.................... 153
Greece, manufactures in,................... 21
GROUND NUTS, profits in,................... 184
GUANO, great speculation in,............. 31
GUM, a new,...................................... 285
" Arabic, ... 180
GUNS, rules for loading,..................... 397
Gutta Percha, artificial,.................... 312

HAIR, specifics for,........................... 398
" dyes, for,...................................... 398
" to remove superfluous,............. 399
HEMP, new varieties of,..................... 145
" the Sisal,.................................... 146
HENS, how to make lay,..................... 101
" number in United States,.......... 99
" proper food for,........................ 100
HOMINY, how to cook,....................... 62
Horse Chestnuts for Starch,............... 377
HORSES, Rarey's method of taming,399–404
HYDROPHOBIA, cures for,................... 404

ICE, how to make artificially,............ 314
ICE-CREAM, how to make,.................. 405
Illinois, profits of farming in,........... 74
India Rubber, artificial, ... 312
INDIGO cultivation and profit of,....202–205
INKS, receipts for,............................. 406
Ink, Indelible, and how to take out,. 407
INVENTIONS, to make money in,.....289–356
IRON AND STEEL, improvements in,..... 293
" Meteoric,................................... 297

JACKS, new breed of,......................... 93
JAMAICA, chances in,........................ 218
JAPAN, ... 268
" profits of Dutch trade with,.... 269
JEWS, as merchants,.......................... 21
JEWELRY, imitation,.......................... 310
Jujube Paste, receipt for, ... 407
JUTE, Indian,.................................... 156
" manufacture of,........................ 157

PAGE
KANSAS, lands in, ... 368

LABOR, the father of capital,............ 66
" chances for,.........................66–81
" profits of free over slave in the Mauritius, ... 124
Land Warrants, locating, ... 368
Larch, the Russian,........................... 180
LEAD MINES, new value of,................ 330
" " Zinc in,.......................... 330
LEAD PENCILS, fortune made in,......... 44
" " how to tell good,......... 305
LEATHER, new kinds of,..................... 333
" Porpoise and Alligator,...... 334
LEMONS AND ORANGES,....................... 159
Light-Houses, oil for,........................ 183
Linen, how to detect cotton in,........... 393
Liquorice,... 170
LITTLE, J., stock operations of,.......... 33
LLAMA AND ALPACA,........................... 363
Locomotives, alloys for,..................... 388
Longworth, Nicholas,.....................38, 105
LOSSES, great, from small causes, illustrated, ... 65
Low spirits, cure for,......................... 391

Manilla Hemp, ... 243
Mangel Wurzel Coffee,...................... 328
MANUFACTURES, chances in,...........289–357
MAPLE SUGAR, profits in,...............130–132
MARBLE, new deposit of,.................... 283
" artificial,.................................. 316
" coating for plaster,.............. 317
" facing for buildings,............ 317
MAURITIUS, cyclones in, ... 9
" superiority of free over slave labor in,.............. 124
" Sugar in,.......................... 124
MEADOWS, ARTIFICIAL,........................ 369
MEAT, how to preserve in a fresh state, 85
" putrid, how restored,............... 87
" Biscuit, value of,...................... 87
MEATS, salted,.................................. 234
" European demand for,............. 235
Medicinal Plants and Extracts,......169–176
MEXICO, Cotton in,........................... 213
" NEW, Soap Weed in,............. 189
" " gum in,.......................... 285
Mice, to drive away, ... 350
MILK, Artificial,................................ 313
" how to keep sweet,................. 409
" preservation of, ... 234
" solidified, ... 234
MILLIONAIRES, not always Ricardos,... 15
" of Boston,.................. 51
" of New York,.............. 52
" of Philadelphia,.......... 52
Milk of Wax, an excellent cosmetic,.. 393
MINERALS, neglected varieties of,....... 299
MINES, SILVER,.................................. 374
" profits of quartz,................... 370
" science applied to, ... 329
Mistakes, common and fatal,............. 79
MONEY GETTING, not a lost art,.......... 11
MONOPOLIES, English,...... 30
" in land,........................ 36
Morris, Robert, losses of,.................. 366
MULES, profits of raising, ... 92

PAGE

MULES, speculation in, 92
" best breed of, 94
MUSEUMS, for manufactures, 384
Muslins, fineness of in India, 24
MUSQUITOES, how exterminated in China, 349–352

Natural History Depot, universal, 384
Negroes, a good chance for, 219
Newspapers and Magazines, 50
Nickel, 297, 388
NOVELTIES in commerce, 272
" in manufactures, 293–357
Nurseries, profits of, 77

OAKS, new varieties of, 179–180
Oatmeal Porridge, excellence of, 61
Oca Plant, the, 164
OILS, a great variety of plants yielding, 181–187
" essential, how made, 311
" how to bleach cheaply, 409
" a good filter for, 409
" machinery for, 181
" seeds for, 182
OLIVE TREE, the 161
" production of, 161
" cultivation of the, 162
OPIUM, growing of in U. States, 170
" importation of, 171
" cost of producing, 172
" profits of shipping, 30
ORANGES AND LEMONS, groves of in Florida, 159
OTTOMAN EMPIRE, a field for commerce, 248
" to establish manufactures in, 249
Ouvrard, speculations of, 43
OYSTERS, a great trade in, 227
" a new chance for profit in, 228

PACKING GOODS, hints for, 286
Panic and Commercial Revulsion, different, 10
PANICS, Letters to a victim of, 9
PAPER, new materials for, 382
" from the Sorgho Cane, 133
" mills in the South, 290
Paraffine, profits of making, 338
PARAGUAY, trade with, 259
" Tea, or *Maté*, 168
" products of, 260
Paste, an excellent, for envelopes, 409
PATENTS for improved liquors, 340
" the most profitable, 50
Pearls, artificial, how made, 309
PERFUMERY, art of, 393
" essential oils for, 311
PERRY, how made, 344
Peruvian Bark, for quinine, 275
Petroleum, value of, 336
Peppermint, cultivation of, in U. S., 187
Pewter, how made, 388
PHILIPPINE ISLANDS, trade with, 243
Phœnicians, achievements of, 21
Photography, foundation of, 20
PLANTAINS AND BANANAS, 208
" dried, value of, 209

PAGE

PLANTAINS, growing in United States, 210
PLANTS, new varieties of, 149–176
" Medicinal, 169–176
" Oleaginous, 181
" Saponaceous, 189
" a new kind wanted, 353
PLUMBAGO, uses of, 305
" whence obtained, 305
" reward for discovery in, 306
Pomades from flowers, 181
Ponies, Canadian, value of, 366
Poppy, cultivation of, 170
PORK, how to pack, 237
Pork and Beans, as food, 62
Poultry, (see *Hens*), 99–102
POTATOES, a new use for, 377
" substitutes for, 150–153
" unsound, for Starch, 377
POTTERY AND PORCELAIN, chances in, 379
PRICES of 11 articles for 31 years, 288
" of Sugar, 123
" of Cotton, 107
Produce, Western, chance in, 285
Provisions, hints to shippers of, 235
Publishing, a precarious business, 50

Quassia Plant, the, 173
Quinine from new substances, 306

REINDEER, fleetness of the, 364
Rhatany Plant, 173
Rhubarb Plant, 174
" Chinese, 175
RICE, a quick ripening, 157
Rome, source of fortunes in, 22
Rouge, an excellent cosmetic, 393
ROTHSCHILD'S mode of speculating in Stocks, 32
Rubies, how to make, 308
RUSSIA, trade with, 252
" what to ship to, 253–255
" what we may import from, 256

SALT, Liverpool, 237
" manufacture of, 375
Salts, new from sea-water, 377
SAPPHIRES, how to make, 308
SARDINES, in California, 374
SAVINGS, accumulation of small, 64
Schools, Cookery, 382
SCIENCE, progress of, 306
SEA SLUG, description of, 80
" profits of trade in, 81
SEEDS, produce of oil from, 182
" and plants, new varieties of, 146
SECRETS AND RECEIPTS, 387
SEWING AND STITCHING MACHINES, 355
SHEEP, quantity of in U. States, 94
" cost of raising in the South, 95
" profits of raising, 95
" raising in New Zealand, 97
" varieties of, 98
" a new breed, 98
" raising among the Hebrews, 18
SHIPPING, Chances in, 225
SIAM, trade with, 245
" produce of, 246
" articles adapted for shipment to, 247

PAGE
SILK, in the East, ... 25
" wild, in Nicaragua, ... 284
Silk Cotton, ... 285
SILVER in Mexico and Peru, ... 29
Silicic Acid, remarkable qualities of, .. 382
Silicium, worth five times as much as Silver, ... 332
SINGAPORE, a good market, ... 244
SLATE, new uses for, ... 303
SLAVES, profits of trade in, ... 34
" raising, ... 35
" cost of keeping, ... 56
Small-wares, making of, ... 381
SOAPS, plants yielding, ... 189–192
SOAPSTONE, or Steatite, ... 302
Soda, a great deposit of, ... 277
Solder, composition of, ... 324–388
SOUPS, receipts for cheap, ... 410
Speculum Metal, composition of, ... 388
SPECULATIONS, good, *passim* ...
" losses by, in wild lands, 366
Spices, former profits in, ... 26
Steam Carriages for common roads, ... 378
Steam Engines in Russia, ... 254
STEEL, ... 293
" Hindoo process of making, ... 294
STOCKS, fortunes made and lost in, ... 33
STOCK RAISING, ... 88–92
STONES, Artificial, how made, ... 319
Solomon, mercantile adventures of, ... 21
SOUTH AMERICA, trade with, ... 258
" productiveness of, ... 258
SUBSTITUTES, Artificial, for Natural Objects, ... 306
SUGAR, profit of cultivating, in Louisiana, Florida, Texas, etc., 121–135
" Beet Root, ... 127–130
" Maple, profits of, ... 132
" " in Michigan, ... 131
" " in Canada, ... 131
" from Sorghum or Chinese Cane, 132
" results of experiments with, ... 134
SUGAR MILLS in Siam, ... 292
SULPHUR in Mexico, ... 282
Sulphuric Acid from Pyrites, ... 283
SYRIA, trade with, ... 250

TALLOW, trees yielding, ... 191
" how to purify, ... 391
Tamarind tree, the, ... 180
TANNING, short process for, ... 333
" new substances for, ... 278
TEA, grown in U. States, ... 166
" packing, fortune made in, ... 79
Teel tree, the ... 187
TEXAS, profits of farming in, ... 73
" stock-raising in, ... 88–92
TIMBER, cheap method of preserving, .. 412
" for Russia, ... 254
" profit of shipping, ... 225
" American appreciated, ... 225
TOBACCO growing in the United States, Cuba, etc., ... 135–140
" seed for oil, ... 187
" and profit of shipping, ... 226
" substitutes for, ... 339
" Glycerin, ... 339
Tooth Powders, receipts for, ... 413

PAGE
TREES, growing of, ... 176–181
" valuable kinds of, ... 180
" profits of, ... 176
" promote health, ... 179
" best fertilizer for, ... 180
" a good speculation in, ... 177
Trinidad, chances in, ... 192
Turning Lathes, alloys for, ... 388
TURKEY, trade with, ... 248–251
Type-Metal, composition of, ... 388
Tyre and Sidon, riches of, ... 20

UMBRELLAS, novelties in, ... 381

Vanilla Plant, the, ... 174
VAN RENSELLAERS, family of, ... 37
VEGETABLES, dried, profit of shipping, 229
" mode of preparing, ... 229
VENEZUELA, cattle in, ... 85
" trade with, ... 261
Vessels and Steamboats, demand for, . 269
" line of, to circumnavigate the globe, ... 271
VIRGINIA, richest man in, ... 36
VINEGAR, from Cane juice, ... 126
" new source of, ... 127
VINEYARDS in France, ... 102
" in United States, ... 103
" best locality for, ... 104

WANTS, fortunes in supplying certain, 356
War, cost of Russian, ... 42
Water Companies, profits of, in California, ... 373
WATER, how to make hard soft, ... 413
" as a fertilizer, ... 370
Wax, trees bearing, ... 191
Welding Powder, receipts for, ... 324
WEST INDIES, British, chances in, .192–220
West India products, table of, ... 197
WHEAT, Turkish Flint, ... 147
" Adelaide or Australian, ... 148
" for Coffee, ... 329
WHITTINGTON, RICHARD, singular history of, ... 28
WILLOW, cultivation of the, ... 357
" varieties of, ... 358
Wind-mills, improvements in, ... 290
WINE, profits of making, ... 102
" prices of, ... 103
" manufacture of, an art, ... 105
" how to secure great profits in, .. 106
" from Pears, ... 345
" substitutes for Grapes in making, ... 345
" from Pine Apples, exquisite, ... 346
" domestic receipts for, ... 413
WOMEN, earnings of, ... 70
WOOD, effect of Silicic acid on, ... 331
" how to render fire-proof, ... 349
" compared with Coal, ... 353
WOODS, Dye, profits in, ... 279
" IMITATION, ... 324–327
" how to color, ... 325
WOOL, average price of, ... 96

YAM, the Chinese, ... 150
Yarns, profits of making, ... 120

OPPORTUNITIES FOR INDUSTRY.

A LETTER TO A VICTIM OF THE LATE PANIC.

My Dear Sir

You inform me that you are one of the sufferers by the financial tornado which, stealthily as a pestilence, recently visited our land, eclipsing the cyclones of the Mauritius and the simoom of Arabia in power of destruction, utterly prostrating houses whose foundations, it was supposed, were laid upon boulders of gold, and teaching a new generation the old lesson of the uncertainty of fortune. Your anathemas upon those who intensified what would have been simply a Commercial Revulsion, making it a fearful Panic, can only be justified in view of the magnitude of your losses. You forget, momentarily, moderation and law and order, in contending that their property should be taken from them and divided amongst their victims, and they whipped, as rascals, naked through the land. You do not admit, that even in a free country, proud of its liberal legislation, men should be permitted to speculate in distress; and argue that something stronger than conscience is necessary to restrain them from so speculating, whether in Sugar, Cotton, or Stocks, that war, pestilence, blight, monetary disturbances, and especially panics, will be to them a godsend. Human nature under such circumstances, it is evident, is quite too weak to resist the temptation to aid in producing what would be so manifestly profitable Every artifice that can be devised is resorted to, to frighten men; past troubles are pointed to as portents of future sorrows; and the cloud, no bigger than a man's hand, is persistently magnified into an omen of terrible import. How destructive an agent fear may be, is not by any means a modern discovery. Fear was worshiped as a god by the Lacedemonians; Solomon noted its influence and observed that men sometimes draw those misfortunes they suspect upon their own heads, and that which they fear shall come upon them; physicians have remarked that predictions of sickness by strolling soothsayers have come to pass, and been literally fulfilled, through the agency of the imagination in producing sickness at the time predicted; and in more than one instance, the dread of dying or apprehension of death has driven men to suicide. The fears of mankind are like enraged elephants in battle, as dangerous to friend as to foe. In the commercial world especially, resting as the superstructure does upon man's confidence in his neighbor, it is not difficult, at certain times, when the air is surcharged with the miasma of extravagance, for designing men to strike away the prop, cause a sudden affright or panic, and induce their neighbors to pull those misfortunes they apprehend upon their own heads. A Commercial Revulsion ordinarily results from a combination of circumstances over which individuals can hardly be said to have any control; a Commercial Panic is very different in its essence, nature, and consequences; and, unlike the former, may be produced by instruments in themselves very contemptible.

But the *causes* of the late financial disasters seem at this day, probably, to their involuntary victims, a matter of minor concern. The man whose wagon is overturned into the gutter, is in no fit mood to discuss the philosophy of accidents. Even the stereotyped phrases of consolation sound like a mockery of distress. You are now in doubt whether, "whatever is, is right." Fortune, you say, may be a fickle jade, but "why did she kick me down stairs?" It is difficult for you to understand that "partial evil" can be "universal good." To be *sans argent*, says Burton in his inimitable *Anatomy*, will cause a deep and grievous melancholy. Many persons are affected like Irishmen in this behalf, who, if they have a good cimeter, had rather have a blow on their arm than their weapon hurt: they will sooner lose their life than their goods. He instances that a poor fellow went to hang himself, but finding by chance a pot of money, flung away the rope and went merrily home; but he that hid the gold, when he missed it, hanged himself with that rope which the other man had left. I will only recommend to you the example and philosophy of David, who said: "While the child was yet alive, I fasted and wept; but being now dead, why should I fast? Can I bring him back again?"

You ask me—and the query is symptomatic of improved mental health—"Is money-getting a lost art? Are all sorts of business equally uncertain in their results? Are the wings of riches always outspread for flight?" I am happy to reply to these interrogatories in the negative. Money-getting is not a lost art; all sorts of business are uncertain, but not equally so. It is probable that we are at the commencement of an era when fortunes will be acquired with a rapidity unknown, save in rare instances, in past times. The percentage of profits will gradually be less, but the aggregate of profits, as well as of business accruing to individuals, will be unprecedented and astounding. For the last half century the world has been "putting up its machinery"—its railways, steamships, telegraphs and lightning presses—and is now, we may say, for the first time, ready to do business. Never before were there such facilities for converting raw materials into finished fabrics—never before could an agriculturist, or manufacturer, or merchant, apprize so many people simultaneously that he can supply a want. So far from being a lost art, it is probable that Money-getting will become so common an art, that the possession of wealth will not be esteemed a claim to consideration. Even now when fortunes it is known are made while standing in mud-puddles in the gold diggings of California and Australia, or by accidentally betting right on the "little joker" of the stock market, the man of wealth is looked upon much in the light of a money-bag—useful, but not necessarily respectable. It is certainly poor consolation to him who has strained every faculty of body and mind, throughout a long life, in accumulating Money, to discover, when at length he has succeeded, that the journeyman gas-fitter of last year, can to-day, in consequence of a series of fortunate speculations, buy him out, and give his life-long accumulations away without impoverishing himself. But what more than any thing else tends to degrade wealth, as a test of final success, is its fleeting, transient, and unreliable nature. When a gale may burst out of a clear sky, like the Panic of 1857, and dissipate the accumulations of years as the dew of the morning; and especially when the wealthiest may calculate, with reasonable certainty, that his descendants, even in the third generation, will probably be candidates for the almshouse, the dullest perception realizes that the merchandise of wisdom is better than the merchandise of silver. Impressed, perhaps, with conviction of this truth, some of our men of money very wisely expend a small portion of their fortune in hiring men of brains to transmit their names to posterity in writings; whilst others seek a refuge from immediate annihilation by piling up bricks or stones, in monuments upon their bones.

But while much wealth is only rarely a blessing, the want of money is nearly always an evil. The very poor, God help them! Your other inquiry, therefore, is one entitled to very respectful and careful consideration, viz.: WHAT ARE THE CHANCES TO MAKE MONEY? You say, that being compelled to begin the world anew, you wish to select wisely from a variety of well-defined opportunities, open to a man of enterprise with some capital; and you inquire from what published source you can obtain the desired information. Books have been written on the principles of doing business, and on the Laws of Business, on Accounts, etc., but I know of no book detailing the openings for trade and the Chances for profitable industry, or, in a word, showing *how fortunes have been made and can be made.* Our professional authors entertain a profound contempt for Money, Money-getting, and Money-makers, and they, of course, will not write such books. It is true publishers do say that valuable manuscripts cannot be obtained, except for a valuable consideration; and that the author of the "Sin of Covetousness" higgled for a long time about a penny more copyright; but has not Bulwer demonstrated in that novel of his, *Zanoni,* that "our *opinions* are the angel part of us, our *acts* the earthly"? The literary celebrities of the world would, I imagine, be sorely puzzled to answer your question. Bulwer would be more perplexed *what to do with it*, than with the disposal of "Jasper Loseley" or "Guy Darrell." Dickens would rather write another "Bleak House," detailing how money can be lost in Chancery, and Thackeray, another "Vanity Fair." Even our distinguished poet, the author of "*Hiawatha*" and "*Miles Standish*," could hardly be expected to originate any thing better on the subject than the following epigram of his brother poet:

"I will tell you a plan for gaining wealth,
Better than banking, trading, or leases;
Take a bank note and fold it up,
And then you will find your wealth *increases*.

"This wonderful plan, without danger or loss,
Keeps your cash in your hand, and with nothing to trouble it;
And every time that you fold it across,
'Tis plain, as the light of the day, that you *double it*."

I once had occasion to put a query, similar to the one with which you have honored me, to one of our most distinguished writers, and his reply was worthy of a romancer—Light cities by balloons and ventilate them with fans propelled by steam! This idea is far more grand, though perhaps less practical, than that of the wiseacre, who advised his friends always to have two strings to their bow—and illustrated it by reference to the practice of medicine combined with dealing in gravestones. Franklin, you may remember, attempted to teach how to make money plenty in every man's pocket; but, alas, even he, with all his practical wisdom, stopped short at such aphorisms as these: First, *Let honesty and industry be thy constant companions;* and Secondly, *Spend one penny less than thy clear gains.* Benjamin forgot to tell us how we could certainly make such clear gains that we could afford to spend one penny less. From these and other reasons you will understand why such a book as you now desire has not been written by the magnates of literature; and for different, but equally satisfactory and comprehensive reasons, millionaires are not authors on this subject, as it is probable you may have observed, they are not invariably all Roscoes or Ricardos. Even men's past successes and misfortunes, their triumphs and failures—in a word, the daguerreotype of man's material condition is only imperfectly preserved in history. Some writer has forcibly said: "The world might well afford to lose all record of a hundred ancient battles or sieges, if it could thereby gain the knowledge of one lost art; and even the pyramids bequeathed to us by Egypt in her glory, would be well exchanged for a few of her humble workshops and manufactories, as they stood in the days of the Pharaohs. Of the true history of mankind, only a few chapters have yet been written; and now, when the deficiencies of that we have are beginning to be realized, we find the materials for supplying them have in good part perished in the lapse of time, or been trampled recklessly beneath the hoofs of the war-horse." How many items of practical knowledge have thus been forever lost—how many foot-prints obliterated—

> "Footprints which, perhaps, another
> Sailing o'er life's solemn main,
> A forlorn and shipwrecked brother,—
> Seeing, shall take heart again."

Xenophon, I think it was, who said, that any one who discovered a new source of gain, without detriment to the community, deserved a mark of honor, for public spirit would then never be extinguished. Stimulated by the hope of making some humble discovery, perhaps bringing to light a diamond long buried in the dust of forgetfulness, I have devoted some leisure hours to researches and reflection upon the topic suggested by you ; and though I hardly presume to offer you any thing novel, I may, nevertheless, be able to present some suggestions that may be regarded as of value, with respect to the chances for profit not as yet entirely developed, and which, without much attempt at arrangement according to the bookmaker's art, I place at your disposal; and, if you think them worthy, or likely to revive the courage of one other "forlorn and shipwrecked" brother, you may submit them to the consideration of the public. I do this the more cheerfully, because I know that my crudities will be regarded with tenderness, and any errors into which I may have fallen, will be pardoned or overlooked, or what is better, corrected by superior information. But in the event of publication, you will please remember, that my name is like a miser's gift, "nothing to nobody."

> " Ay free, aff han' your story tell
> When wi' a bosom crony,
> *But still keep something to yoursel*
> Ye scarcely tell to ony."

LETTER II.

HOW FORTUNES WERE MADE IN ANCIENT TIMES.

BEFORE proceeding to consider the opportunities now open for the exercise of industry profitably, it may afford us some instruction, and certainly the satisfaction of having commenced at the beginning, to review the sources of the fortunes of the Ancients and of our immediate predecessors. It is obvious, however, that in a review so comprehensive, no account can be taken of moderate fortunes; and in endeavoring to trace to its origin, social and individual prosperity in ancient times, it is evidently impracticable, even if desirable, to prosecute the inquiry with much minuteness. Mercantile biographies and magazines did not probably flourish in primeval ages; and the favorites of fortune were debarred the privilege of transmitting the barren incidents of inglorious lives to succeeding generations.

The earliest, as well as the best history of our race, is the BIBLE; and going back to that fountain of historical lore, as well as of poetry and truth, we learn that the first occupations of mankind were *sheep husbandry* and *tillage*. "And Abel was a keeper of sheep, but Cain was a tiller of the ground." Whether the subsequent crime of Cain, in murdering his brother, cast a stigma upon his occupation, or whether a pastoral life was found more congenial and profitable than tillage, we know not, but certainly stock-raising, among the Hebrews, was the favorite pursuit. The history of the sacrifices, both before and after the giving of the Mosaic Law, establishes this point. The wealth of the patriarchs, Abraham, Isaac, and Jacob, consisted principally in their flocks. "Mesha, king of Moab," the Scriptures inform us (2 Kings iii. 4), "was a *sheep master*, and rendered unto the king of Israel an hundred thousand lambs, and an hundred thousand rams, with the wool." The flocks of the Midianites were so vast, that the sheep taken from them by Moses, after his victory, amounted to six hundred and seventy-five thousand. (Num. xxxi. 32.) Nabal had three thousand sheep and one thousand goats (1 Sam. xxv. 2); and as his wealth was said to be "very great," we learn the current idea of what constituted wealth in those days. Some of the most beautiful metaphors in the Scriptures are derived from a shepherd's life. "The Lord is my shepherd, I shall not want. He maketh me to lie down in green pastures; he leadeth me beside the still waters. Yea, though I walk through the valley of the shadow of death, I will fear no evil; for thou art with me; thy rod and thy staff, they comfort me." (Ps. xxiii. 1, 2, 4.) And again: "He shall feed his flock like a shepherd; he shall gather the lambs with his arm, and carry them in his bosom, and shall gently lead those that are with young." (Isa. xl. 11.)

The ancient poets also derived inspiration from the same fountain. Homer, in his "Odyssey," speaks of—

> "That happy clime! where each revolving year,
> The teeming ewes a triple offspring bear;
> And two fair crescents of translucent horn,
> The brows of all their young increase adorn;
> The shepherd swains, with sure abundance blest,
> On the fat flock and rural dainties feast;

> Nor want of herbage makes the dairy fail,
> But every season fills the foaming pail."

In *Egypt*, on the other hand, the *cultivation of the soil* seems to have been the most profitable occupation. All nations, in the time of Joseph, we learn, went to Egypt to buy Corn. The annual overflowing of the Nile enabled the farmers to produce two, and sometimes three crops a year. The river, says a historian, begins to rise in the latter end of June, and attains its utmost height about the middle of August, when Egypt presents the appearance of a vast sea, while the cities and towns appear like so many islands; after this the waters gradually subside, and about the end of November the river has returned to its ordinary limits. During this period the earth, or mud, which the waters held in solution, has fallen on the soil; and on the retiring of the waters, the whole land is covered with a rich manure, and, according to Herodotus, required so little cultivation, that in some cases it was only necessary that the seed should be thrown upon the surface, and trodden down by beasts. In animals, Egypt did not abound; and in some one or other of the provinces, the ox, the sheep, and the goat, were held sacred, and hence not used for food. The Egyptians had such an abhorrence of pork, that they would not intermarry with persons engaged in the keeping of pigs. This prejudice arose probably, in the first instance, from the circumstance, that in a warm climate the eating of pork was found to produce cutaneous disorders, especially the leprosy.

Agriculture, therefore, may safely be said to have been the source of the early prosperity of Egypt; but at a later period—when Tyre had been destroyed, and Alexandria built—immense fortunes were acquired by the Egyptians in traffic. Egypt became the *entrepot* of the commerce between Europe and all the vast countries stretching east from Arabia to China. The silks, spices, precious stones, and other products of Arabia and India, passed through Alexandria; and besides, an immense number of vessels was employed in conveying corn from Egypt to Rome. This trade was exceedingly lucrative, and Alexandria waxed great, and became the seat of commerce and dominion. At the present time, it is said, there are about two millions of acres in that country, which are capable of producing *four crops* per year; and Egypt is again a highway over which traffic passes between England and India, offering, in its resources and situation, excellent opportunities both for cultivators and merchants, as I may subsequently show.

Agriculture and stock-raising, as we have stated, are the original and primitive sources of individual wealth. As soon, however, as some surplus accumulation, called capital, has been secured, a desire for other and additional luxuries arises in the human heart, which can only be gratified by exchanging commodities, or in other words, establishing *commerce*. Then a new and boundless field for acquiring fortune is opened to enterprise. The sagacious merchant is often better rewarded than the laborious producer. The influence of commerce in building up cities, effulgent with luxury, is early exemplified; and nowhere more strikingly than in the growth of the chief cities of Phœnicia, Tyre and Sidon. Their wealth and magnificence are pictured by the prophets, in the glowing language of Oriental hyperbolism: "Tyrus did build herself a stronghold, and heaped up silver as the dust, and fine gold as the mire of the street." "When thy wares went forth out of the seas, thou filledst many people; thou didst enrich the kings of the earth with the multitudes of thy riches and of thy merchandise." This people of whom Ezekiel speaks, the Phœnicians, were an ingenious and inventive as well as a commercial people. They invented ship-building, discovered the manufacture of glass and woolen cloth, and established the fundamental principles of Geography and Astronomy. The origin of Arithmetic and Book-keeping is also traced to them; but probably the greatest of all their many inventions was that of the *Alphabet.* At all events, so great was commercial Phœnicia, that Carthage, a mere colony, planted on the coast of Africa, was able, by its wealth, to resist for a considerable period the mailed legions of Rome.

The reports of the great wealth acquired by the Phœnicians in commerce, excited a desire in the Jews to share in its results; and in the reigns of David and Solomon, some very successful ventures were made by them. The return of one voyage to Ophir, we are told, produced four hundred and fifty talents of gold, about $12,500,000, which far exceeds the semi-monthly shipments of our modern Ophir, generally called California. Solomon himself was a merchant, and traded with his brother king-merchant, Hiram of Tyre—his navy bringing back "gold and silver, ivory and apes and peacocks." We are told he "made silver in Jerusalem as stones, and cedar trees as sycamores that grow in the plains."

In *Greece*, the principal source of large fortunes, honestly acquired, was Manufactures; though her Commerce at one period was also very considerable. The most celebrated manufacturing city of ancient times was Corinth, one of the chief cities of Greece. *Coverlets* made in this city were sought after in foreign countries, and the importance of this manufacture may be inferred from the fact, that Nero paid no less than four million sesterces—about $150,000—for one; and in Cato's time, (Metellus Scipio brought it as an accusation), coverlets were sold for eight hundred thousand sesterces, about $30,000. Philadelphia, which is known to excel in manufactures, I need not tell you, could supply a much better article at a less price. Corinth also excelled in the manufacture of brass and earthenware; and although she possessed no copper mines, her workmen contrived, by mixing that which she received from other countries with a small quantity of gold and silver, to compose a metal extremely brilliant, and almost proof against rust. Of these we are told they made cuirasses, helmets, small figures, cups and vessels, no less esteemed for the workmanship than for the material, which were enriched with foliage and other chased ornaments. Those on their pottery were equally beautiful.

Rome, in this connexion, would principally illustrate getting money by *conquest*, or what plain people would call robbery. The conquered provinces were compelled to pay one-tenth, occasionally one-twentieth, of their produce to Rome; and estates in the provinces were divided amongst influential Roman citizens. The fortunes of some of the old Romans undoubtedly far surpassed those of private individuals in modern times; but the astounding statistics floating about on the waves of *newspaperdom*, I give to you without vouching for their correctness. The philosopher Seneca had a fortune of $17,500,000, which, it seems, caused him so much trouble, that he declaimed loudly in praise of *poverty* and wrote three books "On Anger." Claudius, a freedman, saved by some "hook or crook" $12,500,000. The debts of Milo, it is said, amounted to $3,000,000; and the inference is, I presume, that if he compromised as discriminatingly as some of our modern financiers, he must have become a rich man. Cæsar, before he entered upon any office, owed $14,975,000. He had purchased the friendship of Curio for $250,000, and that of Lucius Paulus for $1,500,000. At the time of the assassination of Julius Cæsar, Antony was in debt to the amount of $15,000,000; he owed this sum on the ides of March, and it was paid by the kalends of April; he squandered $735,000,000. Appius squandered in debauchery $2,500,000, and finding, on examination of the state of his affairs, that he had only $400,000, remaining, poisoned himself, because he considered that sum insufficient for his maintenance. Cæsar gave Satulla, the mother of Brutus, a pearl of the value of $50,000. Cleopatra, at an entertainment she gave to Antony, dissolved in vinegar a pearl worth $400,000, and he swallowed it. Claudius, the son of Esopus the comedian, swallowed one worth $40,000. One single dish cost Esopus $400,000. Caligula spent for one supper $400,000, and Heliogabalus $100,000. The usual cost for a repast for Lucullus was $100,000; the fish from his fish-ponds were sold for $175,000.

Crœsus, the last king of Lydia, made his money by subduing the Phrygians, Paphlagonians, Thracians, and others. His fortune amounted to $17,000,000; and he used to say that a citizen who had not a sum sufficient to support an army or a legion did not deserve to be called a rich man.

Laying aside Conquest as an unjustifiable means of making money, no better than some of the modern schemes, we find that probably the largest fortunes of ancient times had their origin in *trade with India*. It has been well remarked, that nations are some actively commercial, and others passively commercial; the former being those who build ships and go out to trade, the latter being those who either confine their trade to themselves, or wait for foreigners to visit them. The actively commercial, almost invariably, are enabled to drive good bargains with those who wait for their periodical visits, and are enriched. India from time immemorial until recently, when England's machines have eclipsed her glory, was the place of production of the choicest fabrics that luxury can desire. She has ever waited for neighboring nations to come and get her spices and aromatics, her precious stones and silks and linens, and those Dacca muslins, which have been called "webs of woven wind." No nation has equaled the Hindoos in the fineness of their muslins. "Muslins are made by a few families," says the late Rev. William Ward, "so exceedingly fine, that four months are required to weave one piece, which sells at five hundred rupees. When the muslin is laid on the grass, and the dew has fallen upon it, *it is no longer discernible*." Tavernier, who was a merchant as well as a traveler, and therefore accustomed to judge of the qualities of goods, and who wrote in the middle of the seventeenth century, says "The white calicuts" (calicoes, or rather muslins, so called from the great commercial city of Calicut, whence the Portuguese and Dutch first brought them), "are woven in several places in Bengal and Mogulistan, and are carried to Raioxsary and Baroche to be whitened, because of the large meadows and plenty of lemons that grow thereabouts, for they are never so white as they should be till they are dipped in *lemon water*. Some calicuts are made so fine *you can hardly feel them in your hand*, and the thread, when spun, is scarce discernible." The same writer says: "There is made at Seconge (in the province of Malwa) a sort of calicut so fine, that when a man puts it on, *his skin shall appear as plainly through it as if he was quite naked*, but the merchants are not permitted to transport it, for the governor is obliged to send it all to the Great Mogul's seraglio, and the principal lords of the court, to make the sultanesses and noblemen's wives shifts and garments for the hot weather; and the king and lords take great pleasure to behold them in these shifts." He also mentions turbans of such fine cloth, that 25 or 30 ells will not weigh four ounces; and another writer refers to entire garments that can be drawn through a lady's finger ring. Those swarthy natives had a delicacy of touch which enabled them to produce effects that transcend the powers of the most wonderful of our modern machines.

But the staple commodity of the East for a long period was *Silk*. This article, at one time, sold at Rome for its weight in gold; and for about a thousand years the demand throughout Europe was supplied entirely from Asia. Between the sixth and seventh centuries, however, two Persian monks, at the instigation of the emperor Justinian, contrived to transport, in a hollow cane, the eggs of the silkworm from China to Europe, where they were hatched by means of heat, and thus Asia was robbed of an ancient and lucrative monopoly. During the dark ages which succeeded, Commerce, it is probable, suffered by the general paralysis. Men sought wealth, not by ventures to India, but by dark mysterious researches in Alchemy and Astrology. When, however, the lights of Commerce and Civilization, which had been extinguished for a time, again shone in the firmament, we find that trade with the East became again the elixir of wealth. Commerce with the East made Venice and Genoa, in the middle ages, what Tyre and Carthage were before the Christian Era. In the tenth century, says a historian, Venice had established commercial intercourse with the Saracens of Egypt and Syria for their staples of sugar and rice—for dates, senna, cassia, flax, linen, balm, perfumes, galls, wrought silks, soaps, etc. She traded, too, for the rich spices and precious stones of India; and with merchandise so rare and rich, entered the markets of Western Europe and commanded the whole of its valuable trade. Genoa also, even before the time of Peter the Hermit, had opened a flourishing commerce with Asia, and when the Crusaders had planted their ensigns on the battlements of Jerusalem, the Red Cross in the white field was among them; and by diplomacy or conquest she gained a strong foothold in the Black Sea, where she founded a powerful colony that augmented her wealth incredibly.

In the sixteenth century Spices were so precious in Europe, that the profits of commercial adventures to the Indies were in some instances enormous. Crawfurd, in his history of the Indian Archipelago, says that cloves, pepper, and nutmegs, were in that age the principal, if not the only objects of mercantile adventure; an artificial value was conferred on these articles, and commodities, which had been bought at the "rate of nearly six hundred pounds for ten yards of good scarlet cloth, worth £7, sold in England at three thousand per cent. above their original price."

The discovery of America even may be said to be one of the fruits of commerce with the Indies; for when the Portuguese mariners found a new passage to the East, viz., around the Cape of Good Hope, Spain was induced to listen to the arguments and entreaties of Columbus, principally through the hope of finding a shorter route to the spice regions of Eastern Asia; and this enterprise resulted in the discovery of an India in the West,* which, as we fondly hope, is destined to become the central planet in the universe of Nations, the Mecca of the lovers of liberty in all lands, and a country meriting the eulogium:

> "Patient of toil; serene amidst alarms;
> Inflexible in faith; invincible in arms."

* Columbus and Vespucius both died believing that they had reached Eastern Asia, and thus a geographical mistake led to the greatest discovery that has ever been made. In proof of these assertions, we may state, that Columbus designed delivering *at Cuba* the missives of the Spanish king to the great Khan of the Mongols, and that he imagined himself in Mangi, the capital of the southern region of Cathay or China. "The island of Hispaniola" (Hayti), he declares to Pope Alexander VI., in a letter found in the archives of the Duke of Varaguas, "is Tarshish, Ophir, and Zipangon. In my second voyage I have discovered fourteen hundred islands, and a shore of three hundred and thirty-three miles belonging to the continent of Asia." This *West Indian* Zipangon produced golden fragments, or spangles, weighing eight, ten, and even twenty pounds. (See Humboldt's Essay on the Production of Gold and Silver, in the "Journal des Economistes," for March, April, and May, 1838.)

LETTER III.

HOW FORTUNES HAVE BEEN MADE IN MODERN TIMES.

IN my preceding letter a rapid review was taken of the origin of fortunes in ancient times, with some reference to events as late as the discovery of America by Columbus. In the fourteenth century a gentleman is said to have laid the foundation of his fortune in an extraordinary manner; and though the story bears the impress of the fabulous, it may nevertheless be referred to in illustration of one way of making money, since become quite common, viz., by *Accident.*

A wealthy merchant of London was in the habit of making all his servants share in his adventures by putting something at risk. A poor scullion-boy in his employ was called upon to conform to the custom, and deposit something on board a ship just starting for Algiers; but he had nothing in the world that he could call his own except a cat, which he had purchased at the cost of one penny, to save himself from being eaten up by the rats which infested the garret in which he slept. This he brought, shedding tears, and placed it on board the ship as his share in the adventure. On arrival it was ascertained that the Dey of Algiers was exceedingly troubled by rats in his palace; and the captain of the ship loaned him the cat, which proved such a source of satisfaction that he proposed to purchase her at any price. The captain was shrewd enough to ask a very high price, which was readily paid; and Tabby proved so satisfactory as a mouser, that the Dey sent additional valuable presents of pearls to her owner. On the return of the ship it was discovered, to the surprise of all, that the most valuable part of the cargo belonged to the shipper of the cat—the scullion-boy. His master proposed partnership, which was accepted. His business prospered—he loaned money to the king when he was in straits; was appointed Mayor of London, was knighted, became second man in the kingdom, and his name is transmitted to us as—SIR RICHARD WHITTINGTON.

This will recall to your recollection the brilliant exploit of our friend Lord Timothy Dexter, and his shipment of warming-pans to the West Indies. He always silenced cavillers, who ventured to insinuate any thing unfavorable to his geographical acquirements, by pointing to the profits of the speculation; and no one could prove that he had not foreseen that the articles, though not wanted as warming-pans in that climate, would be sought after for some other purpose.

After the discovery of America, by Columbus, immense fortunes were made—

First, *By Mining Silver in Mexico and Peru.*

The conquest of a portion of America by the Spaniards, revealed to the civilized world the riches of the Silver Mines of Mexico and Peru. Masses of silver, such as had never before been seen in Europe, became common, and aroused the fever for adventure to a degree only paralleled by the recent discovery of gold in California. Mining became the goddess of fortune, and richly did she repay some of her devotees. Baron Humboldt states that in Mexico, near Sombrerete, where mines were opened as far back as 1555, the family of Tagoaga, (Marquises de Apartado) derived, in the short space of *five months*, from a front of one hundred and two feet in the outcropping of a silver mine, a net profit of $4,000,000; while in the mining district of Catorce, in the space of *two years and a half*, between 1781 and the end of 1783, an ecclesiastic named Juan Flores, gained $3,500,000 on ground full of chloride of silver and of *Colorados*."

2. Another source of great fortunes, especially in England, was *Monopolies of certain trades, granted by Royalty* to favored individuals.

In the infancy of England's commercial history, which may be said to date from the time of Queen Elizabeth, it was deemed a stroke of good policy to stimulate enterprise by royal monopolies. To one company was granted a monopoly of sweet wines; to another of licenses; the successors of the Dutch traders were alone permitted to export woolen cloths; the Turkish Company possessed the exclusive privilege of trading with India; the Russia Company with Russia. Burleigh probably shook his head at the establishment of monopolies like these, foreseeing the injury likely to result from them in the future; but if so, he discovered that a shake of the head will not deter an obstinate woman from her purpose, much less a virgin queen. But though these companies proved so detrimental to the national prosperity, that in 1624 monopolies were generally abolished, the proprietors of many of them became enormously wealthy, and the East India Company, until recently abrogated, was the most gigantic monopoly for private emolument in the world. Its shipments of Opium to China alone, in the years 1848–9, were 57,918 chests, which, at $600 per chest, amounted to $34,750,800. Who can calculate what an amount of misery was produced by one single year's trade!

The English have always had a *penchant* for governmental monopolies; and when these were no longer tolerated by law, enterprising Englishmen sought them from other and less scrupulous sovereigns. The latest success in this branch of engineering that I know of, is the *Guano contract.* In December, 1847, a firm in London obtained from the Peruvian government the exclusive privilege of shipping and selling Guano, for account of the Government, at four per cent. commission on the gross amount of sales, and the valuable coincident of paying for one-fourth of the net proceeds of the sales in the scrip of the government, at par value, with interest added. This scrip was purchased, it is said, by the contractors, at ten cents for the dollar, and it is estimated their profits in one year exceeded a million of dollars.*

3. Next to government patronage, *Speculation in Government Securities, with the advantage of early information as to circumstances affecting their market value, has resulted in the accumulation of great fortunes.*

Rothschild, the present founder of the house of N.

---

* How much the contractor realized from the contract of December, 1847, cannot well be known—the following estimate, however, has been made:

Gross sales of 130,000 tons of Guano, at $50 per ton, $6,500,000, on which the commission at 4 per cent., was	$260,000
Estimated net proceeds, at $20 per ton, of which one fourth part was accounted for to the Government in its own scrip, costing the contractors, (*with interest added,*) about ten cents per dollar, leaving a profit of ninety per cent. on the whole amount, say, $650,000,	$585,000
Probable gain in exchange, (at $5 per pound sterling) at least ten per cent. on total net proceeds, say $2,600,000,	$260,000
Total estimated profits,	$1,105,000

Rothschild & Sons, was the master-spirit in this sort of speculation. By a series of fortunate operations he attained the enviable position of being able to cause a rise or a fall in stocks to a certain extent, whenever he pleased, by the mere influence of his example. One great cause of his success was the secrecy in which he contrived to shroud all his transactions. He had certain men whom he employed as brokers, on ordinary occasions; but whenever it suited his purpose, or when he supposed that by employing them, it would be ascertained that he wished to effect a rise or a fall, he took care to commission a new set of brokers to act for him. His mode of doing business, when engaged in large transactions, has been described to be this:—

"Supposing he possessed exclusively, which he often did a day or two before it could be generally known, intelligence of some event which had occurred in any part of the Continent, sufficiently important to cause a rise in the French funds, and through them in the English funds, he would employ the brokers he usually employed to sell out stock, say to the amount of $2,500,000. The news spread in a moment in Capel Court that Rothschild was selling out, and a general alarm followed. Every one apprehended he had received intelligence from some foreign port of some important event which would produce a fall in prices; as might, under such circumstances, be expected, all became sellers at once. This of necessity caused the funds, to use Stock Exchange phraseology, 'to tumble down at a fearful rate.' Next day, when they had fallen, perhaps, one or two per cent., he would make purchases, say to the amount of $7,500,000, taking care, however. to employ a number of brokers whom he was not in the habit of employing, and commissioning each to purchase to a certain extent, and giving all of them strict orders to preserve secrecy in the matter. Each of the persons so employed was by this means ignorant of the commission given to others. Had it been known the purchases were made for him, there would have been as great and sudden a rise in the prices as there had been in the fall, so that he could not purchase to the intended extent on such advantageous terms. On the third day, perhaps, the intelligence which had been expected by the jobbers to be unfavorable, arrives, and instead of being so, turns out to be highly favorable. Prices instantaneously rise again, and possibly they may get one and a half, or even two per cent. higher than they were when he sold out his $2,500,000. He now sells out at the advanced price the entire $7,500,000 he had purchased at the reduced prices. The gains by such extensive transactions, when so skillfully managed, will be at once seen to be enormous; by the supposed transactions, assuming the rise to be two per cent., the gain would be $175,000. But this is not the greatest gain which the late Leviathan of modern capitalists has made by such transactions. He has, on more than one occasion, made upward of $500,000 on one account."

Stock-jobbing, one might hence conclude, must be the famous Lamp of Aladdin—rub it, and the genii appear, bringing gold and all desirable things, but modern experience has demonstrated, a thousand times, that one is more likely to rub the wrong than the right way: and then appear the horrid gnomes—losses, mental anxiety, and speedy bankruptcy. No business is in fact more uncertain or more certainly disastrous than stock speculating. It has been calculated that the number of persons that are struck by lightning, every year, is twice as great as those who draw first prizes in lotteries; and the number who have become rich by operating in Stocks, is probably not greater than those who have made fortunes by gambling. Temporary success, in both, is generally the syren that sings to ruin. The Leviathan of our New York Stock-jobbers has undoubtedly made more than one fortune; and in the year succeeding his first failure, he is said to have paid off his debts, which were about a million, and made one million two hundred thousand dollars besides; but notwithstanding these large gains, he is now indebted for his seat at the Board to the courtesy of his *confrères*, who probably hope, in the violent fluctuations to which his gigantic operations give rise, to come in with the tide, or swim to port.

4. Another source of colossal fortunes in Europe, was unrestricted commerce with Africa, commonly called the *Slave Trade.*

The English were formerly the great slave-traders of the world; and it is said by the initiated, that individuals of that nation continue to share largely in its profits. For the fifty years immediately preceding the abolition of the trade by Brazil, it is known that 80,000 slaves on an average were annually exported from Africa by traders; and supposing that each cost thirty-five dollars, or $140,000,000 for the four millions, and that the sale price was $300, or $900,000,000 for all the survivors—assuming that twenty-five per cent. or one million of slaves was lost on the passage—the profits of the traffic would nevertheless amount to the enormous sum of SEVEN HUNDRED AND SIXTY MILLIONS OF DOLLARS! Do these statistics afford any information respecting fortunes mysteriously and suddenly acquired, and often ostentatiously expended in palaces on the Fifth Avenue, the Boulevards, and the West End? It is at least certain that the income of the King of Dahomey from the exportation of slaves, which a few years ago amounted to $300,000 per year, enabling him to enjoy the luxury of having *eighteen hundred wives,* was an unfair proportion of the aggregate profit. He had evidently been overreached; and we are not surprised that he was moved to address, as he did not long since, a modest petition to the Queen of England, with his compliments, begging her to stop the Slave trade everywhere else, but "*allow him to continue it.*"

At the present time, it is calculated that not more than 30,000 Africans are annually exported from Africa to Cuba and the Brazils; but the profits of this limited traffic, notwithstanding many unusual expenses, as gratuities to high officials, etc., amount to about *eleven millions of dollars* annually.*

Slave Raising, we should judge, in view of the high price of slaves, has also been, in some instances at least, a source of fortune. The author of *Slavery by an Eye-witness*, as quoted by the *Liverpool Albion*, furnishes an insight of its profits in the following illustration.

---

* The *New York Herald* gives the following as the expenses and profits of a slaver at the present time:

EXPENSES AND OUTFIT.

Cost of a two-hundred-and-fifty-ton-vessel,	$8,000
Sailmaker's, carpenter's, and cooper's bills,	3,000
Provisions for crew and slaves,	1,000
Wages advanced,	1,000
Stealings in New York by the agent,	4,000
Commission of ten per cent. on the whole expenses,	1,700
Cost of 400 negroes at $50 per head,	20,000
Pay of crew and officers on the coast,	500
Gratification money to the American captain,	1,000
Captain's head money, averaging $15 per head on 380 negroes, allowing for twenty deaths on the passage,	5,700
Head money to officers at $7.50 per head,	2,850
Wages of crew and officers,	2,500
Gratification money to the Captain-General at $51 a head	19,380
Landing expenses, at $34 a head,	12,920
Commission of five per cent. on sale,	11,400
Total expenses,	$94,950

RECEIPTS.

For 380 negroes in market, at $600 a head	228,000
Total profits on cargo,	$133,050

Suppose that the slave is a blacksmith. He will readily earn $130 a year, which in thirty years will amount to $3,900. He will probably have eight children, who, at twenty-one, will sell for $800 each, or $6,400. Total product of one blacksmith, $10,300. A slave woman will bring her owner $100 a year, or in thirty years, $3,000. She may have eleven children, who will sell for $800 each, or $8,800 for all. Total product of slave woman, $11,800.*

5. Another source of great fortunes has been *Land Monopoly.*

In England, the appreciation of landed property may be said to date from the Battle of Hastings, when William

---

* The *Richmond Whig*, some years ago, published the biography of "the richest man in Virginia," which contained the following interesting particulars: "Samuel Hairston, of Pittsylvania, was, a year or two ago, the owner of between 1,600 and 1,700 slaves, in his own right, having but a little while before taken a census. He also has a prospective right to about 1,000 slaves more, which are now owned by his mother-in-law, Mrs. K. Hairston, he having married her only child. He now has the management of them, which makes the number of his slaves reach near 3,000. They increase at the rate of near one hundred every year; he has to purchase a large plantation every year to settle them on. A large number of his plantations are in Henry and Patrick counties, Virginia. He has large estates in North Carolina; his landed property in Stokes is alone assessed at $600,000. His wealth is differently estimated at from $3,000,000 to $5,000,000, and I should think it was nearer the latter. You think he has a hard lot; but I assure you Mr. Hairston manages all his matters as easy as most persons would an estate of $10,000. He has overseers who are compelled to give him a written statement of what has been made and spent on each plantation; and his negroes are all clothed and fed from his own domestic manufacture. And raising his own tobacco crop, which is immensely large, is so much clear gain every year, *besides his increase in negroes, which is a fortune of itself.*"

the Norman divided the forfeited estates of the English among his followers, on condition of faithful service, or fealty. The abolition of the feudal tenures increased rather than diminished the passion for large possessions in land; and, at the present time, one-fourth of the real property of Great Britain is monopolized by a few ducal houses, and the balance is distributed among less than 30,000 persons. The Marquis of Westminster, it is stated, has an annual income of $3,500,000, chiefly, we presume, from landed property; and it is therefore not surprising, as statistics show, that one sixth of the population of Great Britain is dependent on the poor rates for subsistence. In the United States, the law, by abolishing primogeniture and perpetual entails, has done something to discourage land monopoly; while its vast abundance, extending as its area does to over three millions of square miles, occupied by about 29,000,000 of people, although capable of supporting *five hundred millions* without exceeding France in density, or *six hundred and sixty millions* without being more dense than Great Britain now is, has retarded the accumulation of many very large fortunes from this source.

The most notable instance in American history of a fortune acquired directly from a rise in the value of land, is that of the Van Rensselaers in New York, whose manor was obtained by grant from the Dutch government, before the country had passed under the dominion of the English, and which was confirmed by James II. in 1685, and in 1704 by Queen Anne. The Van Rensselaer name, however, is not indebted solely to wealth in the family for its claims to respect. The liberality and virtues of STEPHEN VAN RENSSELAER, and his patronage of science, will be treasured up in grateful memories when the manorial grants are wholly forgotten.

In cities, some very large fortunes have been made by *the rise, in value, of town lots.* NICHOLAS LONGWORTH, of Cincinnati, has made a fortune of several millions by the rise of property, a portion of which he was compelled to take from debtors against his inclinations. The most valuable portion of the Pepper Estate of Philadelphia, it is said, consists of a piece of property which the founder of that fortune was compelled to buy under a mortgage, so sorely against his will, that he is reported to have shed tears over the consummation of the transfer.

In the city of New York there are no doubt several wealthy families whose founders were cabbage-gardeners in the vicinity of the city, and who managed to eke out their existence until the city crawled up to them, and their small farms became as valuable as dukedoms. The rapid growth of Chicago, in Illinois, has necessarily resulted in some astonishing instances of suddenly-acquired fortunes. One philosopher states that, about ten years ago, he sold two lots for $2500, that are now worth $80,000, being those on which the New Richmond Hotel stands; and he congratulates himself for his narrow escape from being a rich man, and thus, probably, ruining his boys. Large fortunes have also been made, quite recently, by the development of the Anthracite *Coal Lands* of Pennsylvania. Hills that were purchased for the taxes, have proved as valuable as gold mines. To get rich by a rise in real estate, it would seem, requires no more sagacity than is ordinarily displayed by going under shelter when it rains. Purchase a rood in the vicinity of a growing city, and maintain your personal sovereignty against sheriffs and all law officers. That is all. Perhaps, however, if we try it, we shall discover that we are of those unfortunates whose bread, when it falls, as it has been classically expressed, always falls on the buttered side.

6. Again, *Trading in Furs has yielded large returns to enterprising adventurers.*

The Hon. Wm. Sturges, who, in early life was engaged in this trade on the Northwest coast, states that on one occasion he purchased from the Indians in one forenoon five hundred and sixty prime sea-otter skins, at that time worth fifty dollars a piece at Canton, giving for each five ermine skins, that cost less than thirty cents each in Boston. He says that more than once he had known a capital of $40,000, employed in a Northwest voyage, yield a return exceeding $150,000; and in one instance, an outfit not exceeding $50,000, gave a gross return of $284,000. It was while the trade was flourishing as just described, Astor, during a detention by ice in the Chesapeake Bay, on his first voyage from Heidelberg to this country, was advised by a fellow-passenger and countryman, a furrier by trade, to invest the proceeds of his merchandise—a portion of which consisted of musical instruments from a brother's manufactory—in furs. He did so, and in less than twenty years he had amassed something like $250,000. As his capital increased, he widened the range of his operations, until, says a biographer, "his ships plowed every sea—now freighted with furs for France, England, Germany, or Russia, and now with peltries, ginseng and dollars for China; in one case bringing home wines and silks, the motley wares of Indian traffic, wool, fine linens and amber, hareskins and duck; and in the other, the valuable products of the Celestial Empire. His inventive mind organized every possible variety of profitable adventure; and his minute acquaintance with the character of the various European markets, and of the prices of all the articles it could advantageously provide him with, enabled him to furnish his captains, supercargoes and agents, with instructions as precise, and as well adapted to every emergency, as those which Captain Thorn lost his life in disobeying. If it is borne, in mind that he thus sold his own merchandise, obtained at a comparatively cheap price, by the ramifications of the Fur Company through the Indian country, in the best foreign market, and ordered back from thence, not only the means of prosecuting the fur traffic, blankets, knives, scissors, guns, trinkets, &c., but the wares that were then most in demand at home, we shall see how great and rapid must have been the multiplication of his gains."

Mr. Astor also invested largely in real estate in the city of New York, and the rise in its value contributed to swell his fortune. "He early foresaw the greatness to which New York was destined, and always kept a large proportion of his property invested in lots, or rather acres. At a certain period he was wont to convert two-thirds of his annual gains into land; and it is a singular feature in the history of one dealing so constantly, and for so long a period with such large sums—nay, whose whole wealth was perhaps at times upon the bosom of the ocean—that he should never have been known to mortgage a lot."

7. The Philadelphia millionaire, STEPHEN GIRARD, made his fortune *in commerce with the East and West Indies*, attended with a large share of extraordinary good luck. His first adventures were limited, I believe, to the West Indies; and it was while engaged in this trade that he received the well-known handsome accession to his capital, by the slave insurrection at St. Domingo. Two of his vessels—a schooner and a brig—were in the harbor

of *Cape Française*, when the negroes rose upon the planters, and the latter attempted to save their most precious valuables by depositing them in the ships; but neither they nor their heirs—in many instances, whole families being totally extinguished—ever called to reclaim their deposit. Subsequently Mr. Girard embarked extensively in the Canton and Calcutta trade; and fortune having favored the most of his commercial adventures, his capital rapidly accumulated, and he invested a large part of it in banking. Shortly after he had established his bank, another notable instance of sheer good luck occurred. His biographer, Simpson, thus relates it:

"His ship 'Montesquieu' had been captured by a British frigate at the mouth of the river Delaware; perhaps at the identical spot from which he so narrowly escaped with his little schooner, when he was encountered by Captain King, off the Capes at this port, in 1776, a coincidence of peril and escape, in the commencement of our two great wars with England, which constitute no inconsiderable feature in the life of this extraordinary man; every event of whose career seems touched with circumstances out of the ordinary routine of life. The commander of the British frigate, aware of the danger of attempting to carry his prize to an English port, wisely adopted the resolution to send a flag of truce to Mr. Girard, to negotiate for ransom in preference to running the risk of recapture by our American frigates. The Montesquieu had an invoice cargo of two hundred thousand dollars, and it was concluded by Mr. Girard to pay ninety-three thousand dollars in doubloons as her ransom. At that period, it would have been utterly impossible even for Mr. Girard to have procured this amount of gold, but for the fortunate existence of his 'little Institution,' a term that he sometimes applied to his bank. Specie payments were even then suspended in fact—nor could that amount of gold easily have been purchased; but it was with the utmost ease that his overcrammed vaults disgorged this—to him a small sum—so that the ransom was immediately transmitted to the British commander; and the 'Montesquieu' was liberated. This cargo was immensely valuable at that time; consisting of teas, silks and nankeens from Canton—all of which had advanced in price one or two hundred per cent.; so that, notwithstanding the additional expense of ransom, his great profits in this adventure must have added at least *half a million* to his fortune."

8. *Large fortunes have also been made by Army and Navy Contracts, especially in war times.*

An abstract has recently been published in France, giving a detailed account of all the supplies furnished by France for carrying on the late war with Russia, and the figures indicate the opportunities for speculation. The *food* sent out to the French army included, among many smaller items, about 30,000,000 pounds of biscuit, 50,000,000 pounds of flour, 7,000,000 pounds of preserved beef, 14,000,000 pounds of salt beef and lard, 8,000,000 pounds of rice, 4,500,000 pounds of coffee, and 6,000,000 pounds of sugar; these, with 10,000 head of live cattle, and 2,500,000 gallons of wine, were the main supplies for provisioning the troops. No less than 260,000 chests and barrels were required to contain the biscuits alone, and 1,000,000 sacks and bags for the other articles. The summary of horse food contains a few items like these: 170,000,000 pounds of hay, and 180,000,000 pounds of oats and barley. The total of food, fodder, and fuel was about 500,000 tons weight, requiring 1800 voyages of ships to convey them to the Crimea. Among the accessories we find the not very pleasing items of over 27,000 bedsteads for invalids, about the same number of mattrasses, and 40 000 coverlets. There were materials for ambulances for 24,000 sick men, 600 cases of surgical instruments, and no less than 700,000 pounds weight of lint, bandages, and dressings of various kinds. We can thus understand why speculators have not invariably been on the side of peace, and have sometimes been accused of fomenting strife between nations.

Perhaps the most extensive and successful army and navy contractor of modern times was M. OUVRARD, of Paris. A single bill of his for supplies furnished the French Marine, in the time of the Directory, amounted to 63,973,494 francs. By his contract for provisioning the Spanish fleet at Brest and Cadiz, he pocketed a clear gain of fifteen millions of francs. In 1804, Ouvrard assumed a contract for supplying all the requirements and wants of the Treasury for the year, an amount which reached the sum of 400,000,000 francs. His last exploit was the collection of 72,000,000 francs, which Spain had agreed to pay France. Her Treasury was bankrupt, but large treasures were lying at her command in Mexico, Peru, and elsewhere, which, however, could not be easily reached on account of the wars then raging. How he effected this, forms an interesting portion of a garrulous book written by Vincent Nolte, late of New Orleans, entitled, *Fifty Years in both Hemispheres.*

9. Fortunes have been made rapidly by the *extensive sale of Specific Articles through the agency of Advertising.*

It is an established principle, that advertising, in some form, is essential to the successful prosecution of mercantile business: the master's art being shown in the mode of advertising. Even those who say they never advertise, generally falsify their assertions by putting a sign over the store-door behind which they sit, waiting for customers, sometimes until hope deferred maketh the heart sick, or the Sheriff ousts them. Some advertise their wares by sending out special agents to introduce them and solicit custom—a mode of advertising of limited range, and very costly. Others erect mammoth buildings, or construct wonderful machines; and a few go out into the streets and harangue crowds at the corners on the merits of their magic razor-strops, their imperishable lead-pencils,* or medicated soaps, so wonderful in curing

* Probably the most noted of these peripatetic merchants was MENGIN, the lead-pencil dealer, who recently died in Paris, leaving behind him a fortune of 400,000 francs. A correspondent of the *London News* describes him as a tall, handsome man, with a brass helmet and plumes, and a beard—the very model of that of Hudibras, "in shape and hue most like a tile"—standing on the box of a light cart, and haranguing a crowd. He wore a costly mantle of green velvet embroidered with gold, and on the fingers of his white hands were many rings of great price. Behind him was a squire, who, from time to time, blew a trumpet to attract public attention, and whose garments were only less splendid than those of his master. The only end and aim of all this pomp and circumstance were the sale of lead-pencils at two sous a piece. Mengin possessed, in a high degree, the art of commanding the attention of his audience. The laughs he raised were rare, but his face was full of promise of something good coming, and thus he kept alive curiosity. Though his speeches took a long time in the delivery, he was essentially a man of few words. He made long pauses, which were filled up by pantomime, and making grotesque sketches on a slate to show the quality of his pencils. The substance of every one of his discourses was that he had originally set up in a quiet shop, but finding that he could not get a living in it, he had resolved to become a quack, and that, from the hour of his taking that resolution, he had done well. "Why," he would say, "do I rig myself up in this ludicrous costume? I will tell you candidly: because by going about in this dress I sell a great many pencils, and if I stayed at home in a warehouse coat I should sell very few. I am a quack, I admit—but I am an honest one, for I sell a good article; and if you want a pencil, I doubt whether you will get as good a one anywhere else for the money." The speech was always followed by numerous demands, which he supplied from cases packed in the body of the cart. Of late he was wont to speak of the large fortune he had made, and he would not unfrequently turn out the contents of several *rouleaux*

cutaneous affections that, if properly applied and in sufficient quantity, there can be no doubt they would cure the eruption of Vesuvius.

But the largest fortunes have been made by those who, without neglecting other auxiliaries, have placed their reliance principally on Printer's ink as an agent of advertising. A host of names, now synonymous with pecuniary success, is recalled at once to every one's recollection. Prof. Holloway, of London, spends $150,000 per year in making the virtues of his Pills known through all lands, and has an annual income of probably quite as much. Dr. Jayne, of Philadelphia, expends $100,000 per year in advertising, and prints annually 2,600,000 almanacs, in eight different languages, for gratuitous distribution, consuming 14,000 reams of paper, at a cost of $40,000. But we suppose that the greatest master of the advertising art in modern times was Barnum; for no matter how unattractive the subject of his speculation —whether an old negro woman, a mermaid, a dwarf, or a wooly horse—it became, through the magic of his art, an object of decided interest, amply repaying all who were attracted to view it. The receipts of Jenny Lind's concerts—a lady, by the way, but very little known in the United States before Barnum advertised her into notoriety—amounted to the snug sum of $712,161.34; and the details are well worthy of being given, as facts and figures illustrative of the virtues of extensive and systematic advertising.

---

of gold, and count them in the public view. He was a remarkably healthy-looking man, and could not have been more than forty years old; but he was carried off by a fit of apoplexy.

	CONCERTS.	RECEIPTS.	AVERAGE.
New York	35	$286,216.64	$8,177.50
Philadelphia	8	48,884.41	6,110.55
Boston	7	70,388.16	10,055.45
Providence	1	6,525.54	6,525.54
Baltimore	4	32,001.88	8,000.47
Washington	2	15,385.60	7,692.80
Richmond	1	12,385.21	12,385.21
Charleston	2	10,428.75	5,214.37
Havana	3	10,436.04	3,478.68
New Orleans	12	87,646.12	7,308.84
Natchez	1	5,000.00	5,000.00
Memphis	1	4,539.56	4,539.56
St. Louis	5	30,613.67	6,122.73
Nashville	2	12,034.30	6,017.15
Louisville	3	19,429.50	6,476.50
Madison	1	3,693.25	3,693.25
Cincinnati	5	44,242.13	8,848.43
Wheeling	1	5,000.00	5,000.00
Pittsburg	1	7,210.58	7,210.58
Total	95	$712,161.34	$7,496.43

Jenny Lind's net avails of 95 concerts................$176,675.09
P. T. Barnum's gross receipts, after paying Miss Lind..$535,486.25

Total Receipts of 95 concerts......................$712,161.34

The magician who could produce results like these, has favored the world with the secrets of his success, and, among other good things, *vide Freedley's Practical Treatise on Business*, has given the following advice for the benefit of those who would do likewise.

" *Advertise your business. Do not hide your light under a bushel.* Whatever your occupation or calling may be, if it needs support from the public, advertise it thoroughly and efficiently in some shape or other that will arrest public attention. I freely confess that what success I have had in my life may fairly be attributed more to the public press, than nearly all other causes combined. There may possibly be occupations that do not require advertising, but I cannot well conceive what they are.

"Men in business will sometimes tell you that they have tried advertising, and that it did not pay. This is only when advertising is done sparingly and grudgingly. Homœopathic doses of advertising will not pay perhaps—it is like a half potion of physic, making the patient sick, but effecting nothing. Administer liberally, and the cure will be sure and permanent. Some say 'they cannot afford to advertise'—they mistake, they cannot afford *not* to advertise. In this country, where everybody reads the newspapers, the man must have a thick skull who does not see that these are the cheapest and best media through which he can speak to the public, where he is to find his customers. Put on the *appearance* of business, and generally the *reality* will follow. The farmer plants his seed, and while he is sleeping, his corn and potatoes are growing. So with advertising: while you are sleeping, or eating, or conversing with one set of customers, your advertisement is being read by hundreds and thousands of persons who never saw you, nor heard of your business; and never would, had it not been for your advertisement appearing in the newspapers. The business men of this country do not, as a general thing, appreciate the advantages of advertising thoroughly. Occasionally the public are aroused at witnessing the success of a Swaim, a Brandreth, a Townsend, a Genin, or a Root, and express astonishment at the rapidity with which these gentlemen acquire fortunes, not reflecting that the same path is open to all who dare pursue it. But it needs *nerve* and *faith*. The former, to enable you to launch out thousands on the uncertain waters of the future; the latter, to teach you that, after many days, it shall surely return, bringing a hundred or a thousand fold to him who appreciates the advantages of printer's ink, properly applied."

Barnum's subsequent embarrassments may serve as a warning against endorsing clock, or any other accommodation notes, and writing autobiographies, but they do not militate in the slightest against the soundness of his observations which we have quoted, nor do they disparage his skill in the art of Making Money. Recently, a Mr. Bonner by chequering whole pages of costly dailies with monotonous advertisements, that could not fail to attract attention, has run up the circulation of a hebdomadal, in the form of a quarto newspaper, from ten to over three hundred thousand copies per week.

Advertising acts with twofold power; it creates a want for the article advertised while notifying the source of supply. It invests goods with virtues even if they have them not; and the advertiser with something of the halo that surrounds an author or a hero. Next to godliness, there is nothing that a merchant should so ardently pray for as the *courage* to advertise. Moreover, money expended in advertising in a reputable newspaper, besides bringing greater or less profit to the advertiser, performs an important service in enlarging the scope and power of that newspaper for good, and thus indirectly elevating the standard of journalistic literature. The superiority of one newspaper over another depends more upon the extent of its advertising patronage than upon any other one thing. An increase of means almost invariably results in an improvement in the medium diffusing intelligence; and he who desires to benefit his race, cannot probably adopt a more effectual plan than in sustaining the organs of social and intellectual progress. Especially should a country merchant strengthen the backbone of the best newspaper in his county, both by advertising in it himself and inducing others to do so.

10. Within a few years, some very *large fortunes have rewarded important Inventions and Discoveries secured by Patents.*

Invention and discovery are not by any means a novel direction for the exercise of wit; but the rewards which in certain instances have recently attended them are un precedented. The desire to find a short cut to fortune, though often resulting in evil, has been the parent of much of our most valuable knowledge, notwithstanding for many hundreds of years, and even as late as the beginning of the eighteenth century, the best mechanical and inventive genius of the world was absorbed in endeavoring to discover that mysterious "stone" which should transmute comparatively valueless metals into precious gold. Again and again it was announced that the discovery had been made; but as frequently the discoverer ended his days in jail for want of a little of that gold which he said he could *project* at will. It is believed, however, by many—and even Lord Bacon admits the possibility of transmutation—that gold, in more than one instance, has been made artificially. Raymond Sully, who visited England in the reign of Edward I., changed at one operation, we are told, 50,000 pounds weight of quicksilver, lead and tin, into pure gold; and according to credible authorities, he furnished his majesty's Mint, first and last, with bullion to the amount of six millions sterling. (Quar. Rev., XXVI., 200.) It appears that they had bargained that the money which he should make was to be employed in making war upon infidels and unbelievers; and when the monarch appropriated a portion of the supplies to making war upon the Scots, Sully refused to make any more money for King Edward, and was thrown into the Tower—from which, however, after a long imprisonment, he escaped in the disguise of a leper. Thus ended the career of one who, had he been kept in good humor, would have saved England's Chancellors of the Exchequer, all trouble in future. In modern times, the genius which before was wasted in abstruse, mysterious studies, has been directed to benefitting the world by subjugating the powers of nature to man's uses; and thus, indirectly, by this means men have discovered the philosopher's stone. The rewards which have attended successful invention have recently, in many instances, been most munificent. Morse has been most handsomely rewarded by the governments of Europe for his discoveries in Telegraphy; Colt has made a large fortune by his revolving fire-arms; Goodyear by his discovery of vulcanizing India Rubber; but probably the most profitable invention secured by patent, ever made, was that known as Howard's Patent for Refining Sugar, and the use of the Vacuum Pan. The real inventor, it is said, was the illustrious Davy, who, however, derived but little benefit from it—though the annual income for many years was between $100,000 and $150,000—one house in London alone having paid for its use $20,000 per annum.

In our own country, one of the most remarkable instances of pecuniary success attained through invention, is afforded in the life of Dr. NOTT of Schenectady, N. Y. The son of a widowed mother, from the day he was nine years old he supported himself; and within a period of twenty years, though all the while actively engaged in various cares as President and Treasurer of Union College, his inventions in machinery have brought him about a *million of dollars.* This large sum—the fruit of his inventive and scientific labors—he has bestowed by trust deed on Union College; though his own estimate of the value of the investment is $600,000. Truly the philosopher's stone has been discovered, and Alchemy has been verified.

Magazine and Newspaper Publishing has also within a few years yielded brilliant returns in some instances, though it is now, as it has been heretofore, the grave of many sanguine projectors. The London *Times* made its founder a millionaire and a Member of Parliament. *Harper's Magazine* must yield its publishers a profit of over $50,000 per year. The shareholders of the *New York Tribune* are said to have divided a profit, a few years ago, at the rate of 120 per cent. per annum on the capital stock. The *Public Ledger*, of Philadelphia, is reported to pay its proprietors six per cent. on one million of dollars. But it is unnecessary to prosecute our researches as to the sources of Fortunes in Modern Times with any greater degree of minuteness. We have gone far enough to justify us in concluding that money can be made in almost any thing, including "trees, stones, and running brooks"; and if we turn to the lives of rich men, they "all remind us" that any one with moderate qualifications may reasonably hope to acquire fortune.

Let us glance for a moment, more for the sake of completeness than for instruction, to the lives of millionaires. The Boston millionaires generally laid the foundation of their fortunes in foreign commerce. THOMAS H. PERKINS traded extensively with Batavia, Canton, and other parts of Asia and Europe. PETER C. BROOKS was in an Insurance Office, and the information which he acquired in that position he used judiciously and to good advantage in sending out what were called "adventures." During the war in Europe, between the years 1789 and 1803, America conducted almost the entire carrying trade of the world, and Mr. Brooks made rapid accumulations. Some of his business principles were, never to borrow money; never to take more than legal interest for money loaned; and never to invest in wild lands or rail-road stocks. The LAWRENCES were engaged in selling imported goods; but the bulk of their fortune was made by monopolizing as much as possible the sale on commission of the fabrics of American factories, which they had aided to establish. Nobly, however, did Amos and Abbott expend their fortunes—the former having given, in benevolence, over $600,000 during his life. EBENEZER FRANCIS, recently deceased with over two millions of dollars in cash on deposit in the Boston banks, was once engaged in foreign trade, and latterly in dealing in negotiable paper, commonly called note-shaving. NICHOLAS BROWN, the millionaire of Providence, inherited a handsome fortune, with which he embarked heavily and successfully in commerce, extending his operations to almost every clime. Our New York millionaires made their money miscellaneously. JACOB LORILLARD, by dealing in Tobacco; PETER COOPER, the founder of the noble Cooper Institute, by dealing in Tin; SAMUEL WARD, by Banking; VANDERBILT, by Steamboating and Shipping; GEORGE LAW, by bridge and other contracts; and so on. In Philadelphia, the author of "Philadelphia and its Manufactures" states that there are at least twenty-five individuals "who are generally accredited by their intimate acquaintances with the ownership of a million and more." The lives of none of them, so far as we know, have been very illustrious. They are, no doubt, men of considerable force of character, with probably the ordinary admixture of those whose biographies, if faithfully written, always afford great consolation to blockheads. Among them, but not of the latter number, is one whose destiny it has been to be one of the standard-bearers of American mechanism in Russia; his establishment there being one of the most remarkable of which we have any record in the annals of industrial enterprises.* His career, moreover, has been adverted to, to illustrate the pecuniary advantages resulting from civility to strangers—a quality which, it is to be hoped, he will never lose in view of the urgent necessity for a good example, in this particular, to millionaires generally.

Franklin has said that the way to wealth is as plain as the way to market. This is no doubt true; but it is a road that has so many diverging paths, side-tracks and turn-outs, by which one is so continually liable to be switched off the rail, that few arrive at the station. It may be compared to Pearl fishing, in which one diver, at the first plunge, may bring up a pearl of great value, while another, equally expert, may dive for a week and

* The *Miner's Journal*, in 1846, spoke of this establishment as one of immense extent, in which 3,500 men are constantly employed, and in the conducting of which there are some curious features. "To keep order among such a congregation—exceeding the whole population of a good-sized town, and consisting of English, American, Scotch, Irish, German, and Russian—a company of soldiers is kept on duty at the Works, and a perfect police force, whose duties are confined to the establishment. Refractory men of every nation are discharged for irregular conduct, excepting Russians; and these are, for all slight offenses, immediately tied up to the triangles, roundly flogged, and sent back to their work again. It is but justice to the proprietors to say, that they have strongly appealed against this treatment, so peculiar to the Russian nation, but without effect. The plan of paying this enormous multitude is ingenious. On being engaged, the man's name is, we believe, not even asked, but he is presented with a medal number. In the pay-house are 3,500 wooden boxes, numbered; and, on presenting himself on Saturday night for his pay, the clerk hands him his money, takes his medal for a receipt, which is dropped in the box of its number, and gives him another medal as a pledge of engagement for the following week."

get little or nothing. It is impossible, moreover, that all can be millionaires — though all blessed with health, strength, and simple tastes, may attain an independence. It is not for the best interests of a state or nation that individuals should accumulate very large fortunes. Individuals, says Mr. Rae—and the remark is a forcible one—grow rich by the acquisition of wealth previously existing: nations, by the creation of wealth that did not before exist. "It is not that a duke has £50,000 a year," says Laing, "but that a thousand fathers of families have £50 a year—that is true national wealth and well-being." Let ours be the prayer of Agur: Give us neither poverty nor riches; feed us with food convenient for us, lest we be full and deny thee.

LETTER IV.

HOW TO GET THE FIRST THOUSAND DOLLARS.

JOHN JACOB ASTOR is reported to have said that it cost him more severe effort to get the first thousand dollars, than all the others. If he had bequeathed to mankind an easy and certain method of overcoming the difficulty, the bequest would have been a far more valuable one than all his fortune; entitling him to the most conspicuous niche in the gallery of the world's benefactors. The task, however, was beyond his powers, as it has proved too vast for abler men. Franklin attempted to teach the true secret of money-catching—the certain way to fill empty pockets—with what success we have seen. Millionaires have favored the world with their dicta and opinions; but the world has not attached any great importance to their sayings, and certainly not been much benefitted by their observations. Mankind generally have probably abandoned the idea of discovering a royal road to wealth, and concluded that an individual, or nation, in order to accumulate capital, must earn something by labor, and then save a portion of the product. Something, however, may be done—and a good deal more than has been done—to facilitate this accumulation; to show labor how, without extra exertion, it can increase its rewards; and show economy how, without injury to the physical system, less may be consumed. Let us consider,

First, HOW TO SAVE. The human mind receives its first practical lessons in the realities of life at a very early period. The child is initiated and instructed in one of the fundamental principles of social science when he discovers that he cannot purchase a cake and also keep his penny—that he must forego the one or part with the other. As a corollary from the proposition, he then comprehends that, to keep his pennies, he must deny himself cakes; and thus, by involuntary deduction, he arrives at a fundamental principle of economy, viz.: *Self-denial in expenditures for personal gratification.* The limit to which it is possible to carry this self-denial without injury to health, or diminution of power for production, is somewhat remarkable. The cost of what are absolute and actual necessaries of life is, in most countries, comparatively little — as is evidenced in cases where stern necessity affixes the bounds of possible expenditure. In France, for instance, there are tens of thousands of peasants and of operatives whose daily earnings do not exced ten cents, and yet they contrive to live gayly on that sum. As a consequence, in no other country has the art of Cookery made equal progress. In Paris, an enterprising woman, Madame Robert, furnishes a dinner daily to six thousand workmen for two pence each, her bill of fare being cabbage soup, a slice of *bouilli* (boiled beef), a piece of bread, and a glass of wine. In our Southern States, the food of the chief laborers—the men who produce an export value of over two hundred millions of dollars per annum in Cotton, Sugar, Tobacco, and Rice—does not probably cost their providers ten cents per day.* We might still further

* "The full allowance for a laboring man and woman—one that toils all the hours of daylight in the field—is a peck and a half of

illustrate the principle that the cost of the substances actually necessary for the support of life is small, by reference to the self-imposed abstinence of misers and the compulsory abstinence of prisoners.*

A few years ago, a Yankee philosopher of the school of Diogenes, endeavored to ascertain, by actual experiment, how cheaply a man could live; and his experience he has recorded in a volume entitled "Walden; or, Life in the Woods."

M. Thoreau, the gentleman referred to, being possessed of a capital of about $25, took possession of a few acres of land esteemed worthless, and proceeded to erect a

---

corn meal, and three and a half pounds of fat bacon. In the cotton States, the average price of the corn is about seventy-five cents a bushel, and the price of bacon eight cents a pound. This would make the week's rations cost fifty-six cents. At still higher rates it would not be a dime a day—in many places, not half that. In many places, though, the negroes do not get half the above rations." —Solon Robinson, formerly a South Carolina agriculturist.

* An item has been circulating in the newspapers, purporting to be the result of some experiments made in a prison, where it was found that ten persons gained four pounds of flesh each in two months, eating, for breakfast, eight ounces of oatmeal made into porridge, with a pint of butter-milk; for dinner, three pounds of boiled potatoes, with salt; for supper, five ounces of oatmeal porridge, with one pint of butter-milk, which cost two pence three farthings per day. Ten others gained three and a half pounds of flesh eating six pounds of boiled potatoes daily, taking nothing with them but salt. Ten others ate the same amount of porridge and butter-milk, with the potatoes, as the first ten, but for dinner had soup; they lost one and a quarter pounds of flesh each: and twenty others who had less, diminished in size likewise.

From this it would seem that potatoes are better diet than smaller quantities of animal food, at least for persons in confinement. The meat-eaters, if they had been allowed ordinary exercise, might have exhibited a very different result.

cabin by his own labor. The result of his building operations he gives as follows:—

"I have thus a tight-shingled and plastered house, ten feet wide by fifteen feet long, and eight feet posts, with a garret and closet, a large window on each side, two trap-doors, one door at the end, and a brick fire-place opposite. The exact cost of my house, paying the usual price for such materials as I used, but not counting the work, all of which was done by myself, was as follows—and I give the details because very few are able to tell exactly what their houses cost, and fewer still, if any, the separate cost of the various materials which compose them:—

Boards, mostly shanty boards	$8.03½
Refuse shingles for roof and sides	4.00
Laths	1.25
Two second-hand windows, with glass	2.43
One thousand old brick	4.00
Two casks of lime	2.40
Hair	.31
Mantle-tree Iron	.15
Nails	3.90
Hinges and screws	.14
Latch	.10
Chalk	.01
Transportation	1.40
In all	$28.12½

These are all the materials, excepting the timber, stones, and sand which I claimed by squatter's right. I have also a small woodshed adjoining, made chiefly of the stuff which was left after building the house."

Obtaining his fuel in an adjacent wood, at the cost merely of gathering it, he details his house-keeping expenses as follows:—

"The expense of food for eight months, from July 4th to March

1st, the time when these estimates were made—*though I lived there more than two years*—not counting potatoes, a little green corn and some peas which I had raised, nor considering the value of what was on hand at last date, was—

Rice,	$1.73½	Lard,	0.65
Molasses,	1.73	Apples,	0.25
Rye Meal,	1.04¾	Dried Apples,	0.22
Indian Meal,	0.99¾	Sweet Potatoes,	0.10
Pork,	0.22	One Pumpkin,	0.06
Flour,	0.88	One Watermelon,	0.02
Sugar,	0.80	Salt,	0.03
		Amount,	$8.74

It will thus be perceived that his food cost him in money about twenty-seven cents per week. For nearly two years after this he states that it consisted of rye and Indian meal (without yeast), potatoes, rice, a very little salt pork and molasses; and his drink was water. The cost of his clothing for eight months he estimates at $8 40¾, exclusive of washing and mending; and his other household expenses, oil, &c., at two dollars—making his whole expenses for eight months less than twenty-five dollars. "I learned from my two years' experience," he says, "that it would cost incredibly little trouble to obtain one's necessary food even in this latitude; that a man may use as simple diet as the animals, and yet retain health and strength."*

Another consoling fact is presented in the fruitfulness of the earth, or in the amount of food that can be produced upon an acre. Nearly every one in our country

* SOLON ROBINSON, in a little pamphlet on "The Economy of Food," published by Fowler & Wells, gives some excellent practical directions for living well at a trifling cost He shows what food is the cheapest and best for the economical to buy, and gives the following

can command the use of an acre of soil, and let us see how much, it is within the bounds of physical possibility, it may be made to produce. Simmonds in his "Vegetable

---

as "the proportion of nutritious matter and water in each of the following substances:"

Lbs.	Substances.	Lbs. nut. mat.	Lbs. water.
100	Wheat flour	90	10
100	Corn meal	91	9
100	Rice	86	14
100	Barley meal	88	12
100	Rye flour	79	21
100	Oatmeal	75	25
100	Potatoes	22½	77½
100	White beans	95	5
100	Carrots	10	90
100	Turnips	4½	95½
100	Cabbage	7½	92½
100	Beets	15	85
100	Strawberries	10	90
100	Pears	16	84
100	Apples	16	84
100	Cherries	25	75
100	Plums	29	71
100	Apricots	26	74
100	Peaches	20	80
100	Grapes	27	73
100	Melons	3	97
100	Cucumbers	2½	97½

"Meats, generally, are about three-fourths water; and milk, as it comes from the cow, over ninety per cent. How is it, as it comes from the milkman?

"It is true that this chemical analysis does not give us the exact comparative value of food, but with that, and the prices of the various articles, it cannot be a hard matter to determine what is the cheapest or most economical kind of food for us to use.

"Perhaps of all the articles named, taking into account the price and nutritious qualities, oatmeal will give the greatest amount of nutri-

Kingdom" remarks, with regard to the comparative productiveness of crops of human food, that one hundred bushels of Indian corn per acre is not an uncommon crop.

---

ment for the least money. But where will you find it in use? Not one family in a thousand ever saw the article; not one in a hundred ever heard of it; and many who have heard of it have a vague impression that none but starving Scotch or Irish ever use it; and, in short, that oats, in America, are only fit food for pigs and horses.

"It is a great mistake. Oatmeal is excellent in porridge, and all sorts of cooking of that sort, and oatmeal cakes are sweet, nutritious, and an antidote for dyspepsia. Just now, we believe oats are the cheapest of any grain in market, and it is a settled fact that oats give the greatest amount of power of any grain consumed by man or beast.

"This cheap food only needs to be fashionable, to be extremely popular among all laborers, all of whom, to say nothing of other classes, eat too much fine flour bread."

Again he says, "Look at the Scotch with their oatmeal porridge, as robust a set of men as ever lived.

"A Highlander will scale mountains all day upon a diet of oatmeal stirred in water fresh from a gurgling spring with his finger, in a leather cup. Another excellent, though little used breadstuff, particularly for the sedentary, or persons of costive habits, is cracked wheat, or wheaten grits, as the article is called. That and Graham flour should be used in preference, at the same price per pound, to white flour, because more healthy and more nutritious. One hundred pounds of Graham flour is worth full as much in a family as one hundred and thirty-three pounds of superfine white flour. Corn meal usually costs less than half the price of flour. It is worth twice as much. It is not so economical in summer, because it takes so much fire to cook it. The first great error in preparing corn meal is in grinding it too much, and next in not cooking it enough. Corn-meal mush should boil two hours; it is better if boiled four, and not fit to eat if boiled less than one hour. Buckwheat flour should never be purchased by a family who are obliged to economize food. It is dear at any price, because it must be floated in dear butter to be eaten, and then it is not healthy Oatmeal makes as

One peck per week will not only sustain life, but give a man strength to labor, if the stomach is properly toned to the amount of food. This, then, would feed one man four

---

good cakes as buckwheat, and far more nutritious. But it is more nutritious and is particularly healthy for children, in the form of porridge.

"PORK AND BEANS.—Perhaps I run the risk of ridicule by reiterating here, what I have so often asserted, that white beans, at the ordinary prices in most places, if not all, are the cheapest, because the most nutritious of all vegetables. Beans enter very largely into the diet of the inhabitants of some countries. This is particularly the ease in Mexico. Baked beans, with salt pork, used to be one of the most common dishes in New England. I have read somewhere that Professor Liebig has stated that pork and beans form a compound of substances peculiarly adapted to furnish all that is necessary to support life, and give bone, muscle, and fat, in proper proportions, to a man. This food will enable one to perform more labor at less cost, than any other substance. A quart of beans, eight cents, half a pound of pork, six cents, will feed a large family for a day, with good strengthening food.

"BEAN PORRIDGE is another of the old-fashioned dishes of New England. We should call it bean soup now. Four quarts of beans and two pounds of corned beef, 'boiled to rags' in fifty quarts of water, would give a good meal to fifty men—one cent a meal."

On the subject of Hominy he discourseth as follows: "Hominy, too, is a dish almost as universally liked as potatoes, and at the South it is more freely eaten; while at the North it is seldom seen. In fact, it is an unknown food except to a few persons in cities. By hominy, we do not mean a sort of coarse meal, but grains of white corn from which the hull and chit, or eye, has been removed by moistening and pounding in a wooden mortar, or patent hulling machine, leaving the grains almost whole, and composed of little else but starch. It has often been said, that not one cook in ten knows how to boil a potato. We may add another cipher when speaking of the very simple process of cooking hominy. We give formula from our own experience, and from instructions received in a land where 'hog and hominy' are well understood. Wash slightly

hundred weeks, or almost eight years. "Four hundred bushels of potatoes can also be raised upon an acre; this would be a bushel a week for the same length of time; and the actual weight of an acre of sweet potatoes is 21,344 pounds, which is not considered an extraordinary crop. This would feed a man (six pounds a day) for 3,557 days, or nine years and two-thirds. To vary the

---

in cold water, and soak twelve hours in tepid, soft water, then boil slowly from three to six hours in same water, with plenty more added from time to time with great care to prevent burning. *Don't salt while cooking*, as that or *hard water* will harden the corn; so it will peas or beans, green or dry, and rice also. When done, add butter and salt; or a better way is to let each one season to suit the taste. It may be eaten with meat in lieu of vegetables, or with sugar or syrup. It is good, hot or cold, and the more frequently it is warmed over; it is like the old-fashioned pot of

> "Bean porridge hot, or bean porridge cold,
> Bean porridge best at nine days old."

"So is hominy; it is good always, and very wholesome, and, like tomatoes, only requires to be eaten once or twice to fix the taste in its favor.

"In this city this article is called *samp*, and the name hominy is given to corn cracked in a mill, and winnowed and sifted, and numbered according to its fineness. It is cheap, healthy food. I have thought proper to add a few of the ways in which hominy may be used.

"HOMINY BREAKFAST CAKES.—Mash the cold hominy with a rolling-pin, and add a little flour and milk batter, so as to make the whole thick enough to form into little cakes in the hand, or it may be put upon the griddle with a spoon. Bake brown, eat hot, and declare you never ate any thing better of the batter-cake kind.

"HOMINY AND MILK, hot or cold, is as much better than mush and milk as that is better than rye-meal porridge.

"HOMINY PUDDING.—Prepare as for batter cakes, add one egg to each pint, some whole cinnamon, sugar to suit the taste, and a few raisins, and bake like rice pudding. A little butter or chopped suet may be added. Served hot or cold, with or without sauce."

diet, we will occasionally give rice, which has been grown at the rate of ninety-three bushels to the acre over an entire field. This, at forty-five pounds to the bushel, would be 4,185 pounds; or, at twenty-eight pounds to the bushel when husked, 2,604 pounds; which, at two pounds a day, would feed a man 1,302 days, or more than three and a half years!

Such considerations as these are full of consolation to the aspiring and of encouragement to the very poor. None need despair, and moreover, none need be dishonest. It is possible to accumulate capital, aye, to get the first thousand dollars from an income not exceeding the most moderate earnings or wages. And let it be inscribed on the lintel of every dwelling—on the desks in every counting-house—on the pericardium of every heart—*It is better to live on ten cents a day than to do a wrong for the sake of money.*

2. Again, the Economy that leads to wealth implies a *judicious use and profitable investment of savings.* A saving of even a small sum will amount, it is true, within the limits of an ordinary life, to a handsome aggregate; but rapid accumulation in this way, can only be attained when money reproduces itself through the agency of compound interest. The wonderful ratio of increase effected by this means, can only be understood by those who have experienced it—though a glimmering of the reality may be obtained by a glance at the following familiar table, interest being calculated at six per cent.:

Savings in 1 Year.	In Ten Years.	In Twenty Years.	In Thirty Years.	In Forty Years.	In Fifty Years	Savings in One Day.
$10	$130	$360	$790	$1,540	$2,900	2¾cts.
20	260	720	1,580	3,080	5,800	5½
30	390	1,080	2,370	4,620	8,700	8¼
40	520	1,440	3,160	5,160	11,600	11
50	650	1,860	3,950	7,700	14,600	13¾

The most notable instance that now occurs to me of remarkable success attained through attention to the prompt investment of small sums, is afforded in the annals of Abraham Shriver, of Frederick County, Maryland. With no other resources than a salary of $1400 a year as judge of a court of inferior jurisdiction, and a small farm of fourteen acres, he succeeded in keeping his personal expenditures within the receipts from his farm, which he cultivated like a garden; and by promptly investing his salary every quarter-day—sometimes borrowing for the purpose of anticipating or securing an investment promptly at the time, he accumulated an estate of $150,000. Among the records of Saving Banks, which perform a most useful purpose in collecting and rendering available the dribblets of wealth, no doubt there are many other remarkable instances. In Massachusetts the deposits in Savings Banks amount to over $23,000,000.

3. Another element of Economy, essential to the accumulation of capital, is *protection against great losses by carefully providing against small ones.* The importance of this principle is thus illustrated by M. Say, the political economist:

"Being in the country, I had an example of one of those small losses which a family is exposed to through negligence. From the want of a latch of small value, the wicket of a barn yard, looking to the field, was left open. Every one who went through, drew the door to; but having no means to fasten it, it reopened. One day a fine pig got out and ran into the woods, and immediately all the world was after it. The gardener, the cook, dairy-maid, all ran to recover the swine. The gardener got sight of him first, and jumping over a ditch to stop him, he sprained his ancle, and was confined a fortnight to the house. The cook, on her return, found all the linen she had left to dry by the fire burned; and the dairy maid having ran off before she tied the cows, one of them broke the leg of a colt in the stable. The gardener's lost time was worth twenty crowns, valuing his pains at nothing. The linen burned and the colt spoiled were worth as much more. Here is a loss of forty crowns, and much pain and trouble, vexation and inconvenience, for the want of a latch, which would have cost three pence; and the loss, through careless neglect, falls on a family little able to support it."

Proceeding now to inquire how to *labor with profit,* we remark, *first,* that Capital is a general term for the accumulated stock of former labor. Its father is Labor, and its mother Economy. Ties of consanguinity, however, it was long ago discovered, are no preventive against unseemly contention. It is an old proverb, "When two men ride on one horse, one must ride behind," but it is not always easy to decide the question of precedence between them. In primitive and unsettled states of society, Labor is more powerful than Capital. In pruning the luxuriance of nature, and subjugating it to man's uses, the capitalist shrinks into insignificance beside the man of the strong arm and the sharp axe. But as soon as population approaches density, Capital vaults into the saddle, and Labor must ride on the crupper. In society as at present developed, especially in the old world, a man who has nothing but ordinary unskilled labor to offer in the market finds that

"To beg, or to borrow, or to get one's own—
This is the very worst world that ever was known."

Wages would seem to be regulated by the cost of the things supposed to be necessary to support life; and he who would save a portion of his earnings, must reduce his expenditures for living to a very low standard. Nevertheless, there are many well-authenticated instances of men who, even in the old world, accumulated some capital from the proceeds of day-labor, and eventually became wealthy. How much may be accomplished by an indomitable will—a resolute determination to overcome all obstacles—Foster has illustrated in his "Essay on Decision of Character." He refers to a young man who, having expended a large fortune in prodigality, sat him down on the brow of an eminence overlooking what were lately his estates, and there resolved that all these estates should be his again.

"He had formed his plan, too, which he instantly began to execute. He walked hastily forward, determined to seize the very first opportunity, of however humble a kind, to gain any money, though it were ever so despicable a trifle, and resolved absolutely not to spend, if he could help it, a farthing of whatever he might obtain. The first thing that drew his attention was a heap of coals, shot out of a cart on a pavement before a house. He offered himself to shovel or wheel them into the place where they were to be laid, and was employed. He received a few pence for the labor; and then, in pursuance of the saving part of his plan, requested some small gratuity of meat and drink, which was given him. He then looked out for the next thing that might chance to offer, and went with indefatigable industry through a succession of servile employments, in different places, of longer and shorter duration, still scrupulously avoiding, as far as possible, the expense of a penny. He promptly seized every opportunity which could advance his design, without regarding the meanness of occupation or appearance. By this method he had gained, after a considerable time, money enough to purchase, in order to sell again, a few cattle, of which he had taken pains to understand the value. He speedily but cautiously turned his first gains into second advantages; retained, without a single deviation, his extreme parsimony; and thus advanced, by degrees, into larger transactions and incipient wealth. I did not hear, or have forgotten, the continued course of his life; but the final result was, that he more than recovered his lost possessions, and died an inveterate miser, worth £60,000."

In the United States, similar instances of moderate fortunes acquired through persevering industry, and acquired too without the sin of covetousness, are so numerous, that a volume would hardly contain them.* A leading

---

* The following sketch of a Chinaman in a foreign country is an interesting delineation of one who is bound to succeed; and, though by no means a commendable example, tends to elevate our ideas, now too low, of the Chinese character:

"No sooner does he put his foot among strangers, than he begins to work. No office is too menial or too laborious for him. He has come to make money, and he will make it. His frugality requires but little: he barely lives, but he saves what he gets; commences trade in the smallest possible way, and is continually adding to his store. The native scorns such drudgery, and remains poor; the Chinaman toils patiently on, and grows rich. A few years pass by, and he has warehouses; becomes a contractor for produce; buys foreign goods by the cargo; and employs his newly-imported countrymen, who have come to seek their fortunes as he did. He is not particularly scrupulous in matters of opinion. He never meddles with politics, for they are dangerous and not profitable; but he will adopt any creed, and carefully follow any observances, if, by so doing, he can confirm or improve his position. If it is expedient for him to become a Catholic, he punctually attends Mass, walks in processions, clings to his rosary or his reliquary with an excess of devotion, until he sails for home, when he tosses them overboard. He thrives with the Spaniard, and works while the latter sleeps. He is too quick for the Dutchman, and can smoke and bargain at the same time, turning his relaxation to account. He has harder work with the Englishman, but still he is too much for him, and succeeds. Climate has no effect on him; it cannot stop his hands, unless it kills him; and if it does, he dies in harness, battling for money till his last breath. Wherever he may be, and in whatever position, whether in his own or in a foreign country, he is diligent, temperate, and uncomplaining. He will compare in good qualities with men of other lands, and is, if any thing, more generally honest. He keeps the word he pledges, pays his debts, and is capable of generous and noble actions. It has been customary to speak lightly of him, and to judge of a whole people by a few vagabonds in a provincial seaport, whose morals and manners have not been improved by foreign society."

builder in New York city, now entitled to a place in the book of the "Rich Men," was some years ago a brick-layer's laborer at one dollar per day. He states that out of this sum he always contrived to save fifty cents per day, and laid by $180 the first year. Robert Fleming, of Philadelphia, was a drayman; as also several others equally or more successful. The senior members of many a stanch firm commenced their connection with mercantile life by sweeping out the store in which their fortunes were afterward acquired. But, notwithstanding the many cheering exceptions to the rule, it is nevertheless true, that ordinary unskilled labor can at best make but slow progress toward the accumulation of Capital.

Secondly. The rewards of labor and the facility for the acquisition of capital are increased by the possession of some *peculiar knowledge or skill.* A man's pecuniary value may be said to augment in exact proportion to the amount of his effective intelligence, superadded to ordinary physical power. The demand for *educated* labor in progressive countries so far exceeds the supply, that it may, to a certain extent, dictate its rewards. Men, animals, and machines are everywhere working fruitlessly or unprofitably for want of suitable persons to direct their movements; enterprises of the first magnitude languish for want of competent managers; and regions where nature has been most bounteous in her gifts, are yet comparatively a wilderness, because the arts and mechanism of civilization have not been introduced. The soil of Uruguay,* for instance, would produce wheat and Indian corn abundantly and luxuriantly; but its adaptation for the growth of these cereals is rendered comparatively worthless by the absence of suitable mills to grind the products. The sugar cane of the Southern States, and especially in the Tropics, is wasted immensely, for want of the proper machines and the requisite skill to extract all the sugar from the juice. There are dyes in the Indies rarer than the cochineal; fibrous plants more valuable than any flax or hemp; substances more oleaginous than linseed: but they are unappreciated, because the educated mechanician has not as yet prepared them for the world's markets. A quick brain and a ready hand constitute a man Fortune's master. Even women, limited as their opportunities are for gaining a livelihood, independently of being a helpmeet to man, wonderfully enlarge the scope of their powers when they combine administrative and manipulative skill. As managers of workrooms, superintendents, etc., women are especially in demand; and, if qualified, can readily earn from $6 to $12 per week.

Thirdly. Again, the accumulation of Capital may be accelerated by *associating with personal labor some responsibility.* Capitalists in general are timid, and desire to protect themselves against extraordinary expenses. It is in the nature of Capital to surround itself with safeguards, and it willingly pays a premium for guarantees. Thus, though an employer may be able to calculate the cost of an undertaking as measured by the labor involved, he would yet prefer to pay something additional to insure its execution for a definite sum. There are many instances, however, where the skilled laborer alone can form an estimate of the actual cost; and in such cases he may, by shrewd bargaining, obtain liberal compensation for the work. Many of those who have been remarkably successful in accumulating Capital have done so by advancing, as soon as possible, from the position of simple laborer to that of contractor.*

Fourthly. But the lever of greatest efficiency in pro-

---

* A slip from a Trenton newspaper, now before me, records the following illustration:

"Some years ago an individual, well known in Trenton, concluded to try the experiment of bettering his condition by adventuring to the Western country. Leaving his family behind, he bade farewell to Trenton one fine morning, and, with little else than a light heart and a good constitution in the way of capital, he commenced his journey. In a few weeks he found himself in the city of St. Louis, without a solitary acquaintance in the place, and but a solitary shilling in his pocket. This he reserved to pay for an obscure lodging, and went supperless to bed. The next morning he went to look for work, and soon got a contract to dig a well. On this job he cleared several dollars; and we next find him building a mill-dam for some person in St. Louis, which he accomplished with his own labor, to the decided advantage of his hitherto lean purse. By thus turning his hands to whatever they could find to do, without regard to the humbleness of the occupation, our adventurer returned, after an absence of a year, with seven hundred dollars in clear cash, and no unpaid debts to harass his fears. In a short time he sought his new home, and arrived in St. Louis in the heat of a copper-mine mania, which had sprung up from the discoveries about Lake Superior. Without friends, without education, without experience in the matter, he put out for the mining region, to see what could be done by such a person as himself. In an open boat, he minutely explored the rock-bound coast of the mighty Lake for several hundred miles; and, after an absence of some years, returned again to Trenton with several thousand dollars in hard cash, and with deeds in his pocket that showed him to be the owner of some of the West.

With the knowledge he had thus acquired by patient assiduity, our whilom well-digger went to Flemington, New Jersey, and succeeded in instilling new life into the owners of the well-known copper mine of that place, and in a few months sold out his interest in that concern at an advance of over ten thousand dollars. A few days since he returned to Missouri, where he has stores, lead, copper

moting accumulation, is *association of several for a common purpose.* Man, however skillful, is, if unaided by others, a very helpless being. There are tribes, we are told, whose cardinal principle it is for each individual to act independently of his fellows, never helping each other; but their condition, as may be supposed, is but little better than that of the wild animals with which they are surrounded. All of man's most wonderful achievements, those which, if considered disconnectedly from their performance, seem practically and physically impossible, are explained by the mystical power embodied in a combination of numbers for a common purpose. Many of the plans and projects to which I may invite your attention in the succeeding papers will, it is probable, be utterly impracticable unless you can associate others with you, in the faith that in union there is strength.

And *lastly,* the accumulated stock of the products of labor may be vastly increased by the judicious use of *Credit.* Credit is the offspring of good laws and good character. It is one of the advantages of legal protection for person and property that the owners of capital are willing to lend it, trusting to the honesty of the borrower that he will return it, or its equivalent, with rent or interest for its use. It is one of the advantages of good character, and known or presumed punctuality in dealing, that a man may, on his own security, obtain the possession and use of a reasonable amount of Capital.

---

mines, &c., all in the full tide of successful operation. All these results have been achieved by individual sagacity, aided by unyielding perseverance. Meanness and parsimony have had no share in the success we have recorded, for our hero is as open-handed as a prince. His generosity is unlimited, as more than one person, who owe all they possess to his friendly munificence, can testify."

Credit, being the representative of Capital, performs many of its functions, and confers upon the borrower the same benefits, less the charge for its use. The advantages of credit are nowhere more strikingly exemplified than in the rapid material progress of the United States; and in no other country are the profits from its use so large, when combined with industry or mechanical skill.

In the new States of the Union, an industrious man, who can command the use of some capital, can hardly fail to carve out for himself an independence. In Texas, for instance, it is said that a farm the second year will yield double the outlay; and a settler who commenced with $500 may, "within that time, have a property worth $1200 or $1500, and the original purchase-money returned with interest, besides maintaining himself and family for two years."* In Florida we are told of one

* I have no doubt this may be done in Texas, but the illustration given for the purpose of establishing it is, I suspect, slightly defective. I refer to the following:

"Let those who reside in cities, and cannot find profitable employment, go to Texas and raise their food out of the bosom of the earth. Any man, with five hundred dollars, can become an independent farmer; and, with industry and economy, may continue independent for life, and have a good home for his family at his death.

Thus, 100 acres of good land will cost	$200
Of this land 20 acres can be fenced, and a good crop put into the ground for	50
A good log-house will cost about	50
Expenses of voyage or journey	50
Add, for support of family till the crop is gathered, and incidental expenses	100
For purchase of horse and cow, and pair of oxen	50
	$500

The crop, when gathered, will be sufficient to maintain a family till

instance among hundreds, where one man, "*without assistance, and solely by his own labor*," made, in one season, over three hundred dollars from cultivating sugar-cane on one acre of land, and a large amount from raising other products, besides maintaining his family. The chronicles of the West record still more remarkable instances. A correspondent of the *Hunterdon Gazette*, endorsed as a prominent citizen of the State of New Jersey, writes from Illinois:

"I saw a farmer in Peoria County, who lived on a rented farm of eighty acres, for which he paid two hundred dollars rent for the land, and twenty-six dollars for the house; he did all his work himself, except some help in planting corn; had one team of horses; and, after paying his rent and supporting his family, would clear one thousand dollars this year."*

---

another and a larger crop can be raised, as more land could be fenced and cultivated the next year by the settler himself, say ten acres. The twenty acres will yield two crops of corn, in all about 1000 bushels, worth one dollar per bushel, or $1000 ; besides sweet potatoes to any desired quantity. This would be more than enough to maintain the family the second year. In addition to which, they would have the produce of their garden and dairy, and the increase of stock, swine, sheep, poultry, &c., which is of great value."

* The Rev. John S. Barger, a Methodist clergyman in Illinois, furnishes the following interesting account of two Mr. Funks, Jesse and Isaac—no relation of Peter. Peter's address, as heretofore, is New York city.

"I will now give you a concise history of the operations of Mr. Funk. Both before and after his marriage, he had made rails for his neighbors at twenty-five cents per one hundred. But when the lands where he lived came into market, twenty-five years ago, he had saved of his five years' earnings $1400, and says, if he had invested it all in lands, he would now have been rich. With two hundred dollars he bought his first quarter-section, and loaned to his neigh-

In California, farming has yielded equally good returns. A gentleman writes:

"The following facts have come under our knowledge. A German farmer squatted on one hundred and sixty acres of ground, some four years ago. Although he began without a halfpenny, he made in the first year by wheat growing the handsome sum of nine hundred dollars, besides paying for his land at one dollar per acre, and for his implements, and buying horses, cows, and oxen, building his house, and completing his fence. For the last two years his field of forty acres has yielded him 1,100 bushels of wheat per annum, selling for net $1400; his eggs, poultry, vegetables, fruit, &c., brought in four hundred dollars. He estimates his increase in cattle at eight hundred dollars, and the increase in the value of the land at three hundred and twenty dollars. Besides this, according to his own account, he had $2,500 cash in the bank; and, in fact, considered he was worth $10,000, and all this the result of four years judicious labor, single-handed, and commencing totally without capital.

"A field of 500 acres of wheat has produced, within the last four years, a total of 63,220 bushels, of the value of $108,000.

"An Irish farmer began farming in 1853 with the small sum of three hundred dollars, made in the mines in company with his nephew, a young lad. He first bought two hundred acres of land, paying a deposit on the same; and the rest of the money was invested in a horse, a cow, and the necessary implements. The first

---

bors eight hundred dollars to buy their homes; and with the remaining four hundred dollars he purchased a lot of cattle. With this beginning, Mr. Funk now owns seven thousand acres of land, has near twenty-seven hundred in cultivation, and his last year's sales of cattle and hogs, at the Chicago market, amounted to a little over forty-four thousand dollars.

"Mr. Isaac Funk, of Funk's Grove, nine miles distant from his brother Jessie, and ten miles north-west from Bloomington, on the Mississippi and Chicago Railroad, began the world in Illinois at the same time, having a little the advantage of Jesse, so far as having a little borrowed capital. He now owns about twenty-seven thousand acres of land; has about four thousand acres in cultivation; and his last sales of cattle at Chicago amounted to $60,000."

year his fenced-in field yielded wheat to the value of eight hundred dollars, which enabled him to pay the remainder of his money for his land, besides repaying him for that expended on his stock. He owns six hundred acres of land, and twenty-eight head of cattle, including seven horses; together with lots of pigs, sheep and poultry. His arable land is now forty-five acres, besides which he has a large orchard and kitchen-garden. In a word, he has made himself a very snug comfortable home and something like four thousand dollars to boot.

In 1852 an Englishman and two Germans came from the mines, with a united capital of thirteen hundred dollars. They bought six hundred and forty acres of land and farmed it. Last year one of the Germans sold his share in the increased concern for nine thousand dollars.

"Some years ago, an intimate acquaintance of ours, a German, in company with another as partner, bought a farm, and took to cultivating it and raising cattle. He now owns upward of fifteen thousand acres of land, and is worth pretty nearly one hundred thousand dollars. This person, too, began without a halfpenny."*

The cultivation of *fruits and vegetables*, especially in the vicinity of large cities, is, if skillfully managed, almost uniformly a profitable business. An acre of superior pear trees has produced to their owner $2,650 in one season; and supposing thirteen bushels to the tree, and the price

---

* The Germans are proverbially a frugal, money-making people. One of the Teutons, in reply to a question propounded at the Philadelphia Board of Trade in relation to discounts, is reported to have revealed the secret of his success as follows: "I commenced bisiness two year ago mit out capital. I open von grocery, mit cot-fish and molasses and one barrel of viskey. Vell, I goes on und by and by I gets a box of sugar and one box of tea; und by and by I gets a big grocery store mit a box China man in der winder and a horse and wagon to go to market. But I know notin about der book-keeping nor dishkounts nor der per cents, but den I tells you vat I knows; *I knows, ven I buys sugar for a five cent and sells it for a ten cent, den I makes money*"

four dollars per bushel, it is possible for an acre to produce $5,200. A gentleman who is engaged in cultivating strawberries on ten acres, eight miles from Cincinnati, states that the gross receipts of his patch, in a single season, were $2,210. The expense of picking, including the boarding of hands, was two hundred and twenty-five dollars, and expenses of marketing seventy-five dollars. The probable cost of cultivation per annum is fifteen dollars per acre. This gentleman cultivates all his strawbrries on new but very hilly ground.

In the vicinity of the Southern cities there is an excellent opportunity for profitable occupation in market-gardening. The attention of producers is so exclusively devoted to the raising of staples, that the markets of the cities are often illy supplied with garden fruit and vegetables. Besides strawberries, peas, potatoes, etc., will ripen at least six weeks earlier in the Southern than in the Northern States; and a very profitable and extensive business may be done in shipping them to Philadelphia, New York and Boston. Within a few miles of some of the Southern cities land may be purchased for five dollars per acre, which, if employed in this way, will produce three hundred dollars per acre.

Nurseries generally yield excellent returns for the skill and well-directed labor expended upon them, though to conduct them successfully considerable capital is also required. A nursery in the western part of the State of New York, is reported to have made a profit of $80,000 in one year, and another of $20,000. A writer describes a half acre of seedling pears that he saw, as worth, at market prices, ten thousand dollars.

Agricultural operations in general are undoubtedly the safest, and permanently the most lucrative; but those who have a special aptitude for trading or bargaining, can readily find other occupations equally lucrative and more congenial to their tastes. Efficient Agents are in great demand—Book Agents, Mercantile Agents, Agents to introduce novel machines. In every settled county throughout the Union, there should be at least one person acting as middle-man between the inhabitants of that county and the publishers, merchants, and manufacturers of the cities, for the purpose of introducing new things that seem calculated to benefit his neighbors. The draw-back to the successful prosecution of these kinds of agency business, hitherto has been, that so many of those who have undertaken it have been wanting in moral character and mercantile honesty—cheating by false representations those who buy from them, and defrauding those who entrust them with goods by not paying for them. A reliable, honest, persevering agent is always in demand; and if located in a populous district, he can accumulate his first thousand dollars with ease.

But the foundation of a fortune can be laid, probably, in all the established pursuits, especially by *expending more than the usual care and labor in having the stock in trade of superior quality.* Even in bread, pie, or cake baking—numerous as the bakers are—I doubt not many more could do well by producing these articles of a quality better than the average. A lady, the widow of a Boston merchant, who, though once opulent, had failed, a few years ago made an independence by baking what is called Domestic bread in contradistinction to what is known as Baker's bread. Her fresh-looking, sweet-tasted loaves, of full weight, were so much choicer than the ordinary bread, that customers flocked to her little store; and in a very few years she had accumulated enough to purchase five hundred acres of land in Michigan, three hundred of which, we were told—five years ago—were in a high state of cultivation; and from these three hundred acres she had raised in one year $6,000 worth of wheat.

The principle is equally applicable to mercantile as to mechanical pursuits. A firm in Philadelphia has made a fortune by putting-up teas in a more neat and convenient form than ordinary, supplying California and other markets with the packages. A mercantile house in New York received satisfactory returns from a voyage to Australia, at a time when all other shippers lost money, simply because their goods were of a superior quality, put up in a secure and attractive form, and they arrived out in good order and condition. The United States supply eighty-four per cent. of the Cotton consumed in England, principally because the American Cotton arrives out in the best possible condition for the subsequent operations of the manufacturer—is better ginned, cleaned, and packed than that from any other country. And again, England sells to the United States millions of manufactured goods annually, to the injury of American manufacturers, mainly because there is an impression abroad—daily, however, becoming more unfounded and erroneous—that English goods, at the same price, are superior in quality to the American. The world wants commodities both cheap and good, if possible; but, at all events, good.

Perhaps the most common and fatal mistake that aspirants for fortune make, is in despising small improvements, small savings, small inventions, small things generally. We forget that an acorn contains the germ of an oak, and that an ignited coal may result in the world's conflagration. Franklin's experiments with a boy's kite were probably regarded as a very small business, for a grave man, by his kite-despising cotemporaries; but the manufacturers of lightning rods have, no doubt, satisfactory and substantial reasons for entertaining a very different opinion. Daguerre threw the sun's light on a silvered plate—seemingly a small affair; but this was the foundation of the great business now extended throughout almost all lands—of Photography. The despised sea-slug, or *Biche de Mar*, has enabled supercargoes to meet their employers with smiling faces;* while the cargo of Silks, Teas, Sugar, and of other products pompously imposing on the manifest, has proved the bankruptcy of its owner. Perhaps the best general advice that can be given to him who seeks his first thousand

---

* *Biche de Mar*, or the Sea-slug, is found among the Feejee group of islands, and belongs to the *Holothuria*. When prepared, it finds a ready sale in China, where it is used as an ingredient in rich soups. There are several varieties of the article, distinguishable both by shape and color, but more particularly by the latter. The valuable kinds are six in number, some of which are from two to nine inches in length, when cured, resembling crape. The kinds most esteemed are found on the reefs, in water from one to two fathoms in depth, where they are caught by diving. The inferior sorts are found on the reefs at low water, and picked up by the natives.

The motions of the animal resemble those of the caterpillar; it feeds by suction, and draws in with its food much fine coral and some small shells. Firewood is indispensable in the curing process, each picul of *Biche de Mar* requiring about half a cord of wood to cure it. This fuel is purchased from the chiefs, who sometimes furnish as much as twenty cords for a single musket. The usual price paid for the animals is a whale's tooth for a hogshead; but they are also exchanged for muskets, powder, balls, vermilion, paint, axes, hatchets, beads, knives, scissors, chisels, plane-irons, gauges, fish-hooks, small glasses, flints, cotton cloths, chests, trunks, etc. Of beads blue are preferred, and cotton cloth of the same color is most in demand. In the process of drying, the *Biche de Mar* loses two-thirds both of its weight and bulk, and, when cured, resembles a

dollars is—*Do that which you can do better than others,* and *do not despise small things.* For your sake the writen would repeat the latter admonition, Do not despise small things—and for his own—or the accompanying papers will be consigned to the tomb of the Capulets.

---

smoked sausage. In this state it is sold by the picul (133 pounds), which brings from fifteen to twenty dollars. The *Biche de Mar* is sometimes carried to Canton, but more usually to Manilla, whence it is shipped to China.

In order to show the profits which arise from the trade in the article, the following table, showing the returns of five voyages to the Feejee group, furnished by an American long engaged in the business, is appended to "Wilkes' Sketch":

Voyage.	Piculs.	Cost of Outfit.	Produce of Sales.
First	617	$1,101.00	$ 8,021.00
Second	700	1,200.00	17,500.00
Third	1,080	3,396.00	15,120.00
Fourth	840	1,200,00	12,600.00
Fifth	1,200	3,500.00	27,000.00

A further profit, it is stated, also arises from the investment of proceeds in China.—*Commercial Relations.*

OPPORTUNITIES FOR LUCRATIVE INDUSTRY

AND

THE SAFE INVESTMENT OF CAPITAL;

OR,

CHANCES TO MAKE MONEY.

Now, assuming that you are possessed of some capital, or its approximate equivalent, Credit; assuming that you are blessed with health and strength, a sound mind in a sound body, and that you command that precious gift—more valuable in the race for Fortune than genius or learning—TACT; assuming that you are theoretically and practically acquainted with the principles which underlie all pursuits, and the laws and customs which regulate them; assuming that you are endowed with varied propensities, having an aptitude for many occupations, without being exactly that phenomenon familiarly distinguished as a jack-of-all-trades; assuming that you are without partiality for any locality, that the world is your home, where to choose—and without partiality for any pursuit, except such as, while profitable to yourself, is of benefit to your country; assuming that, though ever ready to receive suggestions, you always act upon the dictates of your own judgment, which you endeavor to enlighten by procuring all the information within your reach bearing on the subject of your reflections, and, consequently, you hold no one but yourself responsible for your acts; assuming that you prefer the results of experiment and research to imaginary speculations and theories however ingenious, and that you expect principally from me a digest of what others have tested, adhering closely to safe authorities;—assuming, in a word, all that it is necessary to assume in order to establish between us that magnetic sympathy which makes a writer intelligible to a reader, giving the latter a clairvoyant perception to see beneath the surface, and discover harmony and congruity where another would be involved in the clouds of skepticism, if not the darkness of unbelief, I shall proceed to offer such suggestions as occur to me, and submit such information as I am possessed of with regard to the Opportunities or Chances now open for the exercise of industry profitably, and the safe investment of Capital.

It is true, as a general rule, that the average profit of all established pursuits is nearly equal; for no sooner is it ascertained that one pays better than another, competition comes in and reduces profits to the general level. Yet, it is nevertheless true, that some kinds of business can be shown to be more uniformly safe and profitable than others; and in new branches of industry, especially, a large percentage of profits is often attainable before others appreciate their advantages. Consequently, in my researches for your benefit, I have directed my attention rather to the new or comparatively undeveloped openings for Industry and Trade, than to those which are well-established and organized in settled communities, and so well conducted that no improvement can be suggested. In none, however, would it be consistent with a plan embracing a great variety of suggestions, to give practical details respecting modes and processes; and this is the less necessary, because it is assumed that the reader will investigate further, diligently seeking information, and not despising any because it is printed, on the particular subject toward which his inclinations may tend. The writer's attention, it will be of course observed, has been directed to the bright side of the schemes and projects which he ventures to submit; and it may happen, as it has often happened before, that some of them have latent, inherent, and unforeseen difficulties, that may prove insuperable obstacles to their successful execution in practice. He would therefore remark, that "Look before you leap" is a maxim as sound as that "The best laid schemes o' mice and men aft gang agley" is true. In illustration of the concealed obstacles that test the fortitude of projectors, I might allude to the one recently broached, and so favorably entertained—of transporting cattle from South America to New York in propellers specially constructed for the trade. Inasmuch as it was known that cattle could be purchased on shore in the northern parts of South America, for three dollars and even one dollar per head, and freighted to New York for ten or fifteen dollars per head, and when there readily salable at eight or ten cents per pound, live weight, the undertaking looked most promising. But, alas! it was discovered that wild cattle, raised upon the Savannas of Venezuela, will not eat hay, and cannot be forced to eat it; nor will they drink water except from the running stream. They would thus die of hunger or thirst on the voyage, and consequently, are not transportable by sea farther than they can stand the deprivation of food and water. But though this scheme thus became impracticable, it must, nevertheless, be practicable to effect the object in another way. And I mention as—

CHANCE I.—*To make Money render available the products of the Cattle of South America, and transport them to the chief markets of America and Europe.*

In Venezuela and other portions of South America, thousands of cattle are annually slaughtered, for no other commercial advantage than the sale of the hides and tallow. Meat which would certainly command a fair price in the markets of the United States, especially when beefsteaks are worth 18 cents per pound in New York, is left to decay in the fields. The preparation of what is termed jerked beef, is carried on to a considerable extent; and a few Englishmen are utilizing the products of cattle so far as to grind up the bones and ship them to England for manure; but what would probably prove the most lucrative branch of the business is comparatively neglected. Certainly, in this advanced era of chemical science, a mode must have been discovered of preserving beef in its fresh state on a voyage from South America to the United States, or to any of the European ports. Some ten or more years ago, a paper was read at the Parisian Academy of Sciences, by M. Dussourde, stating that meat which has been steeped in ferruginous or iron syrup, dries with only a slight diminution of volume, and is not affected by the most active agents of putrefaction. When required for use, the meat is put into cold water, and it soon assumes its original size. Its color and odor are then like those of fresh meat, of which it has all the properties.

During the late Russian war, a large business was done in supplying the army with fresh meat, obtained on the Danube and its tributary streams, where cattle were sold alive for about the value of their hides, bones, and horns. The mode of preparing the meat was as follows. The beef, with the bones extracted, was cut up into small pieces and put into tin boxes, with a small quantity of water. No salt was used. The tin box was then soldered up on all sides, and only a very small hole was left in the corner of the lid. The boxes were then set in a large iron vessel containing water, and boiled over a brisk fire until all the liquor in the tin boxes had escaped. The small hole left in each was then speedily closed with solder; and being thus free of air, the beef is kept for several years as fresh as on the day when it was put up. The expeditions to the Arctic Sea, under Sir John Franklin and Captain Ross, were furnished with fresh beef preserved in this manner.

Casareep, a delicious sauce made from the Cassava plant, is said to be so powerfully antiseptic that it preserves animal food for a length of time, even in the Tropics. But probably the most available substance, (unless refrigerators can be substituted,) will prove to be pyroligneous acid. Mr. Bancroft, of Providence, in a communication to the *Scientific American,* July 4, 1857, stated: "Meat can be preserved any length of time by merely plunging it in pyroligneous acid for a few moments, and drying it in the shade. This effect is partly ascribed to the empyreumatic oil or tar contained in the liquid; and this would account for the use of smoke for preserving hams fish, tongues, &c., as pyroligneous acid is obtained by the destructive distillation of wood. The harder woods, such as oak, beech, ash, and birch, are used. Pyroligneous acid is a brown, transparent vinegar, and has a strong smell; its acid powers are said to be superior to those of the best wine or malt vinegar, in the proportion of three to two. It has been in use with calico printers for a long time. By perusing an article on this acid in 'Pilkington's Mechanic's Own Book,' I was led to make several experiments with a view to test the truth of its property of preserving flesh from putrefaction, and the result of my experiments was to prove it beyond doubt."*

At the London Exhibition in 1851, one of the substances that excited a great deal of interest was a certain Meat Biscuit, introduced by Mr. Gail Borden from Texas. In connection with dried vegetables, it was supposed that this meat biscuit would prove of the greatest value, especially in supplying the navy. It is a composition of the essence of meat and the finest flour. Dr. Lindley, F.R.S., pronounced it one of the most important substances which the Exhibition had brought to their knowledge, and said: "When we consider that by this method, in such places as Buenos Ayres, animals which are there of little or no value, instead of being destroyed as they often are for their bones, may be boiled down and mixed with the flour which all such countries produce, and so converted into a substance of such durability that it may be preserved with the greatest ease, and sent to distant

* The same writer states, as an extraordinary fact, that pyroligneous acid will not only preserve, but restore putrid meats to a fresh condition. Dr. Jarg, of Leipsic, has made numerous experiments with this acid, and recovered quite a number of anatomical preparations from incipient corruption by simply pouring it over them. By smearing pieces of flesh (already in a state of corruption) with empyreumatic oil, or tar, he succeeded in restoring them dry and sound. Vanquelin proved that this acid was simply an acetic contamination with empyreumatic oil and bitumen.

countries, it seems as if a new means of subsistence was actually offered to us. Take the Argentine Republic—take Australia—and consider what they do with their meat there in time of drought. When they cannot get rid of it whilst it is fresh—they may boil it down, and mix the essence with flour (and we know they have the finest in the world), and so prepare a substance that can be preserved for times when food is not so plentiful, or sent to countries where it is always more difficult to procure food. Is not this a very great gain?"

CHANCE II.—*Good profits can be made by Stock-raising in various parts of the United States, especially in Texas.*

Texas has a peculiar adaptation for raising Stock, in consequence of the excellence and abundance of her pastures, and the mildness of her climate, which saves the expense of winter feeding. Five hundred dollars, it is said, invested in Cows and Calves in Western Texas, will yield, allowing for ordinary casualities, $2,000 in six years. Without vouching for the accuracy of this statement, it is nevertheless evident that the business will pay a large percentage of profit, and is probably attended with fewer risks than almost any other regular business. It possesses an additional advantage in the fact, that a large or a small capital can be employed with a like certainty of success.

Braman, in his "Information about Texas," furnishes the following remarks and advice upon the subject:

"A stock-raiser commencing business purchases his one or two hundred acres of land, near to or at the edge of a prairie, and on the border of a creek, spring, or water-course of some kind; for here he can always find timber for his buildings and fences, and the protection of the shade trees from the summer sun and northern blasts.

Usually these favorite situations are on the outskirts or surroundings of the prairies; but in many instances the prairies themselves are interspersed with 'motts' or 'islands' of timber, containing from a few rods to many acres; and sometimes they are covered with a growth of majestic live oaks: nevertheless, with this seeming contradiction of terms, these are prairies, there being neither underbrush nor shrub, but the oaks growing singly and sufficiently near to shade the ground without deteriorating the grass. A person can ride through them with as little trouble as he can traverse an orchard. When the stock-raiser has made his selection, the first business is to build a pen for the herding of his cattle, and then a small log or frame house covered with oak boards; next he fences in a few acres of the rich prairie, for the culture of his corn and garden 'stuff;' as he expresses it 'Makes a patch large enough to bread his family'—and in truth, all the space that this family will occupy out of the whole prairie before them is but a patch; and hundreds of other patches might be appropriated, without apparently diminishing the great whole. The cattle-raiser supplies himself with two or three Mexican horses for herding, a few hogs and other domestic animals; and having a small stock of cattle, no family, with moderate means, can, under any other circumstances, begin to feel so soon independent of the world for all the comforts of life.

"In commencing, it would be best to purchase one hundred head of cows with their calves, and two or three bulls. A stock started in this way, remain more gentle, and are not so apt to stray as an average stock: they can be purchased in this way for ten dollars, the cow and calf. The increase is very rapid and soon outnumbers the highest calculation of the sanguine owner. The stock requires very little attention, except in the spring and fall: in March, the herding and marking and branding the young calves are performed; where there are many stocks commingled in one range, the owners club together and drive herds of one or two hundred into a pen, when each owner singles out his calves, ropes and brands them. This herding is continued until all but a few scattering ones are gone through with. In the fall season, when the weather becomes cool, the herding, marking, branding, and altering, are again done in the same way: this time includes all the stragglers left at any previous branding, and all that have been dropped since spring. In a small stock, whose range is near no others, so that the owner has to depend for its management on his own force, it is deemed best to be frequently among them, and to mark, brand, and alter the calves as soon as they are old enough, always having regard to the proper seasons. This keeps the stock more tractable, and familiarizes them with man; and the owners soon come to know every animal in the herd, and one cannot get astray without being missed. Stocks of cattle will thrive and increase, with very little care and attention; but it is found from experience, that the bestowal of a considerable degree of attention on them is well remunerated, and that they become more docile.

"There is always a demand for beef and stock cattle. Men come here, and buy up large droves of the latter for the Missouri and Illinois farms and California rancheros: in those places the cattle are more valuable than in Texas. Many beef cattle are shipped from here to New Orleans; and much of the regular supply for said city comes from Texas. Indianola, on Matagorda Bay, is the principal shipping-port for cattle. There are several persons at that place who make regular shipments every week by the steamers. Galveston and Corpus Christi have participated in this trade; but many more beeves are shipped from Matagorda Bay than all other ports. The high value of hides, for the last year, has added much to the profits of stock-raisers. They used to be thought hardly worth saving; and, when saved, the stretching and curing were so carelessly performed, that very little was received for them. Of late, a better economy has dictated more care; and our hides, which are really of extra quality intrinsically, are becoming quite an article of commerce. During our war with Mexico, I have seen thirty beeves killed every other day, and the hides thrown to the vultures. Steers at three and four years old are considered beeves, and are sold to contractors, who ship them to New Orleans or to the planters here. The value of a four-year-old is about fifteen dollars. The stock-raisers who have families, generally, during the spring and summer months, have their pens full of milch-cows, from each of which they take but little milk, and are continually replenishing their yards from the prairies. The calves of the milking-cows are kept up as long as their dams are required, and they and the milker divide the product of the udder, the calves getting the greater share. Large quantities of butter and cheese might be made by the stock-raisers; but an improvident neglect in our people allows these articles to be imported from abroad in large quantities—foreign butter in the winter frequently selling at fifty cents per pound, cheese twenty-five cents.

" The term ' stock-cattle' is conventional, and means, in five hundred head, the following proportions, viz.:

170 Cows, with their calves.
65 Steer Calves under one year old.
65 Heifer Calves " " "
55 Two-year-old Steers.
55 " Heifers.
45 Three-year-old Steers.
45 " Heifers.

Making 500 head of all varieties; and such a stock of cattle is worth $2,500, at the rate of $5 per head. The selling price per head does not vary, whether the stock be large or small. There are laws requiring every stock-owner to adopt a mark and brand different from any of his neighbors, and to have the same recorded in the County Clerk's office. The criminal laws have several provisions for the protection of stock-owners' rights against dishonest persons: there is also an estray law, which obliges the taker-up of a strange animal to give sufficient publicity.

" The cattle of this State have never been subject to any endemical, epidemical, or contagious diseases, to make the business of stock-raising precarious and uncertain; and very few die, excepting the old cows. These generally live to the age of twenty years, and frequently have calves the last year. However, the inclement winter of 1855–6 was extremely disastrous to stock of all kinds, and even to wild animals. In Texas it is estimated that at least twenty-five per cent. of all the neat cattle in the State died from the effects of cold. Some of the older States are said to have lost over fifty per cent. from the same cause: but such a season was never before experienced. Thousands of cattle in good order became so paralyzed with intense cold, that they dropped down while feeding, and perished where they fell.

" The seaboard countries, and all of that region of country lying west of the Colorado, are well adapted to stock-raising; but the coast countries are preferable to the interior. The former combine many advantages, the prairies being larger than in the interior, winters shorter, and the grass continues good the whole year—the heat of summer being tempered by the delightful breezes of the Gulf of Mexico; and at no time is the weather on the prairies oppressive.

"Another great advantage to large stock-raisers is, that shipping depots are handy from any point in those countries; and agents are constantly scouring the country, gathering in beeves for New Orleans. Matagorda and Jackson counties I think preferable to any others; and the prairies of Trespalacios and Harankawa are certainly unsurpassed in the requisites for this business."

CHANCE III.—*Good profits can also be made by breeding American Jacks from imported Stock, and raising Mules in favorable localities.*

The raising of Mules in several of the States is a very profitable business. In Missouri, a mule at weaning time is said to be worth $50; at one year old, $60; at two years old, $85; and three years old, about $100: while the cost of keeping, when the prairie grass is good through the warm season, does not exceed $10 per year. Mules, it is probable, will every year be better appreciated as draught animals. Requiring far less food than the horse to keep him in good condition, yet capable of more constant labor, the Mule, as soon as the best mode of managing him is understood, will probably supersede the horse in team, draught, and all slow and heavy work.

In Northern Mexico, it is said that mares can be purchased for $7, and even $5 each, while mules are worth $40 to $60. Land can be bought for a nominal price, and labor is very cheap. A capital of say $50,000 invested in land, the necessary appurtenances, and in 3000 brood mares, would, at the end of three years, yield mules that could be sold for more than $100,000, with a lot of one and two-year olds on hand and the original stock not materially impaired. Some very large fortunes have been made in this business, and others equally as large can and will be made in future.

The importation of Jacks, as a commercial adventure, has, in some instances, yielded very large returns; and we should think that the raising of them would be found profitable in suitable localities. Jacks of large size, purchased in Spain for $50 or $60, have been sold on arrival in the United States for $1500, and perhaps in some instances more. It is now, however, difficult to procure superior jacks in Spain or elsewhere; hence the importance and inducements for raising an original breed, and, if possible, superior to any that can be imported.

Heretofore it has been the ambition of mule-breeders in the United States to raise mules of the greatest possible height. All their efforts have been directed to this end. This, however, a very sensible writer on the subject in the *New York Tribune* considers a radical error in the American system of breeding. For all purposes of labor to which mules are principally applied in this country, he argues, a small-sized mule is superior to one of great size, while it will consume considerably less provender. On the subject of raising American Jacks, he says:

"It is our belief that the Andalusian jack, if it can be procured, is the most eligible sire for the United States; but as it is understood to be difficult to procure this race, it would be perhaps advisable to commence from the commencement, and proceed to breed our own jacks for the purpose of breeding our own mules, instead of having recourse to constant importation of mules. This in the end would prove to be not only the surest but the cheapest method; and it is confidently believed that a superior jack to any now existing, for American breeding purposes, might thus be produced. In the islands of Majorca and Minorca, to which the ravages of foreign and civil war have not, so far, extended, it is well ascertained that the large, coarse, slouch-eared Spanish breed still exists in perfection; and thence it would be easy to procure jennies—as the females of the ass are technically termed—by breeding which to the finest Maltese jacks, there can be no doubt that stallions might be reared superior in the combination of bone with beauty and spirit to any breed of original jacks now in existence. The choice of mares from which to breed mules by such jacks is an easy matter. They should on no account be blood mares, or highly-bred mares, or tall mares. Fifteen hands in height is abundant stature, and fifteen two is too large; but they should be rather long-bodied, roomy, and, above all, bony. They should have long shoulders, as oblique as possible, since those of the ass are very straight, a peculiarity which it is desirable to correct; and, for analogous reasons, they should *not* have the pasterns too stiff and erect; and they *should* have the hoofs large, round and well opened. The better their necks, withers and heads, the neater in all probability will be the produce. On the whole, we have little doubt that fine, well-selected Canadian or Norman mares, will prove to be the best mule mothers—as thorough-breds will prove to be the worst—while Andalusian jacks, or half-breeds between the Maltese and great Majorca race of asses, will prove the best possible sires. It only remains to be stated that, in order to have mules docile and gentle, they should be handled as young as possible, and invariably altered before they are six months old. The longer that operation is deferred, the more indocile, obstinate, and perhaps vicious they will become, which is the greatest defect in the character of the mule, and that against which it behooves the breeder most to be on his guard."

CHANCE IV.—*Money can be made by raising Sheep where Pasturage is cheap, and the Climate most favorable for the production of Wool.*

John Randolph, of Roanoke, is reported to have said, on the floor of Congress, that he would at any time go out of his way "to kick a sheep." Others less eccentric than he, have shared this antipathy; but as there were 21,571,306 sheep in the United States in 1850, the prejudice cannot be very deep-rooted or wide-spread.

From an examination of what has been written on the

subject, I infer that sheep-husbandry, to be profitable, must be conducted on a large scale, and in localities where the expenses for keeping are small. A small flock, unless the breed be very superior, would not justify the employment of proper persons to guard them constantly, and they would be liable to destruction by disease, and particularly by dogs. Regarded solely with reference to the expenses for keeping sheep, Texas must offer special advantages, if it be true, as stated in the Patent Office Report for 1849, that the annual expense does not exceed 25 cents per head. Olmsted, in his recent work entitled, "A Journey through Texas," gives the following statement of the comparative returns for Wool and Cotton, assuming the capital to be the same. The allowance for lambs, it will be remarked, is considerable.

Sheep on a Large Scale.

Land, 1000 acres, at $2,	$2,000
House and Furniture,	4,000
Fencing and Plowing by contract,	2,000
Tools, Horses and Wagons,	1,500
24,125 Northern Sheep, at $4,	96,500
Improved Bucks,	14,000
	$120,000

Annual Production.

40,000 lbs. Wool, at 25 cents,	$10,000	
18,000 Lambs (25 per cent. lost), at $4,	72,000	
		$82,000
Deduct Wages 100 Mexican Shepherds, at $180	$18,000	
" 10 Head do. 500	5,000	
" 1 Bailiff, at $1400,	1,400	
" 14 Farm hands, at $200,	2,800	
" 1 " Foreman, at $500,	500	
Interest on $115,000, at 8 per cent.,	9,200	
		$36,900
Clear returns,		$45,100

Cotton on a Large Scale.

Land, 2,000 acres, bottom, at $8.50,		$17,000
50 prime field hands, at $1,000.00,		50,000
50 half-hands,	600.00,	30,000
50 quarter-hands,	300.00,	15,000
House and Furniture,		4,000
Quarters and Overseers' houses,		2,000
Mules and Tools,		2,000
Capital outlay,		$120,000

Annual Production.

At 4 bales per hand of 450 lbs., 158,400 lbs. at 8 cents,	$12,672	
Increase of Slaves at 5 per cent.,	4,750	
		$17,422
Deduct annual expenses,	$1,000	
Interest on $120,000, at 8 per cent.,	9,600	10,600
Clear returns,		$6,822

Southern writers claim that the South is at present the only portion of the Union where wool-growing can be prosecuted profitably. The "worn-out" lands would undoubtedly support immense flocks; and there are many situations where sheep would be no expense to the owner for food or shelter even during the winter. The Hon. Mr. Coles, a member of Congress, some years ago, from Virginia, stated, that his flock of 200 sheep, kept in good condition summer and winter, did not cost him $10 a year. Their wool at three pounds per head would be worth, say 600 lbs., at 30 cents, $180. Randall, in his work on Sheep Husbandry, gives eight cents as the highest estimate of the cost of producing a pound of wool in the Southern States; in New York, 27¼ cents. The average price of ordinary wool in England for 32 years is 37½ cents a pound, the lowest price being 21 cents in 1848, the highest being 48 cents in 1836. A great drawback to Sheep-raising in the South, however, is—the immense number of worthless curs that infest the country.

In New Zealand, which is peculiarly adapted for wool-growing, the "squatting" system is generally adopted. The author of "New Zealand, the Britain of the South," states, that the smallest capital on which the business can be fairly commenced is about $5,000, starting with a flock of some 700 ewes; but a more economical and profitable commencement is one with a capital of about $10,000. Any young man landing with $2,500 or $3,000, and desirous of embarking in the business, he advises to entrust his flock to a flock-master, who will generally take them on condition of receiving one-third of the wool and the annual increase; and sometimes he will also initiate the tyro into the mysteries of the business. With regard to the profits of the pursuit, the author says:

"Of a dozen squatting 'balance-sheets,' composed by lettered shepherds of the plains, I give the reader the gist of two. No. 1, the result of a balance sheet drawn up by my Australian friend, whose calculation is most careful and minute; and No. 2, the mean result of various balance-sheets drawn up by myself and by other New Zealand colonists, who have paid attention to the subject.

	Capital to start with.	Flock to start with.	Net cash profit at the end of 5 Years.
No. 1,	£1,000	say 700	£800
No. 2,	£1,000	say 700	£900

The mean profit here, £850, is a profit of not more than seventeen per cent. per annum on the capital employed; and if the reader assumes £1,500 to £2,000 to be the 'commencing-capital,' and will estimate the profit to be about twenty per cent. per annum, he will obtain a fair idea of the first profits of squatting begun on a *small* scale, and on a *moderate* scale. Those larger cumulative profits of colonial sheep-farming of which we read, are not pocketed until a later period than five years, when annual clip and increase of flock have become considerably greater, under the figures of arithmetical progression."

In the Patent Office Report for 1851, there is a noticeable article on "Sheep-Breeding," by PETER A. BROWNE, LL.D., of Philadelphia, in which he maintains that there are two species of sheep—the *hairy* sheep and the *wooly* sheep —that the sheep-breeder should never cross these species; and that "if a line be drawn diagonally through the United States, beginning at the south-east corner of New Hampshire, pursuing pretty much the course of the line of tide-water, and ending in Texas, it will be found that everywhere north-west of it, the *wooly* sheep may be bred, and will thrive provided the blood of his species be kept pure; and everywhere southeast of this line, the *hairy* sheep may be bred, and will thrive, provided the blood of his species be kept pure; but that neither will thrive on the other side, respectively, of that line, nor will they if the species are crossed."

The Agricultural Reports for the last ten years are full of information on sheep and wool growing, well worthy the attention of those about embarking in the pursuit; and in the *Report of the Juries* of the World's Exhibition in 1851 (Vol. I., 168), may be found an account of the success of M. Graux, in obtaining, by crossing and inter-breeding Merinos, a flock possessing a long, fine, silky fleece, pronounced second only to the true Cachemere in flexible delicacy of fibre, and superior even to the pure Cachemere in some respects. A Council Medal—the highest testimony of the Jury's appreciation—was awarded to him. In the Catalogue of that Exhibition may also be found a reference to a *Siphon Apparatus for washing* sheep, which, besides conducing to the health of the animal, will, it is believed, "improve the wool by fibre, by precluding irregular growth, and the formation of knots or joints."

CHANCE V.—*The Poultry and Egg Trade, if conducted scientifically, and on a large scale, in the vicinity of cities, yields good profits.*

A statement has been published, made I know not on what basis, that there are 103,500,000 laying fowls in the United States, of which 50,000,000 lay one egg a day throughout the year. This would give an annual product of 18,250,000,000 eggs, worth, at eight cents per dozen, $121,666,666. The feathery tribe, it is therefore evident, are favorites in this country; but, nevertheless, there are not, as I am aware of, any extensive heneries. In the vicinity of Paris, however, a gentleman by the name of De Sora is said to make the very respectable sum of $175,000 per annum from the sale of eggs and fowls; and his success would argue that an extensive establishment in the vicinity of all large cities would probably be profitable. M. de Sora feeds his fowls on horse flesh, purchasing the old hacks of the city, and slaughtering them for the purpose; and by the sale of the skin, blood, hoofs, bones, etc., is generally enabled to reduce the cost of the food for poultry to nothing. The following is a description of his mode of preparing the food, and of his establishment, as published in the *Saturday Evening Post*, of Philadelphia.

"The flesh is carefully dissected off the frame, of course, and being cut into suitable proportions, it is run through a series of revolving knives, the apparatus being similar to a sausage-machine on an immense scale, and is delivered in the shape of a homogeneous mass of mince-meat, slightly seasoned, into casks, which are instantly headed up and conveyed, per rail-road, to the egg plantation of M. de Sora.

"The consumption of horses for this purpose, by M. de Sora, has been at the average rate of twenty-two per day for the last twelve months; and so perfectly economical and extensive are all his arrangements, that he is enabled to make a profit on the cost of the animals by the sale of the extraneous substances enumerated above, thus furnishing to himself the mince-meat for less than nothing, delivered at his henery.

"It has been ascertained that a slight addition of salt and ground pepper to the mass is beneficial to the fowls, yet M. de Sora does not depend on these condiments alone to prevent putrefaction, but has his store-rooms so contrived as to be kept at a temperature just removed from the freezing-point through all the months of the year, so that the mince-meat never becomes sour or offensive; the fowls eat it with avidity, they are ever in good condition, and they lay an egg almost daily, in all weathers and in all seasons.

"The sheds, offices, and other buildings are built around a quadrangle, enclosing about twenty acres, the general feeding ground. This latter is subdivided by fences of open paling, so that only a limited number of fowls is allowed to herd together, and these are ranged in different apartments according to their age, no bird being allowed to exceed the duration of four years of life. At the end of the fourth year, they are placed in the fattening coops for about three weeks, fed entirely on crushed grain, and sent alive to Paris.

"As one item alone in this immense business, it may be mentioned that, in the months of September, October, and November last, M. de Sora sent nearly 1,000 dozens of capons to the metropolis. He never allows a hen to set.

"The breeding-rooms are warmed by steam, and the heat is kept up with remarkable uniformity to that evolved by the female fowl during the process of incubation, which is known to mark higher on the thermometer than at any other period. A series of shelves, one above the other, form the nests, while blankets are spread over the eggs, to exclude any accidental light. The hatched chicks are removed to the nursery each morning, and fresh eggs laid in to supply the place of empty shells. A constant succession of chickens is thus insured; and, moreover, the feathers are always free from vermin. Indeed, a lousy fowl is unknown upon the premises.

"M. de Sora permits the males and females to mingle freely at all seasons, and, after a fair trial of all the various breeds, has cleared his establishment of every Shanghai, Cochin-China, or other outlandish fowl, breeding only from old-fashioned barn-yard chanticleers and the feminines of the same species. He contends that the extra size of body and eggs pertaining to these foreign breeds can only be produced and sustained by extra food; while for capon raising, the flesh is neither so delicate nor juicy as that of the native breed.

"The manure produced in this French establishment is no small item; and since it forms the very best fertilizer for many descriptions of plants, it is eagerly sought for at high prices by market-gardeners in the vicinity. The proprietor estimates the yield this year at about 100 cords. He employs nearly one hundred persons in different departments, three-fourths of whom, however, are females. The sale of eggs during the past winter has averaged about 40,000 dozen per week, at the rate of six dozen for four francs, bringing the actual sales up to $5,000 in round numbers for every seven days, or $250,000 per annum. The expenses of M. de Sora's henery, including wages, interest, and a fair margin for repairs, &c., are in the neighborhood of $75,000, leaving a balance in his favor of $175,000 per year."

A writer in the *London Gardeners' Chronicle* gives the following directions to make hens lay all winter, which would appear to be worthy of consideration by those who are engaged in the business of raising poultry:

"Keep no roosters; give the hens fresh meat, chopped up like sausage meat, once a day, a very small portion, say one half an ounce a day to each hen during the winter, or from the time insects disappear in the fall till they appear again in the spring. Never allow any eggs to remain in the nest for what are called nest eggs. When the roosters do not run with the hens, and no nest eggs are left in the nest, the hens will not cease laying after the production of twelve or fifteen eggs—as they always do when roosters and nest eggs are allowed—but continue laying perpetually. My hens lay all winter, and each from seventy to one hundred eggs in succession. The only reason why hens do not lay in winter as freely as in summer, is the want of animal food, which they get in the summer in abundance in the form of insects. I have for several winters reduced my theory to practice, and proved its entire correctness."

It is stated that a bushel of corn will last twice as long for hens as a bushel of buckwheat; but the latter will make hens lay more eggs than any other grain, and the profit overbalances the cost.

CHANCE VI.—*The Establishment of Vineyards and the Manufacture of Wines from the juice of the grape, afford an excellent chance for profitable occupation to thousands.*

France contains about five million acres of Vineyards which yield, it is estimated, eighty million barrels of Wine annually, worth about $600,000,000—the greater portion of which is consumed by the French people. The profit of Wine-making is established by the fact, that notwithstanding the demand for cereals and the cheapness of wines in Europe, every acre is appropriated to the vine that is suitable to its growth. In the United States, breadstuffs are lower in price than in Europe, and wines from two hundred to five hundred per cent. higher—hence the greater opportunity for realizing large profits. An acre of well-set vineyard in some of the Departments in France is worth four thousand dollars, and one thousand dollars is about its lowest assessed value.

The centre of the Wine Manufacture in the United States, is at present in the vicinity of Cincinnati, Ohio, though very probably that is by no means the best locality. In 1854 it was stated there were about twelve hundred acres of Vines planted within a circle of twenty miles around that city—eight hundred of which were in bearing, and produced on an average four hundred gallons to the acre, or in all 320,000 gallons of wine. Some of the best Vineyards yielded six hundred to eight hundred gallons to the acre; but others, in localities where the "rot" prevailed, did not produce over one hundred and fifty gallons per acre; the average for a series of years in that vicinity being estimated at two hundred or two hundred and fifty gallons to the acre.

The Vineyards are planted in April with cuttings, which cost $2.50 per thousand, or roots one year old costing $25 per thousand, usually three feet apart by six feet in the rows, and 2,420 vines to the acre. The whole cost of a Vineyard up to the fourth year, when it becomes fully productive, ranges from $200 to $550 per acre. The Wine when *new* sells at one dollar to one dollar and ten cents for the best, seventy-five to ninety cents for second quality, and forty to fifty cents per gallon for inferior. Some has been exported to Europe, and very highly spoken of by European connoisseurs in the article.

Within the last three or four years, Vineyards have been established successfully in several States besides Ohio—in Massachusetts, Missouri, Kansas, Georgia, California, Texas, and probably others. The Catawba grape vine, which is principally used for the making of Wine, was first found growing wild in Buncombe County, North Carolina. Its most productive yield, if we can believe recent accounts, is in Georgia, where a gentleman engaged in the business promises from 2,000 to 2,500 gallons to the acre for the fourth and successive years, from only sixteen hundred vines. This, if true, would incontrovertibly demonstrate that Ohio will not long maintain her pre-eminence.

The selection of the best locality is one of the first importance to him who contemplates engaging in the Cultivation of the Vine. Mr. Blodget, in his "Climatology," gives a table, to which we refer, of the *climate of the Vine-growing Districts of the United States,* embracing latitude, altitude, temperature, amount of rain for the seasons and for the year, and remarks,—

"In the districts where the temperature and amount of rain are less excessive in summer, the opposite extremes of winter and spring temperatures are quite certain to become injurious. A district bordering the southern and western portions of Lake Erie, is more favorable in this respect than any other on the Atlantic side of the Rocky Mountains; and it will ultimately prove capable of a very liberal extension of vine culture. None of the stations given in the table represent it precisely, though Oberlin, Ohio, and Ann Arbor, Michigan, differ only in being somewhat more exposed and extreme in temperature at the colder seasons. The amount of humidity is much lower here in summer than elsewhere; and it corresponds more nearly than any other district with the vine-growing districts of the Rhine, both in temperature and amount of rain. The southern portions of the Alleghany Mountains, bordering the South Atlantic States and those of the Gulf, possess general characteristics, greatly favorable. They have less humidity than the plains below them, reversing the European law of humidity and aqueous precipitation in this respect; and their exposures southward and sheltered valleys must favor the cultivation to a very great degree. The present wine districts of Cincinnati, and other localities on the Ohio, and those on the Missouri at Herman, are very successful in every point, except the liability to injury from excess of humidity and of rains. The general climate will always present difficulties in this respect, which the utmost care in cultivation and choice of position can modify only in degree. In the lower portion of the valley of the Rio Grande, in New Mexico—the nearest approach to equable temperatures and the requisite low humidity is attained. In the vicinity of El Paso, Vineyards are numerous and successful; the rarefied atmosphere and slight precipitation of rain being more signally favorable than in any portion of the continent eastward. The cultivated districts in the latitude toward the Pacific, must present many localities of proper adaptation in their peculiar conditions—though the extent of those is not great; and the southern valleys of California sufficiently distant from the sea-coast, and from the loftier Sierras, would be unusually favorable in regard to these primary conditions."

In California the vine was introduced more than a century ago by cuttings from Madeira, and flourishes with a luxuriance that designates that State as among the most promising for the production of Wine in the Union. The flavor of the grape is so well preserved, that no admixture of other juices is required to give the product an acceptable taste. In Los Angeles County, one firm, in 1857, manufactured 75,000 gallons, consuming 830,000 pounds, or over 377 tons of grapes. In Kentucky and Tennessee there are very extensive tracts of unproductive land, known by the appellation of the "Barrens," which Prof. Swallow, the State Geologist of Missouri, asserts may be converted into fruitful Vineyards. He also asserts that there are *twenty million acres* of land in Missouri, Kentucky, and Tennessee, in which the vine will succeed as well as in France or Germany.

The manufacture of Wine is an art requiring attention, but involves no particular mystery that cannot easily be mastered. It is probable, however, that it will be found most advantageous that the manufacture be conducted as a pursuit distinct from the cultivation of the grape. Ten years ago Mr. N. Longworth, the great patron of this branch of industry, remarked:—

"The cultivation of the grape for Wine will be profitable where persons do their own work. It is seldom that any farming pays well where there is much hiring of hands. Our German emigrants can cultivate the grape to most profit, for the greater part of the work in the vineyard is performed by their wives and daughters, without interfering with household affairs. A greater profit would accrue to a man of observation and skill, who would devote much time to the subject, be certain to have clean casks, gather his grapes at the proper moment, use great care in picking, selecting, and pressing, and a clean press, a cool cellar, care and skill in the fermentation, racking at the proper time, and always keeping the casks full, never to bottle it till four or five years of age, and never to sell any wine with his name, in seasons when the wine is not of the best quality. Such a manufacturer may sell his wine from twelve to eighteen dollars per dozen, when his less skillful and careful neighbor may find his wine a dull sale at seventy-five cents per gallon, with the same exposure and a soil equally favorable for the grape. I have never given the subject the personal attention necessary to the most perfect success. I am now too old to undertake it; and beneficial as the experiment might be, it would form no grounds should I apply to Providence to extend my life for twenty years more, for having it granted. I must leave it in younger hands.

"It would be a valuable business could a skillful wine merchant be found, who would buy the wines at the press, have them brought immediately to the city to his wine cellar, which should be cool, and there personally attend to the fermentation, racking, &c., till ready to bottle for sale. It would require capital and time before the business would be available. The profit would be certain."

CHANCE VII.—*Money can be made in Planting Cotton in favorable localities; and especially by an Association of Individuals who will secure a suitable Tract of Cotton Lands, provide the most improved Implements, and combine Manufacturing, to a certain extent, with Planting.*

Whether the growing of Cotton, as at present conducted in the United States, is a profitable business or not, seems to be a mooted question. It is contended by some, that it is the most profitable business in the United States; while others furnish "facts and figures" to demonstrate that the cotton-planter's profits have not averaged more than fair interest on the capital invested. In 1832, HENRY CLAY, in reply to General Hayne, stated, that in his opinion Cotton-growing was "the most profitable investment of capital of any branch of business in the Union;" and produced a series of particulars showing, that in a crop of $10,000 the expenses fluctuated between $2,800 and $3,200. He observed: "A friend now in my eye, a member of this body, upon a capital of less than $70,000, invested in a plantation and slaves, made the year before last $16,000. A member of the other House, I understand, who, without removing himself, sent some of his slaves to Mississippi, made last year twenty per cent. Two friends of mine in the latter State, whose annual income is from $30,000 to $60,000, being desirous to curtail their business, have offered cotton estates for sale, which they are ready to show, by vouchers, or receipts and disbursements, yield eighteen per cent. per annum. One of my most opulent acquaintances, in the county adjoining that in which I reside, having married in Georgia, has derived a large portion of his wealth from a cotton estate there situated."

It must be remembered, however, that up to this period, that is for forty-three years, from 1790 to 1832 inclusive, the price of Cotton ranged from 9¼ cents per pound, the minimum, to 44 cents the maximum, the average being 21½ cents per pound. For the twelve succeeding years, from 1833 to 1844 inclusive, the price ranged from 8 to 16 cents per pound; and the average was reduced to 11 cents per pound. In the latter year, 1844, a Southern Planter published a work, entitled, "NOTES ON POLITICAL ECONOMY," in which he stated, that the actual expenses of raising Cotton, not counting interest on capital, do not exceed two cents a pound on the product, or crop. He says: "I will give the details to make this clear. A plantation, of 50 hands, makes the average of seven bales to the hand, weighing 450 pounds. This is 350 bales. Suppose two cents for expenses, this amounts to $3,150 on the crop. The crop sells say for four cents a pound net, and, clear of charges for transportation, insurance, commission for selling, leaves $3,150 profit for the luxuries of the owner, who gets his necessaries out of the plantation by living on it. This is a very pretty sum, and half of it would be ample for him, which would reduce Cotton to three cents. As to insurance, the slaves not only insure themselves, but give a large increase, which grows up with the owner's children, and furnishes them with outfits by the time they need them. Now, I will go into a calculation to show that two cents a pound cover the annual expenses. Here follow the items, taking a plantation of 50 hands for a basis—For overseer, $500; for salt, $20; iron, $30; medicines, $20; doctor's bill, $100, for you can contract by the year, which is often done at two dollars a head; bagging and rope to wrap it, at 12½ for the one and five cents for the other, amounts to $300; taxes, $100; sundry small things, $100, all told. The writer speaks from experience, for he is a planter of Cotton and owns slaves. All this amounts to $1,170, much below the allowance of two cents a pound, amounting, as we have seen, to $3,150. I wish only to show, that we can grow cotton *for three cents a pound, and have a living profit.*"

On the other hand, the *Soil of the South* asserts, that the present cost of raising a pound of Cotton is at least *eight cents*, and enters into an elaborate calculation to prove the assertion. (See *De Bow's Review*, 18, p. 469.) If this be the state of facts at present, and inasmuch as the price of

Cotton in the Mobile market for the last fourteen years, from 1844 to 1858, has not averaged more than $9\frac{1}{2}$ cents, the profits cannot be large; and though individuals in this, as in all other pursuits, can be pointed to who have been remarkably successful, the majority have not, probably, made much more than ordinary interest on the capital invested. Valuing slaves at their present high market price, when good field-hands cannot be purchased for less than $1200 each, and money commands an interest of 10 per cent. per annum, their annual cost is equal to wages of $10 a month, or $120 a year, besides board, clothing, taxes, medical attendance, and the risk of the original capital being destroyed.

But however profitable any pursuit may be, I presume that Money, under no circumstances, would be an inducement for you to incur the tremendous moral risks necessarily involved in deliberately, voluntarily, and persistently doing unto others as you would not they should do unto you. The ingenious and fine-spun arguments of hired theologians, when designed as anodynes and opiates for conscience, would not weigh in a wise man's balances as a feather against the imminent danger of being entrapped in a snare from which you may never escape. No financier, and certainly no theologian, is fit to be trusted as an adviser who, in a doubtful question, does not advocate the SAFE side. Hence, unless some plan can be devised by which you can share its profits in undoubted and indubitable consistency with whatever is of more intrinsic value and importance than Money, you are debarred from Cotton Planting. To determine whether this is practicable, let us inquire—First, *What are the Operations or Processes essential for the Cultivation of Cotton;* and secondly, *What are the Localities in which the Plant will flourish best.*

In that very excellent periodical, *Harper's Magazine*, Mr. T. B. THORPE, of Louisiana, published in 1855, an interesting article on "Cotton and its Cultivation," from which we extract the following account of the successive operations in Cotton planting:

"The preparations for planting Cotton begin in January; at this time the fields are covered with the dry and standing stalks of the last year's crop. The first care of the planter is to 'clean up' for plowing. To do this the 'hands' commence by breaking down the cotton stalks with a heavy club, or pulling them up by the roots. These stalks are then gathered into piles, and at night-fall set on fire. This labor, together with 'housing the corn,' repairing fences and farming implements, consumes the time up to the middle of March, or the beginning of April, when the plow for the 'next crop' begins its work. First, the 'water furrows' are run from five to six feet apart, and made by a heavy plow, drawn either by a team of oxen, or mules. This labor, as it will be perceived, makes the surface of the ground in ridges, in the centre of which is next run a light plow, making what is termed 'the drill,' or depository of the seed. A girl follows the light plow carrying in her apron the cotton-seed, which she profusely scatters in the newly-made drill; behind this sower follows the 'harrow;' and by these various labors the planting is temporarily completed.

"From two to three bushels of cotton-seed are necessary to plant an acre of ground; the quantity used, however, is but of little consequence, unless the seed is imported, for the annual amount collected at the gin-house is enormous, and the surplus after planting is either left to rot, to be eaten by the cattle, or scattered upon the fields for manure.

"If the weather be favorable, the young plant is discovered making its way through in six or ten days, and the 'scraping' of the crop, as it is termed, now begins. A light plow is again called into requisition, which is run along the drill, throwing the *earth away from the plant;* then come the laborers with their hoes, who dexterously cut away the superabundant shoots and the intruding weeds, and leave a single cotton-plant, in little hills generally two feet apart.

"Of all the labors of the field, the dexterity displayed by the negroes in 'scraping cotton' is most calculated to call forth the admiration of the novice spectator. The hoe is a rude instrument, however well made and handled; the young cotton plant is as delicate as vegetation can be, and springs up in lines of solid masses composed of hundreds of plants. The field-hand, however, will single one delicate shoot from the surrounding multitude, and with his rude hoe he will trim away the remainder with all the boldness of touch of a master, leaving the incipient stalk unharmed and alone in its glory; and at night-fall you can look along the extending rows, and find the plants correct in line, and of the required distance of separation from each other.

"The planter who can look over his field in early Spring, and find his Cotton 'cleanly scraped,' and his 'stand' good, is fortunate; still the vicissitudes attending the cultivation of the crop have only commenced. Many rows, from the operations of the 'cut-worm,' and from multitudinous causes unknown, have to be replanted; and an unusually late frost may destroy all his labors, and compel him to commence again. But if no untoward accident occurs in two weeks after the 'scraping,' another hoeing takes place, at which time the plow throws the furrows on the roots of the now strengthening plant, and the increasing heat of the sun also justifies the sinking of the roots deeper in the earth. The pleasant month of May is now drawing to a close, and vegetation of all kinds is struggling for precedence in the fields. Grasses and weeds of every variety, with vines and wild flowers, luxuriate in the newly-turned sod, and seem to be determined to choke out of existence the useful and still delicately grown cotton.

"It is a season of unusual industry on the Cotton Plantations, and woe to the planter who is outstripped in his labors, and finds himself 'overtaken by the grass.' The plow tears up the surplus vegetation, and the hoe tops it off in its luxuriance. The race is a hard one, but industry conquers; and when the third working over of the crops takes place, the cotton plant, so much cherished and favored, begins to overtop its rivals in the fields—begins to cast a *chilling shade of superiority* over its now intimidated groundlings, and commences to reign supreme.

"Through the month of July, the crop is wrought over for the last time; the plant, heretofore of slow growth, now makes rapid advances toward perfection. The plow and hoe are still in requisition. The 'water furrows' between the Cotton rows are deepened, leaving the Cotton growing as it were upon a slight ridge. This accomplished, the crop is prepared for the 'rainy season,' should it ensue, and so far advanced that it is, under any circumstances, beyond the control of art. Nature must now have her sway.

"On some plantations there is no 'overseer;' the owner manages his place with the help of a skillful and trustworthy negro, termed the 'driver.' These drivers are very ambitious, and are, like their masters, exceedingly sensitive if a stranger, or other disinterested person, gives an unfavorable opinion of the general appearance of the crop under their management. If much grass is seen in the cotton field, it is supposed to be an unfavorable testimony of the industry or skill of the driver. Upon a certain occasion, a gentleman, riding along a cotton field, remarked to the negro manager, 'You have a good deal of grass in your crop.' The negro felt mortified, and anxious to break the force of the insinuation, coolly replied, 'It is poor ground, master, that wont bring grass.' The finest intellect could not, under the circumstances, have said a better thing.

"The 'cotton bloom,' under the matured sun of July, begins to make its appearance. The announcement of the 'first blossom' of the neighborhood is a matter of general interest; it is an unfailing sign of the approach of the busy season of Fall; it is the evidence that soon the labor of man will, under a kind Providence, receive its reward.

* * * * *

"The season of cotton-picking commences in the latter part of July, and continues without intermission to the Christmas holidays. The work is not heavy, but becomes tedious from its sameness. The field hands are each supplied with a basket and a bag. The basket is left at the head of the 'cotton rows;' the bag is suspended from the 'picker's' neck by a strap, and is used to hold the Cotton as it is taken from the boll. When the bag is filled, it is emptied into the basket; and this routine is continued through the day. Each hand picks from 250 to 300 pounds of 'seed cotton' each day, though some negroes of extraordinary ability go beyond this amount.

"If the weather be very fine, the Cotton is carried from the field direct to the packing-house; but generally it is first spread out on scaffolds, where it is left to dry, and picked clean of any 'trash' that may be perceived mixed up with the Cotton. Among the most characteristic scenes of plantation life, is the returning of the hands at night-fall from the field, with their well-filled baskets of Cotton upon their heads. Falling unconsciously 'into line,' the stoutest leading the way, they move along in the dim twilight of a winter day, with the quietness of spirits rather than human beings.

"The packing-room is the loft of the gin-house, and is over the gin-stand. By this arrangement the cotton is conveniently shoved down a causeway into the 'gin hopper.' We have spoken of the importance of Whitney's great invention, and we must now say that much of the comparative value of the staple of Cotton depends upon the excellence of the cotton-gin. Some separate the staple from the seed far better than others; while all are dependent more or less for their excellence upon the judicious manner they are used. With constant attention, a gin-stand, impelled by four mules, will work out four bales, of 450 lbs. each, a day; but this is more than the average amount. Upon large plantations, the steam-engine is brought into requisition, which, carrying any number of gins required, will turn out the necessary number of bales per day.

"The *baling* of the Cotton ends the labor of its production on the plantation. The power which is used to accomplish this end is generally a single but powerful screw. The ginned Cotton is thrown from the packing-room down into a reservoir or press, which being filled, is trampled down by the negroes engaged in the business. When a sufficient quantity has been forced by 'foot labor' into the press, the upper door is shut down, and the screw is applied, worked by horse. By this process the staple becomes almost as solid a mass as stone. By previous arrangement, strong Kentucky bagging has been so placed as to cover the upper and lower sides of the pressed Cotton. Ropes are now passed round the whole, and secured by a knot; a long needle and a piece of twine close up the openings in the bagging; the screw is then run up, the cotton swells with tremendous power inside of its ribs of rope, the baling is completed—and the Cotton is ready for shipment to any part of the world."

Such are the sequences in the operations of Cotton Planting. There is, of course, a diversity of practice in details according to soil and circumstances generally; but it is evident that the opportunity is yet open for the application of that genius, so signally manifested in the construction of automatic machines for the manufacture of cotton goods, to the invention of contrivances adapted to the production of the raw material. It seems remarkable, that so much labor should be required for the growth of a plant that springs up spontaneously in three-fourths of the warm climates of the world; and it is certainly remarkable that, in an age of steam-engines and steam-plows—of seed-sowers, horse-hoes, and drills of infinite variety—an era of chemical progress that has discovered substances that will keep down weeds and grasses better than the hoe—of patent cotton-pickers (see *Scientific American*)—and of rail-roads that can transport laborers to a given point in almost any given time—the man who would produce the most wonderful staple of modern commerce, must first invest more capital for a hoe and a negro than for all the improved implements of successful tillage. Is there not a hint in this which a shrewd inventive genius could turn to valuable account?

With regard to *localities*, I think experience has demonstrated that there are places on the globe where, by the exercise of as much diligence and intelligence as are now displayed in this branch of industry, Cotton can be grown with greater profit to the producer than in any of our leading Cotton States. In the last century, the West Indies supplied all the finest Cotton; and probably the finest quality ever brought to the English market, and, it is said, ever grown, was that raised by a Mr. Robley, on the Island of Tobago, between the years 1789 and 1792.*

* The Agricultural Report of the Patent Office for 1856 contains

In the Pinos of Texas the plant is said to be extraordinary for length and fineness of staple; and the Cotton

---

a large number of replies from Commercial Agents of the United States, in answer to inquiries with regard to advantages for Cotton Planting in various parts of the world. A. V. COLVIN, Consul for the United States at Demerara, British Guiana, says, with regard to Cotton:

"I believe that no deterioration has ever been evinced in its fibre. On the contrary, it seems extremely well suited to the climate and soil of this region. The product of an acre is from three hundred to six hundred pounds. When it was in cultivation here, it was ginned with rollers manufactured in the colony. Any quantity of unginned Cotton will yield about a third of its weight of fibre. The mode of packing was altogether by hand. I think the soil and climate are *better adapted to its profitable cultivation than any part of the United States.* We have no winter, and the tree grows, blossoms, and bears all the year. The hoe and the spade were the only implements used, and manure was never applied. I do not believe that the soil would be exhausted by the culture of Cotton for a whole century. Planting may be performed any month of the year, but April is usually preferred. A tree will no doubt bear for fifty years, if kept so trimmed that a man may reach to the top.

"Cotton lands may be purchased at one dollar an acre, but often for from fifty cents to one dollar. With respect to the causes operating injuriously to the culture of Cotton, I would express the opinion, that nothing more is needed than to induce the people to work."

G. EUSTIS HUBBARD, Commercial Agent for the United States at Cape Haytien, says:

"The seeds are planted or sown in plowed ground in the month of May; the plants are in flower in October; and the Cotton is harvested from January to March. Cotton land may be purchased at from $3 to $10 an acre.

"The quality of the Cotton raised in Hayti has been pronounced superior, particularly that cultivated in the district of Tiburon, in the southern part. Nothing is wanted but industry and enterprise to render the Cotton of Hayti a large and profitable article of export."

produced by the Germans, by their own labor, commands, we are told, in the Galveston market, a small premium over any other of the same quality. In the southern portions of that State, the expense of cultivation is said to be less than in the other States, in consequence not only of the great richness of the soil, but also of the peculiar mildness of the climate. Planters of acknowledged veracity state, that it is not uncommon to pick four thousand pounds of seed Cotton from an acre.

Mr. Featherstonhaugh, after crossing into Northern Texas, in about latitude 33° 40′, observes, that he never had seen the Cotton plant growing in greater perfection before; for in the Cotton districts he had passed through, the plant was a low, dwarfy bush, not exceeding two feet in height; but here the plants were five feet high, often bearing 300 bolls, and yielding from 1500 to 2500 lbs. of seed Cotton to the acre, which gives from 25 to 30 per cent. in weight of raw marketable fibre.

In Mexico there is a wide extent of country, particularly the Gulf Coast, admirably adapted for growing Cotton; and some very successful experiments have been made on a large scale, even at an elevation of from 5,000 to 7,000 feet above the level of the sea. In California the indigenous growth gives evidence that Cotton can be raised of a very superior quality. THOMAS SPRAGUE, Commercial Agent of the United States at La Paz, Lower California, says: "It is my opinion that the Sea Island Cotton of the United States can be grown to a great advantage here, and that the lands of this country are unsurpassed for producing sugar, rice, coffee, and grapes. Although the temperature of this place is but 24° north, the climate is so happily tempered by sea breezes, that labor can be performed by any race of men, without inconvenience or detriment to health." Col. Gray, in his Report of Surveys for a Rail-road Route, says of the country near the Gila River, in Sonora and California: "Large tracts of land on the Gila and in other portions of the district, appear to possess the requisite properties of soil; and I have no doubt the finest Cotton will soon be raised and brought to its highest state of perfection by proper cultivation. The Cotton of which I procured specimens, though cultivated by the Indians in the most primitive manner, exhibited a texture not unlike the celebrated Sea Island Cotton. Its fibre is exceedingly soft and silky, though not of the longest staple."

It has been stated that there are more than a hundred known varieties of the Cotton Plant; and it therefore is an important consideration for him who contemplates embarking in Cotton-planting, to select that which will produce the finest staple, without a proportionate increase in the expense of production. Formerly, the West India Cotton was deemed the choicest variety, of which the Bourbon Cotton is now the representative in the markets. Prof. Royle states that the Cotton of Porto Rico was at one time considered to be the best; and that from St. Domingo has been spun into No. 100 yarn. But at the present time, the *Sea Island*, or *Long-stapled* Cotton takes precedence over all others, commanding readily double, and sometimes quadruple the price of ordinary Upland; and it has been sold in the Liverpool market for one dollar and seventy-five cents per pound. Opinions differ as to the causes of its superiority. Some scientific men ascribe it to the saline qualities of the sea air; whilst others attribute it to the equable temperature and humidity of the atmosphere, and the absence of disturbing circumstances during its growth. The average temperature of Whitemarsh Island, which is usually regarded as the central point of the production of this variety, is 64.8°, and the quantity of rain that falls averages 39.1.

But probably the best opportunity for profit, in this connection, that can be suggested, is in the combination of Manufacturing, to a certain extent, with Planting. A cotton-mill in convenient proximity to the plantation, would seem to be as desirable in the Cotton-producing States as the flour-mill in the Wheat-growing States. The most gigantic folly of modern times is, that cotton-growers often go four thousand miles to mill. The cost of getting the Cotton to its principal mill in Europe, and bringing back the finished product, including the items of warehouse charges, freight, insurance, drayages, storages, weighages, pickages, pressages, commissions, postage, bills-of-lading, dock dues, etc., is necessarily a formidable summary, and falls mainly upon the grower. The true theory would seem to be, that the hands which cultivate the Cotton in the summer should spin it in the winter; but, at all events, it is suggested that every fifteen planters, growing three thousand bales, should consider a mill for producing yarns or coarse goods an indispensable adjunct to their plantation. Cotton manufactories have already been established to some extent in the Southern States; and the profits of some of them foreshadow what may be expected with a superior organized system of available labor.*

Among the modern improvements tending to facilitate

---

* A work now in course of preparation, on the Manufactures of the United States, by J. Leander Bishop, M.D., will, I am informed, give some astonishing facts with regard to the development of Manufactures in the Southern States.

the combination of which we speak, perhaps the most noteworthy is the invention of Mr. Henry, a merchant of standing in Mobile, and familiar with the Cotton product. He has invented a plan for combining the spinning with the ginning, by which he manufactures seed Cotton into yarns of every size, and excludes several machines now used for similar purposes. With any gin that the planter may prefer, whether it be the old Whitney gin or the modern improved gin made by BARTON H. JENKS, of Philadelphia, he can effect this combination, converting it into a *preparation carder*, and sending the ginned Cotton out in a sheet, and make it form a *lamina;* and this lamina he takes to the place assigned for it at the carders. "Thus attached," says the inventor, "it passes through the cards by the railway, in the form of a sliver, to the drawing-head, thence to the drawing-frames, thence to the spinning-frames, thence to the reels, from which the hanks are taken; and the wrapping paper and baling having been previously arranged to receive it, some 300 to 350 pounds are pressed and turned out in a bale of yarns. My gin and spinning machinery is geared, as before remarked, to one shaft; and, as in the cotton factory, all may run, or any part of it may be stopped as desired.

"Planters making one hundred bales or less may use their mules; for, as my gin turns off two-thirds less, I divert two-thirds of the power thus economized to my machinery; and as I exclude from use the picker, or devil of the factories, and as my gin, spreader, beater, and carders, may be driven with less speed, hence with less power than the present process, six mules—certainly not over eight—will be enough for the one hundred bale planter to gin and spin his crop in six months. Those making one hundred bales and above are adopting the steam-engine for their ginning and other plantation purposes; so the water or steam-power they now use, which they can so economically get, will both gin and spin their crops.

"In every department of the process of spinning, an elastic and flexible fibre is important; and hence in dry, hot weather, to run factories rapidly, working old Cotton, breaks the slivers and thread very much. But taking the fibre as I do, just from the seed, in its oily, elastic, and flexible state, is of incalculable advantage to its manufacture, as it admits of the drawing and eliminating with the utmost freedom, and parts with the impurities without rupturing or breaking the filaments."

With regard to the advantage of converting Cotton into yarns, the inventor of the above-mentioned machine makes the following interesting and pertinent remarks, which we extract from his article on the "Revolution in the Cotton Industry," *De Bow's Rev.*, 22, p. 398:

"Yarns range at prices from about 22 cents to $1 a pound in Europe, and I would class them thus:

"Say a crop of 3,000,000 bales of cotton, at 450 pounds to the bale, weighs 1,350,000,000 pounds, which, at twelve cents per pound, is equal to $162,000,000. One half of this—675,000,000 pounds—I put into yarns at an average of 22 cents, which would amount to $148,500,000; one fourth of the remainder, 337,500,000 pounds, at 28 cents, $94,000,000; one fourth, or balance, 337,500,000 pounds, at 40 cents, $135,000,000—in all $378,000,000.

"To make this plain, let me say that yarns are made from No. 5 to No. 200; that the lower numbers are the sizes mostly used, and are made of the poorest Cotton. I have allowed that one half of our crop was consumed in the coarsest quality of goods, and hence I put them at the lowest price of yarns—22 cents; one fourth, a small grade finer, at 28 cents; and one fourth, finer still, at 40 cents. To-day, that I might be certain, and give you the latest quotations, I sent to two eminent firms, one buyers, and the other sellers of yarns, for their quotations, and to specify numbers. The buyers responded: '22 cents, manufacturer's price, from Nos. 5 to 9.' The sellers responded: '21 to 22 cents per pound for numbers ranging from 5 to 12—principally 6's to 9's—with an increasing demand: that they could not get a half supply; that their prices, from 1852 to 1856, had been from 18 to 19 cents—same numbers.' During these years, from '52 to '56, the average price of Cotton was about 9, as it is now about 11½ to 11¾ cents. Here you see for these lowest numbers (and the lower the number, the lower the price) the yarns command about double the average price of Cotton: and it must be especially borne in mind, that those yarns are made of the lowest class and cheapest Cottons. Below I give the quotations of Cotton in our market (3d February), by an eminent brokerage firm:

	Cts.	Cts.
Inferior	10 @	10½
Ordinary	11 @	11½
Middling	12 @	12⅜
Fair		13

You perceive that 3,000,000 bales of Cotton at 12 cents per pound, are worth	$162,000,000
That the crop spun into yarns—½ of the coarsest, ¼ a shade finer, and ¼ a few shades finer, will amount to,	$378,000,000
Difference	$216,000,000

"Here we have $216,000,000, or nearly 150 per cent. more than the cotton sells for; and putting Cotton at the extreme prices, and yarns below the actual rates. So a planter whose crop of cotton amounts to $5,000, would get for it in yarns $12,500—say $7,500 for spinning it, and $5,000 for the ginned cotton, if spun into the average qualities. When we get under way, we can spin the kinds they want in France and Italy to mix with the heavy satins and moire-antique silks we prize so highly."

CHANCE VIII.—*Money can be made in the Production of Sugar, and especially by Manufacturing Sugar from other Plants than the Cane.*

The history of the cultivation of Cane Sugar in the United States does not awaken any very flattering expectations of its success in the future. Introduced about

1751, the Cane, notwithstanding its cultivation for more than a century, is limited to a very narrow range; and within that limit has been subject to so many discouraging vicissitudes, and even deterioration, that unless renewed, its extinction may reasonably be apprehended.* The product of cane Sugar, which in 1853 was 449,324 hogsheads, the maximum, was in 1856 only 73,976 hogsheads, while the consumption of sugar in the United States is annually increasing, and has trebled, it is said, within ten years, amounting now, it is supposed, to 900,000,000 pounds, which, excluding from the population three million slaves who probably do not consume sugar, is an average of about 40 pounds for each person. In Great Britain, the consumption averages 28½ pounds per head; in France, nine pounds; while in Prussia it is only six pounds. [For PRODUCTION, see STATEMENT on the following page.]

---

* That there has been a degeneracy in the cane, caused by exhaustion of the soil and injudicious rotation, is obvious from the fact that the same lands which have been under cultivation for a long period have yielded more than three times the amount of Sugar to the acre in some years than in others, the productiveness having been in those cases in which the soil was in its primitive fertility, or when enriched by guano and other appropriate manures. In seeking a remedy for the evil here complained of in Louisiana, the minds of many have very naturally been turned to the project of replenishing the cane fields of that State by the importation of a fresh supply of cuttings, of such varieties as may be found best suited to the soil and climate. Resort to this means of restoration should be promptly made on a liberal and extensive scale, so that the experiment may be thorough, and, if possible, effectual in its results.—An intelligent agent should be selected for the purpose, well acquainted with the character of the cane and the nature of the soils and climates in which it grows, as well as the best modes of packing and transporting it to distant parts, either by land or sea.—*Cy. of Com.*

A Statement of the Total Production, Average Price per Hogshead, and Value of the Sugar Crop of the United States, from 1834 to 1857 inclusive.

Years.	Total Crop.		Average Price per Hogsh'd.	Total Value.
	Hogsheads.	Pounds.		
1834	100,000	100,000,000	$60.00	$6,000,000
1835	30,000	30,000,000	90.00	2,700,000
1836	70,000	70,000,000	60.00	4,200,000
1837	65,000	65,000,000	62.50	5,062,500
1838	70,000	70,000,000	62.50	4,375,000
1839	115,000	115,000,000	50.00	5,750,000
1840	87,000	87,000,000	55.00	4,785,000
1841	90,000	90,000,000	40.00	3,600,000
1842	140,000	140,000,000	42.50	4,750,000
1843	100,000	100,000,000	60.00	6,000,000
1844	200,000	200,000,000	45.00	9,000,000
1845	186.650	186,650,000	55.00	10,265,750
1846	140,000	140,000,000	70.00	9,800,000
1847	240,000	240,000,000	40.00	9,600,000
1848	220,000	220,000,000	40.00	8,800,000
1849	247,923	269,769,000	50.00	12,396,150
1850	211,303	231,194,000	60.00	12,678,180
1851	236,547	257,138,000	50.00	11,827,350
1852	321,931	368,129,000	48.00	15,452.688
1853	449,324	495,156,000	55.00	15,726,340
1854	346,635	385,726,000	72.00	12,025,020
1855	231,427	254,569,000	30.00	16,199,890
1856	73,976	81,373,000	110.00	8,137,260
1857	279,697	307,666,700		
Total,	4,252,413	4,504,370,700		$199,131,128

The amount of raw Sugar produced by the acre is less in Louisiana than in any of the principal Sugar-growing countries, being only 1,000 pounds; while in the Mauritius, it is 6,000 pounds; in Brazil, 5,000; in Cuba, 4,000; in the Isle of Bourbon, 3,300; Guadaloupe, 2,000; Vera Cruz, 1,900. The Island of Mauritius is now in advance of all others in relative productiveness for Sugar growing, and it is indebted for this enviable position to Guano and to free labor. Previous to the introduction of

Guano upon the estates, the average product did not exceed 2,000 pounds of Sugar per acre; and previous to the introduction of free labor, a much larger number of persons, at a higher cost, were required to produce a less quantity of pounds, as appears by the following advices.

"The importance of free labor to the cultivation of the estates has now become fully appreciated by the planters; it being found that an equal amount of work can be obtained by this means from a less number of hands, and that at lower rates of wages than were current in previous years, the average of which is shown in the following table.

Years.	Number of Coolies employed.	Aggregate am't of wages paid per week.	Average wages per head per week.
1846	47,733	£33,484	14*s*. 0*d*.
1847	48,314	35,338	14*s*. 9*d*.
1848	41,777	26,627	12*s*. 9*d*.
1849	45,384	27,625	12*s*. 2*d*.
1850	47,912	31,664	12*s*. 3*d*.
1851	42,275	27,832	12*s*. 2*d*.

"In 1826, to make from 25,000,000 to 30,000,000 pounds of sugar it required 30,000 laborers (slaves); at the present time, with less than 45,000 (from which number fully 5,000 must be deducted as absent from work from various causes), 135,000,000 pounds are produced, or about five times the quantity under slavery. The Coolies are found to be an intelligent race, who have become inured to the work required, and by whose labor this small island can produce the fifth part of the consumption of the United Kingdom, and that with only about 70,00 acres under cane cultivation."

Whether the production of Cane Sugar in the United States will be profitable or not in future, depends, it is evident, upon a variety of circumstances that cannot readily be foreseen or precalculated. Unless a plant can be discovered that will ripen earlier than the present Cane, or prove hardy enough to withstand the frost, the prospects are not brilliant. The capital required to start a Sugar Plantation is now very large; and as respects profits, it is doubtful whether they equal the interest which could be obtained upon the investment if loaned out in the Western States. The following is a statement of the value, product, etc., of one of the largest and most flourishing Sugar Estates in Louisiana.

The Estate of St. James for the Year 1852.

Land, 9,000 acres, of which about 1500 are under cultivation, 800 being in Cane, balance forest, worth $40 per acre	$360,000
Buildings	100,000
Machinery, including sugar-mill and apparatus for making and refining 25,000 pounds of Sugar by steam every 24 hours	60,000
215 Slaves, including 109 field hands, and 64 children under five years of age	170,000
Stock, 64 mules, 12 horses, 16 oxen, 145 sheep, 80 cows and beeves	11,000
Total	$701,000

PRODUCTION OF THE ESTATE IN 1852.

Sugar, 1,300,000 lbs. at 6 cts. per pound	$78,000	
Syrup, 60,000 gallons at 36 cts. per gallon	21,600	
		99,600
Corn and Wood, estimated value		14,400
		$114,000

Cash expenses annually, $20,000.

The net product, it will be perceived, is about thirteen per cent. on the capital invested.

In Florida, there are said to be hundreds of thousands of acres of land, worth from $1.25 to $10 per acre, in bodies of from 100 to 1,000 acres, admirably adapted for Sugar-growing, having an advantage of at least six weeks in the duration of the growing season over Louisiana; while in Texas the production of Sugar is becoming rapidly established as a prominent pursuit. On the Rio Grande, a number of persons have recently commenced making Sugar with the aid of native laborers. A Southern newspaper considers these far cheaper than slaves, and says:

"A native field-hand seldom receives more than six dollars per month, which, with a ration of an 'almude,' or peck of corn per week, comprises the whole expense of the employer; and we think will be found much cheaper than slave-labor, when the cost of purchase, food, clothing, and doctor's bills are estimated."

The manufacture of Sugar involves chemical principles of such nicety, that success in its production may be said to depend more upon the science of the manufacturer than upon the character of the labor employed. Within a few years a very important improvement has been made in the purification of Sugar, by means of an improved lime process, which prevents the formation of molasses, and consequently effects an increase in the Sugar product of about twenty-five per cent. A saturated mixture of alum and lime is applied to the juice in the proportion of two pounds of the mixture to a hundred gallons of the juice. These being intimately mixed, the acid is then neutralized by the application of milk of lime in the proportion of about three pounds to a hundred gallons. When the mixture ceases to affect the usual tests for an excess of acids, or alkalies, the impurities are precipitated, and the juice thus purified is subjected to the usual mode of clarification and concentration.

One suggestion, however, may be made, that may increase the profits of Sugar-growing from the Cane, and that is, to *manufacture Vinegar from the sour cane juice.*

The commercial value of Acetic Acid is high; and the planters, when overtaken by severe frosts, often sacrifice their cane altogether from the rapid spontaneous passage of the Sugar into Vinegar, and thus sustain an unnecessary loss.

Sugar can be produced from a great variety of substances; but the best known, next to the Cane, are the Sugar Beet, Sugar Maple, and the Sorghum, or *Chinese Sugar Cane.*

1. BEET-ROOT SUGAR.

The manufacture of Sugar from the Beet-root is indebted mainly to French perseverance and enterprise for its present prominence and importance. As early as 1747, Margraf, a chemist, discovered that Sugar could be made from the Beet-root; but its importance, as a manufacture, dates from Napoleon's attempts to injure Great Britain by prohibiting the importation of produce from the West Indies. He offered a magnificent premium to the discoverer of a permanent home-supply of Sugar; and when the Beet was fixed upon as the most promising plant, he was zealous in encouraging its growth, in spite of ridicule and repeated failures. At the present time, the production of Beet-root Sugar in France exceeds one hundred and fifty thousand tons a year; and half as much more is made in all the other parts of the Continent of Europe.

Of the Beet-root there are several kinds. That which is considered to yield the most Sugar is the White or Silesian Beet; then the Yellow, then the Red, and lastly, the common or field Beet. The Silesian Beet is smaller than the mangel-wurzel, more like the Swedish turnip; and the smaller kinds, those of which the roots weigh only one or two pounds, are preferred by some of the most successful makers of Sugar. The quantity of Sugar produced from a ton of roots varies; but, with the successive improvements in machinery that have been made, it has risen from two to ten and a half per cent. Count Chaptal, a grower of the root, and a manufacturer of Sugar, reports that five tons of clean roots produced about 4½ cwt. of coarse Sugar, which gave about one hundred and sixty pounds of double-refined Sugar, and sixty pounds of inferior lump Sugar; the rest being molasses, from which a good spirit is distilled. Achard, the first manufacturer of Beet-root Sugar in Silesia, says that about a ton of roots produced one hundred pounds of raw Sugar, which gave fifty-five pounds of refined Sugar and fifteen pounds of treacle. The conclusion is, that six thousand tons of Beet-root will yield four hundred tons of Sugar and one hundred tons of Molasses.

Many of the operations in manufacturing Beet-root Sugar are nearly the same as those by which the juice of the Sugar Cane is prepared for use: much greater skill and nicety, however, being required in rendering juice crystallizable, on account of its greater rareness, and the small quantity of Sugar it contains. But when the Sugar is refined, it is said that the most experienced judges cannot distinguish it from Cane Sugar, either in taste or appearance. "Beet-root Sugar," says Simmonds, "when it is completely refined, differs in no sensible degree from refined Cane Sugar. In appearance, it is quite equal to Cane Sugar, and the process of refining it is more easy than for the latter." (See *Simmonds' Vegetable Products.* Art. SUGAR, pp. 190–205.)

Within the last few years some very important improvements have been made in the manufacture of Beet-root Sugar, as we have stated, increasing its yield largely. One of the most important of these is M. Dubranfaut's process for extracting Sugar from the residuum—the molasses of the Beet-root, which is nauseous, and uneatable except by pigs. To this useless molasses he adds hydrate of baryta, which combines with the saccharic acid, or sweet principle, and produces a Saccharate, or Sucrate of Baryta, an insoluble substance. The coloring and other soluble matters are then washed out. Thus, from this dark substance, acted upon in the first instance by the hydrate of baryta, he obtains a body which is perfectly colorless. It is next necessary to get rid of the baryta, it being poisonous; and carbonic acid is used for that purpose. Carbonic acid being introduced, a carbonate of baryta is formed: the baryta goes over to the carbonic acid, and the Sugar left. The sweet fluid is then subjected to clarification by straining through animal charcoal and sulphate of lime, and becomes a colorless substance, extremely sweet and perfectly free from baryta. Thus is obtained a kind of *Eau sucre* from the black and fètid molasses: the final result being the recovery of from thirty-five to forty-five per cent. of Sugar.

The Beet-root grows very luxuriantly and abundantly in the United States; but, so far, little attention has been paid to the production of Sugar from it. This is probably because the processes of manufacture require considerable skill and knowledge, not as yet possessed by those who command the requisite facilities for growing the root. It is probable that the culture and the manufacture should be carried on separately, as the growing and grinding of wheat now are; and if proper encouragement were offered to persons skilled in the manufacture, to erect mills in or adjacent to localities well suited for the growth of the root, and who, in turn, could hold out inducements to the growers, both cultivators and manufacturers would do well, and the country would be greatly benefitted.

In New Mexico, Sugar, in consequence of the immense cost of transportation from the Mississippi to Santa Fé, ranges in price, we are informed, from nineteen to twenty-five cents per pound; and Molasses, made from corn-stalks, is purchased at $1.50 per gallon, while all kinds of grain and vegetables in that climate are remarkable for their extraordinary sweetness. The Beet, especially, contains an unusual amount of saccharine matter; and it is supposed the business of manufacturing Sugar from it would be found very profitable.

"The experience of France," says the author whom we quoted before, "ought to be a sufficient guarantee that the manufacture of Beet-root Sugar is not a speculative but a great staple trade, in which the supply is regulated by the demand, with a precision scarcely attainable in any other case; and where, in addition, this demand tends rather to increase than to diminish. That the trade is profitable there can also be no doubt, from the large capital embarked in it on the Continent—a capital which is steadily increasing, even in France, where protection has been gradually withdrawn, and where, since 1848, it has competed on equal terms with colonial Sugars."

2. MAPLE SUGAR.

The whole amount of Maple Sugar manufactured in the United States in the year 1850, according to the returns of the last Census, was 34,249,886 pounds. This amount, it is supposed, falls short of the real quantity by at least one third. In addition to the Sugar crop, there was produced from the Sugar Maple, in 1850, Molasses to the amount of 40,000,000 of gallons. But notwithstanding this seemingly large production, there is room for a vast increase, especially in the North-Western States.

Professor CHARLES U. SHEPHARD, of Charleston adverts to the subject in a letter to the writer, and says:

"Having been employed, about twenty-five years ago, under the directions of the Secretary of the Treasury (L. McLane), to aid in making a report upon the subject of Cane Sugar in the United States, my attention was also slightly directed to the same product as afforded by the Sugar Maple; and I was lead to believe, that in many situations of our country, particularly in Michigan, immense areas existed more or less covered with this growth and in an excellent condition for affording the staple in question. The Manitouline Islands were mentioned to me as abounding in the Sugar Maple. At that period, such lands could be bought at $1.25 per acre, with a standing crop (so to speak) of the trees, capable of yielding, with the most trifling outlay, one thousand or fifteen hundred pounds of sugar per acre annually; and with suitable precaution, encouraging the young trees' growth, a succession of trees could be kept up through all time. The kettles and huts and living of the workmen (for about one month of the year) would be all that would be required as outlay; the rest would be clear profit—no cultivation, no fencing, next to no taxation. The years are not equally prolific in the yield, but the crop never fails any more than the market for it. The labor is performed moreover at a season when it is most at command."

In Canada, the Sugar Maples are sufficiently abundant to supply the whole population of that province with Sugar. On the south shore of Lake Huron and the islands of that lake, there are said to be more than a million of trees; and if, as reported, one hundred and fifty trees of medium growth will yield an amount of sap that would make three hundred pounds of Sugar and twenty-five gallons of Molasses, the aggregate production, it will be seen, would be immense. Every farmer having Sugar Maples should certainly supply his own consumption; and if he extend his production, he will find it as profitable as any other branch of his business.

Maple Sugar, when thoroughly refined, is equal in quality to the best West India Sugar.

In 1847, a premium was awarded by the Oswego County Agricultural Society, New York, to Mr. R. Tinker, for the following improved method of preparing Maple Sugar:—The sap is boiled in a potash and caldron kettle to a thick syrup; strain it when warm; let it stand twenty-four hours to settle; then pour it off, heaving back all that is impure. To clarify fifty pounds, take one quart of milk, one ounce of saleratus, and the whites of two eggs, well mixed; boil the Sugar again until it is hard enough to lay upon a saucer; then let it stand in the kettle and cool. Stir it a very little, to prevent caking in the kettle. For draining, use a tube, funnel-shaped, fifteen inches square at the top, and coming to a point at the bottom. Put in the Sugar when cold, tap it at the bottom, and keep a damp flannel, of two or three thicknesses on the top of the mass. When drained, dissolve the Sugar in pure warm water, and clarify and drain as before.

3. SORGHUM, OR CHINESE SUGAR-CANE.

For this plant, as for the Beet root, we are indebted mainly to French enterprise. In 1851, Count de Montigny, Consul of France at Shanghae in China, sent, in compliance with the request of the Geographical Society of Paris, a collection of plants and seeds which he had found in China, and which he thought would succeed in his own country. Among these were the Chinese Yam, and the *Holcus Saccharatus*, under the name of "The Sugar Cane of the North of China." Only one single seed of the package of Cane seeds germinated; but this had fallen into careful hands, who tenderly nursed it to maturity. Some of the seeds of this plant were received by a gardener, who the next year gathered eight hundred and sold them to the house of Vilmorin, Andrieux & Co., seed merchants at Paris, for eight hundred francs, or nearly twenty cents for a seed. In 1854, D. Jay Browne, Esq., of the United States Patent Office, brought with him from Europe a quantity of the seed; and thus had the satisfaction of introducing to American agriculturists a plant that has already excited a great deal of interest, and in the opinion of many is destined to take a rank among the most valuable of economical plants.

We must concede to a Frenchman, moreover, the credit of having been most successful in developing the useful qualities of this plant. Dr. Sicard, of Marseilles, has manufactured from it excellent sugar, which will favorably compare with any other whatever. By grinding the seed, he has obtained flour and fecula, of which he has made bread and chocolate that many tasters have found palatable. He extracts, further, from the plant an abundance of alchohol of superior quality; and, besides, a most agreeable wine, containing in large quantities all the tonic and other salutary elements of the juice of the grape. In addition, he has made paper out of it, and exhibits superior samples. By chemical agents he gets from it Gamboge,

Ginseng and Carbon, and has dyed skeins of cotton, wool and thread, in those delicate and varying shades which hitherto have been found only in the stuffs and articles coming directly from China. We should add, that the new derivations (as we may style them) from the cane are complete, and can be delivered to trade and industry at determinate prices.

In the United States, the results of experiments so far as made are conflicting, and it is somewhat difficult to predict the precise position which this plant will hereafter occupy in the scale of value. With regard to the point, at one time disputed, whether crystallizable Sugar can be made from the Sorghum, we consider it definitively settled in the affirmative by the experiments of Joseph S. Lovering, Esq., a prominent Sugar Refiner of Philadelphia, and a scientific man. We extract from his pamphlet a summary of the conclusions at which he has arrived, viz.:

"1st. That it is obvious that there is a culminating point in the development of the Sugar in the Cane, which is the best time for Sugar-making. This point or season I consider to be when most, if not all the seeds are ripe, and after several frosts, say when the temperature falls to 25° or 30° F.

"2d. That frost, or even hard freezing, does not injure the juice nor the Sugar; but that warm, Indian summer weather, after the frost and hard freezing, does injure them very materially, and reduces both quantity and quality.

"3. That if the Cane is cut and housed or shocked in the field, when in its most favorable condition, it will probably keep unchanged for a long time.

"4th. That when the juice is obtained, the process should proceed continuously and without delay.

"5th. That the clarification should be as perfect as possible by the time the density reaches 15° Beaume, the syrup having the appearance of good brandy.

"6th. That although eggs were used in these small experiments, on account of their convenience, bullock's blood, if to be had, is equally good; and the milk of lime alone will answer the purpose. In the latter case, however, more constant and prolonged skimming will be required to produce a perfect clarification, which is highly important.

"7th. That the concentration, or boiling down, after clarification, should be as rapid as possible without scorching—shallow evaporators being the best.

"With these conditions secured, it is about as easy to make good sugar from the Chinese Cane as to make a pot of good mush, and much easier than to make a kettle of good apple-butter."

The day is not distant, we may reasonably hope, when America will produce enough Sugar for her own consumption and some for export. Before this period will arrive, however, new sources of Cane Sugar must be discovered, and the chemist must make known improved processes for the production of *syrup from plants affording only glucose.*

For elaborate and valuable articles on Sugar and Cotton, see "De Bow's Industrial Resources," and "Review," "Homan's Cyclopedia of Commerce," "Merchant's Magazine," etc.

CHANCE IX.—*Money can be made by growing Tobacco, especially by Cultivating qualities equal to the Havana Tobacco, on soils adapted for it.*

The United States export about two-fifths of all the

Tobacco consumed in Europe, and to some of the countries with which we have commercial relations, Tobacco constitutes the chief article of export. The principal drawback to the extension of our trade in this product is its inferior quality, though it is stated that the very best Tobacco in the world is a mixture of the United States article and Tobacco the produce of tropical countries; for while the former has too much essential oil, the latter has too little; and that by combination the peculiar qualities of each are brought out without being impaired.

In 1850, there were about 400,000 acres in the United States devoted to the cultivation of Tobacco, embracing some in nearly every State in the Union. The product per acre varied in different States, Kentucky producing 575 lbs.; Maryland, 650 lbs.; Missouri, 775 lbs.; Tennessee 750 lbs.; Ohio, 730 lbs.; Virginia, 660 lbs. But supposing an average of 600 lbs. to the acre, the product was 240,000,000 lbs. Since the census of 1850 was taken, the cultivation of this article has greatly increased; and what constitutes the most hopeful prospect for the future importance of the crop is, it has taken deep root in the New England and the Western States. In the Connecticut Valley the crop is already an important one. A Hartford Journal says:

"It is unquestionably the most remunerative crop grown, taking its average price and product for the last twenty years. We believe 1,500 lbs per. acre is the average yield in this section, and ten or twelve cents per pound the average price. The more perfect the leaf the higher the price. The manner in which Tobacco is prepared for market, after it reaches second hands, is an enigma to most growers. By some wonderful hocus-pocus, it increases very rapidly in value; so the same article which to-day was sold for twelve cents by the producer, to-morrow is repacked and sold for from twenty-five to fifty cents. Tobacco speculators make money even in hard times. We have a man in memory, who, in a little country village is reported to have thus made $65,000 last year. We believe it. There are some men that annually double and quadruple their money in Tobacco. We believe a book containing the secrets of the craft would pay. There is no use in decrying book-farming any longer. The great unanswerable argument in its favor is that it fattens the purse. The muscle and bone can do a great deal, but mind and brain can do more."

There is a large quantity of Tobacco raised in the southern part of Indiana annually, said to be equal in quality to the Tobacco raised in Kentucky. In some counties the article is extensively cultivated, and generally pays the producer a handsome profit on the labor bestowed on it. The cultivation of it is becoming more extensive every year. Nearly all this crop is taken to Louisville, and sold in that market for account of the producer.

Within a few years past, considerable progress has been made in raising Tobacco in Ohio. One county alone is reported to have raised, in a single year, Tobacco of the value of $800,000. The average price approximates to six cents per pound, which, we are told, makes a good crop yield $100 per acre.

In Florida, the cultivation of Tobacco has taken root, especially in Gadsden County, and the product is shipped to Bremen, paying the planter as high as twenty-five cents per pound for the first quality. The cultivation, however, is confined to the new lands, the cut-worm which prevails in the old lands being very destructive to the plant.

While it is thus evident that more attention is being paid to the cultivation of Tobacco every year, and in all parts of the Union, and while the business, even as at present conducted, is a profitable one, it may nevertheless be safely asserted, that far more magnificent results than any that have been realized can be attained by cultivating the finer qualities. Cuba, in this particular, surpasses all other countries, and no doubt many valuable lessons could be borrowed from her experience. Even in Cuba, however, the quantity of the very first-class Tobacco produced is quite limited. The best Havana Tobacco farms are confined to an area about eighty miles long and twenty-one broad, in the south-western part of Cuba. This district is bounded on the north by mountains, on the south and west by the ocean, whilst eastward, though there is no natural limit, the Tobacco sensibly degenerates in quality. A light sandy soil, and a rather low situation, seem essential for the production of the best quality.*

The profits of growing Tobacco in Cuba are said to exceed $800 per parallelogram of two hundred yards in length and fifty in breadth. An illustration of the great variety of prices, and the mode adopted in curing the leaf, will be seen from the following extract from the Report of the American Consul to the State Department:

---

* The best ground for raising the plant, according to Capt. Carver ("Treatise on Culture of Tobacco," &c.), is a warm, rich soil, not subject to be overrun with weeds. The soil in which it grows in Virginia is inclining to sandy, consequently warm and light; the nearer, therefore, the nature of the land approaches to that, the greater probability there is of its flourishing. The situation most preferable for a plantation is the southern declivity of a hill, or a spot sheltered from the blighting north winds; but at the same time the plants must enjoy a free current of air, for if that be obstructed they will not prosper.

"HAVANA LEAF TOBACCO.—Tobacco is one of the most important articles of production in the Island. The planters commence to plant in August or September, after the heavy rains are over, and the northers may be looked for, which generally come accompanied by a drizzling rain that is favorable to the plant. In February or March, and as late as April, the Tobacco is cut and taken to a house or shed, erected for the purpose of affording shade, and at the same time a free circulation of air; it is placed on *cujes* (poles), laid horizontally at some distance from the ground, where it is allowed to become perfectly dry until the spring rains commence, when the humidity seizes the leaf, causes it to swell and to take the silky appearance peculiar to it. It is then taken from the poles and laid in heaps on the ground, the leaves being slightly sprinkled with water; in this state it undergoes a species of fermentation. After this operation is gone through, the leaves are placed in *manojos* (hands); afterward it is a very common practice to take a quantity of refuse leaves and infuse them in a quantity of water, and, in some instances, wine, and even alcohol, or rather tafia, is used when the Tobacco is light-colored and weak, and it is desired to give it increased strength. This infusion undergoes a state of fermentation, after which the refuse leaves deposit themselves at the bottom. The Tobacco is dipped into this preparation before being hung up in a room almost air-tight, where it undergoes the sweating to which the name of *calentura* (fever) is given; the process of dipping is performed as many times as the Tobacco may require. I am under the impression that this process might be used to a great advantage with the Connecticut Tobacco.

* * * * * * * *

"It would be difficult indeed, for any one to attempt to fix prices for Tobacco; they vary from $10 to $170, generally; but occasionally fabulous prices are paid for that which is very good in quality, and which offers a fair prospect of yielding a large number of cigars. I have it from a very reliable source, that a little over a month since, the celebrated factory of 'La Hija de Cabanas y Carbafal' paid the sum of $10,000 cash for a lot of only forty-five bales, none of which exceeded one hundred pounds in weight. By the following quotations, given by our latest price current, it will be perceived how varied the prices are for Tobacco:

$120 to $140 for firsts, seconds, and thirds.

60 to	80 for fourths,	According to quality, selection and renown, all is Vuelta Abajo.
40 to	50 for fifths,	
20 to	30 for sixths,	
17 to	20 for sevenths and Capadura,	

When tobacco is shipped, it is generally covered with crash."

In Appendix No. 9 of the *Patent Office Report* for 1847, may be found an account of a method of raising Tobacco in Cuba, which was considered of such value, that it was forbidden to be sent from the Island. In the Report for 1854, J. M. Hernandez gives a statement of the best method of raising Cuba Tobacco in Florida.

The Tobacco grown in the Island of Trinidad is said to be fully equal to the Tobacco of Cuba in quality; but all raised in that colony is generally consumed there, and is consequently little known in the English market. Trinidad, it would seem, is worth a visit, if in search of a good site for a Tobacco plantation.

CHANCE X.—*The Cultivation of Flax and Hemp, especially Flax, is worthy of your attention, as likely to be profitable in future.*

Flax and Hemp, though among the earliest of the staples, have never been elevated to a very prominent position in the agriculture of the American people. Flax has been grown principally for its seed, the fibre being burned for manure, or thrown into the highway. In Europe, in the meantime, it has become a very important article of production and manufacture, and whole communities are occupied almost exclusively in its cultivation. In Ireland, of late years, considerable progress has been made in Flax growing; and a Royal Society has been established for the improvement of its cultivation. England consumes immense quantities of both Flax and Hemp in her manufactures, and has imported from Russia in a single year, fifty-five million pounds of Hemp, and from the United States in the same year 127,806 pounds; making, however, a difference to the advantage of Russia of 54,872,200 pounds. Our Consul in Liverpool wrote in 1854:

"American Hemp, if due attention were bestowed on the improvement of the quality, might be profitably sent hither to a considerable extent. Heretofore it has been found so much inferior to the Hemp received from Russia, that scarcely any but experimental importations, (and mostly, I am told, at a loss), have taken place. Whether our Hemp cannot be so improved as to compete successfully with that of Russia in the English market, is a point well worth the attention of American agriculturists."

In Flanders, the average annual value of the Flax crop is $8,000,000, and the mode of dressing and preparing Flax for the loom is deemed superior to that in any other country. In its culture, the order of the crops, the preparation of the soil, the system of manuring, and the process of steaming, the inhabitants of Flanders are considered unrivaled in the world; and hence the linens of Belgium have long been celebrated for their excellence and beauty. No others equal them in the fineness of their quality or the evenness of their tissue.

In the United States, within a few years, several linen mills have been established, though the average number of spindles now in operation probably does not exceed 40,000. The erection of more manufactories of this description at an early day may, however, be anticipated, and the time is not remote when the home market for the fibre of Flax will be an important one; and if its cultivation was profitable before, when the seed alone was available, the future of this staple cannot be other than promising. What, however, offers additional encouragement and inducement to embark in Flax-growing is, that the business is no longer the laborious and disagreeable one it once was. Various improvements have been successively and rapidly made, that have revolutionized the mode of preparing the fibre for market.

Some ten years ago, a Mr. Schenck patented a process —said, however, to have been known long before—for retting Flax by steeping it in water heated to a temperature of about 80°, by which the desired effect is produced in from 70 to 90 hours, instead of weeks, as formerly. "The practical result," says Prof. Solly, F. R. S., "which may now be considered as satisfactorily established, is, that Flax retted by Schenck's warm-water process is equal to the best Flax prepared under the old methods, and that whilst time and money are economized, and some of the objections of the old methods are removed, there is less danger of injuring the fibre, and hence, a far more uniform fibre is obtained; in fact, the average product of the new mode, is superior to the average product under the old process."

In the Transactions of the New York State Agricultural Society for 1853 may be found an address from John Wilson, containing a resumé of the various improvements, in the order of their occurrence, that had been made up to that period, in the preparation of Flax; and stating that processes have been invented by which the entire operation of converting straw into dressed fibre may be effected in *twelve hours.*

In 1854, Dr. O. S. Leavitt submitted to the American Institute of New York plans of machinery and processes for preparing Flax for manufacture, after being stripped of the seed, *without being rotted;* and the committee stated that they believed that Flax cleaned, bleached and formed into rovings by this machinery, can be produced at a much less cost than that of rotted and hackled flax unbleached. The inventor himself claims that, by his mode of manufacture, linens can be made for about the cost of cotton goods of the same weight and fineness, at the average prices of cotton. "With straw at $10 per ton, the amount paid the farmer is five cents per pound for fibre, and the cost of bleaching and refining enough for a pound will be less than five cents more, making the refined material, like that exhibited, less than ten cents per pound, about the average price of cotton. If the Flax that is cut with a scythe like hay, such as can be bought at the West for $5 per ton, be used, of course the fibre would cost less. At any rate, very large profits must be made at the linen business for many years, until competition shall eventually bring down prices. Shirt linen will average 14½ yards to the pound, so that the raw material would cost less than 1½ cents per yard, all the rest being labor in the factory. There is no doubt that such goods can be produced for ten to twelve cents per yard."

It will thus be seen that Flax-growing no longer involves the tedious and laborious processes formerly necessary for its preparation, and that a market for the fibre is now established both at home and abroad.

With regard to the relative or comparative profits of growing Flax and Hemp, it may may be said, generally, that the former is the more profitable, first, because the seed pays for the crop; and, secondly, because it requires a far less rich soil than Hemp. To raise Hemp, a deep, rich loam, containing a very large per centage of decomposed vegetable matter, is almost essential. As respects the *actual profits* of raising Flax, they of course vary with the market value of the product, which in England, we are told by the Jury on the "Vegetable Substances used in Manufactures," (Rep. I. 228), range "from £40 to £180 per ton," that is from $200 to $900. On Western alluvial soils, that can be purchased for $1.25 per acre, Flax can be raised successively for many years without manure; and if the product will command in the English market an approximation to the prices above stated, Flax may be made uniformly one of the most profitable of crops. In England, one agriculturist, among others, it is reported, hires 300 acres of land at $40 per acre, that is $12,000 rent per annum, and raises upon it nothing but Flax, which yields him satisfactory profits. In the United States, I know of no statistics like these, but Mr. Blakeslee, of Waterbury, Conn., states that he has made a clear profit of $60 per acre in raising Flax, and that three pecks of good seed yielded four hundred pounds weight of fibre and seventeen bushels of seed. The "Scientific American," in an article on "the Management of the Flax Crop," May 16, 1857, recommends that "plump, heavy, shining seed alone should be used, and care exercised in its selection. American Flax seed generally produces a coarse, branchy stem. Dutch and Riga seed are held to be the best. If farmers wish to cultivate Flax for fine fibre, it should be sown thick, not less than two bushels to the acre, we believe; if for the seed, they should sow it thin, one bushel to the acre. Thick-sown Flax grows tall and straight, producing fine fibre but little seed: thin-sown Flax grows coarse and branches out, producing a great quantity of good seed but coarse fibre."

Within a few years several new varieties of Flax and Hemp have been introduced to the notice of agriculturists, among which the most promising are the *New Zealand Flax* and the *Sisal Hemp*.

The native Flax of New Zealand is a plant essentially different from the European or American Flax. Its fibre is described as three times as strong as *Agave Americana*, twice as strong as Flax, and excels in strength the Hemp of Russia; in fact, it is said to be the strongest of known vegetable fibres. A single three-inch leaf, split into strips, will, when knotted together, form a flat green cord fifty feet long, which no slight strain will break. The natives use its leaves for girths, halters, measuring-tapes, boot-laces, and common strings; and if a *pig* or *sheep* has to be tied, a couple of leaves, split or whole, form a cord which no pig can break. Poinsett recommends the introduction of this plant to Southern planters, even when it may not be advisable to raise it for sale. The leaves, he says, form strong and durable baskets, plow-lines, and such cords as we daily use on a farm, and may be fabricated by any common laborer; offsets of this plant may be procured from France at a cheap rate, and from the Nurseries in our Northern States at from twenty-five to thirty cents a plant. But besides its great strength, New Zealand Flax has the advantage of hackling out to an almost inconceivable fineness; and it is remarkable that it has not advanced more rapidly in popularity with Flax growers.

The *Sisal Hemp* has been cultivated for some time in Florida, and its success is no longer doubtful. A number of tons, we are told, (see Patent Office Report, 1855,) have been sent to market, where it brought within half a cent a pound as much as Manilla Hemp, that is about $250 per ton. A gentleman writing from Florida says:

"The *Sisal Hemp* is very successful. The plant (*Agava Sisalana*, or *Americana*) grows in the poorest kind of land; and even on a stony, barren island, it grows very well. There are a few acres here just ready to be cleaned out for market; and it has been ascertained by experiment that an acre will yield *one thousand dollars per annum* after the fourth year. It requires no cultivation. Just drop the seed in the ground, and you have nothing more to do with it for four years, when you can begin to cut and clean. The suckers are constantly springing up, so that by the time you cut down the first crop, the second is ready to begin with; and so on until the land is entirely exhausted."

This reference to new Varieties of Plants suggests a comprehensive consideration, in which it may be stated there are, at least, a hundred chances to make money; viz.:

CHANCES XI.—C.—*By introducing New Things, and by especially enlisting popular interest in Agricultural Products that are of economical value in foreign countries, and which experiment has shown can be successfully cultivated in the United States.*

It may be axiomatically stated that Americans are fond of novelties. Their political individuality had its origin in the upturning of established systems, and their industrial progress and social advancement have for their basis a proverbial readiness in originating and adopting improvements. Wide awake to the "main chance," whoever can offer them what combines novelty and utility, can be assured of an attentive hearing, and often of a munificent patronage. The agricultural class is, in general, the slowest to manifest faith in things unseen; but when partially convinced, skepticism with them is apt to give way to credulity. Within a single generation, the agriculturists have been the victims of three great popular fevers, which depleted their purses and prejudiced their minds against Merinoes, Morus Multicaulis, and Shanghais, but fortunately without destroying their confidence in all future progress.

Confining my observations mainly to Seeds, Plants, and Cuttings which are highly esteemed in distant parts of the world, I shall not attempt more than to illustrate the subject by reference to a few which seem the most important, and the culture of which is apparently well adapted for the United States.

1. THE TURKISH FLINT WHEAT.—The Patent Office recommends this as a hardy fall variety, with a dark-colored chaff, a very heavy beard, and a long, flinty, light-colored berry, which will prove highly profitable to the farmer and miller, from its superior weight and the excellence of the flour it will produce. It appears to be well adapted to the soil and climate of the Middle States, and has even improved in the quality of its grain, both in regard to its color and size. It withstood the severity of severe winters without much injury from the cold; and from its very long and thick beard, it doubtless will be protected in a measure from the depredations of insects in the field, as well as from the heating or molding in the stack. The hardness of the grain, too, when dry, is a sufficient guarantee against ordinary moisture in transportation and the perforation of the weevil in the bin.

From several reliable experiments made with this Wheat in Virginia, with ordinarily good cultivation, the yield was thirty bushels to an acre. Estimating the present annual crops of Wheat grown in the Middle and Southern portions of the United States to be 100,000,000 bushels—averaging, say twenty bushels to the acre—the increased production in those sections, if the Turkish Flint Wheat alone were cultivated, and the ratio of yield as above, would be 50,000,000 bushels, which would often add to the resources of a single farm $500, and of the country at least $50,000,000.

2. THE ADELAIDE, OR AUSTRALIAN WHEAT.—At the London Exhibition in 1851, the cereal which attracted the greatest attention from corn factors and competent judges, was a sample of Wheat from South Australia, and which was pronounced "the most beautiful specimen of Wheat that had ever been brought to market in any country." It was a white Wheat, in which every grain appeared to be like every other grain—plump, clear-skinned, dry, and heavy, weighing, what may seem incredible to those who are only accustomed to common Wheat, *seventy pounds to the bushel.* Various attempts have been made in England to raise this magnificent Wheat, but without success—the crop from the seeds sown being of a very inferior description, "ugly, coarse, and bearded." The conclusion, as stated by JOHN LINDLEY, F. R. S., is, that the "Wheat of Australia is no peculiar kind of Wheat; it has no peculiar constitutional characteristic by which it may be in any way distinguished from Wheat cultivated in this country; it is not essentially different from the fine Wheat which Prince Albert sent to the Exhibition, or from others

which we grow or sell. Its quality is owing to local condition, that is to say, to the peculiar temperature, the brilliant light, the soil, and those other circumstances which characterize the climate of South Australia, in which it is produced; and therefore there would be no advantage gained by introducing this Wheat for the purpose of sowing it here. Its value consists in what it is in South Australia, not what it would become in England." While this may be true as respects England, it must be remembered that the United States have a much greater diversity of climate and soil than Great Britain; and it is believed, as it is certainly to be hoped, that there are localities possessing the requisites for cultivating a Wheat that would command a preference over all others in the markets of the world.

3. THE IMPROVED KING PHILIP, OR BROWN CORN.—The seed of this was obtained about 1852, from an island in a lake in New Hampshire, and was extensively disseminated in all the States north of New Jersey, and throughout the mountainous districts of Pennsylvania, Maryland, and Virginia. The result has been "that it usually matures within the period of ninety days from the time of planting (from the first to the middle of June), and yields, with good cultivation, in most cases, from *eighty to one hundred bushels of shelled Corn to an acre.* It is well adapted to high latitudes and elevated valleys and plains, where, from the shortness of summer, other varieties of Corn are liable to be killed by late spring or early autumnal frosts. The quality of the grain is good, being heavy, well filled with oil, and suitable for fattening animals, or for transportation by sea, without injury from moisture in vessels. This Corn also possesses an-

other valuable property, in being susceptible of close planting, and consequently is of a dwarfy growth, which renders the entire stalks and blades suitable for fodder when cured.

"Estimating the present annual Corn crop of New England, New York, Michigan, Wisconsin, Minnesota, Utah, Washington, and Oregon, at 50,000,000 bushels, say thirty bushels per acre, if the variety of Corn in question were solely cultivated in these States, the increased yield, allowing the product to be fifty bushels (one half of the maximum) to the acre, would be more than 33,000,000 bushels, the value of which would be at least $20,000,000."

4. Within the last ten years attention has been considerably directed to the discovery of *substitutes for the Potato,* in case the rot should render the cultivation of that vegetable unprofitable. The prosecution of researches in this direction, though they have not resulted in the discovery of any substitute, has made known the value of several roots and vegetables, that may be in the future welcome additions in domestic economy. Among them are the *Chinese Yam* and the *Saa-ga-ban.* The Chinese Yam, we are informed, has succeeded well in several parts of the Union, and promises to serve as an excellent substitute both for the common and sweet Potato. It possesses the remarkable property of remaining sound in the earth for several years, without either deteriorating in its edible qualities, or sustaining injury from frost, which adds much to its value, in being always in readiness for the kitchen; and this, too, often at a time when the Potato is shriveled or otherwise impaired. But the *Saa-ga-ban* is probably the most promising substitute that has yet been suggested, and certainly is worthy of experi-

mental investigation. Attention was first directed to this vegetable, in 1846, by Dr. Gesner, in the "Colonial Magazine," as follows:

A. tuberosa (Boerhaave) or *Glycine Apios.*—This plant is common throughout the Northern and Southern States of America, and is also met with in the lower British North American provinces. It is known under the native name of *Saa-ga-ban* by the Macinac Indians, by whom the pear-shaped roots are used as an article of food. Like the *Arachis hypogoea,* it belongs to the *Leguminosæ* family. The fruit and flowers resemble those of the wood vetch. It is thus described in Professor Eaton's "Manual of Botany for North America," published in 1836:—"Color of corolla, blue and purple; time of flowering, July (and August in Nova Scotia); perennial; stem, twining; leaves, pinnate, with seven lanceolate leaflets; racemes, shorter than the leaves; axillary; root, tuberous. Root very nutritive; ought to be generally cultivated." Dr. Gesner shipped several bushels of the Saa-ga-ban to the principal Agricultural Societies in Great Britain, also to Halifax, Nova Scotia. "The ordinary Potato of this country," says Simmonds, "does not yield more than fourteen per cent. of starch, and contains seventy-six per cent. of water. From the best Saa-ga-ban Dr. Gesner obtained twenty-one per cent. of starch; and the quantity of water is reduced to fifty per cent. It also contains vegetable albumen, gum, and sugar. From these facts, it is evident that the Saa-ga-ban is much more nutritive than the Potato; and the weight of the tubers in their wild state, compared with the weight of the slender vine in the best samples, is equal in proportion to the common cultivated Potato in its ordinary growth. The starch is very white, and closely resembles that made from the arrow-root. It is not improbable that the quantity of water in the tuber will be increasd by cultivation; yet the fibrous parenchyma will be reduced—and, taken altogether, the nutritive properties will be increased. And if the plant improve as much by cultivation as the Potato and many others have done, its success is certain."

Besides these, Mr. Simmonds, in his "Vegetable Kingdom," refers to numerous roots which serve as sustenance to the Indians and to the aborigines of various countries; some of which may prove to be very superior food-producing plants, if not a substitute for the Potato, viz.:

The MENDO, or *Wild Sweet Potato*—Root similar in taste and growth to the ordinary Sweet Potato.

WABESSEPIN, or *Wild Potato*—Grows only in wet ground

PRAIRIE TURNIP—Form and size like a hen's or goose's egg. M. Lamare Picot, a French naturalist, believes the seed of this is capable of cultivation; and that it may form a substitute both for the Potato and for Wheat.

The WILD BEAN—Has a rich and very pleasant flavor, and it would be a most desirable garden vegetable.

The EARTH MOUSE (*Lathyrus tuberosus*)—Found in Lorraine and Burgundy, resembles an earth-mouse in form and an earth-chestnut in taste. The French peasants have a prejudice against cultivating it, because they say it walks underground, and leaves the place it is planted in to go to a neighboring field.

The ARRACACHA ESCULENTA—A native of South America. Unites the taste of the Potato and the Parsnip, but said to be superior to both. Highly recommended by the Rev. J. M. Wilson in the "Rural Encyclopedia."

The AIPI—Grown in Brazil, may be boiled and eaten, or dissolved and drank.

The TAPIOCA, or BAY RUSH—Grows in the Bahamas group, in the form of a large beet, from twelve to sixteen inches in length. Makes good bread, and was of great use to the inhabitants of Long Island during a scarcity of food, occasioned by drought in 1843.

The KOOYAH PLANT (*Valeriana edulis*)—Much used by the North American Indians, and sometimes called the "Tobacco Root."

The KAMAS ROOT (*Camassia esculenta*)—The bulb has a sweet, pleasant flavor, somewhat of the taste of preserved quince.

The AURACANIAN PINE—The seeds have a flavor not unlike the chestnut. Constitute a great part of the diet of the Auracanians.

The NUT PINE (*Pinus monophyllus*)—Alluded to by Fremont, in his Exploring Expedition to the Rocky Mountains, as largely used by the Indians—said to be very nutritious.

The AUSTRALIAN PINE (*Auracaria bidwillii*)—The aborigines fatten and grow sleek on the seeds roasted.

The SINGHARA, or WATER NUT—Extensively eaten in Cashmere and other parts of the East.

Besides these, there is also a great variety of mosses and Ferns; as Iceland Moss, Ceylon Moss, Sea Wrack, Mushrooms, which furnish food to many; some of which may be a valuable addition to our list of culinary vegetables.

5. GRASSES.—Of Grasses there is also an infinite variety, and many natives of distant countries, as the Tussock Grass of the Falkland Islands, could be profitably introduced into our own country, in some portions of which, at certain seasons, fodder is scarce. Most Grasses, it has

been remarked, will be found to be of a social character, and to do best in a large mixture with other varieties; and we may remark that most pastures could be improved by suitable admixture of those that grow early and luxuriantly with those of which the chief recommendation is their nutritive qualities. It would be presumptuous to enter upon so comprehensive a subject, largely treated of in agricultural works (see "*Farmer's and Planter's Encyclopedia,*" in particular); and I advert to it only for the purpose of directing your attention to one variety—the *Sweet-scented Vernal Grass*, which is said to impart to the Philadelphia butter its well known high and delicate flavor for which it is remarkable, especially in the Spring. Dr. Mease referred to its celebrity as long ago as 1811, in his "Picture of Philadelphia." The discovery that the Philadelphia butter is indebted for its peculiar and superior flavor to the Sweet-scented Vernal Grass, with which the pastures in the vicinity of the city abound with a luxuriance unknown in any other part of the country, was made by Dr. G. EMMERSON, of Philadelphia, who, in 1850, wrote as follows:

"Extensive operations, and many experiments made and continued through many years, have convinced me that the proximate source of the high flavor of our Philadelphia May butter is the *Sweet-scented Vernal Grass*, abounding in the old pastures, fields, and meadows of the adjacent counties. Some of the facts and reasons upon which I found this conclusion are the following:

"1st. In the dairy region around Philadelphia, the Sweet-scented Vernal Grass, with its peculiar vanilla-like fragrance, constitutes the predominant spring herbage on all the pastures, fields and meadows several years unplowed. The longer the pastures have been left unbroken, the greater the proportion of the Vernal Grass, and the higher the flavor of the butter produced from the cows fed upon them. Many of the meadows and pasture fields have remained ten twenty, thirty, and more years unbroken by the plow. In such cases the Sweet-scented Vernal Grass affords almost the exclusive spring herbage.

"2d. The high flavor continues in the butter during the development of the Grass, and invariably declines with the maturing of the seed; after which, the stems become dry and hard, and the cattle push them aside, in search of fresher and greener herbage.

"3d. The Sweet-scented Vernal Grass is shown, by chemical analysis, to contain an aromatic essential oil, of which *benzoic acid*, or flowers of benzoin, is the base.

"This aromatic principle is abundant, and can readily be obtained by distillation, furnishing a delightful perfume and source of flavor. As the milk of all animals is so very susceptible of acquiring disagreeable tastes from substances eaten, such as garlic, turnips, &c., it is natural to infer that it may likewise be imbued with agreeable flavors when the proper agents for such a purpose are presented in the food.

"4th. That the *benzoic acid* is the principal agent in producing the peculiarly agreeable flavor of butter made from pastures abounding in the Sweet-scented Vernal Grass, I have rendered probable, if not a demonstrated fact, by several experiments, in which the flowers of benzoin given to cows imparted to the butter made from them the characteristic flavor. In such cases, twenty or thirty grains of the benzoin were given twice a day, previously dissolved in hot water, which was stirred into some flour and meal, and then mingled with the customary mess. The cows receive not the slightest injury from this or a larger quantity of the benzoin."

He says further: "I consider the Sweet-scented Vernal Grass worthy the attention of all farmers desirous of obtaining butter and other dairy products in the highest perfection, and of having in their fields and meadows one of the earliest, if not the very earliest, pasture Grasses known."

It must be understood that the Sweet-scented Vernal is recommended as a pasture, not as a hay Grass. An additional recommendation for sowing it, is found in the fact that it improves mutton, the places in which it grows naturally being said to produce the finest mutton.

6. THE CHINA GRASS.—China Grass-cloth has been known as an article of commerce for many years, but the plant furnishing the material was only identified about the commencement of this century; and the product only obtained the notice of the public generally at the London Exhibition in 1851, where it was presented in every condition, from the crude article to the woven fabric, showing a fibre of such beauty and strength, that three prize medals were awarded to different persons for specimens in the prepared state.

The value of this fibre will be understood from the statement of Dr. Royle, that, as imported into England, it has "sold for £60 to £80, and even for £120 a ton." A simple but efficacious method of preparing this valuable fibre has lately been devised in England, depending chiefly on the solvent powers of a hot solution of carbonate of soda; and its use is consequently rapidly increasing, particularly in the formation of mixed fabrics. When well prepared, it has all the lustre and brilliancy of silk.

7. JUTE.—This plant is of the hemp species, and, like hemp, is a native of India. It consists of the fibres of two plants called *Chonch* and *Isbund*, and constitutes the material of which gunny bags and gunny cloth are made. In the period of its first production, it is a remarkably beautiful fibre — pearly-white, soft, silky, and easily spun. But it is said to be deficient in strength and durability; and moisture is particularly injurious to it.

Jute is now largely consumed in various manufactures

in Great Britain, particularly for cheap carpets, rugs, etc.; and it is supposed it could be turned to good account in the shawl trade, as a substitute for cotton. In and around Dundee, in Scotland, there are no fewer than seventy-six mills all engaged spinning this Jute and Flax, the principal of which is said to be the largest mill in Scotland. There are in this mill some two thousand hands, all wholly employed in spinning Jute, which is used to a large extent in the manufacture of carpets and rugs. Some three houses in that vicinity dye for this branch of trade alone, some seven tons a day. The carpets are sold as low as from seven pence to eleven pence per yard, and the rugs as low as three shillings.

8. Imperial, or Chinese Rice.—The ordinary Rice cultivated in our Southern States, requires a warm climate and an abundance of water. In China, there is a very superior quick-ripening Rice, adapted for cold climates and dry countries, and seemingly well worthy of introduction into the United States.

One of the Chinese Emperors, in his Memoirs, says: "I was walking, on the first day of the sixth moon, in some fields where Rice was sown, which was not expected to yield its harvest till the ninth. I happened to notice a Rice plant which had already come into ear; it rose above all the rest, and was already ripe. I had it gathered and brought to me; the grain was very fine and full, and I was induced to keep it for an experiment, and see whether it would, in the following year, retain this precocity; and, in fact, it did. All the plants that proceeded from it came into ear before the ordinary time, and yielded their harvest in the sixth moon. Every year has multiplied the produce of the preceding; and now, for thirty years, it has been the Rice served on my table. The grain is long, and of a rather reddish color, but of a sweet perfume and very pleasant flavor. It has been named *Ya-mi*, or Imperial Rice, because it was in my garden that it was first cultivated. It is the only kind that can ripen north of the Great Wall, where the cold begins very early and ends very late. But in the provinces of the South, where the climate is milder and the soil more fertile, it is easy to obtain two harvests a year from it; and it is a sweet consolation to me to have procured this advantage for my people."

M. Huc observes: "The Emperor Tkhan-hi did render in fact an immense service to the population of Maatchuria, by encouraging the culture of this new kind of Rice, which succeeds admirably in dry countries, and has no need, like the common Rice, of perpetual irrigation. It would certainly prosper in France; and it is not the fault of the missionaries that it has not long since been acclimated there."

9. THE BAMBOO.—Huc claims that it is no exaggeration to say that the mines of China are less valuable than her Bamboo; and, after rice and silk, there is nothing that yields so great a revenue. Bowring, in his "Siam," says:

"It is employed for building, for baskets, mats, and vessels of every sort, In some shape or other, it is used for food, for clothing, for shelter, for navigation, for comfort, for ornament. It is a plant alike of the utilitarian and the poet—one perpetually turning to account its infinite variety of uses, the other celebrating its multifarious beauties. It is the raw material of the shipwright and the builder, the tool-maker and the carver; out of it are constructed instruments of music and weapons of war. The hardness of the wood, the facility with which it is split into the minutest thread, the straightness and regularity of its fibre, its smoothness of surface, the rapidity of its growth—all add to its value. It lends itself from the most exquisite and minute carving, to the coarsest usages of the crate and the hurdle, collecting, conveying, or distributing every species of fluid. It supplies fire by friction, and is the great water conductor, being an almost ready-formed conduit. In some species the knots of separation in the stalk are distant six or seven feet; in others they are adjacent. For boxes, for nets, for cordage, for thread, for numerous instruments and implements, it is the ever-present material. Perhaps, among the many gifts of Providence to a tropical region, the Bamboo is the most benignant, appropriate, and accessible. The author, the sculptor, the architect, and the painter, have all laid it under contribution in the field of imagination, and the development of art; and if the camel is characteristic of the desert, the Bamboo may be considered typical of Indo-Chinese nations. Its leaves, its stems, its branches, its roots—all contribute to multitudinous objects, a detailed description of which would fill a thousand pages."

The Bamboo is of rapid growth, and in four or five years it is fit for many uses. Though generally issuing from the ground, like the asparagus, some varieties grow so as to become two feet in circumference; and single knees of these are used as pails or buckets. The Chinese are believed to manufacture their cheap and common paper from macerated Bamboo.

10. The Orange and the Lemon.—A gentleman, in a communication respecting the Soil, Climate, and adaptations of Florida, some years ago, remarked:

"There is no culture in the world by which the foundation of an independent income can be laid at the expense of so small an outlay, as the culture of the Orange and the Lemon in East Florida. The method of establishing groves, by transporting the sour Orange Trees from the hummocks, where they abound in the wild state, and which has been in successful practice for several years, is of great importance; in the first place, because it does away with the difficulty and expense of procuring sweet trees, and, in the second place, because sour trees, planted and budded, will bear much sooner than sweet trees from a Nursery. The sour trees may be dug carefully in the hummocks at any time from October to June. They should be topped about four feet from the ground, and carefully planted and watered. In about three months, shoots large enough to be budded will grow out. The buds are taken from sweet trees and carefully inserted into the young shoots, just as peach trees are budded at the North. It is common for trees to bear the sweet Orange in eighteen months from the budding. If the sour trees are selected from the hummock of good size (and they can be found of all sizes), in three years they will be competent to bear a thousand Oranges each, and will go on every year increasing in size and production.

"This culture is well adapted to persons of small capital, whose health requires a residence in Florida. A suitable piece of land is easily obtained, on which provisions can be raised and an extensive grove established, at a very moderate expense. But, to farmers and planters, this culture presents also advantages over those of any other Southern State; for, without interfering at all with their agricultural operations, they can gradually, and without the outlay of a dollar, plant an Orange grove that may ultimately yield more than all their other productions.

"The longevity of the Orange Tree is another thing which invests it with more permanent character than common fruit trees. It lives and flourishes to a very advanced age. There are Orange Trees now living in the city of Rome that are known to be more than three hundred years old. So that an Orange grove, when once established, will not only last a man's whole lifetime, but become a valuable inheritance for his children."

This is truly a delightful picture; but if report be true, those who have attempted the cultivation of the Orange and the Lemon in Florida, have not as yet realized the results which are so prophetically depictured in this communication. At all events, it is always well, and we here repeat the admonition, to "look before you leap."

11. THE OLIVE TREE.—The commercial importance of the Olive Tree is very great. As early as 1788, France produced Olive Oil of the value of $15,000,000. Yet in one year she imported nearly six million dollars worth. Naples exports annually about seven million gallons, valued at over $3,000,000. In the United States, the consumption of Olive Oil is comparatively limited, and much of that which is purchased as such is manufactured out of lard oil. With the development of Manufactures however, particularly of woolen goods, and of soap, etc., the consumption of Olive Oil must annually increase; and if it were cheaper, it would form a more important constituent than it now does in general domestic economy.

Thomas Jefferson, in a letter written to a South Carolina Agricultural Society, in the last century, advocated in a very earnest manner the importance of cultivating the Olive.

"If," he says, "the memory of those persons is held in great respect by South Carolina who introduced there the culture of *rice*, a plant that sows life and death with equal hand, what obligations would be due to him who should introduce the Olive Tree, and set the example of its culture? Having been myself an eye-witness to the blessings which this tree sheds on the poor, I never had my wishes so kindled for the introduction of any article of new culture into our own country." And he says further, "Wherever the orange will stand at all, experience shows that the Olive will stand well, being a hardier tree."

Since Mr. Jefferson wrote, the culture of the Olive has been attempted in several of our Southern States, principally, however, for pickling. In Mississippi, South Carolina, and Florida, the lands and climate are stated to be as well adapted to the successful cultivation of the Olive for oil, pickles, etc., as any part of Europe. Some hundreds of the trees are grown in South Carolina, and the owner expressed his conviction that this product would succeed well on the sea-coast of Carolina and Georgia. The frosts, though severe, did not destroy or injure the plant; and in one place, where it was supposed to be dead, and corn was planted in its stead, its roots sent out shoots.

"Formerly," says a writer on the subject, "on account of its slow growth, the Olive was not considered very useful; but some years since a new variety was introduced into France, and into some parts of Spain and Portugal, which yields an abundant crop of fruit the *second year* after planting. They are small trees, or rather shrubs, about four or five feet high. The fruit is larger than the common Olive; is of a fine green color when ripe, and contains a great deal of oil. The advantages accruing from this new mode of cultivating the Olive Tree, are beyond all calculation. By the old method the Olive Tree does not attain its full growth, and consequently does not yield any considerable crop under thirty years; whereas the new system of cultivating dwarf trees, especially from cuttings, affords very abundant crops in two or three. An acre of land can easily grow two thousand trees of the new variety, and the gathering of the fruit is easy, as it can be done by small children. At Beaufort, South Carolina, the Olive is cultivated from plants which were obtained in the neighborhood of Florence, Italy.

A gentleman in Mississippi is stated, by an American Agricultural Journal, to have Olive Trees growing, which at five years from the cutting bore fruit, and were as large at that age as they usually are in England at eight years old. The Olive, then, it is added, will yield a fair crop of oil at four years from the Nursery; and in eight years a full crop, or as much as in Europe at from fifteen to twenty years of age."

The Olive Tree, it is well known, is a tree of great longevity, even reaching to a *thousand* and *twelve hundred years*. So that, when once established, its productiveness continues through many successive generations. The expense of extracting the oil is also stated to be but trifling.

12. THE COCA.—This is a very remarkable plant in its effects upon the human constitution. The natives in several parts of Peru chew its leaves as Europeans do tobacco, particularly in the mining districts, when at work in the mines or traveling; and such is the sustenance that they derive from them, that they frequently take no food for four or five days. "I have often (observes Mr. Stevenson, in his 'Travels in South America') been assured by them that, while they have a good supply of Coca, they feel neither hunger, thirst, nor fatigue; and, without impairing their health, they can remain eight to ten days and nights without sleep. The leaves are almost insipid; but, when a small quantity of lime is mixed with them, they have a very agreeable sweet taste. The natives generally carry with them a leather pouch containing Coca, and a small calabash holding lime, or the ashes of the molle, to mix with them."

The Coca plant grows about four or five feet high, with pale, bright green leaves, somewhat resembling in shape those of the orange tree. The leaves are picked from the trees four or five times a year, and carefully dried in the shade; they are then packed in small baskets.

13. THE OCA.—Mr. Stevenson refers to another root that is cultivated in several of the colder provinces of Peru. This plant, he states, is of a moderate size, in appearance something like the acetous trefoil; the roots yellow, each about five or six inches long, and two inches in circumference. They have many eyes, and the roots, several of which are yielded by one plant, are somewhat curved. When boiled, it is much sweeter than the *Camote* or *Batata*—indeed, it appears to contain more saccharine matter than any root I ever tasted. If eaten raw, it is very much like the chestnut. The roots may be kept for many months in a dry place. The transplanting of the Oca, he adds, to England, where I am persuaded it would prosper, would add another agreeable and useful esculent to our tables.

14. THE CAMPHOR TREE.—Prof. Johnston states that the ordinary Camphor Tree belongs to the same family as the common Sassafras of the United States; though, in its general character, it is more nearly related to the Red Bay, so common throughout the Southern country, both being evergreens of similar height, and, at a small distance, looking so much alike as to be easily mistaken for each other. In commerce, two kinds of Camphor are known. The consumption of one of these, however, is monopolized by the Chinese, who, by a mere whim, set a value upon it from seventy to one hundred times the price of the other variety. The kind they so highly esteem is the Malay article, the product of a gigantic tree

which grows wild on the slopes of the Diri mountains in Sumatra, and in the territories of the Sultanate of Brunai in Borneo, a tree which attains a height of one hundred feet, and a diameter of six or seven feet. Siebold describes one which measured fifty feet in circumference. It is known in botanical works as the *Dryobalonops camphora* or *aromatica*. The Camphor is obtained from this tree without employing the process of separation required in producing the other variety. It is found in concrete masses, secreted in longitudinal fissures in the heart-wood, and is extracted by splitting the trunk in pieces, and picking it out with a pointed instrument, or the nail when they are small. Some lumps have been found as large as a man's arm; but the product of a large tree does not often reach twenty pounds. Half this amount is a good yield for a middling-sized tree; and, in hunting for one, many are split up with great labor which furnish no Camphor; hence the high price of the article. The Chinese, it is said, pay for it the amount of from $1000 to $1200 the picul (133 lbs.); or, for a very superior quality, even $3000 per cwt.; while the Japan article obtained in their ports, and hence known as the Chinese Camphor, is worth only from $12 to $15 the picul. The Camphor-wood trunks are supposed to be made of the wood of this tree. It answers well for house and ship-timbers and articles of furniture, especially such as are intended to contain and preserve cloths. It is very easy to work, splits readily, and is never attacked by the many destructive insects in the East which will so speedily devour any European wood, and even those of the East, except the Teak, the Calambuco, and the Camphor. The young trees produce, instead of the full-formed Camphor, a straw-colored fluid, which is called, in the East Indies, the Oil of Camphor, and is used as an external application in rheumatic complaints.—*Am. Cy.:* Art. CAMPHOR.

The younger Michaux, writing to Hon. Joel R. Poinsett, says:

"I have frequently and unremittingly urged my friends in Charleston to cultivate the *Laurus camphora* (Camphor Tree), which is less liable to be injured by the cold than the Orange tree. It is not in the sandy soil of the environs of that town that this tree ought to be planted, but in the fresh swamp land eight or ten miles in the interior, where the Red Bay is found, to which it is analogous. The *Laurus camphora* might very well be grafted upon this tree; but it is commonly found in all the Nurseries around Paris, where it is sold at five francs (one dollar) a plant thirty inches high. This plant reaches the height of thirty or forty feet. What an acquisition it would be to the southern parts of Georgia and Florida!" We hope this experiment will be made, and this valuable plant generally introduced into the Southern States.

15. THE TEA PLANT.—This valuable herb, the cultivation of which has been confined for centuries principally to China and Japan, has, within the last ten years, been introduced into this country; and it is conceded that, in favorable situations, and under proper management, it may be successfully cultivated in most, if not all the Southern States. This was partially realized from an experiment made at Greenville, in the mountainous parts of South Carolina, by the late Junius Smith, in 1848 to 1852. He imported several cases of Black and Green Tea plants, of Chinese stock, of from five to seven years' growth, and planted them in the village bove-named, where they remained about two years. On

their removal to a plantation in that vicinity, in March, 1851, Dr. Smith stated that "they grew remarkably last summer, and are now fully rooted, with fine large main and collateral roots, with an abundance of fibrous radicles. They all stood the snow, eight or nine inches deep upon the level, on the 3d of January, and the severe frosts of winter, without the slightest covering or protection, and without the loss of a single plant. They are now all forming part of the plantation, composed of those received from China last June, and a few planted the first week in June, which germinated the 17th of September. All these young plants were thinly covered with straw. Some of them have lost their foliage—others have not. The stems do not appear to have sustained any injury. The fresh buds are beginning to shoot. I cannot help thinking that we have now demonstrated the adaptation of the Tea plant to the soil and climate of this country, and succeeded in its permanent establishment within our borders."

In South America, as we are informed in a recent work entitled "Brazil and the Brazilians," the cultivation of the Chinese Tea, notwithstanding numerous and long-continued discouragements, has become one of the most flourishing and remunerative branches of Agriculture. At sixteen cents per pound, its cultivation is considered as remunerative as Coffee; but since the disturbances in China, forty cents per pound have been readily obtained for the greater portion of the crop. The culture, gathering, and the preparation of Tea are not difficult; and children are profitably and efficiently employed in the various modes of arranging it for market. The authors remark:

"The Tea plant is a hardy shrub, and can be cultivated in almost any portion of Brazil, though it is perhaps better adapted to the south, where frosts prevail, and which it resists. If left to itself, in the Tropics, it will soon run up to a tree. The coffee tree requires rich and new soil, and a warm climate unknown to frosts: but the Tea plant will flourish in any soil. Dr. ———, who visited various portions of China, is of the opinion that the *Cha* (tea) *can be grown in any part of the United States from Pennsylvania to the Mexican Gulf.* There are not many varieties of the plant, as is often supposed, Black and Green Teas being merely leaves of the same tree, obtained at different seasons of the year. The flavor is sometimes varied, as that of wines from the same species of grape grown on different soils. The plant is not deciduous as in China, and in Brazil is gathered from March to July, which, in the Northern hemisphere, would correspond to the interval between September and January."

16. MATE, OR PARAGUAY TEA.—This is another remarkable shrub, in very great favor with the inhabitants of South America, and of Paraguay in particular, who attribute to it almost fabulous virtues. It is unquestionably aperient and diuretic, and produces effects similar to opium; but most of the qualities so zealously attributed to it may, with some reason, be doubted. Like that drug, however, it excites the torpid and languid, while it calms the restless and induces sleep. "Its effects on the constitution, when used immoderately, are similar to those produced by ardent spirits; and when the habit of drinking it is once acquired, it is equally difficult to leave it off. The leaves of the plant are used by infusion; and all classes of persons partake of it, drinking it all hours of the day—at their various meals rarely, indeed, beginning to eat before tasting their favorite beverage. Not only is this the case in Paraguay, Uruguay, and the Argentine Republic, but in Peru, Chili, and Ecuador it is no less esteemed. They drink the tea from the spout

of a pot which they call *maté,* adding to it a little burnt sugar, cinnamon, or lemon-juice. The wealthier or more refined class draw it into the mouth through a tin or silver tube, called *bombilla,* which, being perforated with holes at one end, is inserted in the *maté* or teapot, enabling them to partake of the liquid without swallowing the smaller particles of the pulverized leaves floating on the surface. The quantity of leaves used by a person who is fond of it is about an ounce. The infusion is generally kept at the boiling temperature; but those who are accustomed to it, drink it thus without inconvenience. In the meantime, hot water is supplied as fast as it is consumed, each visitor being supplied with his *maté* and pipe. If allowed to stand too long, the leaves acquire an inky color. The leaves when fresh, taste something like mallows, or inferior Chinese Green Tea."

Like the sample brick of Æsopus, the foregoing will serve to show how boundless is the field open to speculators in novelties, in introducing new things that are also likely to prove useful.

CHANCE CI.—*Another and somewhat analogous opportunity is presented in the Establishment of Gardens or Farms for the Growth of Medicinal Plants, with the requisite Machinery for converting them into the Drugs of Commerce.*

The consumption of Drugs in the United States, derived principally from importation, is very large; and many of the plants from which they are produced, there is no doubt, could be successfully cultivated at home. Within a few years, establishments have been commenced on an extensive scale for obtaining Medicinal Extracts from vegetables, evaporated in *vacuo;* and one of these, in

15

1852, produced thirty thousand pounds of extracts, consuming nearly a million pounds of material. But this is but a partial development of one of the branches of what may be made a much more extensive, and probably more lucrative business.

In the Patent Office Report for 1855, there are several new Medicinal Plants recommended for cultivation, of which the most important seem to be the following:

1. LIQUORICE.—A quantity of the roots of Liquorice, a somewhat tender perennial, much cultivated in the south of Europe, and to some extent in England, has thus far answered the expectations of the experimenters in several of the Middle and Southern States. From the increasing demands for this root in Pharmacy, or medicinal preparations of various kinds, there is no reason why its culture could not be profitably extended in most localities where it will thrive. The amount annually imported, in a crude and manufactured state, is valued at about $300,000.

For the culture and preparation of this plant, see Agricultural Report of the Patent Office for 1854, page 358.

2. POPPY FOR OPIUM.—A variety of the common, or Opium Poppy, indigenous to the warm and temperate parts of Europe and Asia, from Portugal to Japan, and especially cultivated in China, India, Turkey, Egypt, and in the Morea, "has been introduced, and has proved itself susceptible of easy cultivation on very rich soils, and is well adapted to the climate of the Middle and Southern States. The flowers of the 'White Poppy,' the variety with which the experiment was made, may be either entirely

white or red, or may be fringed with purple, rose, or lilac, variegated and edged with the same colors, but never occur blue nor yellow, nor mixed with these colors, each petal being generally marked at the bottom with a black or purple spot. The seeds are black in the plants having purple flowers, and light-colored in those which are white; although the seeds of the latter, when of spontaneous growth, are sometimes black. The largest heads, which are employed for medical or domestic use, are obtained from the single-flowered kind, not only for the purpose of extracting Opium, but also on account of the bland, esculent oil that is expressed from the seeds, which are simply emulsive, and contain none of the narcotic principle. For the latter purpose, if no other, its culture in this country is worthy of attention.

"With regard to the cultivation of this plant, with the view of obtaining Opium, there can be but little doubt that our clear sky, fervid summer sun, and heavy dews would greatly favor the production of this article; but how far these circumstances, in connection with American ingenuity in devising improved methods for its extraction, would allow us to compete with the cheapness of labor in the East, can only be determined by actual trial. Certainly it is an object worthy of public encouragement, as the annual amount of Opium imported into the United States is valued at upward of $407,000, a considerable portion of which might be saved, and thereby add to our resources. Besides, if we were to raise a surplus, it could be sent to China in exchange for Tea. The successful cultivation of the plant, however, requires the provision of good soil, appropriate manure, and careful management. The strength of the juice, according to Dr. Butler, of British India, depends much upon the quantity of moisture of the climate. A deficiency even of dew prevents the proper flow of the peculiar, narcotic, milky juice which abounds in almost every part of the plant, while an excess, besides washing off this milk, causes additional mischief, by separating the soluble from the insoluble parts of this drug. This not only deteriorates its quality, but increases the quantity of moisture, which must afterward be got rid of."

A writer in "De Bow's Review" says:

"Climate and soil in the vicinity of St. Diego, California, are highly propitious to the production of Opium, better, I dare say, than any part of Asia Minor; and the Pueblo Indians, under proper directions, are as well qualified as the Fellaheens, Osmanlees, and Hindoos of the Eastern hemisphere, to attend to this new, but as I have shown, also easy cultivation. So much more, as it wants neither chemical nor mechanical skill to the production of Opium, as is the case with sugar, Indigo, and the like. In the vicinity of St. Diego, land, labor, and cattle are at normal prices, yet unaltered by gold excitement or immigration. Any amount of Opium produced there would find a ready and very commodious market in the neighboring State, at San Francisco, whose population contains a very large number of Chinamen, and whose commercial relations with Japan and China are improving daily.

"According to good information, collected in Smyrna and Alexandria, the cost of production of one pound of Opium in Egypt is sixty cents, and in Anatolia 75 cents, the climate and the soil of this latter country being less propitious than the Nile valley. In British India, Opium is still a monopoly of the government; the lease-holders of certain districts are bound to produce, and to deliver annually a given quantity of this drug to the East India Company, at the fixed price of $150 the chest of 140 pounds. This price of course leaves a small remuneration to the producer. This traffic amounts to about 50,000 chests a year, and the prices obtained in the Residencies vary from 500 to 700 dollars the chest, according to the quality and demand. The cost of superintending and collecting this important revenue absorbs nearly one and a half million pounds.

"From the preceding it may safely be concluded that the price of *one dollar the pound of Opium* may be considered the *highest term of production of the drug in California*, and *four dollars the lowest price* to be expected for it in the San Francisco market."

3. THE RHATANY PLANT.—This plant, indigenous to several provinces in Peru, delights in dry, sandy soils, and grows on the declivities of mountains, exposed to the intense heat of the sun. "Its root is very extensively used for improving the color, astringency, and richness of red wines. On being slightly masticated, it discovers a very grateful astringency, which is perceptible for some time to the palate, and is slightly aromatic and bitter. These qualities, as well as the coloring matter, are imparted both to cold and boiling water, as well as to proof spirit. The tincture made with brandy approaches very nearly to the flavor of Port wine.

"The simple tincture is made by adding three ounces of the root to a quart of proof spirit, and is much used by dentists, combined with equal parts of rose-water, as a lotion to astringe the gums, and correct any unpleasant fetor of the mouth. Equal parts of powdered rhatany-root, orris-powder and areca-nut charcoal, are stated to form the best tooth-powder in use."

4. THE QUASSIA PLANT.—This is a beautiful shrub or low tree, the roots, bark and wood of which afford the true officinal Quassia of commerce. This plant is sufficiently hardy to withstand the summer climate of England, where it flowers freely for several months, from which circumstance it is believed that it would succeed well in favorable localities in our Southern States.

Aside from its use as a bitter tonic, in materia medica, it is asserted that the brewers in England have, of late years, used Quassia-wood instead of hops. Beer made with it however does not keep well, but soon becomes muddy and flat, has a mawkish taste, and runs into acetous fermentation. Consequently, it is less nutritious and wholesome than that which is properly hopped. This wood, from its narcotic power, is also used to poison flies.

5. THE VANILLA PLANT.—This is a native of the Island of St. Domingo, where it climbs to the tops of the highest trees; and is somewhat extensively cultivated in Mexico, in the vicinity of Vera Cruz. From the great demand, and the high price which it brings in the United States, it doubtless could be grown to advantage in some parts of the South, with a very little protection during the colder months of the year, and perhaps in hot-houses at the North.

The amount of Vanilla imported and consumed in this country, principally for flavoring cake, ice-cream, &c., is believed to exceed 5000 pounds, valued at from $20 to $30 a pound, or $125,000 a year.

6. THE GINGER PLANT.—This is a native of the East Indies, and of various parts of Asia, and extensively cultivated in the West Indies, and other warm parts of America. It doubtless could be grown with advantage in various parts of the South. The amount of Ginger annually imported into the United States is valued at upward of $60,000.

For the cultivation of this Plant, see the Agricultural Report of the Patent Office for 1854, page 354.

7. RHUBARB.—This is a perennial, a "native of Russia and some parts of Asia, whence the dried root is imported

into this country for medicinal purposes. Large quantities of the roots are also annually collected for exportation in the Chinese provinces, within the lofty range of the Himalayas. The best is that which comes by the way of Russia, as greater care is taken in the selection; and, on its arrival at Kiachta, within the Russian frontiers, the roots are all carefully examined, and the damaged pieces destroyed. This is the fine article of the shops, improperly called 'Turkey' Rhubarb. That of the best quality occurs in small pieces, with a hole in the middle of each, made in the fresh root, to facilitate the operation of drying. The color is a lively yellow, streaked with white and red. Its texture is dense, and, when reduced to powder, it is entirely yellow.

"The Chinese Rhubarb, called by the natives *Ta Hroangor Hai-houng*, is cultivated chiefly in the province of Chersee. As imported, it is known by the name of 'East Indian' Rhubarb, and comes in larger masses, more compact and hard, heavier, less friable, and not so fine in the grain as the other, and having less of an aromatic flavor.

"This species has been introduced into England, where it has been extensively cultivated; and there is little doubt, therefore, of its proving perfectly hardy in many parts of our own country. Large quantities are annually imported, the cost of which might be saved if its culture were successfully prosecuted here, and we might thus add to our productive resources."

8. Castor Oil Plant.—This is known in almost every part of the East and West Indies, South America, China, and the countries and islands of the Mediterranean, under the name of "Palma Christi," and has proved itself well

adapted to the soil and climate of our Middle and Southern States; and were its culture extended for the manufacture of Castor Oil, there is no doubt that it would be profitable, under improved methods of extracting it; and we shonld no longer be dependent on other nations for a supply. At present, the culture is confined principally to Illinois and the neighboring States, where it grows abundantly.

9. THE CARDAMOM.—This plant, the seeds of which are imported in considerable quantities, and valued for their pungent taste, is cultivated in plots, on either level or gently sloping surfaces on the highest range of the Ghaûts, between latitude 11° and 12° 30′ N., after passing the first declivity from their base.

In India, the seeds of this plant are highly prized as an agreeable condiment, and, as such, their use is so universal, that they are regarded as a necessary of life by most of the natives of Asia. In fact, their general use in those regions renders the plant a very important and profitable object of culture. How far its adoption could be made applicable to the soil, climate, exposure, and economy of some of our Southern States, can only be determined by trial.

CHANCE CII.—*Groves of rapidly-growing and usefu. Trees can be profitably planted on Prairies, and where land is otherwise worthless, as in Barrens and sandy plains.*

We read that the old Duke of Athol planted a forest on his estate in Perthshire of 15,593 acres, and when he died he had upward of twenty-seven millions of young trees. His successor set out on poor mountain land 6,500 acres with larches, valuable for ship-timber. The land was not worth over twenty-two cents an acre; now, with the timber on it, is valued at $32,500,000.

There are now doubtless in our vast country millions of acres, unproductive and valueless, which if planted with trees would be worth much more than the ordinary price of unimproved land. It would therefore be a likely speculation, to purchase "barrens," as they may generally be purchased for a trifle, and plant them with such rapidly-growing trees as are useful both for timber and fuel. A correspondent of the *New York Tribune*, not long since, recommended for this purpose the Ailanthus tree, and remarked:

"It is not a soft, worthless wood; on the contrary, when seasoned, it is firm, hard, strong and durable. It will make fence-posts nearly as valuable as locust timber, and when seasoned, it will burn freely and give a strong heat. It is good fuel.

"Then, instead of planting Ailanthus trees for shade or ornament let some one establish a plantation of a hundred acres on the cheap, "barren" land of Long Island, or a thousand acres upon the Western prairies, and see what a valuable timber lot you may have in only ten years. In fact there are millions of acres of land in the United States now lying idle, barren, unproductive of any thing valuable to the owners, that might be made to produce a valuable crop of wood, while at the same time becoming renovated so as to be worth cultivating in some food-producing crop.

"We will instance one such tract, because it is one so often seen by numerous persons traveling from New York to Boston; and because it lies so near that beautiful town, the city of New Haven, and in the very midst of the most enterprising people in the world—the most improving of machinery; the most money-making in trade; the most neglectful of any other equally educated people of improvements of the soil. It is the sandy plain through which the railway passes from New Haven to Meriden, that we allude to; once a fine cultivated, productive tract, now a waste of drifting sand.

"Upon this waste, we are confident that Ailanthus trees may be planted, with only a wheel-barrow load of rich loam to a tree, and that in ten years, the growth would not only be such that it would hide the desolate barrenness of the land, but would make it of a salable value of $100 an acre.

"Much of the land called barren upon Long Island, which has not produced the annual interest of a dime an acre since the discovery of America, might be planted in Ailanthus, which in ten years would acquire a growth sufficiently large to afford an annual cutting of fence-posts and fuel, worth more than most of the cultivated farms on the Island have ever netted their owners. Besides the tracts utterly worthless, there are thousands of acres that are kept for wood the owners depending upon the slow growth of oaks and scrubby old 'field-pines,' which are cut off once in twenty or thirty years, when two to four inches in diameter. In place of the oaks and pines, grow Ailanthus, and twice the quantity can be cut in half the time. If such unimproving mortals as some of these wood-cutters ever read and think, let them think of this and profit by it. Upon a hundred hills, denuded of their wood by that insatiable wood-consuming dragon, the New York and Erie Railroad, the Ailanthus might be planted where no food-crop can be profitably cultivated, where it would bring a sure return to the planter. But of all places where it might be grown most rapidly and to the greatest profit, we must look to the great prairies of the West. There, where the richest soil of the world that is susceptible of cultivation without irrigation must lie waste for want of wood, a systematic business of tree-planting might be made the most profitable of any ever practiced in this country. There we would not confine the planting to this one tree but certainly would use it for the first plantation, on account of its easy production from seeds, its rapid growth, its hardy nature withstanding cold and heat, wet and dry, and not being liable to attacks of insects. A belt of these trees would afford shelter for the production of other more valuable ones—such as locust, oak, elm, cedar, pine, sugar maple, and fruit trees.

"'Let it be an edict' that the world shall at once prepare, not for the destruction of this anathematized tree, but for its extended propagation, cultivation and usefulness. Let us cease the insane folly of planting Ailanthus trees under our bed-room windows—as great a folly as it would be to keep a pet skunk in the house—and plant them where we would keep the unsavory, though useful, bug and vermin-destroying animal, in the forest—an Ailanthus-tree forest grown for useful, not ornamental purposes."

The establishment of forests, too, in many localities, particularly near swamps and marshes, will promote health, and thus have an indirect but important bearing upon social prosperity. The leaves of trees act chemically in neutralizing malarial poison by the emision of oxygen. hence it is, as has been frequently noted, (see La Roche on *Pneumonia* and *Malaria,*) a narrow border of forests intervening between residences and a swamp, has protected the inhabitants perfectly from fever and ague, and other malarious fevers; and the removal of trees in such situations has brought on speedily fatal consequences. It is stated that the strong growth of annual vegetation which has been interposed, at the suggestion of Lieut. Maury, between the National Observatory buildings and the shoals of the Potomac, at Washington, has had eminent success in diminishing the unhealthiness of that locality.

In planting groves, or forests, trees of well-known utility, and established value, will of course be preferred; but there are many new varieties that, in certain localities, can be no doubt advantageously introduced. D. J. Browne, Esq., the author of "The Trees of America," in his report to the Commissioner of Patents, from which we have already quoted, recommends several, viz.: the *Boxwood* tree, which supplies the wood principally used in Wood Engraving, and which is sufficiently hardy to stand in the open air near Philadelphia; the *European Sweet Chestnut,* which produces very large excellent nuts, of a rich creamy flavor and aromatic odor, when roasted, that will keep a long time;* the *Grammont,* or *Sweet-*

* The usual modes of cooking Chestnuts in France and Italy are, boiling them in water with simply a little salt, or with leaves of celery, sage, or any other herbs which may impart to them an agree-

acorned Oak, which produces acorns that are edible, and when in perfection are equal, or superior to, the Chestnut; the *Kermes Oak*, which supplies a dye as brilliant as scarlet; the *Gall Nut Oak*, which furnishes the well-known gall nuts, extensively used in the manufacture of writing ink, and in dyeing; the *Valonian Oak*, the acorns of which are believed to contain more tannin than any other vegetable, in proportion to their bulk; the *Date*, a single tree of which will supply from one to three hundred pounds of the dates of commerce, and will continue fruitful for a period of two hundred years; the *Tamarind*, the *Frankincense*, and the *Balm of Gilead* trees; the *Egyptian Gum Arabic*, and the *Deodar*, or *Indian Cedar*, the wood of which is compact, resinous, highly fragrant, of a deep, rich color, which has been compared to that of a polished brown agate.

To these I would add the *Russian Larch*, a very remarkable tree. From its inner bark, when boiled and mixed with rye flour, and afterward buried a few hours in the snow, the Siberian hunters prepare a sort of leaven bread. From the inner bark also, the Russians manufacture fine white gloves, not inferior to those made of the most delicate chamois; and it is said, stronger, cooler, and more pleasant for wearing in the summer. The bark is, besides, nearly as valuable as Oak bark.

To augment the growth of trees, perhaps the most wonderfully beneficial substance that can be employed,

---

able flavor; and roasting them in hot ashes or a coffee-roaster. They are also occasionally scorched before the fire, or on a shovel; but, when thus prepared, are not considered so good. In whatever way they are roasted, the French cooks previously slit the skin, or shell, of all except one; and, when that cracks and flies off, it is an indication that the rest are done.

is the residuum of Soda and Potash works, known by the name of the *Oxy-sulphuret of Calcium.* M. Chevaudier ascertained this by five years study and experiments; and, in a communication to the French Academy of Sciences, stated that, in his opinion, it would augment the growth of forests one hundred per cent. Next to the oxy-sulphuret of calcium, he found the chlorohydrate of ammonia, plaster of Paris, wood-ashes, sulphate of ammonia, lime, non-calcined bones, and poudrette, most beneficial.

CHANCE CIII.—*Establish Flower Farms, and Manufacture Pomades, etc., from Plants.*

Piesse, in his "Art of Perfumery," remarks: "We desire to see Flower Farms and organized Perfumatories established for the extraction of essences and the manufacture of Pomades and Oils, of such flowers as are indigenous, or that thrive in the open fields of our country. Besides opening up a new field of enterprise and good investment for capital, it would give healthy employment to many women and children. Open-air employment for the young is of no little consideration to maintain the stamina of the future generation."

CHANCE CIV.—*Cultivate Oleaginous Plants, and provide the requisite improved Machinery for expressing the Oils.*

The demand for Oils and fatty substances may be said to be increasing every day. They are used in candle and soap-making, for burning, as lubricators for machi nery, and for a great variety of purposes in the Arts and Manufactures. But it is remarkable how limited is the number of substances from which Oils of commercial value are now extracted, in comparison with the

16

variety of plants that are richly oleaginous—the vegetable world, in fact, is overflowing with Oil.

Decandolle states the following as the quantity of Oil obtained from various seeds:

	Per cent. in weight.		Per cent. in weight.
Hazlenut	60	White mustard	36
Garden-cress	57	Tobacco	34
Olive	50	Plum	33
Walnut	50	Woad	30
Poppy	48	Hemp	25
Almond	46	Flax	22
Caper-spurge	41	Sunflower	15
Colza	39	Buckwheat	14
		Grapes	12

Boussingault quotes the following as the result of some experiments by M. Gauzaé.

	Seed produced per acre.			Oil obtained per acre, in lbs.		Oil, per cent.	Cake per cent.
	cwts.	qrs.	lbs.	lbs.	oz.		
Colewort	19	0	15	875	4	40	54
Rocket	15	1	3	320	8	18	73
Winter Rape	16	2	18	641	6	33	62
Swedish Turnip	15	1	25	595	8	33	62
Curled Colewort	16	2	18	641	6	33	62
Turnip Cabbage	13	3	19	565	4	33	61
Gold of Pleasure	17	1	16	545	8	27	72
Sunflower	15	3	14	275	0	15	80
Flax	15	1	25	385	0	22	69
White Poppy	10	1	18	560	8	46	52
Hemp	7	3	21	229	0	25	70
Summer Rape	11	3	17	412	5	30	65

In establishing a plantation for the cultivation of Oleaginous Plants, of course only those could be selected that are adapted for the locality. The United States offer in this particular a less extensive range than the warmer climates of the East; but there are no doubt many vegetables, the seeds of which are extensively used for the production of Oil in other countries, that could be as successfully cultivated in ours. We have already adverted to this in another connection, and indicated the *Olive* and the *Castor-oil Plant*, and would now add the *Colza*, the *Ground-nut*, and the *Bene Plant*.

1. THE COLZA.—This is a species of cabbage, and allied to the Rape—containing, however, about one-third more Oil than the Rape. The light-houses on the coast of France, which are regarded as the best lighted in the world, consume, we are told, Rape-seed Oil exclusively; and the cultivation of the plant from which it is produced is now an extensive and profitable culture in France and Germany. A few years ago, the American Light-House Board induced the Patent Office to import some of the seed, and distribute it for culture; but the experiments seem not to have been very attentively or energetically made. Colza Oil is not limited to light-house uses, but may be employed in common lamps, and is reported to be capable of rivaling Sperm for giving a brilliant light. The mode of cultivating the plant is thus described:

"It requires a rich but light soil, and does not succeed upon either sandy or clayey lands. The ground for it must be deeply plowed, and well dunged. It should be sown in July, and be afterward replanted in a richly-manured field in October. It is to be planted out in beds, fifteen or eighteen inches apart; it may also be sowed in furrows, eight or ten inches asunder. Land which has been just cropped for wheat is that usually destined to Colza; it may be fresh dunged with advantage. The harvest takes place in July, with the sickle, a little before the seeds are completely ripe, lest they should drop off. As the seed is productive of oil, however, only in proportion to its ripeness, the cut plants are allowed to complete their maturation by laying them in heaps, under airy sheds, or placing them in a stack, and thatching it with straw. The stalks are thrashed with flails, the seeds are winnowed, sifted, and spread out in the air to dry, then packed away in sacks, in order to be subjected to the oil mill at the beginning of winter. The oil-cake is a very agreeable and nutritious food for cattle, and serves to fatten them quickly. This alone will defray the cost of the mill. I think it proper to state that Colza impoverishes the soil very much, as do, indeed, all the plants cultivated for the sake of their oleaginous seeds. It must not, therefore, be come back upon again for six years, if fine crops are desired; the double plowing which it receives effectually cleans the ground."

The mode of extracting the oil is thus described in the *Scientific American:* "The seed is first ground to meal, then heated to 200°, placed in bags, and submitted to very severe pressure. As the oil comes from the press, it contains some mucilage, which must be removed to fit it for burning. This is accomplished by stirring about two per cent. of vitriol among it, washing with water in vats, and afterward filtering it. The sulphuric acid unites with the mucilage of the oil, and falls down as a heavy precipitate; the oil floats on the top of the water after standing a few days, and is then drawn off by a syphon or tap."

2. THE GROUND-NUT.—The Ground-nut is one of the great staples of Africa, constituting among many tribes a chief article of food, and over a million bushels, it is presumed, are now annually exported. Within a few years, the cultivation of the Ground-nut has been attempted in the United States, principally in the vicinity of Wilmington, North Carolina, where, from a single tract, 80,000 bushels were carried to the Wilmington market in one year, realizing $1.25 per bushel. The

plant, it is said, has somewhat the appearance of the dwarf garden-pea, though more bushy. It is cultivated in hills, and the pea grows on tendrils, which put out from the plant and take root in the earth, where the nut is produced and ripened. The fruit is pinched from the root by hand, and the vines are favorite food for horses, mules, and cattle. From thirty to eighty bushels are produced on an acre. The Ground-nut is exceedingly prolific, and requires but little care and attention to its culture—almost any kind of soil being adapted for it. Nothing can be more simple than its management. All that is required is, the soil to be turned over, and the seed sown in drills like potatoes; after it begins to shoot, it may be earthed with a hoe or plow.

In the United States, Ground-nuts are a staple article of diet with "Bowery Boys," a luxury for juveniles, and sometimes introduced on tables at dessert. In France, Ground-nuts are largely converted into oil, and thence find their way over the world in the shape of olive oil; the skill of the French chemists enabling them to imitate the real Lucca and Florence oil, so as to deceive the nicest judges. Indeed, says a good authority, the oil from the pea-nut possesses a sweetness and delicacy that cannot be surpassed.

Ground-nut Oil has been manufactured to some extent in Philadelphia by Mr. Carpentier, for several years, but its valuable qualities are not so well appreciated in this country as in France. The immense consumption of Ground-nuts, however, as before stated, must render the cultivation of the plant worthy of consideration by those who have soil adapted to its growth.

3. The Bene Plant.—This is said to excel all other

plants in the quantity of oleaginous matter that it yields and Dr. Cooper, of Philadelphia, who analyzed the oil, pronounced it equal to the finest. The Bene has been introduced to some extent into the Southern States, by negroes from Africa, where it is used for feeding horses, and also for culinary purposes; but it may also be worthy of cultivation in the Middle and Northern States, for its medicinal virtues, if not for oil. A gentleman in Virginia writes as follows respecting it: "It requires to be sown early in April, at a distance of about a foot apart. A few leaves of this plant, when green, plunged a few times in a tumbler of water, make quite a thin jelly, without taste or color, which children affected with the summer complaint will drink freely; and it is said to be the best remedy ever discovered. It has been supposed that the lives of three hundred children were saved by it last summer, in Baltimore; and I know the efficacy of it by experience in my own family." This plant will throw out a great profusion of leaves by breaking off the top when it is about half grown.

Besides those mentioned in the Tables above, a long list of oleaginous plants might be made, some of which will sooner or later be turned to good account; for instance:

Saffron, *Mustard*, *Apricots* and *Cucumbers*.

Spergula Sativa—A variety of the common Cow Spurrey, which affords, on expression, a good lamp oil.

The *Physic-nut*—Used as a medicine and as a lamp oil.

The *Poonay, or Pelang Tree*—Of the East Indies, yields the *Domba Oil* used for burning and for medicinal purposes, being considered a cure for the Itch.

The *Teuss Plant*—Used extenively by the Chinese; the oil affording a clear, bright light, and not so offensive to the smell as train and other common lamp oils.

The *Tobacco Seed*—Yields about fifteen per cent. of a first-rate drying oil.

The *Guiana Carapa*—From which *Carap* or *Crab* oil is made, highly esteemed as an unguent for the hair, for the cure of wounds, and for destroying tics and vermin on cattle.

The *Oil Palm*—Which furnishes the well-known Palm Oil.

The *Cahoun Palm*—See *infra*.

The *Cocoa Nut*—See *infra*.

The *Great Macaw Tree*—Found in South America, furnishes much oil that is largely used in Toilet Soaps, and is said to be a sovereign remedy for pains in the bones, or "bone-ache."

The *Agaiti*—Supplies an oil that commands as high a price as Olive in the Indian market.

The *Madia Sativa*—Of Chili; now extensively cultivated in France, and yields a solid soap similar to that made from Olive Oil.

The *Croton Tiglium*—An evergreen, yielding Croton Oil.

The *Horse-radish Tree*—From which is obtained the *Oil of Ben*, much esteemed by watchmakers and perfumers. Twenty-four pounds of oil have been extracted from one hundred pounds of seed. The Oil of Ben is very expensive, and not often to be obtained pure.

The *Arzo Tree*—Of Morocco, which furnishes Almond Oil worth twenty-five cents a pound.

The *Sesame, or Teel*—Of which there are two or three species. The *Sesamum indicum* affords the *Gingellie* or *Suffed Oil*, already extensively known. The expressed oil is as clear and as sweet as that from almonds; and probably the "Behens Oil" used in varnishes is no other.

The *Melia Azederachta*—From which the well-known *Margose Oil* is made. Said to be equally efficacious as Cod Liver Oil in consumption and scrofula.

The *Bassia*—Which yields the Illepe oil, and the cake of which may be rubbed on the body as soap.

The *Avocado Pear Tree* (*Laurus Persea*)—A native of the West Indies. Yields a large amount of oil, which, when properly prepared, is said by Dr. Hofman to be equal to Sperm for illuminating purposes.

The *Peppermint*, and other plants yielding volatile and essential oils, are already extensively and profitably cultivated in some of the Middle and Western States.

There are also numerous and curious empyreumatic volatile oils, obtained from the distillation of the barks of trees, such as the Birch Oil of Russia,used in the manufacture of *Russian Leather*, and from which it derives its well-known fragrant odor, and its power of withstanding the attacks of insects, and the progress of decay. This oil does not appear to be so well known as it deserves. It might probably be used for other purposes besides the preservation of leather; it is possible, likewise, that similar oils might be obtained by the destructive distillation of the barks of other trees.

Lastly, COTTON-SEED OIL.—The manufacture of oil from the Cotton Seed may be said to be established in France, England, Egypt, and the United States, though not on a large scale in any. The annotators on the articles exhibited at the Crystal Palace in 1853 remark:

"Each pound of ginned cotton yields three pounds of seed, the total amount in the United States being 3,600,000,000 pounds. One half being retained for planting, there remain 1,800,000,000 pounds which might be manufactured. One hundred pounds of Cotton Seed will yield two gallons of oil, forty-eight pounds of oil-cake, and six pounds of soap-stock; the total estimated value is about $35,000,000, no appreciable part of which is at present realized. The specimens of Cotton Oil prepared by the exhibiter, were used on the machinery in the Crystal Palace, and found to possess excellent lubricating qualities. Soaps of every variety are made from it, and in New Orleans it has been used with commendation as a substitute for the Italian Olive oil."

Flint, in his "Treatise on Milch Cows," asserts that Cotton-seed-meal or cake is superior to linseed-cake as food for cattle; and, as it is richer in oil and albuminous matters, three pounds of Cotton Seed are equivalent to four of linseed-cake of average quality. It has been stated that the quantity of oil in Cotton Seed is not sufficiently large to allow transportation to distant points for manufacture; and consequently the mill must be in close proximity to the plantation. Recently a machine has been invented in Antwerp for cleansing Cotton Seed, by which from two to three tons of seed can be cleaned per day, by four-horse power, with the assistance of three persons. The cotton surrounding the seed is taken off clean, and is sold to carpet manufacturers and paper-makers at from thirty to fifty francs the one hundred kilogrammes—about ten dollars the two hundred pounds. The cost of the machinery for the purpose is said not to be expensive.

CHANCE CV.—*There are Saponaceous Plants readily convertible into substitutes for Soap; and Trees yielding substances that can be profitably converted into Vegetable Tallow and Wax.*

In New Mexico there is a weed denominated by the natives *Lechu-guill*, or *Soap Weed*, of which the root is very extensively used as a substitute for Soap, and it is said to be superior to ordinary soap for washing woolens. This singular shrub, which is to be met with on the prairies, but where it never grows to any considerable size, consists of a trunk very pithy, surmounted by a fine head of stiff leaves, each of which is about two feet and a half in length, and armed at the end with a long thorn. The leaves, which are of a dark green color, project from the stalk on all sides, and sit as closely as possible. The flower is white and very pretty. As each year's foliage decays, it drops down against the trunk, and is of a light brown color. These dry leaves, when fire is applied, flash up like gunpowder, and burn with a bright light.

This plant is applied to many uses by the natives; of

its leaves they make their hats; when dressed like hemp, it is formed into ropes and sacks, having something of the appearance of Manilla hemp, though coarser.

The author of "A Campaign in Mexico" observes:—"These plants have a singularly provoking quality; being from two to eight feet in height, they will assume to the eye in twilight the most deceptive forms. To the sentinel they will appear as the forms of men; and many an unconscious Soap Weed has run the chance of a sentry's shot for not answering the challenge 'Who goes there?' If your mule or horse has strayed from camp, and you start to hunt him in the gray of the morning, you are sure to be led first in one direction and then in another, by one of these shrubs, which from a short distance has taken the form of your animal. Time after time you may be thus deceived, yet never seeming to learn experience from a Soap Weed."

In South America and the West Indies, there are many plants that furnish useful substitutes for common soaps. The seeds of the *Sapindus saponaria* will cleanse more linen than thirty times their weight of soap; but after a time, it is said, they will corrode or burn the linen. The fruit of this tree is however largely used, as we are informed by Humboldt, for washing linen, by the Indian women along the Gulf of Cariaco. In Chili, there is a Soap tree known as the *Quillaya saponaria*, of which the bark pulverized makes a Soap instantaneously that cleanses silks, velvets, and woolen cloths, but it is said to turn linen yellow. It is exported to some extent. In Brazil Soap is made of the ashes of the Bassura or Brown plant (*Sidu lanceolata*), which abounds with alkali. The leaves of the American Aloe (*Agave Americana*,) were formerly extensively converted in Jamaica into a Vegetable Soap that was "as detergent as Castile Soap for washing linens, and had the remarkable quality of mixing and forming a lather *with salt water as well as fresh.*" Dr. Robinson, the naturalist, thus describes the process he adopted in 1767, and for which he was awarded a grant by the House of Assembly: "The lower leaves of the Curaca or Coratoe (*Agave karatu*) were passed between heavy rollers to express the juice, which, after being strained through a hair cloth, was merely inspissated by the action of the sun or a slow fire, and cast into balls or casks. The only precaution necessary was to allow no mixture of any unctuous materials which destroyed the efficacy of the Soap. A Vegetable Soap which has been found excellent for washing silks, &c., may be thus obtained: To one part of the skin of the Ackee add one and a half parts of the *Agave karatu,* macerated in one part of boiling water for twenty-four hours, and with the extract from this decoction mix four per cent. of resin."

There are also numerous plants that yield a vegetable tallow and wax, the most remarkable, probably, being the *Stillingia sebifera,* or TALLOW TREE OF CHINA.

The fruit of this tree contains a substance identical, it is said, with the two proximate principles which compose animal tallow, viz., *stearine* and *elaine.* When the nuts are ripe they are cut off with the twigs, and by a simple process a tallow is extracted, which when cool is "hard, brittle, white, opaque, without taste, and without the odor of animal tallow. Under high pressure it scarcely stains bibulous paper; melts at 104° Fahrenheit. It may be regarded as nearly pure stearine, the slight difference is doubtless owing to the admixture of oil expressed from the seed. The seeds yield about eight per cent. of this vegetable stearine, which sells for about five cents per pound."

In addition to the tallow, the nut in its kernel contains about thirty per cent. of oil, which, besides heing useful in lamps, has a place in the Chinese Pharmacopœia, because of its quality of changing gray hair black, and other perhaps imaginary virtues. The husks and shell are used in China to feed the furnaces, and the residuary tallow cakes are also employed as fuel, a small quantity remaining ignited for a whole day. Finally, the cakes which remain after the oil is pressed are valuable as manure, and are found especially serviceable in restoring impoverished tobacco fields. The candles made of this vegetable stearine are frequently and readily converted into wax candles by dipping them into a mixture of the same material and insect or other wax. The cost, even when they are colored red, is only about eight cents per pound.

The tree is evidently a valuable one, and should be introduced into this country, and cultivated wherever it will grow. (For further information, see Macgowan's article, *Sill. Jour.*, Vol. 12, p. 17, 2d *Series.*)

CHANCES CVI.—CC.—*Purchase or lease a Plantation in the British West Indies, and cultivate such Tropical Products as require the employment of comparatively little labor; or, what is better, form Associations for the purpose.*

The British West Indies comprise a large number of fertile islands, extending south-westwardly from the coast of Florida, through many degrees of latitude and longitude, the principal being *Jamaica*, which contains about 4,000,000, acres; *Trinidad,* second only to Jamaica; *Antigua*, which is eighteen miles long, and twelve in breadth; *Barbadoes,* twenty miles long and about fifteen broad; *Grenada,* area 80,000 acres; *St. Christopher's,* area 43,720 acres; *St. Vincent,* 85,000 acres; the *Bahamas,* which consist of several hundred islands between Florida and Hayti; the *Bermudas,* a group of three hundred and fifty islands; *Anguilla, Dominica, Montserrat, Nevis, St. Lucia, Tobago, Tortola, The Virgin Isles* and the *Grenadines,* with *Honduras* and *Guiana,* which though not islands are included in the British West Indies. The products include all the usual productions of the Tropics, Sugar, Coffee, Cotton, Rum, Tobacco, Cacao, Arrow-root, Potatoes, Corn, etc.

The productive capacity and resources of many of these Islands are unsurpassed by any in the world. Jamaica contains about 4,000,000 acres, of which it has been said there are not, probably, ten lying adjacent to each other which are not susceptible of the highest cultivation; while not more than 500,000 acres have ever been reclaimed or even appropriated. Sugar ratoons on most of the plantations three or four times. Very little of the soil, says Bigelow, in his "*Jamaica in* 1850," has been manured or requires to be, and such a thing as exhaustion is unknown. Vegetation is not suspended by the approach of Winter, which averages a temperature only ten or fifteen degrees lower than that of Summer. The fruits are of infinite variety, and most of them grow spontaneously, or with very little culture. The Island also abounds in the rarest cabinet-woods, and in dye-stuffs, drugs, and spices of the greatest value. There is also good reason to believe that the copper mines of Jamaica are inferior in richness to none in the world; and that coal will be mined there extensively before many years.

Contrasted with their natural advantages, the present condition of most of these Islands is remarkably deplorable. Since 1833, when the British Government emancipated 780,993 men, at a cost of nearly one hundred millions of dollars, paid principally to creditors of absentee planters who had been bankrupted by their bad management and extravagance, about two hundred Sugar estates and over five hundred Coffee plantations have been abandoned in Jamaica alone—that is, the movable property has been taken away, and the plantation left to weeds and idleness. Land has depreciated in value until in many instances it will not bring one-tenth of the amount for which it was originally mortgaged. The author before quoted, notes that the Spring Valley Estate, embracing 1,244 acres, had been sold once for $90,000 and recently for $5000. The Caen Wood Estate, which once cost $90,000, was offered by its present owners but found no purchasers, at £1500, or less than $7,500. The overseer of Friendship's Valley Estate, who used to receive a salary of $600 per annum for his services, has been offered the whole estate for $600. Bunker Hill Estate, which had been mortgaged for $150,000, was at last sold for $12,500. The Governor, Sir Charles Grey, stated that he knew of ten thousand acres of land lying all together which could be bought for about fifty cents an acre; and what is more extraordinary, a cultivated sugar estate of two thousand acres, was sold quite recently for $3000. It would lead us too far from the main subject of our inquiries to attempt to consider the various circumstances which have co-operated and combined to produce this disastrous state of things; suffice it to say, that Bigelow in his volume before referred to, has given a detailed and seemingly satisfactory explanation of the bankrupt condition of the planters at the time the Emancipation Act was passed, rendering a great depreciation in the marketable value of property sooner or later an inevitable certainty: and that the reason that this retrograde movement has continued without cessation to this day, is generally said to be that the cost of labor is too great to enable absentee planters, who continue to own the principal estates, to compete with resident slave-owning planters in Cuba and elsewhere, in the cultivation of such staples as Sugar, Tobacco, Rum, etc.; and that they are not prepared to give attention to other products of minor commercial importance.* Consequently the stagnation and deterioration must continue until the attention of small capitalists is directed to the natural resources of these Islands, and *they* enter upon the work of developing them. This period, it would seem, has now arrived. An improved estate of highly

---

* ROBERT M. HARRISON, United States Consul at Kingston, writes: "In the cultivation of estates, what is termed a day's labor is paid for at the rate of one shilling to one shilling and sixpence, regulated by various circumstances; but as the day's labor usually produces but small results, where the planters can make any arrangement with the laborer the work is done by the job; that is, by the acre, cart-load, or otherwise—by which, generally, the laborer can obtain a much better remuneration, and the work of the planter progresses more favorably. In this way, also, the mines now in operation, are carried forward, either at the rate of one shilling and sixpence, or two shillings per day, or by the fathom, according to the difficulty of the ground. The principal difficulty, particularly with the planter, is to obtain *continuous work*. The old people who were accustomed to labor as slaves, are disappearing, and the present race, who were in the first instance taken from labor by too sudden an emancipation, afterward had such a high rate of wages during the time of protection, that they are now indisposed from taking what can be given in these days of free-trade and competition."

productive land in an Italian climate, warm but generally healthy, where planting and harvesting go on throughout the year, can be purchased for less than the cost of an equal quantity of wild land in States covered with snow for five months in the year. Colored people are availing themselves of the opportunity, and becoming landowners in the West Indies—there being now in Jamaica alone, over *one hundred thousand Africans* who own from three to five acres, and maintain themselves, by cultivating them, but they have not the tools nor the requisite knowledge to render available the natural fertility of the soil. Looking then solely at the chances for profit, and dismissing from the mind all considerations associated with a desirable residence, it is probable that a moderate fortune can be made as speedily in the West Indies as in the most favored portion of the globe.

Before proceeding to an enumeration of the products which a West India colonist could cultivate at the present time with the most profit, we submit a table from the proceedings of an Agricultural Society of Grenada, showing the climate, duration, and production of certain plants. The second column gives the altitude, in English yards, above the level of the sea. The third, the mean temperature, by Fahrenheit's thermometer. The fourth, the average time required to commence bearing. The fifth, the number of plants in a Spanish "fanegada" of one hundred and seventy varras, about one hundred and fifty-three square yards. The sixth, the average duration of each plant. The seventh, the average product of each plant in the year.

	Level of the sea, to	Mean Temp. in Degrees.	Time required.	No. of Plants.	Years.	Average produce.
CACAO	587 yds.	81.17 46.00	6½ years.	1,156	40	1¼ lb. per tree.
PLANTAIN	630 to 1077	81.17 46.00 40.61	9 mths. 9½ " 11 "	3,613	30	50 plantains.
INDIAN CORN	1077 1260 to 1890 2880	81.17 40.61 36 to 37.80 25.20 to 27	90 days. 110 " 120 " 180 "	28,900	Annual.	238 for every seed planted.
MANIOC, or CASSAVA	1077 1195	81.17 40.61 43.00	10 mths. 12 " 120 days.	28,900	Biennial.	One w'gh-ing ¾ lb.; ¼oz. st'ch.
COCOA-NUT	630	81.17 46.00	5 years. 6 "	452	60	4 bottles oil pr tree.
TOBACCO	630 1077 1980	81.17 46.00 40.61 33.30	150 days. 170 " 180 " 225 "	28,900	Annual.	½ lb. *dried* to every 5 plants.
COTTON	630 1077 1415	81.17 46.00 40.61 34.61	6½ mths. 7 " 7½ " 9 "	28,900	3½	½ lb. net. per plant.
COFFEE	230 630 1077 to 2250 2453	47 46 37.80 to 39.60 33.30	24 mths. 25 " 28 " 36 "	5,300	45	1½ lb. per tree.
SUGAR CANE	630 1080	84.17 46.00 41.40	11 mths. 12 " 14 "	28,900	5	10 pr ct. of sug. on wt raw cane.
INDIGO	90 630 1077	48.60 46.00 40.61	2½ mths. 3 " 3½ "	57,800	1½	70 plants give 1 lb. col. matter
POTATO	1080 1980 2700	38.70 33.30 27.00	140 days. 165 " 210 "	116,600	Annual.	4½ pounds each plant.
WHEAT	567 1170 2520	42.30 38.70 32.99	80 days. 100 " 120 "	57,800	Annual.	37 for every seed planted.

Bearing in mind that the principal embarrassment to which an agriculturist in the West Indies is or may be subjected, is the inability to procure efficient laborers at such times as he may need them, prudence will dictate to him to make a selection of crops which, while highly remunerative, require comparatively little labor, or a low order of labor, in their cultivation. I invite attention to a few articles that seem to come within the category of requiring but a small capital and little labor.

1. CACAO, OR COCOA.

The fruit of this tree is an article of enormous consumption, and is the basis of Chocolate, which, in an economical and medicinal point of view, is a highly-important dietetic. (See *infra.*) It grows abundantly in the Islands of Trinidad, St. Lucia, and Grenada; and though the West India Cacao has not the marketable reputation of the Socomesco, yet the sample from Trinidad, produced at the Great Exhibition in London, was pronounced quite equal to any in the world.

The cultivation of Cacao requires but little labor and outlay; and it is therefore suitable to a country where labor is unreliable, and is also adapted for persons of small capital. Humboldt observes, alluding to Spanish America, "that Cacao plantations are occupied by persons of humble position, who prepare for themselves and their children a slow but certain fortune; a single laborer is sufficient to aid them in their plantation, and thirty thousand trees, once established, assure competence for a generation and a half." The tree, however, it will be seen by the Table, requires several years before it bears; and the Cacao planter must have patience if not capital.

Joseph, in his "History of Trinidad," remarks that there are few, perhaps no agricultural or horticultural pursuits so delightful as that of the cultivation of Cacao.

"It is planted in rows intersecting each other at right angles, at the distance of from twelve to fifteen feet, according to the nature of the soil. The tree is not suffered to grow higher than about fifteen feet; and its broad, rich foliage, the hues of which vary from a light green to a dark red, loaded with yellow and dark-red pods, which contain the chocolate bean, are beautiful objects. The alleys are shaded by rows of beautiful trees, called *Bois Immortel* by the French and English, by the Spaniards the *Madre de Cacao*. It is the *Erythrina umbrosa*, or *Arborea* of Linnæus. Like the Bignonia or Pouie, this tree at particular seasons throws off its foliage, and is covered with blossoms. Those of the Erythrina are of a brilliant red color, justifying its Greek appellation. In this state they are literally dazzling to behold—no object in the vegetable world looks more striking than the alleys of a Cacao walk, shaded by a forest above them of the Bois Immortel."

2. COFFEE.

For many years after the introduction of Coffee as a beverage, its use, like that of tobacco, was an object of execration with many. Lieber, in the *Cyclopedia Americana*, states that he recollects having heard an old preacher hurl a thunderbolt like this at the smokers and coffee-drinkers among his parishioners: "They cannot wait till the smoke of the infernal regions surrounds them, but encompass themselves with smoke of their own accord, and drink a poison which God made black that it might bear the devil's color." Whatever effect this counterblast may have had upon his immediate hearers, the world evidently is "not afraid," for it consumes annually of tobacco over nine hundred million pounds, and of Coffee about six hundred million pounds.*

The Coffee plant is an evergreen, and is described by La Roque as follows: "The Coffee tree is from six to twelve feet high, the stem ten, twelve, and fifteen inches in circumference. When full grown it much resembles our apple trees of eight or ten years' standing. The lower branches ordinarily bend when the tree begins to grow old, and extend themselves into a round form somewhat like an umbrella; and the wood is so very limber and pliable, that the ends of the longest branches may be bent down within two or three feet of the earth. The

* The following is the production of Tobacco in the world, as estimated by the Richmond *South.*

	Pounds.
Asia	399,900,000
Europe	281,844,500
America	248,280,500
Africa	24,300,000
Australia	714,000
	955,039,000

The consumption of Coffee in 1855 is stated in *Commercial Relations* as follows:

	Pounds.
Brazil	320,000,000
Java	120,000,000
St. Domingo	35,000,000
Cuba and Porto Rico	20,000,000
British West Indies	5,000,000
Sumatra	15,000,000
Mocha, &c	5,000,000
Ceylon, India	50,000,000
Venezuela	20,000,000
Costa Rica	9,000,000
Total	599,000,000

bark is whitish and somewhat rough; its leaf is much like that of the Citron tree. It continues green all the year, and the tree is never without leaves, which are ranged almost opposite on each side of the bough, and at small distance from each other. Nothing is more singular in its kind than its production; for in almost all seasons of the year blossoms, and green fruit, and ripe, may be seen on the same tree at the same time. When the blossom falls off there remains, in its room, or rather springs from each blossom, a small fruit, green at first, but which becomes red as it ripens, and is not unlike a large cherry, and is very good to eat. Under the flesh of this cherry, instead of the stone, is found the bean or berry we call Coffee, wrapped around in a fine thin skin. The berry is then very thin and of a disagreeable taste; but as the cherry ripens the berry in the inside grows harder, and the dried-up fruit being the flesh or pulp of it, which was before eatable, becomes a shell or pod of a deep brown color. The berry is now solid, and of a clear transparent green. Each shell contains one berry, which splits into two equal parts. When the fruit is sufficiently ripe to be shaken from the tree, the husks are separated from the berries, and are used in Arabia by the natives, while the berries are exported for the European markets."

The Coffee tree grows spontaneously in many countries; and in Hayti what is called a Coffee plantation, is said to be nothing more than a large tract of land covered with a spontaneous growth of the tree. The cost of producing a pound of Coffee berries varies according to location and other circumstances. In Brazil the average cost is about four and a half cents, the transportion to a central market being estimated at two cents per pound. Mr. Baird, in his "Impressions of the West Indies," &c., thus speaks of a Coffee plantation:

"Any thing in the way of cultivation more beautiful or more fragrant than a Coffee plantation, I had not conceived; and oft did I say to myself, that if ever I became, from health and otherwise, a cultivator of the soil within the Tropics, I would cultivate the Coffee plant, even though I did so irrespective altogether of the profits that might be derived from so doing. Much has been written, and not without justice, of the rich fragrance of an Orange grove; and at home we oftimes hear of the sweet odors of a bean-field. I have, too, often enjoyed in the Carse of Stirling, and elsewhere in Scotland, the balmy breezes as they swept over the latter, particularly when the sun had burst out with unusual strength after a shower of rain. I have likewise, in Martinique, Santa Cruz, Jamaica, and Cuba, inhaled the gales wafted from the orangeries; but not for a moment would I compare either with the exquisite aromatic odors of a Coffee plantation in full blow, where the hill-side, covered over with regular rows of the tree-like shrubs, with their millions of jessamine-like flowers, showers down upon you as you ride up between the plants, a perfume of the most delicately delicious description. 'Tis worth going to the West Indies to see the sight and inhale the perfume."

A discovery has recently been made which may prove to be very important, viz., that the leaves of the Coffee plant contain the same essential principle for which the berry is so much valued. In the Dutch Island of Sumatra, in the Indian Archipelago, the natives scarcely use any thing else, and greatly prefer a beverage made from the leaf to the berry itself. The leaves undergo a process of curing similar to tea, and they possess all the virtues of either tea or Coffee. The discovery is probably important, because while the culture of the Coffee plant for the sake of its fruit is limited to particular soils and high temperatures, the tree produces leaves in abundance anywhere within the Tropics where the soil is sufficiently fertile.

3. INDIGO.

Indigo is now principally grown in India, of which

it constitutes one of the great staples. Formerly it was very extensively cultivated in the West Indies; and in South Carolina, some sixty years ago, a quality of Indigo was made superior to the finest Guatemala or the best Bengal. With regard to the productiveness of the crop, and the causes of the decline in its cultivation, Bridges, in his "Annals of Jamaica," remarks: "The labor of a single negro would often bring to his owner £30 sterling clear profit—a sum which was at the time the laborer's highest price. It continued the staple of Jamaica till an intolerable tax oppressed it, while its price was lowered by the competition of other Colonies. Its cultivation immediately declined throughout them all, but nowhere so rapidly as here. The financial error was quickly discovered—a remedy was attempted by a bounty; but it came too late—the plantations were thrown up, and the planters, attracted by the temporary gain, abused the tardy boon by introducing, as of their own growth, large quantities of foreign Indigo."

Another reason assigned for the neglect of the Indigo manufacture within the West Indies, and in the United States, is the unhealthiness of the vapor arising from the fermented liquor. To this it is replied that the *original* growers did not complain of the mortality attending the cultivation; and Dr. Edward Binns, of Jamaica, adds:

"There is nothing whatever in the manufacture of Indigo, either in the cultivation or the granulation, or even the maceration or fermentation of the plant, which is directly or indirectly, *per se*, injurious to human life. I have certainly never seen the Indigo macerated on a large scale, but I have myself steeped much of it in water, and allowed it even to rot, and found nothing in the mass differing in any marked degree from decomposed vegetable matter. It seems to me that this idea of the manufacture of Indigo being especially inimical to human life is as unfounded as the belief, even by Humboldt, up to a very recent period, that none of the Cerealia would grow in tropical climates. In conversing with an old gentleman in Jamaica some twelve years since, who had tried the manufacture of Indigo, and with every prospect of success, but abandoned it, as he confessed, for the cultivation of the sugar-cane, since it was then more profitable, he suggested the solution that as the manufacture was light work, probably aged and debilitated in place of youthful and vigorous slaves, were too frequently employed in the process—hence the mortality. This may be correct to a certain extent; but I am also inclined to think that another cause of mortality might be found in the mode and manner in which the negro was fed and clothed, and not because aged persons were exclusively engaged in the manufacture. I believe I may state without contradiction, that the real cause of the decline and consequent abandonment of the Indigo plant was the monstrous duty levied upon it by the English government. Indeed, this has been already stated in an extract from Bridges; while the cause of the failure of the attempt to renew it, over and above the reasons we have given, was the greater temptation to embark capital in sugar plantations—the West Indies enjoying a monopoly in this article, while they had competitors in the Southern States of America in the other. I have therefore no hesitation in saying, that with a trifling capital, under prudent management, Indigo might be cultivated to a very great extent and with considerable profit even now, in Jamaica. But the adventurer is not to expect to count his gains, as the original growers did, by the thousands; he must be content with hundreds if not fifties; for at the present day every branch of industry is laden with difficulties, encumbered by taxation, and obstructed by competition."

Mr. Bonynge, who was a successful Indigo and Tea planter in the East, published a book some years ago, in which he calculated that the expense of raising seventy-five pounds of Indigo, supposing labor could be procured for fifty cents a day, would be—

Preparing and sowing land,	six men,	per acre	$3.00
Weeding,	" two "	"	1.00
Cutting plants,	six "	"	3.00

Conveying to factory	$1.00
Vats, filling and emptying, two men per acre	1.00
Beating vats, " "	1.00
Boiling	.10
Firewood, etc	.25
Packing in chest 3½ monds, 75 cts., 1-5	.15
Raising water	.20
	$10.70

"Say 220 monds at 75 lbs. of Indigo. Therefore, as 130 : $10.70 : : 220 : $18.10 for 75 lbs.

"The lowest description of Indigo sells in Calcutta for not less than $30 for the 75 lbs. The average price for good for the last year would be about $65 for 75 lbs.; but the best Bengal Indigo is rarely under $80, and from that up to $100. Some time ago it had been up as high as 340 Rs. or $170; that is the sale price obtained by the planters at Calcutta for 75 lbs."

The Indigo shrub grows wild in many of the West Indian Islands, and its cultivation does not require one-third of the labor that is generally required for the cultivation of cotton. The manufacture, however, involves some nice points in fermentation and granulation, and several experimenters have failed for want of the requisite knowledge of these processes. No one should attempt the manufacture without the aid of an experienced Indigo cultivator. The fixed capital required is stated as follows: "It consists simply of a few vats of common masonry for steeping the plant, and precipitating the coloring matter, a boiling and drying house, and a dwelling for the planter. Thus a factory of ten pair of vats, capable of producing at an average 12,500 lbs. of Indigo, worth on the spot £2,500, will not cost above £1,500 sterling. The building and machinery necessary to produce an equal value in sugar and rum, would probably cost about £4,000."

The demand for Indigo within the last few years, it is stated, has exceeded the supply, and that a spurious article, not containing one-half the coloring matter of the genuine, sells readily at $1.50 per pound. There are hundreds of persons, we are assured, who would rather pay $2 per pound for the best Bengal, or such as was formerly grown in South Carolina, than seventy-five cents for that with which the market is now principally supplied.

4. CASSAVA, OR MANIOC.

The Cassava is also a shrub-like plant about six feet high, having a root that is exceedingly nutritious, and is largely consumed in the West Indies and South America, in all of which it grows abundantly. There are two kinds of Cassava plants, distinguished as the *sweet* and the *bitter*. The root of the *Sweet* Cassava, when taken from the ground is said to be poisonous, but if exposed to the sun for a short time it becomes innocuous, and when boiled is quite wholesome. When pressed into cakes, it constitutes the principal food laid in by the natives in their voyages on the Amazon; and when sliced and dried in the sun, is marketable in Europe.

From the root of the *Bitter* Cassava, *Tapioca,* which is so often prescribed by physicians as an aliment of easy digestion, is prepared. Also *Casareep,* an antiseptic, previously referred to, and which forms the basis of the West India dish, "pepper pot." The juice of the Bitter Cassava, when distilled, is also a deadly poison, thirty drops of which would kill a man in six minutes; but this property is driven off by roasting, and then the starch is used in the form of Cassava bread.

With regard to the profits of cultivating Cassava, Mr

Simmonds, in his "Vegetable Products," states that the trouble of planting is inconsiderable, while the profit arising from its manufacture, even by the common process of hand-grating, is immense. He refers to a Mr. Glen, proprietor of Haagsbosch Plantation, in Demerara, who, having erected machinery for grinding the root, and preparing the starch of the Bitter Cassava, had already shipped the article in considerable quantities to Europe, where it had been sold at a price which completely distanced the ordinary profits of cultivating sugar. He says:—

"His agent, in Glasgow, writes, that any quantity (like that already shipped), can command a ready sale at 9d. per pound. Its use is coextensive, or nearly so, with that of sugar. The productive capabilities of the soil are not perhaps generally known, nor is it necessary that, to pay the grower there, it should bring even half that price. A sample of a ton, which was prepared at Haagsbosch, in 1841, was submitted for examination to Dr. Shier, at the Colonial Laboratory, Georgetown, who admitted it to be a beautiful specimen of starch, although it had undergone but one washing. The root from which it was made, was planted eight or nine months previously, upon an acre of soil which had never undergone any preparation of plowing, or been broken and turned up in any way. The plants were never weeded after they had begun to spring, nor were they tended or disturbed until they were ripe and pulled up. The expense of planting the acre was $5, and the reaping this crop would, I suppose, amount to as much more, say £2 in all. The green Cassava was never weighed, but the acre yielded fully a ton of starch—equal, at 9d. a pound, to £84.

"The experimental researches of Dr. Shier have led him to believe that the green Bitter Cassava will give one-fifth its weight of starch. If this be the case, the return per acre would, under favorable circumstances, when the land is properly worked, be enormous. On an estate, at Essequibo, a short time ago, an acre of Cassava, grown in fine permeable soil, was lifted and weighed; it yielded twenty-five tons of green Cassava. Such a return as this per acre would enable our West India Colonies to inundate Great Britain with food, and at a rate which would make flour to be considered a luxury. Dr. Shier is convinced that in thorough drained land, where the roots could penetrate the soil, and where its permeability would permit of their indefinite expansion, a return of twenty-five tons an acre might uniformly be calculated upon. What a blessing, not only for those Colonies but for the world, would the introduction be of this cheap and nutritious substitute for the potato."

5. PLANTAINS AND BANANAS.

With regard to the Plantain, M. Humboldt has remarked:—"I doubt whether there be any other plant that produces so great a quantity of nutritive substance in so small a space. Eight or nine months after the sucker is planted, it begins to develop its cluster. The fruit may be gathered in the tenth or eleventh month. When the stalk is cut, there is always found among the numerous shoots that have taken root, a sprout (*pimpollo*) which being two-thirds the length of its parent plant, bears fruit three months later. Thus a plantation of Bananas perpetuates itself without requiring any care on the part of man, further than to cut the stalks when the fruit has ripened, and to stir the earth gently once or twice a year, about the roots. A piece of ground of one hundred square metres of surface will contain from thirty to forty plants. During the course of a year this same piece of ground, reckoning the weight of the cluster at from fifteen to twenty kilogs. only, will yield two thousand kilogs., or more than four thousand pounds of nutritive substance. What a difference between this product, and that of the cereal grasses in most parts of Europe. The same extent of land, planted with wheat, would not produce over thirty pounds, and not more than ninety pounds of potatoes. Hence the product of the Banana is to that of wheat as one hundred and thirty-three to one, and that of the potatoes as forty-four to one." *Essai sur La Nouvelle Espagne.*

In Mexico, the Banana constitutes a principal portion of the food of the inhabitants, and the facility with which it can be grown is said to be one cause of the proverbial indolence of the inhabitants. Plantains are also dried, and from their nutritive qualities and agreeable taste, it is supposed that a profitable business might be done by importing them into Europe, and making known their virtues.*

At a recent meeting of the British Horticultural Society, Dr. Royle exhibited "specimens of paper, rope, cordage, and other substances prepared from the Plantain, and entered into highly interesting details concerning the

* "Dried Plantains possess considerable nutritive value, and are at the same time exceedingly agreeable to the palate, while they are cheap and easy to prepare. But what I would more especially mention in respect to them is, that the Plantains which lie there, perfectly sweet, and having undergone no material change whatever up to the present time, were sent into a baggage warehouse in Wolwich, in the year 1835, and had there been lying until they were transferred to the Exhibition building. So that it appears that dried Plantains are not only exceedingly good to eat, and highly nutritive, but have the property, which many such substances do not possess, of keeping for a very long time—a fact that should interest those who deal in figs and similar articles, which are apt to become mity and dry, and to spoil, to the loss of those who own them. It is certain that there is no good property belonging to the *fig*, which does not also belong to the dried Plantain. It appears from the statements of Colonel Colquhoun, to whom we owe our knowledge of the preparation, that such dried Plantains can be prepared in Mexico and sold in Europe for threepence a pound, allowing ten per cent. profit, supposing there is no duty on their imports." "*Lindley's* Lecture on Substances Used for Food."

amount of produce obtainable from an acre of plantain ground, independently of the fruit, for which alone the plant is now cultivated in the greater part of the Tropics. The paper, though for the most part unbleached, and not prepared with European skill, was of the best quality as regards strength and fineness—some of it was of a delicate cream color." Simmonds states that the fibre of the Plantain is equal to rags in texture, and possesses the superior advantages of being clean, free from vermin, and requiring no sorting of material. He recommends the establishment of mills and machinery for the preparation of the fibre of the Plantain for this purpose. The capital required he estimates, including $5,000 working capital, at $25,000; and the total expense of producing a ton of fibre at $45. In 1848, Manilla rope, or Plantain fibre, of good quality, was worth $190 per ton.

The cultivation of the Plantain has been recommended for the United States. A correspondent of the Commissioner of Patents, writing from New Orleans, says:—

"The Plantain tree (*Musa sapientium*), is superior to the potato or wheat as a staple article for food. This is proved by eminent English chemists, who have analyzed it. It is easy for cultivation —one hand attending to one hundred acres, and is of continuous or spontaneous growth after the first year. In its green state it is used for food; when ripe, for fruit; and makes an acid and cheap vinegar, an intoxicating drink, and flour or gruel. The green leaves are used for fodder, and the dry ones for bedding in all the public hospitals, being cheap and healthy. The tree itself, after yielding its fruit, is cut down, and is now manufactured into writing-paper in England. An indelible ink is also produced from the shells of the green Plantain. I believe no known plant contributes so much to the wants of man.

"It is cultivated in gardens in Louisiana, but its great value to man and beast is neither known nor appreciated. Any number of plants could be procured from British Guiana at 2½ cents each."

6. THE COCO-NUT PALM.

Like the Bamboo, of which we have spoken, the Coco Palm is applied in the East to an infinite variety of uses. It is the Indian nut which alone

> "Is clothing, meat and trencher, drink and can;
> Boat, cable, sail and needle all in one."

Europeans know of no less than forty-three uses to which this palm is applied, and the natives of the Torrid zone know of others. The principal seat of its present cultivation is Ceylon and the South Sea Islands; but a large quantity of Coco-nut oil is made in the West Indies, especially on the east coast of Trinidad, where in one locality there is an uninterrupted belt of Coco-nut Palms, fourteen miles in extent. Essentially a maritime plant, it flourishes best where the roots reach the salt water or salt mud; but in favorable localities it grows rapidly, without much labor or attention, and continues fruitful for more than a hundred years. The author of "The Commercial Products of the Vegetable Kingdom" is enthusiastic in recommending the cultivation of the Coco Palm, and remarks, whether sold at the rate of one dollar per hundred in their natural state to captains of ships, who freely purchase them, or manufactured into oil, they are equally a remunerative product. Having assumed that there are fifty-eight Coco-nut trees on an acre, and that fifty nuts are an annual crop, and that one hundred nuts will give two and a half gallons of oil, he proceeds:

"Take the case now of a plantation of one hundred acres in extent. This would give us five thousand eight hundred trees, which, at fifty nuts per tree, two hundred and ninety thousand nuts, at two and a half gallons of oil per hundred, would yield seven thousand two hundred and fifty gallons of oil, the value of which any person may calculate, but which at the low rate of three shillings over-charges would furnish as the gross plantation return of oil, a sum of £1,087 10*s.* sterling. If the cultivator, instead of making his produce into oil, were to sell it in its natural state, his gross returns, in the West Indies, would be nearly £600 sterling, at the rate of $10 per thousand.

"Either of these sums would be a handsome return from one hundred acres of land, *requiring no care or cultivation whatever after the fourth year, and yielding* the same amount for upward of half a century. But this is not all. An outlay of a few pounds will secure other advantages, and ought to enable the owner of a Coco-nut plantation to turn his gross receipts for oil into net profits. The coir made from the husks of the nut is calculated to realize nearly one-fourth the proceeds of the oil; but if we put it down at one-fifth, we shall have, in addition to the value of the oil, £217 10*s.*, thus making a total of £1,305 sterling. If we obtained sixty nuts from each tree, the return would be £1,566 sterling; and if seventy-five, £1,957 8*s.* sterling; and this from one hundred acres of sea-side sand. But even this does not exhibit the whole return of this article of culture. Each nut may be calculated to give a quarter of a pound of poonac, or oil-cake, being the refuse after expression, fit for feeding all kinds of stock, which may be estimated as worth £10 per ton. We must therefore add, on this account, to our first calculation, the sum of, say £325; to the second, £390; and to the third, £485. This would give in round numbers the entire returns of the one hundred acres planted: at fifty nuts per tree, £1,630; at sixty per tree, £1,957; at seventy-five per tree, £2,446.

"These are striking results, and may anoear exaggerated; but I will—to show how very moderate has been my calculation—give two returns with which I have been favored from Ceylon. These, it will be seen, differ materially; but the latter I can rely on as a practical result from a plantation in Jaffna, the peninsula of the northern portion of the island. After estimating the expense of establishing the plantation, the first writer sets down his returns thus:—

"'The produce, calculating ninety trees to an acre, and seventy-five nuts to a tree, sold at £2 per thousand, would yield 675,000 nuts, worth £1,350; or if converted into oil, calculating thirty to give one gallon, it would produce 22,500 gallons, or about ninety tons from one hundred acres.'

From Jaffna, the following is an abridged estimate of return of one hundred acres in full bearing :—' At twenty-seven feet apart, fifty eight trees per acre, five thousand eight hundred trees at sixty nuts per tree, three thousand four hundred and eighty nuts per acre, one hundred acres, three hundred and forty-eight thousand nuts ; at forty nuts per imperial gallon, eight thousand seven hundred gallons of oil, at 2*s.* per gallon, netted £8 14*s.* per acre. The poonac left will pay the expense of making the oil. If shipped to England at the present time, (close of 1848), the selling price there being 55*s.* per hundred-weight, measuring twelve imperial gallons, say 4*s.* 7*d.* per gallon, and the cost and charges of sending it home, and selling it being 23*s.*, it would leave 3*s.*, per gallon, or £13 per acre.' This sum is net proceeds.

" It will be seen, by the above, that I have been extremely moderate in my computation of the return which may be anticipated ; for there is no doubt that planters can, in favorable localities on the coast of most of our Colonies, cultivate this Palm with as much success as attends its culture in Ceylon. By the first of the calculations I have cited from that island, the gross return appears thus :

	£	*s.*
22,500 gallons, at 4*s.* 7*d.* per gallon	5,156	5
Coir, one-fifth of value	1,031	5
Cake from 675,000 nuts, say ¼ lb. each, 75 tons, at £10	750	0
Total gross return from 100 acres	£6,937	10

" According to the other calculation, the return will stand thus :

	£	*s.*
8700 gallons at 4*s.* 7*d.*	1,993	15
Coir	398	15
Cake from 348,000 nuts, 34 tons	340	00
Total gross return from 100 acres	£2,732	10

" It will be seen that in my calculation I have set down the return lower than it is rendered in the less favorable statement from Ceylon by a sum of upward of £1,000 sterling. But even supposing *one-half* of the amount of the lower Ceylon estimate could be realized, we should have a return of £1,366 5*s.* from one hundred acres of sea-side sand.

"Let us now see what are the *planter's expenses*, making ample allowance on account of each item:—

6000 picked nuts at $10 per thousand	$60
Hire and rations of twelve hands at $16, for three months	576
Two hands at Nursery for same period	96
Purchase of twelve cattle at $20	240
Foddering cattle one month	32
Hire of two extra hands, making tanks and sheds three months	96
Hire of six hands for nine months	864
Tools, including plow	100
Total	$2,064

"About £415 sterling for expenses for the first year.

"Where fencing is required, we must add for making about three miles of fence, say £30 sterling. Two carts will also have to be provided, which will cost, say £20 more. In all, we may compute the first year's expenditure at £460 sterling.

"Second year's expenditure: plowing land or hoeing it twice, watering plants, manuring, repairing fences, and supplying plants, say hire of eight men for six months, about £150 sterling. The same for the third. Fourth year's expenditure: hire of six hands for three months, cleaning land and manuring plants, about £60 sterling and the like at the cultivator's option for the fifth year.

Summary of Expenses.	£
First year	460
Second year	150
Third year	150
Fourth year	60
Fifth year	60
Total expenditure	£880
Add for buildings	80

And we will have a grand total of £960 sterling, expended; for what purpose? to secure a net income of at least £1,200 sterling per annum for at least fifty years!

"The cultivation of this tree deserves much more attention than has hitherto been paid to it, particularly in the East, where it not only forms part of the daily food of all classes of the community, but is an exportable article to neighboring regions, the oil which it yields having of late years become of great demand in England for the manufacture of composite candles and soaps; and there is no doubt of its continually extended application to such purposes. Supposing nevertheless the result of an increased cultivation of the Coco-nut should be such as to cause a fall in price, and sink the net return in England to 2*s*. per gallon; this being clear profit, would make this kind of plantation a safe and sure investment for both capital and labor."

In Belize, Honduras, there are extensive forests of another very valuable Palm, which as yet has been comparatively neglected, viz., the *Cahoun Palm.* The Cahoun tree yields a crop every year, consisting generally of three and sometimes four bunches of nuts of the size of a small turkey's egg, and on an average there are eight hundred of them in one bunch. One quart of oil may be extracted by a very simple process from one hundred nuts; and Mr. Wilson states, in the *Journal of the Society of Arts,* as the result of his experiments, that the commercial value of Cahoun oil equals that of the highest quality of Cocoa-nut oil, which comes from the Malabar coast, and sells at $150 per ton. Judge Temple, formerly British Consul in Honduras, in a communication read before the above Society, in 1857, stated that "in Belize, for miles and miles, you have nothing but forests of it (the Cahoun Palm): and yet, with all these trees bearing nuts from which a most valuable oil can be extracted—an oil for which there would be a ready market in every town of Europe and America—no one has yet been found to turn them to a profitable account."

Besides these, there are numerous products of less commercial importance, but which can be cultivated with considerable profit and without much labor, in certain parts of the West Indies. For instance, Arrow-Root in Bermuda, of which England, in 1852, imported 2,139,930 pounds. A gentleman resident in the Bermudas gives the following statement of his operations in growing Arrow-Root on twenty rods, or the eighth of an acre, and on land which had not been plowed before for twenty years.

"The expense and profit stand thus:

EXPENSE.		£ s. d.
To the plowman, harrowing and planting the Arrow-Root		1 0 0
Arrow-Root plants		16 0
Digging it up	£1 0 0	
Deduct half, as the land was planted for the next year	10 0	10 0
Balance carried down, being net profit		5 14 0
		£8 0 0

PRODUCE.	
By 2,000 lbs. of Arrow-Root at 8*s*. per 100 lbs	£8 0 0
By balance brought down as net profit	5 14 0

"The above £5 14s. clear profit on the twenty rods is at the rate of £45 12*s*. profit for an acre. Now if a small cultivator were to plant three or four acres, and get only one-half the above profit, it would give a good return and would be well worth the trial."

Again he says—

"In 1845, I planted, in the months of January and February, a quarter of an acre of good land in Arrow-Root and Onions. The expense and profit stand as follows:

EXPENSE.	£ s. d.
To digging the ground	1 0 0
Planting Arrow-Root	6 0
Twelve loads of sea-weed at 1*s*	12 0
Rotten manure for Onions, 10 loads at 2*s*	1 0 0
One bottle Onion seed	16 0
Sowing Onion seed and keeping the plants clean	10 0

	£	s.	d.
Planting-out Onions	1	0	0
Cleaning Onions after set out		15	0
Tops and making baskets	1	8	0
Pulling, cutting, and basketing		18	0
Carting and shipping		8	0
Digging Arrow-Root	2	0	0
	£10	13	0
Clear profit on quarter acre	22	13	9
	£33	6	9

PRODUCT.

	£	s.	d.
By Onions sold	£20	16	0
By Arrow-Root	12	10	9
Total	£33	6	9

"This is at the rate of £90 15*s.* clear profit per acre, which is more than double the worth of the land. I have not named the Arrow-Root plants, because I have planted my land with them again; but they might be fairly put to the credit of the account. The above statement shows what may be done with good land and good management; but even if a man can only clear £10 on an acre of land, he ought not to grumble."

Other valuable articles might be referred to, as for instance *Ginger*, and *Pimento* or *Allspice*, of which Jamaica alone has exported in a single year over five million pounds, but I shall allude to only one more, of which the cultivation is of the most simple kind, viz., ALOES. Nothing in fact is required after planting the suckers, except to keep them free from weeds. The Aloe plant, we are told, is indigenous to Jamaica, but though handled by thousands of the peasantry, there is not perhaps one in five thousand who understands its properties or knows its value. The best Barbadoes Aloes has commanded in the market $35 per cwt.; and cables have been made from the fibre of this plant which, in a series of trials recently made at Paris, raised a weight of one-fifth more than that of hemp. Lastly, in addition to the cultivation of such articles as are principally adapted for sale in distant markets, a profitable business is afforded in raising provisions for consumption in the Home markets 'So entirely," says Bigelow, "are the capital and industry of the island (Jamaica) absorbed in the culture of favorite staples on these large estates, that common articles of table consumption in Kingston are higher than in any part of England or the United States. I give below a list of prices paid at the hotel where I stayed, for articles, every one of which could be cultivated in Jamaica with the utmost ease and abundance, and ought to be sold for prices far below the current rates for the same articles in any city in the United States:

	Cents.
Butter, per pound	37½
Cow's milk, per quart	18¾
Goat's milk, per quart	25
American cheese, per pound	25
English cheese, per pound	37½
Potatoes, per pound	6¼
Eggs, two for	6¼
Eggs during the Christmas holidays, each	5
Garlic, per pound	25 @ 37½
Flour, per pound	12 @ 18
Flour, per barrel	$16 @ $18
Corn meal, per barrel	12 @ 14
Hams at retail, per pound	25
Lard, per pound	21
Onions, per pound	12½

"Nothing apparently can be more unnatural than for the people of this Island, in their present poverty-stricken condition, to be paying such prices as these for their daily food; and yet nothing is more inevitable as long as the land is held by a few absentee landlords in such large quantities."*

One suggestion, by way of precaution, it may be necessary to make to Americans who are about to purchase land in the West Indies—and that is, the alien laws require landowners to take an oath of allegiance to the government of Great Britain. It is not supposed that the title of an alien to landed property would ever be disturbed, certainly not in time of peace; but in important cases, it may be an advisable precaution to place the title in the names of one, or what is better, two trusty persons who are British subjects, residing in America or in the West Indies, taking as security a mortgage for a sum equal to the price, and with provisions prescribed, rendering a sale as speedy and as easy as possible.

---

* WM. W. ANDERSON, a resident of Kingston, Jamaica, in a letter dated Sept. 23, 1850, says: "Wheat usually sells at from 75 cents to $1,25 per bushel. For grapes it is not unusual to pay 50 cents per pound. I paid not long ago $4.50 for a barrel of potatoes. These prices will surprise you when I aver that two hours a day of work with the hoe will enable a man to obtain abundance of food for the year. The food of the island which is not imported, is raised, not by farmers using implements of husbandry, but almost entirely by the middle class of negro laborers in the country, who often carry a basketful on their heads fifteen or twenty miles to a market. One of your small farmers would economize his labor, and bring similar products to market in a cart, cheaper, with a profit of seventy-five per cent.

"I wish we had a large, a very large, importation of your *colored people who have been accustomed to farming.* Our climate and whole state of society would suit them infinitely better than Liberia, and it would be a cheaper course for them to a comfortable home."

In accordance with natural laws, Agricultural operations take precedence over all others in a growing society, and are succeeded first by Manufactures, then by foreign Commerce. No apology can be necessary for dwelling on the opportunities for profit, which are afforded in developing the latent resources of the soil; since in no other property can capital be more securely invested than in land, and in no pursuit will intelligent industry be more certainly rewarded than in tilling it. But it may be proper to state, that by giving prominence, as I have done, to articles principally adapted for cultivation in Southern climates, no depreciation is intended of those which are staple products of agriculture in England and the Northern and Western portions of the United States. Farming, *under certain conditions*, may be made as profitable in all these as any regular pursuit that can be named; but to realize such a result requires very considerable knowledge and capital, much technical skill, and a high order of mental and physical qualifications. It is a singular fact, that many of the most important improvements made in Agriculture are traced to men who are not professional farmers. The same remark applies to the best books on agricultural subjects; and the largest comparative or proportional profits have been realized by amateurs in farming—as for instance, merchants who have abandoned the counting-house for a place in the country, or scientific men who have applied science to the cultivation of a small plot of land. Professor Mapes, we are told, made $15,000 from cultivating sixty acres of Jersey soil, in the first five years of his experimental farming. The different results attained by different farmers, having apparently the same advantages, are truly remarkable. An average crop of *Indian Corn*, for instance, throughout the United States, does not exceed twenty-five bushels per acre—some say twenty bushels; while, at the same time, individuals have repeatedly raised over one hundred and fifty bushels per acre. Coleman, in the *American Farmer*, Vol. XV., has cited a number of instances, based on *verified statements for premiums*, of a product of over one hundred bushels per acre. Fifteen cases in Massachusetts are named, occurring from 1820 to 1831, and varying from one hundred and ten to one hundred and forty-two bushels per acre. Others are given for Madison County, New York, in 1821 and 1822, where the product varied from one hundred and fifty to one hundred and seventy, and one hundred and seventy-two bushels per acre. Several other localities in New York yielded one hundred and twenty to one hundred and forty bushels, and seven certified cases in Pennsylvania, mainly in Washington County, are taken from the Memoirs of the Pennsylvania Agricultural Society, ranging from one hundred and eighteen to one hundred and thirty-six bushels per acre. At an Agricultural Exhibition in Harrison County, Ohio, in 1849, Mr. S. B. Lukens furnished evidence satisfactory to the Committee, that he had raised three hundred and seventy-four bushels of Corn on three acres of ground, at a cost not exceeding $17.10 cents, delivered in the crib, being less than five cents per bushel. His statement was at follows:—

"The ground has been in meadow ten years, was plowed six inches deep about the middle of April, was harrowed twice over on the 9th of May, and planted on the 11th four feet by two feet. It came up well, was cultivated and thinned when ten inches high; three stalks were left in a hill. About two weeks afterward it was again cultivated, and the suckers pulled off. About the last of

19*

June it was again cultivated, making three times the same way, as it was laid off but one way.

Expense of culture, gathering, and cribbing,..............	$17 10
Produce of 374⅜ bushels, at 31¼ cents, ...	117 10
Profit on three acres,................................	$100 00

Contrast with this statement the profit that arises from raising twenty-five bushels Corn to the acre, even if fifty cents a bushel is obtained for it. Thus: Proceeds of three acres at $12.50—$37.50. Expense of culture as before, $17.10. Profit, $20.40, instead of $100. In other Agricultural products, Wheat, Oats, Potatoes, Roots, etc., there is a like difference between the average and the exceptional yield and profit, demonstrating, that to those who will study and secure the most favorable condition of soil, climate, and elements of fertility for the plant they cultivate—who are free to operate in the right place, and know how to operate in the right way—there are as brilliant chances for profit in cultivating ordinary staple products as any, not purely accidental and exceptional, that can be suggested.

Within the last quarter of a century, so many changes have been made in the accessories of Farming, that the pursuit is, in a measure, revolutionized. Rail-roads are now the carriers of its products, and Science is its handmaid. Instead of being satisfied with "a hoe, a negro, and a stump-tailed steer," an intelligent farmer, owning one hundred acres of land, considers himself illy provided with tools unless he has three plows, three harrows, two cultivators, a roller, a horse-power corn-sheller, a portable grist-mill, a seed planter and sower, a horse-rake, a combined mower and reaper, and a thrasher and grain-cleaner. The farmer now works most successfully when he employs other agencies than his own physical labor, and consequently the *brains* as well as the "bone and sinew" of the country, are being attracted to the cultivation of the soil.

But however delightful Agricultural pursuits are to those who are so constituted as to enjoy them, or however munificent their rewards to those who observe the conditions essential to the greatest productiveness of plants it is possible that neither the delights nor the profits of farming may tempt you to embark in it. You may be one of those adventurous sons of New England, so graphically referred to by Burke, in one of his orations,* or you may have adopted, as a rule of action, the classical motto, "Make a spoon or spoil a horn;" and in either case a more suitable theatre for the display of your genius, will be found in the speculations

* "While we follow them among the tumbling mountains of ice, and behold them penetrating into the deepest frozen recesses of Hudson's Bay and Davis' Straits; while we are looking for them beneath the Arctic Circle, we hear that they have pierced into the opposite region of polar cold; that they are at the antipodes, and engaged under the frozen Serpent of the South. Falkland Islands, which seem too remote and romantic an object for national ambition to grasp, is but a stage and resting-place in the progress of their vigorous industry. Nor is the Equinoctial heat more discouraging to them than the accumulated winter of both Poles. We know that while some of them draw the line and strike the harpoon on the coasts of Africa, others run the longitude, and pursue their gigantic game along the coast of Brazil. No sea but what is vexed by their fisheries—no climate that is not witness to their toils. Neither the perseverance of Holland, nor the activity of France, nor the dexterous and firm sagacity of English enterprise, ever carried this most perilous mode of hardy industry to the extent to which it has been pushed by this recent people; a people who are still as it were in the gristle, and not yet hardened in the bone of manhood."

and fascinations of FOREIGN COMMERCE. Let us, at all events, in anticipation, inquire whether there are any openings for trade and chances for profit in this direction, and particularly, since so much has been done recently in rendering information about markets common to all, and in placing all nations on an equality with the "most favored," whether any encouragement can safely be extended to those desirous to become commercial adventurers.

Of the goods exported from the United States, about sixty-five per cent. are sent to the West Coast of Europe, and from thence we receive more than fifty per cent. of the imports. In a trade so well established as this, with its steamships, price-currents, correspondence, submarine and incipient ocean telegraphs—it would certainly be presumption to assume that any brilliant opportunities for considerable profit have escaped a thousand Argus-eyed merchants, and are available to adventurers. It is true that local circumstances are at all times lowering or raising the prices of standard products in some of the markets of the world; but these are so purely temporary, and so likely to mislead, that we cannot notice them. By comparing price-currents, establishing correspondence, and reading commercial journals, they can readily be ascertained. Nevertheless, if you desire not merely to make a single fortunate venture, but to embark in a regular business, I would commend to your attention, and state in this form that there are abundant opportunities to make money, viz.

CHANCES CCI.—D.—*By shipping such articles as are not in favor with fancy merchants, and novel articles, and arti-*

cles superior in quality to the average of their kind; and I designate, for instance, *Timber* and *Tobacco*, *Oysters* and *Dried Vegetables*, *Superior Butter* and *Cheese*, *Provisions cured in a superior manner*, *Fine Fruits*, etc. Something perhaps may be said with regard to each of these that may be of value to somebody.

1. TIMBER.

In both France and England the Ship-building Timber of the United States is highly appreciated, and generally commands remunerative prices. The American Red Pine is considered, at Liverpool, preferable to any other Timber for Spars; and the French shipwrights always prefer American Pine for similar purposes, if it can be obtained. Our Consul at Havre, in 1854, wrote—

"Masts, spars, and almost all kinds of Timber of the United States, used in ship-building, would always find a ready and profitable sale, for vessels actually building or about commencing to be built, as such Timber, as before observed, is always preferred; but the extent of profit would depend on the rate of freight paid for its conveyance."

The Oak principally used in France is obtained from the Baltic, and from Africa; the former is inferior to American White Oak in quality, and the latter to American Live Oak. The American Consul at Zante, says, with reference to Timber:—

"This is an article also which I would highly recommend American traders to take into consideration. I cannot, at the present moment, state the amount imported, on account of the difficulty I meet in obtaining the required information; but what I positively know is, that we have frequent arrivals, and that the article is always sold at high prices."

Recently, a cargo of ordinary wood, Walnut, Hickory, Cherry, Ash, etc., was shipped from Cincinnati, O., *via* Quebec to England, and thence to Hamburg, where we are informed by our Minister in Berlin, it was "sold at auction and brought a fair price."

2. TOBACCO.

The United States, I have already stated, export about two-fifths of all the Tobacco consumed in Europe; and with greater attention to the cultivation of this article, the trade in it would be largely increased. In many of the countries of Europe, Tobacco is a Government monopoly. In France, the exclusive right to purchase imported and indigenous Tobacco, is invested in an Association called the *Regie*, under the supervision of the Minister of Finance. No one can purchase Tobacco, at wholesale, of any one but the *Regie;* and no one can retail without a license, which compels the purchaser to sell at prices fixed by that commission. Of late years, however, the system has been so far relaxed as to allow an importation for personal use, of a certain quantity by individuals, upon the payment by the importer of the duties, equal to the profits reaped by the *Regie* upon the sales. The capital of the Association, consisting of houses, offices, machinery, and Tobacco in store, is of the value of about $45,000,000, and there is usually kept on hand a supply of Tobacco sufficient to meet the demand for three years.

In the Northern nations, Denmark, Sweden, and Norway, Tobacco from the United States is largely consumed, but it is generally obtained in an indirect way from Holland, Bremen, and Hamburg. There are no restrictions of any kind on the sale of Tobacco in Denmark, and under the moderate duty of 89⅔ cents per 110⅓ lbs. on

Leaf, and $3.15 on Manufactured Tobacco, it is supposed that direct importations from the United States could not fail to be profitable.

Tobacco is consumed by nearly all the tribes of the East, and it is therefore one of the safest articles of export and barter, commanding in exchange the richest products of Oriental manufacture. It is an article especially worthy of attention by American merchants, who have a prescriptive right to the trade, and who have suffered themselves to be over-reached by foreign houses, as for instance in Morocco and Tunis, by the Greek merchants, and in Russia by two Bremen houses, who monopolize the trade.

3. OYSTERS.

These, and Ice and Granite, are among the great natural products of America. In Virginia alone it is estimated there are 1,580,000 acres of Oyster-beds on the sea-coast, harbors, bays, rivers, and creeks; and allowing *one-eighth of a bushel* to every square yard, there are at least 784,000,000 bushels of Oysters in the natural beds of Virginia. The tonnage employed in carrying these shell-fish from their natural beds, amounts to not less than 100,000 tons, and the quantity carried away annually approximates 30,000,000 bushels. From one hundred and fifty to two hundred vessels, mostly schooners, are employed in carrying Oysters to New Haven alone, the cargoes consisting of from two thousand to six thousand bushels. They are then replanted; where they remain from spring to fall, when they are taken up, opened, put into kegs or cans, which are afterward packed in boxes containing ice, and having a capacity equal to from twelve to twenty gallons each, and then shipped to the West and the South. This branch of the business is engrossed by some twenty firms, of whom at least one sends off daily from one thousand to fifteen hundred gallons; and so remunerative is the business, that we are informed one firm has cleared in four years from $75,000 to $100,000. Failure in the Oyster trade is rarely known, and when ordinary sagacity is exercised, moderate success at least may generally be predicted.

One branch of the trade, however, in which it is supposed a handsome profit could be realized, if properly managed, has not to my knowledge been attempted, and that is—the *exportation of Oysters to Europe.* The London Oyster, as most persons know, is remarkable only for its disagreeable, coppery taste and high price. It is barely possible that, by long use of nauseous bivalves, the taste of our brethren of the "fast-anchored isle" may have become so perverted that at first they may reject our Absecoms and Maurice Coves as insipid; but the time will inevitably come when the American Oyster will crown the board at the London Coffee-houses, and the authors of future *Noctes Ambrosianæ* will improvise songs in its praise. By means of steamships, Oysters can be conveyed to Europe more rapidly than to some portions of the West, at which they are now delivered; and the trade will in time, it is quite probable, amount to more than a million of dollars.

4. DRIED VEGETABLES.

These were among the articles that were first brought prominently into public notice by the London Exhibition of 1851. A Frenchman, by the name of Masson, had invented a simple and cheap process of preparing Vegetables, so that they would preserve their fresh flavor and quality for a long period of time. The samples exhibited by him consisted of White and Red Cabbages, Turnips, Brussels Sprouts, and various other vegetables. The mode of preserving them has been described briefly as follows: They are dried at a certain temperature (from 104° to 118°), which is neither so low as to cause them to dry slowly, nor so high as to cause them to dry too quickly; if the latter happen, they acquire a burnt taste, which destroys their quality. They lose from eighty-seven to eighty-nine per cent. of their water, or seven-eighths of their original weight; after which they are forcibly pressed into cakes, and are ready for use. "I saw," says Mr. Lindley, F. R. S., "a year ago, the original of a letter from the captain of the Astrolabe, a French vessel of war, speaking in the highest terms of the supply of these Vegetables for the use of that vessel during her voyage. The French navy generally mentions them in the most favorable terms, and no reason appears for doubting such statements. The specimens before you are, I repeat, seen under unfavorable circumstances. They ought to have been kept in tin and protected from the air; instead of which, they have been lying about for more than nine months in the Exhibition building, where they have been exposed to considerable dampness. Yet they are not injuriously affected, although they are absorbing moisture, as must necessarily happen in a damp place, and which, if it were to continue, would spoil them. Now, I think this is a matter of more consequence than it may appear to be, for the following reasons: It is usual to supply the Navy with preserved food of different kinds; and I am informed by a distinguished officer of the Antarctic Expedition under Sir James Ross, that although all the preserved meats used on that occasion were excel lent, and there was not the slightest ground for any com plaint of their quality, yet the crew became tired of the meat, but were never tired of the vegetables. This should show us that it is not sufficient to supply ships' crews with preserved meats, but that they should be supplied with vegetables also, the means of doing which is now afforded."

It would seemingly be a profitable as well as a benevolent speculation to prepare Vegetables in this manner in the Western States, where raw material can be obtained at a very low price, and ship them to the Eastern cities and to Europe as cheap food for the economical, and for seamen on long voyages.

5. BUTTER, CHEESE, AND PRESERVED MILK.

These are standard articles of export, but in order to be remunerative to shippers, it is generally essential that they be of first-rate quality. Losses almost invariably attend the shipping of an inferior article of this description. In England, American Butter of inferior quality is classed as grease, and commands the price of grease.

Within the last ten years very considerable progress has been made in the art of making Butter; and generally an important improvement has been effected in the dairy products of the United States, though a vast deal of Butter, which deserves no other designation than grease, is still produced annually, particularly in the West. In the production of superior Butter and Cheese the State of New York takes precedence, Pennsylvania being second, though it is probable that some of the dairies in the vicinity of Philadelphia, which supply that market, are unsurpassed by any in the world.

The importance of procuring Butter of the first quality being conceded, the best mode of doing this, and of preparing it for a distant market, is a consideration of primary importance, both with merchants and dairymen. Flint, in his excellent "Treatise on Milch Cows," states, that—

"A practical butter dealer, in New York, gives the following as the best mode of packing Butter, or putting it up for a distant market. The greatest care should be taken to free the Butter entirely from the milk by washing it, and washing it after churning, at a temperature so low as to prevent it from losing its granular character and becoming greasy. The character of the product depends in a great measure on the temperature of churning and working, which should be between sixty and seventy degrees Fahrenheit. If free from milk, eight ounces of Ashton salt is sufficient for ten pounds. Western salt should never be used, as it injures the flavor. While packing, the contents of the firkin should be kept from the air, by being covered with saturated brine. No undissolved salt should be put in the bottom of the firkin.

"Goshen Butter is reputed best, though much is put up in imitation of it, and sold at the same price. Great care should be taken to have the firkins neat and clean. They should be of white oak, with hickory hoops, and should hold about eighty pounds. Wood excludes air better than stone, and consequently keeps Butter better. Tubs are better than pots. Western Butter comes in coarse, ugly packages; even flour and pork barrels are sometimes used. Much of it must be worked over and repacked here before it will sell. It generally contains a good deal of milk, and if not worked soon becomes rancid. Improper packing in kegs, too large and soiled on the outside, makes at least three cents a pound difference. Whatever the size of the firkin, it must be perfectly tight and quite full of butter, so that when opened, the brine, though present, will not be found on the top. Until the middle of May, dairymen should pack in quarter-firkins or tubs, with white oak covers, and send directly to market as Fresh Butter. From this time until the fall frosts, there is but little change in the color and flavor with the same dairy, and it may be packed in whole firkins, and kept in a cool place. The fall Butter should also be packed separately in tubs.

"In the vicinity of good markets it is most frequently done up in pound lumps, neatly stamped, and tastefully prepared, so as to please the eye as well as the taste. No artificial coloring-matter is needed with Butter from rich milk, and summer pastures. In winter the color will depend somewhat on the richness of the food given to the cows, but it will not be so yellow and rich as at other times. Grains and carrots produce a richer straw-color than dry hay alone. As already seen in the statement of practical dairymen, the greatest care is required in the salting and seasoning. Over-salted Butter is not only less palatable to the taste, but less healthy than fresh, sweet Butter. The same degree of care is needed with respect to the box in which it is packed. I have often seen the best and richest flavored Butter spoiled by sending it to the exhibition, or to market, in new and improper boxes. A new pine-wood box should always be avoided.

"Butter that has been thoroughly worked, and perfectly freed from buttermilk, is of a firm and waxy consistence, so as scarcely to dim the polish of the blade of a knife thrust into it, leaving upon it only a slight dew as it is withdrawn. If it is soft in texture, and leaves greasy streaks of buttermilk upon the knife that cuts it, or upon the cut surface after the blade is withdrawn ; it shows an imperfect and defective process of manufacture, and is of poor quality, and will be liable to become rancid.

"An exceedingly delicate and fine-flavored Butter may be made by wrapping the cream in a napkin or clean cloth, and burying it a foot deep or more in the earth, from twelve to twenty hours. This experiment I have repeatedly tried with complete success, and I have never tasted Butter superior to that produced by this method. It requires to be salted to the taste as much as Butter made by any other process. A tenacious subsoil loam would seem to be best. After putting the cream into a clean cloth, the whole should be surrounded by a coarse towel. The Butter thus produced is white instead of yellow or straw-color."

With respect to firkins, and their size, referred to in the above extract, we may remark, that in shipping to foreign markets, it has been recommended that the kegs should be made of well-seasoned white oak, strongly hooped, and to contain, say, twenty or twenty-five pounds

This is an acceptable quantity to consumers, particularly in foreign markets; when prices are high, it will invariably be preferred even at an advance. The kegs, before being used, should be scalded with a stout pickle made with rock salt, and the pickle left in them until they are perfectly saturated therewith. If the kegs, after being filled with Butter and headed up, are to be packed in tierces; they should be closely packed, and the tierce filled with strong pickle of the same salt.

In Holstein, where very choice Butter is made, the firkins are made of beech-wood, charred on the inside, and made perfectly air-tight. The Butter is packed as closely as possible; then after sprinkling the top with salt, a thin layer of powdered charcoal is spread over the more effectually to exclude the air, and also to absorb those gases, the tendency of which is to hasten decomposition. When thus packed, after being properly salted, it will keep sweet for a long time, even in warm climates. The salt should always be of the purest description. Much Butter is spoilt from using salt containing *sulphate or chloride of lime.* When coarse salt is used, the latter, which adheres to the surface of the crystals, can be removed by pouring upon it a little warm water, and then allowing it to drain off.

Mr. Fogg, in an article on the subject, says: "It may not perhaps be known to all, that rancid Butter can be restored and rendered sweet by a very simple process. This is to work it thoroughly in cold water often changed; and after pressing out the water, salt it anew, and add a little sugar, say half an ounce to the pound. It will thus be rendered much more palatable, although it may not entirely recover that delicate flavor peculiar to new and sweet Butter, which, once lost, can never be restored."

20*

The preservation of *Milk*, to adapt it for sea voyages, is now extensively followed as a business by some dairymen. There are various modes of doing this—the one in most common use being to concentrate it by boiling. Another form is that of *solidified milk*, in which state it is perfectly soluble in water; and when so dissolved, it assumes the original form of Milk, and may be made into butter. A pound of this solidified Milk will make five pints, when dissolved in water. [For a description of the processes of concentrating and solidifying Milk, see "Flint on Milch Cows," pp. 212, 213.]

Of *Cheese* I have nothing to remark, except that it is indigestible stuff; and while it may be proper enough to preserve the art of making it in order to entertain our enemies in the event of war, it can scarcely be called a friendly act to ship it to a people with whom we are at peace. [For modes of making best qualities, see authority above named.]

6. SALTED MEATS—BEEF, PORK, ETC.

In Europe, especially in France, some important movements have recently been made tending to increase the demand for, by stimulating the consumption of, American salted provisions. In the three years from 1852 to 1854 inclusive, the price of fresh provisions in France advanced at such an extraordinary rate as to arrest the attention of the Government, and every means was resorted to, to encourage the use of Salted Beef among the mass of the French people. The duty on Salted Meats was lowered from \$5.58 to \$3.72, then to \$1.86, and in 1855 to 9½ cents per 100 kilogrammes (220 lbs.). Since that period the importation of salted provisions has so increased that it is probable that they will henceforth be a leading staple of export from the United States to France.*

To England, the American trade in this article has been limited by competition from Ireland and Russia, and still more, until recently, by the suspicions with which American-packed Beef and Pork were regarded by the English merchants, in consequence of the immense quantities of damaged provisions which have been exported to their markets. This latter obstacle, however, has been partly neutralized by the successful efforts of a few Beef-packing firms, especially by those in Philadelphia whose exports were so highly commended by the Inspec-

---

* "In 1834, the importation into France of Salted Meats reached only 3,527 quintaux, equal to about 777,844 lbs. After a lapse of twenty-one years, that is to say in January, 1855, and during that single month, the importations reached as high 3,720 quintaux, exceeding the importation of the whole year of 1852 by 203 quintaux, or 44,769 lbs.

"Prime Pork is imported into France in barrels of 331½ lbs. gross, in brine of gray salt, and is usually sold at from $14.80 to $15.81 the barrel.

"For the English markets, such Pork is exported from the United States in tierces of 304, 320, and 336 lbs., and in barrels of 200 lbs. American mess Pork is too fat for the French market, and seldom finds a purchaser. American sugar-cured hams, however, always find a ready market and a brisk competition among purchasers. Shoulders well cured and put up into hogsheads of 994 lbs. are equally in demand, and bring from $18.60 to $19.53 per 220 lbs.

"A similar feeling is manifested in France in behalf of her Colonies. By decree of 10th March, 1855, the duty on Salted Meats has been reduced as follows: Into Martinique, Guadaloupe, Guiana, and Reunion, Salted Meats of whatever origin, under whatever flag, pay 9½ cents per 220 lbs. This measure has attracted the attention of Pork merchants of the United States, and already heavy freights of this article have been forwarded to those islands."—(*Com. Relations*, Vol. I.)

tors for the English Navy, that certain brands of American Beef are now preferred in England when they can be obtained. There are now no insuperable obstructions to an immense increase in this trade; but to effect this desirable result, it is absolutely indispensable to adopt the most approved modes of curing and packing provisions. The enormous quantities of tainted meats of American, principally Western packing, that are sold at auction every year both at home and abroad, is a stigma upon the practical intelligence of the age, besides causing losses to the amount of millions annually. In view of this fact, and also to aid in diffusing information of value in putting up meats for domestic consumption, I have presumed to make and submit an analysis of the opinions of the most extensive and intelligent packers of Beef and Pork.

In 1852, the Secretary of the New York State Agricultural Society published a series of replies to queries propounded to various persons of intelligence and experience in this business; and though the answers, as usual, were contradictory, I deduce that the following points are essential to be observed in order to secure Beef of first-rate quality, and which will retain its quality for any required time.

1. The cattle should be four or five years old, stall-fed for at least six months before being slaughtered; and after being driven to market, a rest of about forty-eight hours should be afforded them, in order, as it is stated in the regulations for the Victuallers of the English Navy, "to give time for them to cool."

2. That the animals should be hung up in the slaughter-house about twenty-four hours before being cut up.

3. That Beef should not, if possible, be packed in warm weather, being liable to discoloration and to taint before the "salt strikes in."

4. That great care must be taken in the salting, both as respects the quality and quantity of salt; that *Liverpool boiled salt* should never be used, nor a superfluous quantity of any salt, however excellent; and that upon the right proportion of the saltpetre in the brine mainly depends the right color of the Beef.

5. That *seasoned* white oak or ash casks alone should be used, inasmuch as green-oak staves contain an acid that blackens the contents of the cask; and every precaution should be taken to preserve the casks in a sweet condition.

C. SEGUINE, Esq., an inspector and packer of Beef and Pork in New York, and under whose observation, it is represented, 25,000 to 50,000 barrels of these articles come annually, makes the following statement:—

"The most approved method of curing and packing Beef is first to 'strike' it in open vats or hogsheads, *i. e.*, pack loosely and cover with a pickle only, the pickle to be as strong as possible, and to contain saltpetre in the proportion of three ounces to the one hundred pounds of Beef. It is in this first process that the red or cherry color is given to Beef, and if not done in the first instance, no after application of saltpetre will supply the deficiency of color. As the market value of the article is greatly influenced by its color, too much care cannot be exercised to obtain this desideratum in perfection, and the process indicated above is decidedly the best. A week or ten days in the vats is sufficient to draw out the blood and fix the color, when it is packed with about twenty-five pounds of salt to the hundred pounds of Beef, and pickled with a strong new pickle. With proper care, Beef packed in this manner will keep for the longest voyages."

For Pork, he says—

"Pack with a light quantity of salt, say thirty pounds per barrel of two hundred pounds, and pickle with a strong pickle. No saltpetre is required for Pork; repack early in the spring with forty pounds of salt and a new strong pickle; hams should be packed with from seven to fifteen pounds of salt, the lesser quantity will make the finer ham; pickle with a strong pickle, adding about a pint of molasses and six ounces of saltpetre for every hundred pounds of ham. All Pork intended for smoking should have saltpetre applied to give the lean a lively cherry color; as also Pork packed for the English market, the use of saltpetre being general with English packers on all descriptions of Pork."

7. FRUITS—APPLES, PEARS, PEACHES, ETC.

European writers admit that the Apple Tree flourishes better in America than in Europe; and I presume that, for the production of fine fruits generally, no country has natural advantages superior to certain portions of the United States, while in none is less attention given, with few exceptions, to the growth of the best varieties of fruit trees, and the preservation of their products. The difference in quality, as affecting the sale price of fruits, is illustrated by the fact that Pears, for instance, are constantly being sold in the confectionery shops at twenty-five and fifty cents a piece, while the ordinary qualities will hardly command as much for a half bushel. In France, a gentleman recently raised three thousand Pears on a half acre, which he disposed of at twenty cents each for the entire lot; and another, it is reported, sold some Pears weighing four pounds, for ten dollars each. An extensive Apple-grower in the State of New York receives six dollars per barrel for all that he ships to Europe, and has realized a handsome fortune; whilst others, shipping inferior qualities at the same time, have lost money. It is certain that no article of produce will better reward attention and intelligence than fruits; and for shippers it is especially important, besides selecting the best qualities, to understand the best mode of preserving them.

Mr. H. MEIGS, of the American Institute of New York, some four or five years ago, recapitulated *eighteen* ways to preserve Apples, Pears, and Vegetables, viz.: 1st, to sweat them, and then put them in single layers on shelves of the fruit-room; 2d, in the same way, but covered with canvas of light kind, which should be dried occasionally when moistened by the fruit; 3d, in close drawers, one or several layers deep; 4th, in dry casks, without any thing, but they must be picked over in a few weeks carefully, the casks made perfectly dry, refilled, and headed up, and not disturbed till wanted for use; 5th, in garden pots of large size, boxes, casks, or jars, with pure and dry sand between the layers; 6th, in jars in which no sand or other things are put, the mouths of the jars covered with pieces of slate, and the whole buried in dry sand some inches below the air; 7th, in a dry, airy loft, with a covering of straw sufficient to keep off the frost; 8th, in baskets lined with straw; 9th, in close cellars, light excluded, for it is very injurious; 10th, in dark but airy vaults; 11th, on a small scale, under bell-glasses cemented down air tight, and this not on wood the least resinous, or the flavor is injured greatly; 12th, buried in boxes, each on four bricks, under other boxes inverted, and all buried so deep that the upper fruit shall be from one to two feet below the level of the earth; 13th, packed in thrashed grain, or in straw sacks; 14th, laid on wheat straw, without any covering; 15th, put in wheat or oat chaff; 16th, in flaxseed chaff; 17th, in pulverized charcoal; 18th, in dry fern leaves. To these I might add another, viz.: *to pack in salt barrels;* for it has been repeatedly ascertained that Apples packed in barrels that have contained coarse salt have been preserved fresh and sound when others, gathered at the same time, and put in other barrels, have wholly decayed. The methods enumerated apply to Pears as well as to Apples.

Mr. ROBERT J. PELL, the extensive and very successful grower of Fruits before referred to, who, by applying to the roots of his trees a compost containing a great variety of such ingredients as he supposed would be proper, has succeeded in making his Apple Trees bear *every year*, remarks:

"It has for years been a desideratum to preserve Fruits for winter store by some method not very costly. To do this reasonably, they should be picked from the tree by hand with great care, so as not to break the skin or bruise the fruit in the slightest degree, as the parts injured immediately decay, and ruin all the fruit coming in contact. Apples shaken from the tree become more or less injured, and totally unfit to be kept through the winter, or even shipped to the nearest ports. My pippin fruit is all picked by hand, by men from ladders, into half-bushel baskets, from them into a bushel and a half basket, in which they are carried in spring wagons, twelve at a time, to store-rooms covered with straw; where they are carefully piled three feet thick, to sweat and discharge by fermentation some thirty per cent. of water, when they are ready for barreling for shipment to Europe or elsewhere. If they reach their destination before the second process of sweating comes on, they will keep perfectly four months. I have kept them sound two years, and exhibited them at the end of that time at the Institute Fair, Castle Garden. They have been sent to Europe and China from my farm, packed in various ways, viz.: in wheat chaff, buckwheat chaff, oats, rye, mahogany sawdust, cork dust, wrapped separately in paper, and in ice. By the mode I now adopt, I can warrant them to bear shipment superior to any other, except ice. Some kinds of Apples are gathered from the trees before they are quite ripe, and the ripening is completed in the fruit-room; this is generally called the maturation of fruit."—For Pell's method of preparing land for Orchards see *Trans. of Am. Inst.*, 1851, p. 493.

Thus, while it is evident there is considerable latitude or diversity of practice in the details of preserving Fruits, it appears that all agree that they must be handled with great care, picked without being bruised, and that they should not be piled upon each other in masses, nor tumbled out of carts or barrels; that they should be kept in perfect darkness, except during an occasional opening to let in a moderate circulation of air. Further, especial attention must be paid to keeping them at a low temperature, always the same; but they should never be placed in damp cellars.

The foregoing observations are intended, while communicating some information on specific points, principally to illustrate the proposition, that a wide range of opportunity for fortune is open to men of enterprise, even in the beaten tracks of Commerce, by an improvement in the quality of common and ordinary articles of export, and in the modes of shipping them. The remarks in this, as in other cases, are intended to be suggestive, not exhaustive. By a little persevering examination, you will readily discover other articles which, by extra care in sending out only the best qualities, and put up in such a manner that they will retain their quality when they arrive, will be certain to bring back satisfactory returns. The influence that a merchant may exert in improving the quality of the staple agricultural products of a country, you will perceive, is very great. Were the merchants and agriculturists of the United States to co-operate and improve the average quality of their products in Tobacco, Salted Provisions, Butter, and Fruits, to the standard of excellence attained by a few individuals, the exports would be profitably increased to the amount of millions annually. And could Cottons be so cheapened in their manufacture in the United States as to successfully compete with those of any other country in the markets of passively commercial nations, as is probable they will be when the factory system is properly organized approximate to the plantation, we may reasonably anticipate that the balance of trade will be permanently in favor of this country.

But this is not the field, or certainly not an inviting field, for the operations of commercial *adventurers*. The man who is ambitious to make a small fortune speedily, —who, for instance, hopes, by chartering a vessel, loading her with a selected cargo, and, after a two or three years' cruise, to return with means sufficient to take his ease in his hotel, must turn her prow away from the beaten tracks of Commerce, and sail for lands where Nature is luxuriant and the most valuable products of Commerce abound, but are unappreciated by the inhabitants. He must seek a people who have few manufactures, little spirit of adventure, and who wait for the foreigner to come and trade with them. Three-fourths of the populous countries of the globe are of this description; and the only difficulty is, to determine upon the choicest localities. By way of suggestion, I would recommend him to direct his attention

First, to the commercial advantages of the *Indian Archipelago;* particularly the *Philippine Islands*, and *Singapore* and *Siam*.

The great fortunes that were formerly made in the East India trade I have already adverted to; and though times have changed, and new fields of commercial adventure have absorbed the attention of merchants, the Indian Archipelago, at this day, presents probably the best opening that can be mentioned for the profitable extension of Commerce. The products that centre there are of the kind that are highly valued in all the markets of the world—Spices, Scented Woods, Camphor, Betel, Ebony, Ivory, Horns, Hides, Tin, Gold-Dust, Tamarinds, Benzoin, Tortoise-shell, Rice, Beeswax, Gutta Percha, Bird of Paradise Feathers, Pearls, etc.; and a number specially adapted for the China market, as Edible Bird's Nests, Shark's Fins, etc. The population of the whole Archipelago is said to exceed twenty-five millions.

The *Philippine Islands* have an area of about 120,000 square miles, and a population of between three and a half and four millions. The two most important products are the *Manilla Hemp*, and *Sugar*, (which is in especial favor with the refiners of the United States); but all the tropical products grow in those Islands. The chief port is Manilla, whose exports include, besides Hemp and Sugar, Sapan-wood, Cigars, Cordage, Indigo, Coffee, Rice, Hides, Mother-of-Pearl Shell, Almaciga, Grass Cloth, Tortoise-shell, etc. The imports include Silks, Woolens, Haberdashery, Drugs, Clocks, Jewelry, and especially Cotton Goods. The following summary of the movements in the Manilla market during one month, (July, 1854), will show the general demand and price for Cotton fabrics:—

"British White Shirting, 14,150 pieces, viz.:

800 at	$1.98¾	per piece.
3,100 at	$2.12½ @ 2.25	"
3,300 at	2.31¼ @ 2.37½	"
4,850 at	2.43¾ @ 2.50	"
1,500 at	2.75	"
600 at	2.87½	"

"British Gray Shirting, 2,100 pieces, viz.:

1,000 pieces, 40 inches, at	$2.18¾	per 40 yards.
500 pieces, 40 inches, at	2.31¼	" " "
250 pieces, 42 inches, at	2.37½	" " "
360 pieces, 45 inches, at	2.62½	" " "

"British Long Cloths, 4,700 pieces, viz.:

4,500 pieces, 39 inches, at	$2.12½	per 40 yards.
200 pieces, 43 inches, at	2.75	" " "

"British Gray Domestics, 2,650 pieces, viz.:

650 pieces, 29 inches, at	$1.62½ @ $1.81¼	per 40 yards.
50 pieces, 27 inches, at	2.22¾	" " "
600 pieces, 36 inches, at	2.09	" " "
1,350 pieces, 39 inches, at	2.50 @ 2.56¼	" " "
British Gray Drills, 300 pieces, 29 inches, at	$2.12½	per 32 yards.
American Brown Jeans, 800 pieces, at	3.06¼	" " "
" " Drills, 2,800 pcs., at	2.37½ @ 2.50	" " "

"The articles designated in the preceding summary are such as command, at all times, a ready market in the trade of these Islands, and generally at the prices indicated.

"When imported, they are subject to a duty of fourteen per cent., as are nearly all other articles from foreign countries. The export duty on Hemp is two per cent., Shells and Ratans one per cent.; all other articles three per cent."—(*Com. Rel.* I., 172.)

Singapore is a city of over 60,000 inhabitants, and one of the most flourishing of the East. To this port some considerable American trade is already established, and Tobacco, Naval Stores, Pitch, Tar, Copper-sheathing and Bolts, and Pine Boards and Spars, generally sell at satisfactory prices; while the *Teas*, which come down from China, and *Wild Cinnamon*, "thin quill, well-cleaned and covered neatly with gunny bags," have often proved a highly remunerative return cargo. *Gambier*, an article that is largely in demand for printing and tanning purposes, is also imported; and *India Rubber* and Tin, (which is produced in quantity,) have for years remunerated importers.

Another, perhaps more novel and attractive opening for trade, is presented in *Siam*, which all writers concur in representing as one of the most fertile countries in the East, distinguished alike for its Mineral and Vegetable products. Until quite recently, the policy of Siam was opposed to trade with foreigners; but in 1855, Sir J. BOWRING succeeded in effecting a Treaty, which is deemed very favorable for future Commerce; and more recently, Mr. TOWNSHEND HARRIS, Commissioner for the United States, concluded a Treaty, containing provisions which are said to be almost identical with the British Treaty. And so radical is the change in the feelings and policy of the present Government, as respects Commerce with foreigners, that it is currently reported an American merchant, established at Shanghai, in China, has taken the King of Siam into partnership with him, as junior partner in his mercantile house.

The contributions which Siam can make to foreign Commerce are very valuable, comprising Sugar, Pepper, Lac, Benzoin, Gamboge, Tin, Cardamoms, Ivory, Horns, Hides, and others of minor importance. The *Sugar*, which constitutes the principal return for British imports, is especially valued for its whiteness and fine strong grain, and the soil is admirably adapted for its cultivation. *Rice* is extremely abundant and consequently cheap; the ordinary price being 61 cents per 133 lbs. *Rosewood* and *Ebony* are shipped largely to China and Singapore. The *Hemp* grown in Siam is just becoming known to foreign traders, and it is particularly recommended on account of its great strength, and its glossy and silky texture, which would allow of its being woven and mixed with silk fabrics. Its moderate price, $6.10

for 133⅓ lbs., would enable it to compete successfully with that of Manilla.

Bowring, in his work on Siam, gives the following as prices of Siamese produce at Bangkok, April, 1855:—

"Sugar, white, 7¼ to 7½ ticals per picul; do., 2d quality, 6¾ to 7 do.; 3d quality, 6½ do.; Sugar, red, 3 do.; Pepper, black, 8 to 9 do.; Lac, old, 11 do.; Lac, new, 8 do,; Gamboge, 30 to 35 do.; Gum Benzoin, 40 to 60 do.; Cardamoms, 230 to 400 do.; Tin, 30 to 35 do.; Tallow, 8 to 12 do.; Cotton, 12 to 13 do.; Cotton uncleaned, 4 do.; Cocoa-nut Oil, 9 do.; Rice, 30 ticals per coyan of 100 baskets; Hides, 4 ticals per picul; Horns, 6 do.; Sapan-wood, ½ to 1 tical; Hemp, 10 ticals per picul.

"Opium has become one of the most important articles of importation; its consumption is said to be about 1,200 chests, which represents a value of nearly £150,000 sterling."*

---

* "The picul is 133⅓ lbs. The money that circulates in Siam consists principally of silver *ticals* or *bats*, of the value of 2*s.* 6*d.* sterling with smaller coins, constituting its subdivisions. The coin is an irregular ball, but has two impressions, made by blows, bearing the King's mark. There is a double tical—a half tical, called *song-salung*—a quarter tical, the *salung*—and the half *salung*, or *fuang*, which represents twelve hundred *cowries*. These shells are generally employed for the small purchases of the people, about one hundred of them representing a farthing. They are collected on the Siamese coast. Pallegoix says, that for a *fuang* (less than 4*d.*) fifty or sixty varieties of vegetables may be purchased in the public markets. Four ticals make the Siamese ounce—twenty ounces the catty, or Siamese pound of silver. The larger amounts are reckoned in pounds of silver, of which the sterling value is about £10. Gold coins, resembling the silver in form and size are issued, but in small quantities. Copper coins are issued by individuals in the provinces; and stamped glass or enamel, bearing inscriptions, is also used as a circulating medium. The Government issues promissory notes of various amounts, even to one-eighth of a tical. They do not seem extensively current, and, I believe, have not experienced any depreciation."

The following list will be found to contain all the manufactures which are most adapted to Siamese consumption:—

White and Gray Long Cloths,
" " Madapollans,
" " Cambrics,
" " Jaconets,
Book Lappets,
Velvets, Plain and Figured,
Checked Fancy Muslins,
American Drills,
Merinos, of assorted colors,
Cotton Umbrellas,
Figured Long Cloths,
Dyed Cambrics,
Dyed Long Cloths,
Prints, Chintzes,
Furniture, and Neutrals,
Siam *Chowls*, or Dresses,
Turkey-red Cloth,
Gray Cotton Twist,
Turkey-red Twist,
Imperial Red and Blue Twist,
Long Ells,
Ladies' Cloth,
Spanish Stripes,
Canvas.
Iron, Steel, Lead, Spelter,
Earthenware, assorted,
Glassware and Lamps, ass'd,
Muskets, Gun-locks,
Brimstone, Beeswax,
Cowries, Flintstone, Musket Flints, etc.

"The imports from China and India are even more varied, and consist of almost every article of manufacture, trifling or important, produced in those countries; these being required not only to meet the tastes and requirements of the Siamese, but also to supply the wants of the natives of India and China, many of whom are domiciled in Siam."—See *Commercial Relations*, Vol. I., Art. SIAM.

A word as to the mode of transacting business with the Islands of the Indian Archipelago. Payments are made principally by "documentary bills," under letters of credit from Brown, Shipley & Co., and Baring Brothers & Co. "The captain or agent draws at six months' sight, as soon as his cargo has been collected, packed up, stowed on board, and bills of lading signed; and then the drafts go forward, the acceptors secured by bills of lading, on the back of which the invoices are indorsed. As the mail going through to England is some two months, the owners of the cargo have the benefit of eight months' credit, or four months' leeway, after the arrival of the property, on an average passage of one hundred and twenty days, thus giving them ample time to dispose of it and realize to meet the bills. The shrewd financier this way, provided he possesses the credit to get a fair start, can do any amount of business, and make or lose a fortune by bold speculations, under good or bad judgment."

Secondly, I would commend to your consideration the *Ottoman Empire*, which embraces Turkey-in-Europe, Asia Minor, Syria, Egypt, and the other tributary States in Africa and Asia. In the London Crystal Palace in 1851, as you may have observed in the Reports, Turkey contributed some of the most valuable raw produce, Gums, Dyes, etc., and some of the richest-embroidered fabrics of Silk and Wool that were there exhibited. An official enumeration of her exports comprises Wool, Goats' Hair, Cattle, Horses, Hides, Hare Skins, Wheat, Raw Cotton and Silk, Tobacco, Raisins, Figs and Almonds, Mastic and other Gums, Gall-nuts, Vallonia, Leeches, Honey, Wax, Saffron, Madder, Anise Seed, Linseed, Turpentine, Safflower, Orpiment, Meerschaum Pipes, Whetstones, Carpets, Silk and Cotton Fabrics, Leather, Copper, and Metallic Wares, with Arabian, Persian, Indian, and Chinese goods. The chief ports, moreover, are centres of trade for a vast country in and beyond her limits. Adrianople, for instance, supplies all the fairs throughout Roumelia and Bulgaria. To Aleppo, caravans bring Pearls, Shawls, Indian and Chinese Goods, from Bussorah and Bagdad; Camels from Arabia, Cotton Stuffs and Thread, Morocco Leather, Goats' Hair, and Galls, from the pachalics of Mosul, Diarbekir, Orfa, and Aintab, &c.:

Furs, Goats' Hair, Wax, Gum, Gum Ammoniac, &c., from Asia Minor; Silk, Mocha Coffee, Soap, Scented Woods, Ambergris, Drugs, and Pearls from Syria and Arabia; Rice, Coffee, and Egyptian produce from Latakia; Silk Manufactures from Brusa and Damascus; European and United States Cotton Stuffs, Woolens, Printed Muslins, Hardware, Watches, Wrought Amber, and Fur from Smyrna and Constantinople.

To the port of Salonica, it is supposed that merchants from the United States, could ship colonial produce advantageously, inasmuch as it is now supplied at second and third hand by England and Austria. The State Department remark, upon information furnished from the Consuls:

> "There is nothing to prevent the United States from participating in the trade in this species of merchandise. Neither Austria nor England could compete with this country in supplying the vast quantities of colonial produce, and the cheap White and Printed Cottons which are required for consumption in this market. In addition to the supplies needed to meet the daily wants of its one hundred thousand inhabitants, Salonica furnishes large quantities of Colonial and Manufactured Goods for the yearly fairs of Parlepi, Lucca, and Seras, where the sales are always made for *cash*. The high price of French Cotton and Woolen Cloths will always preclude the merchants of France from successful competition in this branch of trade; and the heavy expenses attending the circuitous trade through Marseilles, Smyrna, Constantinople,. Trieste, and Venice, would necessarily favor direct exportations from the United States. The prices at Salonica are always from ten to twelve per cent. higher than at Constantinople or Smyrna."

An English authority, referring to this trade, furnishes a hint worthy of attention by those interested in the Turkish trade. He says: "A demand for British cotton manufactures of all descriptions daily increases, and every year there is some new outlet of sufficient importance for the establishment of agencies in the interior, by the importers at Salonica; hence the prospect of an increase of the import trade, in proportion to the increasing value of the export trade. The Austrian and Saxon manufacturers have again turned their attention to this part of Turkey, and are sending larger parcels of low Cotton Goods."

With *Syria* a considerable trade has already been transacted by mercantile houses in Boston, New York, and Philadelphia, particularly in importing the washed and unwashed Wools in which that country excels. In 1854, a cargo of refined Sugar was shipped to Beirût, and sold at a large profit; and it is supposed that Cotton Goods would find a ready sale, if, as in the English goods, a uniformity were established in the number of yards contained in the pieces.*

Egypt, in the valley and delta of the Nile, possesses a large area of exceedingly fertile land; while its principal port, Alexandria, is becoming the seat of very extensive foreign trade, it having amounted, in 1850, to $19,000,000. In 1854, Edwin de Leon, Consul-general of the United States at Alexandria, wrote:

"Egypt has no trade with the United States, but there

---

* The United States Consul at Beirût, writing under date of October 5th, 1855, says: "I learn, upon the best authority, that the people of this country consider the cloth manufactured in the United States superior in quality to that of England; but, since the pieces of American goods do not uniformly contain the same number of yards, like the English pieces, they are slow to purchase, owing to the power of old ideas and habits. It would be of great service to the manufacturers if they understood this fact, and would regard it.'"

is a good field open for something to be done in that way, as the coarse Cotton Goods which we manufacture so extensively for China and South America, and which defy English competition in those markets, are precisely such fabrics as are required by the common people of this country; namely, blue, bleached and unbleached Sheetings and Shirtings, to which might be added Cotton Drills, blue, bleached, and brown Ticks and Stripes. Lumber of all kinds for building purposes might also be introduced, as well as Staves for Sugar Refineries and Distilleries, Boots, Shoes, Wooden-ware, and an infinity of articles manufactured in New England, especially the common kinds of Iron-ware and Edged-tools, which can be furnished from thence cheaper than from England, and of a better quality."

The State Department remark:

"During the year 1855, an English house at Alexandria sent two vessels to New York, and an Austrian house two more to the same destination, loaded chiefly with Gums, Rags, &c. There is no doubt but that a profitable trade might be established between the United States and the port of Alexandria, by sending out such merchandise as usually finds a market in Egypt, and receiving in return the rich and varied exports of that extensive Emporium."

It is said that the necessary capital has been subscribed for constructing the long-talked-of Ship Canal to connect the Mediterranean and Red Seas; and in the event of its completion, a few good American mercantile houses, established at Port Said on the Mediterranean, or Suez on the Red Sea, will undoubtedly command an extensive business.

Thirdly. At no very distant day, *Africa* will present a splendid theatre for the operations of the adventurous trader. The explorations of Livingstone, Barth, and Bowen reveal an unexpected development of civilization, in regions remote from the influence of the slave-trader, alike gratifying to the philanthropist and to the merchant. The United States already participate largely in the trade with the Eastern coast of Africa; but Americans have neglected the Western, of which the central portion alone exports annually to Europe a value of $15,000,000, at a commercial exchange in favor of the European merchants of about five hundred per cent. It is estimated that what is called the Western Coast contains *fifty millions* of inhabitants. Its exports to Great Britain consist of Barwood, Camwood, Ebony, Guano, Gum Animi, Gum Copal, Untanned Hides, Palm Oil, Orchal, Elephants' Teeth, and Bees'-wax — the heaviest item being Palm Oil, of which the value, in 1854, exceeded $7,000,000.

Fourthly. But in the present, there is a less mystical and colder, but more settled and safer country, which invites alike the merchant and the manufacturer. I allude to *Russia.* The great fortunes that have been made there by machinists have been already incidentally mentioned; and judging from the reported prepossession of the Russian Government in favor of uniting the two countries more closely in commercial relations, and from the fact that large quantities of the produce of the United States, particularly Cotton and Tobacco, are shipped to Russia at second and third hand, there are seemingly excellent chances for American merchants to acquire large profits in a direct trade.

Upon this subject, and respecting the commodities that could profitably be shipped to and from Russia, G. M. HUTTON, Esq., American Vice-Consul at St. Petersburg, makes some very valuable suggestions, as will appear by the following lengthy extract from his communication to the Government:

"Having made a list of nearly all the articles of United States production which have been, or may be, imported here, with the present tariff on each reduced to United States weights, measures, and coins, it may be of some service to give it, together with some remarks.

"Cotton, 25 copecks per pood = 52 cents per 100 lbs. avoirdupois, or about $2⅓ per bale.

"Tobacco, in leaves or bundles, six silver rubles per pood = 12½ cents per lb. avoirdupois.

"Cigars, two silver rubles per lb., Russian = $1.35 per lb. avoirdupois; are weighed with the package. These are mostly made in Germany, of mixed Tobacco, though marked and labeled as from Havanna. Tobacco for smoking, in rolls, carrots, or cwt., 60 copecks per lb. Russian = 46½ cents per lb. avoirdupois.

"Biscuit 5–6 cents per lb. avoirdupois. The best American are much admired, and a moderate quantity may be regularly imported.

"Cider in bottles, 22½ cents per bottle; would require to be of first-rate quality; with less duty, the demand would be large.

Apples, per cask of two ancres (= 2½ bushels), 90 cents; large demands and good prices for choice quality.

"*Furs*—Muskrat, at 10⅛ cents per lb. avoirdupois; Raccoon, 54 cents per lb. avoirdupois. *Buffalo Skins*, dressed, 50 1-10 cents per lb. avoirdupois; with a lower duty, a very large quantity of the two latter would be used.

"*Clocks*, wooden, 37½ cents each; may have brass wheels; would require a regular depot; should be ornamented in gay colors.

"*Fish*, salt and smoked, 4⅛ cents per lb. avoirdupois. As the Russians keep Lent very strictly, and have a second one of three weeks in August, the use of Fish is very great; and as a considerable trade in Codfish from Norway has latterly sprung up, I think that first-quality dried Codfish may, hereafter, form an important item in our shipments to Russia.

"*Extracts of Dye-woods*, 4⅙ cents per lb. avoirdupois.

"*India-rubber* and *Gutta-percha* goods, $6.22 per 100 lbs. avoirdupois.

"*Oysters* in cans, 2 1-12 cents per lb. avoirdupois; are weighed with the can.

"*Quicksilver*, 5 cents per lb. avoirdupois; demand regular. A supply may be contracted for from California.

"*Rice*, 1¼ cents per lb. avoirdupois; Carolina preferred, and not received as antagonist to their own grain.

"*Sumac*, same duty.

"*Spermaceti*, $2.95 per 100 lbs. avoirdupois.

"*Spokes* and *Felloes*, 37½ cents per hundred. Machine-made would do well as soon as known. Makers wishing to occupy the market, should stamp their names.

"*Anthracite Coal*, free. The chief Russian mines being of that kind, it is intended to use it in their Navy. A supply from the United States might be contracted for; they will form large depots.

"*Front Brick*—to try the market. Bricks are free, when of the Russian legal forms. The regular size is the same as the French, and nearly the same as ours. St. Petersburg being built mostly of Brick, of quite common quality, requiring to be plastered to protect it, the best Front Brick may prove very acceptable, especially when the required forms for cornices, &c. can be given. The freight would be cheap with cargoes of cotton.

"High-pressure *Steam Engines*, suitable for saw-mills, free when for special use. Must be cheap and substantial; would require a regular depot. Machinery for working wood, free.

"Plows, Harrows, Cultivators and the like, and Agricultural machines, free; only the most approved would sell.

"*Staves*, and *Casks* in pieces, free. A large business may be established, especially as the improvements in the interior communications progress.

"*Ships* free, but with charges on changing flags equal to one per cent. on the price.

"*Timber* for ship-building, masts and spars, free. Woods of all kinds for the use of cabinet-makers and turners, viz., Sassafras, Cypress, Palm, Cedar, Lignumvitæ, Mahogany, and other high-priced woods, 5-12 cents per lb. avoirdupois, or equal to about $23 per thousand feet on Mahogany; about $14.50 on Walnut; and about $16.33 on Maple. A depot well supplied direct could do a steady, good business.

"Contracts might be made for supplying Machine-made Rifles, and Rifled-Muskets, which would be preferred to the Liege hand-made. Liege price of Rifled-muskets, $9.30 This Government could be easily induced to order an extensive set of machinery for making small arms like that made for the English Government.

"Any tools or machinery sent here must be of well-established reputation. They will adopt and use, but dislike experimenting. Cotton and Tobacco seem to be the articles on which a reduction of the Russian tariff would be the most important to us, though the duty on Cotton is only equal to 52 cents per 100 lbs. American weight; yet it amounts to about $400,000 a year, and is rapidly increasing. The duty might be negotiated off for an equivalent. The Russian Tobacco is mostly of an inferior quality; and a large reduction on their specific duty can be made without affecting the Russian planting interest, and with much benefit to their revenue.

Still the only means of obtaining special reductions is by equivalent reductions on Russian articles. Considering that greatly the larger part of the American Cotton, and that nearly all the American Tobacco brought here is at second-hand from England and Germany, and sent by the merchants and in the vessels of those countries, it would seem to me very advisable to confine any negotiation respecting those articles to reduction of duty on the direct importation from the producing country. The object would be more easily attained, as there would not only be less opposition, but a very strong existing feeling here would be gratified thereby. I feel warranted in saying that the American tonnage entering here annually may be speedily doubled, and go on steadily increasing, and the trade pass at the same time into the hands of American merchants. Naturally, our shipping should bring nearly all the transatlantic Tobacco and Cigars; but the latter are mostly made in Germany, and sent from thence, though called and marked as American. A Tobacco depot from which to supply the demand regularly, is now furnished in using the Government warehouses, and paying the duty as withdrawn therefrom provided that be done within twelve months; but the charge for storage should be reduced.

"A reduction of duty and storage would have a most beneficial effect on the direct trade. The foreign Tobacco, though mostly grown in the United States, is nearly all brought from Bremen, and the trade is in the hands of two very respectable houses originally from thence. The partners (five) came here poor, and are now very rich. In future, such fortunes should be made off American produce by American citizens; and I think it is now in the power of our Government to secure that result.

"Having made some observations on the items which I think may add to our exports to Russia, I beg leave to examine those which may add to our future imports therefrom.

"The steady increase of the exportation of Flax to England, along with the great increase of its culture in Ireland, both in face of the immense increase in the manufacture of Cotton, prove clearly that the two materials are not naturally antagonists, else flax could not have sustained the rivalry, and is a fact worthy of serious consideration. I think that our manufacturers would do well to imitate the English in making cloths of Flax and Cotton mixed, which are coming into such extensive use. To do so successfully, Russian Flax must be admitted on as favorable terms as into England.

Eminently agricultural as Russia is, it must of necessity, from its position, and the existence of such extensive regions not otherwise available, continue to be still more specially pastoral, and the various annual productions will constantly increase in importance. It is true that the exportation of Tallow is checked; but as the establishments for changing it into Stearine and Veline extend into the interior, the exportation in these modified forms will again increase.

"The number of Cattle in Russia, equaling that for Austria, Prussia, and France, and of Horses being more than double of that for those three countries together, the excess of disposable raw Hides is evident, and will be more available for exportation as the interior communications improve. But the force of this consideration is increased, especially with reference to the United States, by the fact that nine-tenths of all the cattle slaughtered in Russia are killed during October and November; that is, the Hides are crowded on the market just in time for the last vessels sailing before the close of the navigation.

"The Hides would also arrive out in good condition, on account of the season. Great Britain imports as freely as we do from South America; yet about one-third of all the Hides exported from Russia go to England.

"The Russian Wool is generally of common to inferior quality, 90,000,000 pounds averaging twenty cents per pound; yet over 20,000,000 pounds are exported, chiefly to England. Though England is a large producer of Copper, yet more than one-fourth of the Russian exportation goes there.

"I cite these exportations to England to show that the prices are down to the level of the general market of the world, and that the United States may also be advantageously supplied from Russia.

In low-priced Woolen Cloths, Russia can supply a strong, serviceable, well-dyed article cheaper than England. The Cloths of which the uniform of the Imperial Guards is made cost on an average forty-nine cents per square yard, and the soldiers of the line an average of thirty-eight and a half cents per square yard. But as it is notorious that the Government pays a large per-centage more on contract goods, or when made at Government factories, than the same can be purchased by a merchant for cash, I think that the Cloths for the Guards may be purchased for an average of forty cents, and for the line at thirty-one cents per square yard. The cloths for the Guards are not only good but handsome. In the Government of Moscow alone they are made to the value of $10,000,000 annually; so that a large demand can be easily supplied.

The price of Butchers' Beef in the market, as the hotels buy it, after rejecting the neck and other rough pieces, is five cents per American pound, and choice pieces at eight cents. In Moscow it sells much cheaper. I therefore feel warranted in saying, if good curing and packing houses were established at Moscow, or further south when the rail-roads shall be made, Russia could supply Salt Beef of prime quality for exportation cheaper than any other country, and to a vast amount. The Baltic is the better outlet. I was surprised to find that, from the gradual decline in the exportation of Iron, and the increased production of Copper in Russia, the total average value of the latter exported in 1851–'53 was ninety per cent. greater than that of the former.

"As England takes about one third in competition with her own productions, the price must be within the limits of profitable exportation to the United States; yet none is sent.

"Besides the principal articles named, there are many minor ones, which together would make a sensible addition to the trade. I will now only mention one—a small, red berry, called the *Broosneeka*, a variety of the bilberry, of which the Russians consume a great quantity, and are very fond. They have a slightly astringent taste, and are considered healthy. In their natural state they will only keep a few days in the air; yet they require a very moderate quantity of sugar to make a very cheap preserve, which is used with meat or on the tea-table. But in the country advantage is taken of a peculiarity to keep them fresh. By filling casks three-fourths or four-fifths with the berries, and then completely with pure water, so as to exclude the air, they will remain in good condition in a cool cellar until well into the next summer, and serve as a dessert. As they are gathered in September, they may be taken in water to the United States, and would enter under the twenty per cent. duty."

Fifthly. But nearer home, even in the southernmost part of the great Western Continent, the enterprising Yankee trader may find a land more prodigal in bounties than any of those we have mentioned, where mountains, plains, and valleys teem with mineral and vegetable treasures, and where, if man will labor one day, nature will provide him food for seven. In *South America*, a man combining the qualities which make a successful explorer with a thorough mercantile knowledge of tropical commodities, may place himself in a position to pick up a fortune more speedily than probably in any other country. Difficulties he must encounter, and undergo hardships; but, within a decade, a sensible improvement has been effected in some of the principal States, both in the stability of the Governments and the enterprise of the people. Let him go, for instance, to the Valley of the Amazon, and he will be amazed, almost terrified, at the tremendous productive forces of Nature. Listen to Lieut. Maury:

"From the mouth to the sources of the Amazon, piled up one above the other, and spread out Andean-like over steppe after steppe, in beautiful, unbroken succession, are all the climates and all the soils, with the capacities of production, that are to be found between the regions of everlasting summer and eternal snow. The Valley of the Amazon is the place of production for *India Rubber*—an article of commerce which has no parallel as to the increase of demand for it, save and except in the history of our own great staple since the invention of the Cotton gin. The *Sugar Cane* is found there in its most luxuriant growth, and of the richest saccharine development. It requires to be planted but once in twenty years. *Peruvian Bark*,—cascarilla and cinchona as the Spaniards call it—is found in the Valley of the Amazon, and nowhere else. It is cut from the banks of one of its navigable tributaries, packed upon the backs of Peruvian sheep, carried up beyond the clouds into the regions of perpetual snow on mountain tops, and transported beyond the Andes six hundred miles to the Pacific Ocean; arrived there, the ceroon, which at the place of production in the great Amazon basin, was worth only a few pence, now commands from eighty to one hundred dollars.

"In the valley of the Amazon are mines of silver and gold of immense yield. There, too, are found and wrought the great quicksilver mines of the world; and there, too, situated far down toward the Atlantic, in that valley, are the mines of Diamonds, of Gems, and precious Stones, which have dazzled princes, lent splendor to the crowned heads of Europe, and added brilliancy to the pageants of all people.

"The Cinnamon of Amazonia is superior to that of Ceylon; its Gums and Ornamental Woods are said to be of surpassing beauty, variety, excellence, and value.

"Men of science, who have studied the physical conditions of Amazonia and India, and who have compared the climatology of the two regions, are of the opinion that in this magnificent wilderness of America are to be found both soil and climate suitable for the production of every Spice, Gum, Resin, and Drug that is grown in the East."

In *Paraguay*, the adventurer will find the vegetable kingdom rich, especially in medicinal herbs—Rhubarb, Sarsaparilla, Jalap, Bryonia Indica, Balsam of Copaiva, Nux Vomica, Liquorice, and Ginger. Of dye-stuffs, too, there is an immense variety--the Cochineal, which feeds on a species of the cactus; two distinct kinds of Indigo; vegetable Vermilion; Saffron; Golden Rod; with other plants, producing all the tints of dark red, black, and green. Many of the forest trees yield valuable gums, not yet familiar to commerce or medicine; and they comprise some of the most delicious perfumes and incense that can be imagined. Others, again, are like amber, hard, brittle, and insoluble in water. Some Cedars yield a gum equal to Gum Arabic; others a natural glue, which, when once dried, is unaffected by heat or dampness. On the plains vast quantities of Hides, Hair, Horns, Bones, Tallow, &c., are lost for want of transportation.

In the country bordering on the Upper Paraguay, which, by Treaty between Paraguay and Brazil, ratified June 14, 1856, it is stipulated shall henceforth be free to general commerce and navigation, there is a like or even greater abundance of natural resources and wealth. In the volume recently issued by the State Department, the following remarks are made with regard to the products.

"*Indigo*, not cultivated, but grows wild in abundance; Sarsaparilla, Sassafras, and Ipecacuanha, exceedingly abundant. Coffee grows wild—any quantity may be gathered; and on the Peruvian coast it is preferred to the Mocha. Tamarinds worth from fifty cents to one dollar for twenty-five pounds. Rice, from eighteen to twenty-five cents per arroba. Copaiva and other balsams, abundant. India-rubber exceedingly abundant, and no value attached to it. Raisins of all kinds very abundant; also Gum-lac. Timber of various descriptions—some varieties said to be of good quality for ship-building; cabinet-woods, abundant and beautiful; dye-woods, gums, and drugs of great variety; Nutmegs, different in form from the common article, being oblong; *Almonds* of large size and very agreeable; *Cinnamon* very abundant; *Peruvian Bark* very abundant; can be delivered on the borders of the river for $15 per cwt, exclusive of the duty to the Government, which is now $20 per cwt.: *Sucupira*, a febrifuge, regarded in Bolivia as better than Peruvian Bark, very abundant; *Tar*, very abundant; as also *Vanilla;* a material for cables, ropes and cordage (the bark of a tree, and described by some naturalists as being as durable and strong as the Russian hemp); *Cocoa Nuts*, very abundant; Straw for hats, resembling the Tuscany; *Tropical fruits* in great variety.

"In addition to these vegetable productions, are Gold, Wax Honey, Tortoise, Cattle, Horses, Hides, and Horns, and Skins of wild animals (Tigers, Wolves, &c.); and there may be added, also as productions of the high regions, Skins of the Chinchilla, and Wool of the Llama, Sheep, and Alpaca."

The *Mineral* resources of the country bordering on the Upper Paraguay and its tributaries, are as abundant as the Vegetable and Agricultural. The rich Province of Matto Grosso, in Brazil, abounding in Diamonds, Gold and Silver, can be reached direct from the seaports, Buenos Ayres and Montevideo, by a highway as broad as the Mississippi. In this region, it is stated, there are upward of *one thousand valuable* mines unworked, it having hitherto been found impossible to convey machinery thither across the mountains from the Pacific coast. The expedition now being sent out to Paraguay, it is to be hoped, will give a new impetus to the development of this country.

In *Venezuela*, in the vicinity of Maracaibo, and up the Orinoco, a merchant will see abundant opportunities for profitable trade that will tempt him to share in the profits now being enjoyed almost exclusively by foreigners. With advantage of proximity from port to port, and the real desire of the Government of Venezuela to trade with Americans, it is remarkable that more capital and zeal are not embarked in this trade; especially inasmuch as many important products can be obtained as plentifully and as cheap in those markets, as in any other part of South America. Coffee, Cocoa, Cured Hides, Indigo, Fustic, Tobacco, Cotton, Cattle, Mules and Horses, can generally be obtained on very advantageous terms for Cotton and Woolen goods, Flour, Provisions, Hardware, Soap, Furniture, Glassware, Brandies, Wines, &c.

It is not to be supposed, however, that South America is a *terra incognita* to American citizens. The sappers and miners of the great army of fortune-seekers in that country are already there. The *Commercial Bulletin* of New Orleans, referring to the enterprise of American citizens, remarked: "In Lima they are projecting turnpikes, and teaching the people the best mode of conquering impossibilities; in Brazil, people from the States are growing Cotton, and showing how it can be manufactured without taking it all the way to Liverpool or Manchester. In the States of the Plata, Edward A. Hopkins is building an 'American wharf.' By the last advices from Buenos Ayres, we learn that this company of the 'American Wharf' was in active operation, and the structure daily drawing to completion. The papers publish regular bulletins of its progress, and are loud in their praises of its American projector and engineer. The stock, at latest advices, was sold at twenty-five per cent. premium." [For statistics of present trade with South America, see *Cyclopedia of Commerce, and Commercial Relations;* and for interesting descriptions of the country, see *Herndon's and Gillis' Report, Stevenson's South America,* and other books of travel.]

Fifthly. Passing from South America, let us pay a flying visit to the land toward which the eyes of the whole commercial world are now turned, viz., the flowery kingdom, *China.* In common with the rest of mankind, you are doubtless aware that Treaties have been recently concluded between the United States, Great Britain, and China, securing to merchants of the former countries access for trading purposes to the whole of China, and placing them, if the treaty stipulations be faithfully observed, in a more favorable position, particularly as respects freedom from Mandarin exactions, than the native trader. There can be no doubt that American Commerce will share largely in the benefits to accrue from future trade with China, both because an American merchant will not be embarrassed by the hostile feelings which have been engendered against the English and French by the late war; and because some articles of American manufacture, as coarse Cottons for instance, have already secured the vantage ground of preference. But the danger to be apprehended, if we may judge from past instances, when markets have been opened to which the attention of the world was drawn, is that the influx of foreigners and merchandise may be so great as to deprive, for a long period, all except the very first comers, of any advantage in profit. Dismissing, however, this apprehension from view at present, there can be no question that, sooner or later, very great profits will be realised by the manufacturers and shippers of articles adapted to Chinese wants and tastes. It is highly important, however, for those intending to embark in this trade, to study the idiosyncracies of the Chinese, for without a knowledge of their tastes and preferences, the losses will be very likely to exceed the profits. Cooke, a recent traveler in China, and a correspondent of the *London Times*, offers some very sensible and important suggestions to the manufacturers of Manchester, respecting Cottons and articles of dress intended for the Chinese market, and perhaps American merchants may derive from them a valuable hint. He says:—

"That the Chinese are not easily induced to adopt foreign fashions is true, only to a very partial extent. You cannot make a China woman wear a Cranbourn-street bonnet, nor a Coolie wear a pair of Stuart-plaid trowsers; they are even so bigoted as to consider that their narrow cottons, ten inches broad, are more conveniently made-up than your wide long-cloths. They do not like your flimsy cottons; I have seen them take them between their fists and rub the dressing out. At Ningpo the Chinese can buy the best gray shirtings at fivepence a yard, and they yet prefer to pay sixpence a yard for home-made cotton cloth not quite half the width. But this is not because they are insensible to the superior fineness of the English texture; it is because they cannot afford to buy the British material. The home-made cloth is of thrice the substance, and will last a Chinaman at least two years. The British calico, washed in the Chinese fashion, by beating between stones, will wear out in six weeks. Depend upon it that the Chinaman is, of all human creatures, the most shrewd in all matters of economy; provide him with a cheaper and better thing than he can make at home, and he will buy it. Of course you must give him what he wants. If Yung A'Lung, the tailor of Canton, were to send a circular to the deputy-lieutenants of England, that he had sent to England rich Mandarian dresses much handsomer than the stiff clothes which they wear on grand occasions, and inviting them to go to court *à la Chinoise*, we should scarcely think that Yung A'Lung had made a wise or profitable consignment. Yung A'Lung is not such a fool. He sends us gold lace of the proper width and quality. Surely Manchester can produce a piece of strong thick cotton cloth, ten or twelve inches wide, and put it down at Shanghai at less than sixpence a yard. At this moment narrow thick calicoes, which one of the Hong Kong houses had the wit to order from England, are selling at very remunerative prices. There is also some trade doing in cotton brocades, made in imitation of the Chinese silk brocades, of the same flowered pattern, and dyed to the same colors. These are laid down at Shanghai at three and a half taels; they there readily fetch five taels, and I am told that the Chinese merchants find a ready market for them up in the tea country at thirteen taels. No doubt if the Mandarins find this out, there will be a tremendous squeeze upon the Chinaman's profits of eight taels somewhere. But it is a mistake to suppose that the Chinese are not fond of Western fashions. In going through the house of the richest merchant in

Ningpo, I was surprised to notice that, except in the servants' room, there was not a bit of Ningpo furniture in the house. The furniture was all of Chinese manufacture; but it was of simple fashion, without a mandarin or dragon, or a piece of inlaid ivory about it. I recognized several articles as having been not very successfully imitated from drawings in the *Illustrated News*—a paper which a Chinaman is always anxious to beg, borrow, or steal."

Again he says:—

"Every morning, throughout the Chinese Empire, there are 300,000,000 of blue cotton-breeches drawn over human legs. Men, women, and children, alike wear them. They are loose and shapeless. There are not five different patterns and five different sizes throughout the Empire. My Coolie says that his costs him two hundred cash; but that he is obliged to have a thick quilted pair in the winter, which costs him one thousand cash. Here is a scope for Manchester energy! It is not a changeable fashion, not a perishable production; it is imperishable from the fundamental of Chinese society. Depend upon it, if you can make these blue breeches as strong as they are now made, and cheaper than they are now sold, the Chinaman will gradually surrender to you the trade, grow less cotton and more rice. So of other articles of dress. On the 17th of September, a northwest wind reduced the thermometer to the inclement wintry position of 74° Fahrenheit. That morning the China population of Shanghai were completely changed. The shorn skull which had defied the fierce summer sun, was covered from the cold by a small warm cap or Chinese bonnet. Some of the chair Coolies had even covered their legs. But every man of decent station appeared in a thick, loose, dark-colored tunic or cape. The shape and fashion varied only from the cape to the tunic, but the material was very various. The great majority were satisfied with a thick dark-blue cotton cloth, but many wore woolen cloth; some luxuriated in quilted silk, and a few came forth in capes of black velvet. Do you think that these sensitive Celestials ever asked, when they bought their winter's garb, in what country's looms the fabric was spun? Not they. They chose the cheapest and the best."

Passing to other articles than Textile fabrics, it is

probable that *Clocks* and *Watches* will become important articles of export from the United States to China, when proper modifications in their manufacture are made, in order to adapt them to Chinese horology. Cooke remarks, that the highest ambition of a Chinaman is to have an English watch. He relates that a pirate, who had taken a Missionary as prisoner, but set him free, risked his life by calling on him next day at his house. He produced the reverend gentleman's watch, and the rightful owner thought that the repentant man had come to return it. Not so; the dandy Cantonese pirate had come to beg the Missionary to teach him how to wind up that watch.

D. J. MACGOWAN, M.D., in a letter dated Ningpo, July 4th, 1851, and published in "Silliman's Journal," states that *with a modification to be suggested*, American Clocks can be made an article of extensive import into China:—

"For a long period, the importation of Clocks and Watches, chiefly the former, into this country from the continent of Europe, was little short of half a million of dollars annually. This trade has nearly ceased, partly owing, no doubt, to the rapid impoverishment of the country by the Opium traffic, and partly to the fact that native manufacturers are able to compete with foreigners; yet Clocks are not often met with in China, they are chiefly confined to the public offices, where it is common to find half a dozen, all in a row. The number annually manufactured cannot be large, for in the richest cities in China, clock-makers are not numerous. At Nankin there are forty shops, at Suchau thirty, Hangchau seventeen, and at Ningpo seven. The average number of men employed in each being less than four, who are mostly occupied in repairing Watches and Clocks. The cheapest Clock they make costs $7—some are worth as much as $100—the most common price being about $25 each.

"A manufacturer estimates the number of Clocks made at the above places at one thousand per annum, and probably five hundred more would more than cover the whole annual manufacture of the

Empire. A few Watches are made, with the exception of chains and springs, which are imported. The oil used by Chinese workmen to abate friction appears to be particularly adapted to that purpose, though expensive; it is obtained from the flowers of the *Olea fragrans*. That a time-piece of this description would be in demand in China, I am perfectly satisfied, from inquiries made of natives in various quarters. Chinese merchants say they should be retailed at about $5 or $6 each. If I recollect rightly, they can be made in Connecticut at $2.50, which would afford sufficient profit both for the mechanic and the merchant."—[For a description of the kind of Clock which, in the opinion of the writer, is best adapted for the Chinese market, see *American Journal of Science and Art*, 2d *Series*, 13, 242.]

A *Looking-glass* is also a luxury highly prized by a Chinaman; and an English *Knife* is one of the most acceptable presents that you can make him. But among the most peculiar, and also important constituents in the American trade with China, is a plant that is not, I believe, appreciated anywhere else in the world, viz., GINSENG, which being translated, signifies the *Medicine of Immortality*. It resembles a small carrot, having a root three or four inches in length, and one inch in thickness, grows naturally in Pennsylvania and Virginia, and other of the Middle and Western States, and is esteemed in China for its medicinal virtues, especially its beneficial effects upon the *nerves*. It is recorded, that at one time the Chinese Government sent out a regiment of 30,000 Tartar soldiers to search for the plant, for it also grows in some parts of China, requiring each to bring home two ounces of the root gratis, and paying, for all that a soldier brought above that quantity, its weight in silver.

In 1850, the United States exported to China, Ginseng of the value of $122,916; and in 1854, the price of crude Ginseng in the Canton market was from $70 to $80 per 133 lbs.; and cured or clarified root was sold at $130 to $140. It is supposed that all the American Ginseng is used in the vicinity of the Chinese ports heretofore open to foreigners, none of it probably reaching the interior; and that since communication with the interior is now permitted, the demand will be so largely increased as to repay cultivation, especially on lands not appropriated to other products. In California, especially, where so many Chinese have already settled, as to create to some extent a home demand for this article, its cultivation it is thought would undoubtedly be profitable.

Sixthly. Respecting trade with *Japan*, which has recently manifested a disposition to enter the family of commercial nations, by opening several of her important ports to American and other vessels, expectations have been formed which it is not likely will be realized. It is probable that what are now called advantages, will prove very disadvantageous to many adventurous persons. The Japanese have never given evidence of a desire to procure the commercial products of other nations, by paying a remunerative price for them. Even the Dutch, who for two hundred years have had a monopoly of the Japan trade, have never, if we can believe the abstracts professedly taken from the Company's books at Batavia, made a profit on their outward cargoes. In 1804–'5, an invoice amounting to $212,000, from Java, consisting of Sugar, Rice, Tin, Sapan Wood, Nutmegs, Spices, Pig-lead, and Prints and Cloths, which, after adding all expenses, outfit, &c., cost, laid down at Nangasaiki, $380,000, sold at a loss which was perfectly ruinous—the entire outward cargo only netting $92,000. But the return cargo of Copper and Camphor changed the result of the voyage—realizing $886,000, and giving the Company a clear profit of over a half million of dollars. In 1806, however, the Dutch ship did not do so well; the cargo, costing $394,000, produced only $567,000, thus netting but $173,000. But even this average the English did not keep up, when the Dutch possessions in the East fell into their hands by treaty—the account of a voyage in 1813, made up with the same assorted produce of Java, states that what cost them $298,000, sold at port of destination at a loss of 60 per cent.; and the return cargo sold so as to leave a balance in their favor of only $44,000. At this time it is not probable that Japan exports would sell as well as formerly; and, with the exception of fancy articles, as highly-varnished Furniture and Lacquered-ware, with which the markets can be easily overstocked, the valuable products, so far as known, are identical with those of several other countries offering greater advantages for profitable exchanges. An enumeration of the products comprises—Diamonds, Topaz, Rock Crystal, Gold and Silver, Copper, of which it has many productive mines, Iron, Tin, Lead, Tutenag, Sulphur, Coal, Saltpetre, Salt, Camphor, Pearls, Corals, Ambergris, Rice, Tea, Wrought Silk, Lacquered-ware, and Earthenware.

Seventhly. In at least two of the countries referred to—China and South America—the time is nearly at hand when *American Vessels, Steamboats, and Steamers will be largely in demand to navigate the interior streams, and also to connect the various seaports.* "When I observe," says a recent traveler in China, "the steamers from Hong Kong to Shanghai crowded with Chinese passengers—when I see the boats on Canton River full of living freight, all Celestials, I can but think that a taste for such travel will increase; and once get our boats in the interior, and what a field for enterprise! Imagine the steamboat traffic between such cities as Liverpool and London, New York and Boston, or, perhaps better still in comparison, New Orleans and St. Louis, and then contemplate the populous towns of China, and the extent to which our machinery, our engineers, our enterprise would be employed! It is utterly impossible to reflect upon the complete change this would bring about. Why, all the machinists, all the steamboat men, the Vanderbilts and the George Laws of the day, could not supply the ravenous demand; and the same remark applies to many other notions. Let us once settle on some of the rivers and canals in the country, and look out for what follows." For the advantages to result from establishing American vessels on the great rivers of South America, I would refer to Lieut. Maury's articles on Southern Direct Commerce, republished in *Industrial Resources of the South and West*, Vol. III.

In the meantime, there is an opportunity for the profitable employment of vessels of moderate size, by participation with English vessels in their foreign trades. The legal restrictions upon the employment of foreign tonnage have been abolished; but comparatively little advantage has been taken of this circumstance by American ship-owners. A leading English ship-broker, in a letter to the American Consul at Liverpool in 1854, expressed his surprise, and remarked:

"With the exception of the deal and timber trade, and a few ships to the East Indies and China, American tonnage has scarcely mingled in our wide-spread commerce. In our continental, Baltic, Australian, South American, West Indian, almost nothing has been done. In instances, few and far between, our immense coal trade (now extending to every part of the globe) and our continuous guano trade have been entered into, but no general move toward them has taken place. Comparatively few vessels of moderate size say up to four hundred tons, find their way to our shores. For such there is constant employment in the Baltic, South American, and West Indian trade.

"By the rapid transmission of intelligence, the rates of freight are kept very much at a certain level all over the world; so that it has not been a question of rates that has hitherto prevented the Americans joining in our trade. It is evidently from a disinclination to undertake long and unknown voyages, or from a want of sufficient attention being drawn to the subject, or perhaps from contentment with the remuneration in the beaten tracks. But when the question is properly looked into, and an increase takes place in shipping (which will be a natural consequence of prevailing rates), there must be an increased anxiety to participate in trades yet untried. Briefly, there is a very wide and extending field for the employment of American tonnage by English merchants in every known trade; and it is of great importance for the ship-owners of the United States earnestly to consider the subject."

As has been before stated, all the English trades are open to foreign shipping. The last restriction was removed by the opening of the coasting trade.

Lastly, if your capital is unlimited, and your ambition unbounded, carry out Astor's proposed project of *establishing a Line of Vessels to circumnavigate the globe.* This magnificent plan was suggested, if it originated at all with him, in connection with his celebrated project at Astoria. It was simply to take in at New York a cargo of goods adapted to exchange with the Indians of Oregon, sail down the whole of the Atlantic, double Cape Horn, sail up the whole of the Pacific to Oregon, where they were to exchange their cargo for peltry which had been collected there by his agents. The vessels would then go to Canton, and exchange the peltry for tea and silks, then sail round the Cape of Good Hope, and up the whole Atlantic to Liverpool or London, exchange the Asiatic for European goods, and with these return to New York, to begin again this gigantic circumnavigation. In that way, he would keep some fifteen vessels running around the world, like a line of busy arms, exchanging and re-exchanging. And the old gentleman naively added: "If I had done it, I might have been a rich man."

And now, as a long-winged hawk (adopting a simile of Burton's, with a variation), when he is first whistled off the fist, mounts aloft, and for his pleasure fetcheth many a circuit in the air, still soaring higher and higher, till he come to his full pitch, and in the end, when the game is sprung, comes down amain, and stoops upon a sudden—so I, having wandered into those ample fields of air, wherein I could freely expatiate and exercise myself for my recreation, and having roved awhile around about the world, now descend to my former elements again.

But before descending to my "elements," or abandoning the commercial subdivision of the general subject, I desire to submit for your consideration two or three additional suggestions with respect to importing and exporting

NOVELTIES AND CURIOSITIES, *or such articles as have not as yet entered into general commerce.*

This is a business that requires nerve and courage, and partakes largely of the profits and dangers, and the advantages and disadvantages, of speculation. It is an avocation, moreover, that to a certain extent has been undertaken, as there are now several persons, whose exclusive business it is to buy (in Europe) a certain class of novelties—as curiosities in bijoutry—and sell them at public and private sale in the United States. Allusions, however, are frequently to be met with in books of travel to articles which do not seemingly come within the scope of such operations, and which, of little value in the place of their production, would, if introduced into the centres of wealth and commerce, command a ready sale. A traveler in Belgium states that he is astonished at the abundance and cheapness of superb carvings in oak, splendid Altar Ornaments, Sideboards, Tables, Book-cases, Clothes-Presses, that may be found of the most exquisite cutting, and can be purchased for a trifle. He says, that to those about fitting up their houses in the style of two or three centuries back, he would recommend a visit to Belgium. "Old china," he observes, "is another article to be found very cheap; and to antiquarians would prove invaluable relics of olden times, in the New World. Such is now the mania for all things ancient in this country, that I know no better speculation than for some shrewd American to go to Belgium, travel through Flanders, and purchase a cargo of ancient carved furniture of all kinds, china, &c., and ship to the United States. For every dollar expended in his purchases, he would realize ten, without doubt, in the cities of New York [and Philadelphia,]

"'Where in each gay mansion softest sounds control,
And wealth, with taste and beauty, chain the soul.'"

India, however, and the remark applies to the East generally, offers a much wider field for the speculative explorer than Europe. At the London Crystal Palace, in 1851, the long-established industries of Asia were represented, and excited universal admiration for the excellence of the workmanship in manufactured articles, and astonishment that so few of them had been introduced into European markets. Prof. Royle, who has given much attention to such matters, thinks that the *Calico Prints* and Flowered Silks of India, remarkable as they are for the beauty of their patterns, would, if imported, be applied to a variety of ornamental purposes; if not of dress, still of decorative furniture. He says that the embroidery being equal to any thing produced elsewhere, only requires that the things embroidered be fitted for European use, since the cheapness of all hand-work in India will insure the prices being reasonable.

"The manufacture of lace at Nagercoil may be safely undertaken; and the Carpets, Rugs, and carved Furniture, would command a ready sale if offered at rates moderate in proportion to the cost in India. The *Wootz Steel* might be largely consumed, and the highly-wrought Arms would be bought as curiosities, as well for the artistic skill displayed in the cutlery as in the inlaying. Well-shaped Pottery, and highly-finished Biddery-ware, as well as the lacquered Boxes of Cashmere, would all be bought; as also the various works of Bombay—inlaying of ivory, horn, ebony and sandal-wood; likewise Mats, Baskets of Khuskhus and of other materials, and japanned Boxes. To these we may add the polished Agate-ware of Cambray, and the inlaid Marbles of Agra, and the the Enamels of Cutch, Scinde, and of North-west India; also the Filagree-work of Cuttack, Dacca, and Delhi, as well as of other places; likewise some native Jewelry, if made in the forms fitted for European use. Even the toys would command a sale; and the models of fruits, as well as the figures of natives of different castes and trades, would find purchasers if they could be easily procured."

In Persia and other oriental countries, they practice the ancient art of interweaving gold and silver with silken and linen threads, like that described in *Exodus* xxxix., 3: "They did beat the gold into thin plates, and cut it into wires to work it in the blue, and in the purple, and in the scarlet, and in the fine linen, with cunning work;" and it is probable that some articles of this description would find purchasers in a day of incipient extravagance. For the benefit of those less oriental-extravagantly disposed, the French have succeeded in producing a similar effect by means of glass, and of course at much less cost. At a soiree of philosophers, we read, there were exhibited "rich silk curtains, having all the appearance of being interwoven with gold and silver, in most gorgeous patterns of Arabesque. They looked and felt exactly like the most splendid patterns of Louis Quatorze taste; but their cost is a mere trifle in comparison, for the *gold* and *silver* is merely *woven glass*."

In our own Continent there are also numerous articles, particularly of raw produce, that are as yet novelties in commerce, but which will richly reward those who will devote themselves to making known their valuable properties. Having already instanced several which may be found abundantly in South America, I will at this time allude to only one, which may serve as a substitute for the Peruvian bark in the production of quinine. It is called the *New Granada Bark.*

The State Department, in their volume on Commercial Relations, quote a letter from a mercantile house in London, saying: "We imported last year seventeen thousand seroons (hampers or baskets) of New Granada, and five hundred seroons of Bolivian bark. The New Granada all sold; but the Bolivian, being held for a monopoly price, is still in the market, proving that this kind has very little demand."

Delondre, in his new work on Quinine barks, gives an analysis of a New Granada bark, containing quite as much quinine as Bolivian calisaya. "If the Calisaya of Santa Fé, or *Fusagasuga* and *Pitaya* barks of New

Granada, had been introduced into the market before the Bolivian, there would be no question about the quality of the alkaloids they yield."

In the volume before mentioned it is remarked:—

"There seems a probability that this New Granadian bark will soon enter largely into the export trade of that country. The chemical tests to which it has been subjected in England, has already stamped it as a valuable acquisition to the Materia Medica; and the periodical scarcity of quinine, which sometimes raises that article to a most exorbitant price, will render it still more popular. In reference to this bark, and other valuable products of New Granada, a report submitted in July, 1856, to the French Government, relative to the commercial movements of France in New Granada, says: 'Formerly that republic had no other equivalent to offer in exchange for foreign merchandise than the gold of its mines. The abolition, in 1853, of the monopoly of tobacco, however, has given a new stimulus to agricultural industry, and attracted numbers to the cultivation of that article. This agricultural movement is not the only benefit accruing to New Granada from the suppression of this monopoly. In bringing the capitalists of the country in contact with foreign merchants, it has taught them to appreciate better than formerly the immense wealth to be found in the soil of the republic. Thus *Quinquina*, which has remained almost unknown since the departure of the Spaniards, has been a second time discovered in 1853, and has already entered into their exports, and will soon become a considerable article among the staples of New Granada. The cultivation of cocoa, formerly limited to the consumption of the country, has also been largely extended, and is now become an article of export."

Hooker, in the *Lond. Pharm. Jour.*, X., 344, makes mention of the *Sinaba cedron*, a plant indigenous to Panama, New Granada, as a remarkable substance. So highly is it esteemed by the natives as an antidote for bites of venomous reptiles, and as a specific in intermittents and diseases of the stomach generally, that it commands frequently an enormous price. "Herran (*Comptes Rendus*, 1850), who administered it in eight cases, attests its efficacy. He gave it in doses of five or six grains, mixed with a spoonful of brandy, and at the same time dressed the bitten part with linen saturated with some of the spirituous liquor. After repose, the patient recovered without any repetition of the dose. A similar treatment was equally successful in cases of fever, where quinine had failed."

Quite recently, the immense deposit of SODA, which exists in the form of Nitrate, Carbonate, or Sulphate, in addition to the common Muriate, in one vast tract near the Pacific coast, between Chili and Bolivia, known as the Desert of Acatama, has become of commercial value; and it is probable that since the opening of the Panama Railroad, the other mineral productions which abound in that section of country will come within the range of American and English enterprise.

In South America, the East Indies, and elsewhere, there are numerous localities abounding in *valuable Dye-woods*, many wholly unknown in the Arts; and a very profitable business may be done in collecting and shipping them to European markets. Thousands of tons of dye-stuffs are annually imported into England alone, and the prices of those which are of rare excellence are high. In collecting dye-stuffs, much labor and expense can be avoided by extracting the coloring matter by chemical concentration, and shipping the dye without the useless woody-fibre. This is a highly-important consideration, suggested by Prof. Solly, which has not as yet received the attention it deserves. There are also numerous astringent barks and woods, which are of great value as aids to Oak Bark, if not as substitutes for it, and useful in the preparation of particular kinds of leather. From these, Extracts have been made and shipped either in a dry and solid form, like Catechu and Kino, or as a thick solution, like the Mimosa Extract of New Holland.

The Great Exhibitions in 1851 and in 1853, made known a large number of new Dyes and Tanning substances; and as an important secret in dyeing* or in tan-

---

* Gilbart, in his Lectures on Ancient Commerce, remarks: "Secrets in Dyeing are more easily kept than secrets in most other trades. Dyes usually require an intermediate substance called a 'mordant.' This word means *a biter*. This substance bites the cloth and bites the dye, and so keeps them both together. If you dye a piece of cloth with any color without using a mordant, the color will come out on the first washing. The great secret of dyeing is to find out what particular mordant is adapted to each particular dye; for a different mordant will produce different colors, even with the same dye. If you dip a piece of cloth in a solution of alum, which is a very common mordant, and then dye it with cochineal, it will produce a beautiful scarlet; but if you dip it in oxide of iron, and then dye it with cochineal, it will be a perfect black. Sometimes a color will be produced different from that of either the mordant or the dye. If you boil a piece of cloth in a blue mordant, and then dip it in a yellow dye, the color produced will not be either blue or yellow, but a perfect green."

The Tyrian purple is an illustration of the great value of a superior dye; and if this could be revived, what a fortune for the resuscitator! This dye is said by Pliny to have been obtained from two kinds of shell-fish, the first being called *Buccinum* and the other *Purpura*. A single drop of the liquid dye was obtained from a small vessel or sac, in their throats, to the amount of only *one drop* from *each* animal. A certain quantity of the juice thus collected being heated with sea-salt was allowed to ripen for three days, after which it was diluted with five times its bulk of water, kept at a moderate heat for six days more, occasionally skimmed to separate the animal membranes; and when thus clarified, was applied directly as a dye to white wool, previously prepared for this purpose by the action of lime-water, or of a species of lichen called *Fucus*.

ning is equivalent to a fortune, perhaps I may render you a service by submitting a list of the most valuable, including a few novel Vegetable Dye-stuffs, and Barks for Tanning.

DYES AND COLORING STUFFS.

The *Maklua*—A berry extensively used by the Siamese as a vegetable black dye.

The *Rottlera Tinctoria*—The dried fruit extensively used in the East to dye a brilliant orange.

The *Alkanet-root*—Used to color gun-stocks, furniture, etc., a deep red mahogany and rosewood color.

The *Berberry*—Of which the bark and roots are used in the East to dye yellow.

The *Turkey*, or *French Berries*—Used for dyeing leather yellow; extensively imported from Constantinople.

The *Betel-Nut*—A well-known dye.

The *Awl Tree* and "*Mangkudu*"—Extensively used for dyeing red.

The *Room*—From Borneo, dyes a deep blue; described by Dr. Griffiths as "a valuable dye, and highly worthy of attention."

The *Grana Ponciana*—Growing near Quito; the bark furnishes a purple tint or dye, of which Stevenson says: "If known in Europe, it would undoubtedly become an article of commerce."

The *Bignonia Chica*—Obtained in various parts of South America, furnishes a valuable red coloring matter.

The *Lana Dye*—Procured in Demerara; dyes a bluish-black color, remarkably permanent; honorably mentioned by the Jurors at the London Exhibition in 1851.

The *Wild* and *Cultivated Plantain*—Used for dyes in the West Indies.

Bark of *The Eno*—Used by the natives of New Zealand to dye their mats. Produces a most brilliant blue black. It is important that chemical science should find a means to fix this valuable dye on wool.

Red Sanders Wood—Used to produce a lasting reddish-brown on wool; yields its color to ether or alcohol only. Native of Madras, Ceylon, &c.

Fustic—Supplies derived from Brazil, Cuba, and Jamaica; the best is obtained from Cuba—an ingredient used for dyeing yellow.

Sapan Wood—A considerable article of Eastern commerce; largely imported from Siam and the Philippine Islands. It yields a dye yellow in color, like that of Brazil Wood, but less excellent.

Camwood—Found in great quantities in Africa, thirty miles east of Bassia Cove. A great source of wealth to Liberia. Largely imported to Europe and the United States, and used as a mordant, and for producing the red color in English bandana handkerchiefs.

Gaboon Barwood—Another variety of this dye-wood, imported from Western Africa. The African dyes resist both acids and light in a degree beyond all *other dyes*.

Arnotto—A plant of South America, East and West Indies, and Africa; used to impart a bright orange color to silk goods, and to give simple yellows a deeper shade. Spanish-Americans use it to give a beautiful rich hue to their chocolate.

Chay Root—From the *Chay* plant, a native of the East; not much used in Europe; used by the natives dyers of South Hindostan. Produces a red dye, similar to *Munjeet*.

Bark and Root of *Morinda*—Used in the East Indies, and considered a very valuable red dye. Colors exceedingly brilliant, and the coloring matter is more permanent than many other red dyes. Worthy the attention of dyers.

Mangrove Bark—Used in the East and West Indies to dye a chocolate color. Introduced by Dr. Bancroft, who obtained for its exclusive use an Act of Parliament.

Sumach—Native of Southern Europe; grown also in Syria and Palestine. Has powerful astringent properties. Valuable in tanning light-colored leather, and imparts a beautiful bright yellow to cottons, which proper mordants may render permanent.

Safflower—The dried flowers give a pink dye, used for silks, cottons, and in the rouge manufacture. Color fugitive. The Chinese is worth four or five times as much as the best Bengal.

Gamboge—Much used as a pigment, on account of its bright yellow color.

Cudbear—Used in dyeing woolen yarn.

The *Rocella Tinctoria* furnishes the orchil, or orchilla weed, that sometimes is sold as a moist pulp, but the usual form is that of dry cakes, known as *litmus;* it produces a fine purple color. An exhibitor from the Elbe got a prize medal in 1851, for specimens of the weed, and an extract of red and violet orchil.

Woad, and the dyers *Yellow Woad*, are both well known.

Indigo—Also well known. See *ante*.

Madder—A substance extensively used in dyeing red. Chiefly obtained from Europe, India, and Ceylon, though grown also in the United States, particularly in Ohio, Massachusetts, etc. It is a very certain and profitable crop, but requires from two to four years to attain full maturity.

Logwood—The red heart-wood or duramen of a fine tree growing in Campeachy and the Bay of Honduras. Used by dyers, hatters, and printers, as affording the most durable deep red and black dyes.

Quercitron—An oak bark furnishing a yellow dye.

Brazil Wood—Yields a red or crimson dye when united with alum or tartar; used by silk dyers. Imported from Pernambuco.

The *Cork Tree Bark*—Imported largely into Great Britain from Spain, Italy, and Barbary.

LICHENS.—*Henna*—An important dye-stuff, used in India by Mohammedan women to dye their nails red; also in Arabia; and in these countries used also for dyeing the manes and tails of horses.

Orchilla Weed—The fine purple color it yields is used for coloring, staining, and dyeing.

BARKS FOR TANNING.

Besides Oak bark, there are—

Mimosa Bark—A powerful tanning agent; abounds in Australia and Van Diemen's Land.

Tanahaka Bark—Found in New Zealand; used by the natives as a red dye. Yields sixty-three grains of tannin to the pound. There is another red dye, called the *Tawaiwwai*, much used in tanning.

Rimu Bark—A common tree, superior to any of the Australian barks. One pound of the bark yields eighty-five grains of extract.

Callistemon Ellipticum—A native of New Zealand. Yields sixty grains of tannin to the pound; would be useful in tanning.

The *Towai*—A New Zealand bark, which it is thought would be valuable to the tanner; is said to yield one hundred and four grains of tannin per pound of the bark.

Black Mangrove—Almost every part of this tree, which attains the height of from thirty to fifty feet, abounds in an astringent principle successfully applied to tanning. Said to surpass the Oak bark—completing in *six weeks* what requires the Oak *six months:* and the sole leather thus tanned is quite as durable.

Myrobalans—A name applied to the kernels of a nut or dried fruit, of the plum kind; used in tanning and dyeing.

Kino—The produce of the Iron Bark Tree of Botany Bay and Van Diemen's Land. Found, by Vauquelin, to contain 75 parts of peculiar extractive matter, red gum 24, insoluble matter 1 (= 100). Yields, according to Solly, 73¼ of tannin.

Catechu, Cutch, and *Terra japonica* are peculiarly rich in tannin. A given weight of catechu will tan four times as many skins as the same weight of Oak bark; so that where Oak bark is scarce, it is the cheapest of all tanning materials.

The *Gambier Plant*—An evergreen shrub, like the myrtle. It is cultivated chiefly on the same plantations as pepper. In 1850, there were four hundred plantations of pepper and gambier in Singapore.

Divi Divi—This is the name for the curved pod of a leguminous shrub, imported from the East and West Indies; furnishes nearly fifty per cent. of tannin, and is much used by curriers.

Valonia—The commercial name of the cup of the acorn produced by the Valonia oak. Contains an abundance of tannin. Much used by tanners.

Camata and *Camatini*—Two varieties of valonia, more valuable for some purposes of tanning than the common kinds.

In Mexico, there is a very extensive and valuable deposit of SULPHUR, which sooner or later will become of immense commercial importance. A Mexican journal states that an inexhaustible amount of *pure* Sulphur is springing up every day, in infinite abundance, from the bowels of the volcano of Popocatapetl, and it remarks:—"The United States consume annually in their manufactories Sulphuric Acid to the amount of more than twenty millions of dollars; and Great Britain and France probably each consume an equal amount. The present source of supply for this immense consumption is Mount Vesuvius; and the cost of the article in American or English markets is about fifty dollars per ton. It is averred that gatherers of sulphur from Vesuvius would be unable to compete with the Mexican product from Popocatapetl, for the reason that this sulphur is amalgamated with an infinity of substances, which involve great expense to separate; and the supply from Vesuvius is limited, while that of Popocatapetl would find little diminution in the labor of a century. The ore, too, it is said, can be obtained with great facility; and only a little energy and enterprise are needed to secure a golden harvest. It is supposed that a trade of thirty or fifty millions of dollars annually could be established."

We may note, however, that it has been discovered that Sulphuric Acid, suitable for manufacturing purposes, can be made from Sulphuret of Iron, or pyrites, which is found in great abundance in the United States; and, perhaps the consumption of Sulphur for this purpose may not increase.

In Honduras, in a portion of a mountain chain, back of Omoa, which is a small but *secure seaport*, we are informed by Mr. Squier, that there are vast beds of *White Marble, of spotless purity, fine, compact, and susceptible of exquisite finish.* It more clearly resembles the marble of Carrara, in Italy, than any of those found in the United States. It is easy of access, and may be obtained in any desirable quantity. ("*Squier's States of Central America.*") In the Province of Rio de Janeiro, in Brazil, there is also, it is said, the *finest marble* in places easy of access.

In another direction there are also abundant opportunities for profit by *purchasing staple articles of Commerce, by means of Agencies established in districts abounding in producers who cannot afford to transport their products to distant markets.* In Mexico, for instance, there is a large amount of cotton raised all along the coasts of the Pacific and the Gulf, for about forty leagues inland, principally by small farmers (*rancheros*), who are content to receive fifty cents for twenty-five pounds, which is about one-half the value, and take dry goods and groceries in advance at exorbitant prices. The establishment of Agencies for the purchase of cotton in such localities would also stimulate the production.

In Brazil, the cultivation of Chinese Tea, as I previously stated, has become an important and profitable branch of industry. It would, perhaps, be found a very profitable business to purchase, by means of agencies, the green leaves of tea from the growers in the interior, and forward them to Rio Janeiro, where they could be prepared for market on a large scale by machinery, as is done in China. In Canton, there are thirty thousand people wholly occupied in preparing teas, which had been purchased in their green state from the small growers in the interior.

Formerly, as an old Mexican author states, a considerable business was done in gathering *wild Silk* in the Isthmus of Tehuantepec, and exporting it to Spain. At the present time we learn that in Central America, especially the Province of Olancha, there is found suspended from the trees a sort of sack, some two feet in depth, which is the nest of a species of silk-worm; and over the inside, silk is woven, from which handkerchiefs of excellent quality have been made. It is thought that a profitable trade in this article might be established, as this material can be gathered in any required quantity.*

---

* The *Cyclopedia of Commerce*, Art. SILK COTTON, remarks: "A beautiful silky kind of cotton is obtained from the *Bombax*, and

In the State of Texas, and in New Mexico and the adjacent Indian territory, there is said to be an inexhaustible abundance of a *gum*, for which Dr. Shumard, physician to the expedition that discovered it, proposes the name of *Gum Mezquita.* It is pronounced equal in adhesive or glutinous qualities to gum Arabic; and by the process of vulcanizing gutta-percha it may be adapted for water-proof fabrics. The roving Indians could be induced to gather and deliver it to the frontier ports for a very small compensation.

In the United States, I would instance the *Domestic Produce Business* as one that can be extended with profit to many, without injury to those who are now engaged in it. In the interior counties of the Western States, at no great distance from the leading thoroughfares, it is well known that produce can be purchased for considerably less than the difference in cost of transportation. Money, too, in nearly all the Western States, is a scarce and precious commodity; and for cash in hand, bargains can at nearly all times be secured. There are many articles, besides, that have not as yet been deemed worthy of much attention by the merchants engaged in this trade, as Game, Vegetables, Poultry and Eggs, Butter, Preserves, &c.; and handsome profits on a small capital may be realized by those who will conduct the business so as to

---

other trees; it is short and remarkably elastic, and would be very largely used were it not fragile and tender. The Hindoos spin it into a loose, coarse, warm kind of cloth. In Europe it has not yet been employed; but in America, a method has been discovered of applying it as a covering for so-called silk hats, for which it is said to be admirably adapted. As there is an almost boundless supply of the tree yielding these delicate fibres, there may *here be a great manufacture in the future.*"

deliver articles of this description of the best quality, in the best condition. Very considerable advantages can be gained by those who will give particular attention to the *packing of goods;* especially of such as are intended for re-shipment to foreign markets. Improvements in packing can be effected in at least two ways: first, in the neatness, convenience, and security of packages; and secondly, by compressing bulky articles so as to occupy the least space.

I have already alluded to the advantages to be realized from shipping goods packed in a neat and secure manner; and so important is this, that, to a limited extent, a good business may be done in purchasing certain articles in their original packages, and putting them up in a more desirable form. A firm in Philadelphia, as I mentioned, has made a fortune by repacking teas for miners' use, and shipping them to California and Australia. The quantity of goods that arrive in San Francisco and Melbourne in an unsalable condition, solely through defective packing, is said to be frightful; and trade circulars impressively urge shippers to send only merchandise of a first-rate quality, and in the best packages. "To make the Australian trade profitable," says the *London Times*, and the remark applies to California, "the very best goods must be sent out in such a manner that they may retain their quality when they arrive. If this simple rule is adhered to, these markets may still be reckoned invaluable; and exportations will not only be enormous in statistical amount, but proportionately productive in their material returns."

The adoption of improved methods of compressing bulky articles, so as to occupy less space and save transportation, is also exceedingly important. For instance, a means has recently been invented by which two barrels of raw whisky may be put into one, and be equally good—it is said better—for every use to which it is applied. Supposing this practicable, the shipper of whisky from the West to New York or Philadelphia, will save one-half the freight and the cost of one-half the barrels; or in other words, on every hundred barrels he would save,

Freight, say 50 bbls., $1.25 each..........................	$62.50
Fifty barrels, worth 1.00 "	50.00
	$112.50

and his profit would be $30,000 per annum greater on the same business than his neighbor, who adopted the old method. This is certainly "important if true."

Lastly, if you wish to make a fortune in commercial speculation, *study statistics, attend to great political and commercial changes, and buy such staple commodities as have fallen below their average price for a series of years.* The rule for successful speculation, and it is probably the best that can be given, is stated in the *Practical Treatise on Business,* as follows: "Take a commodity, and find out the average price of years, excluding from consideration extreme cases; and when the price has fallen below the average of years, buy. Thus, let us suppose that this commodity is flour; that there has been a great crop of wheat, or that the price has fallen below the average, or, in other words, it has become cheap; if the harvest be bad, you gain; if otherwise, it does not follow that you are to lose; sell, and replace your old stock by a new one." In this matter the only assistance that I can render you is to prepare, for your convenience, a Table of the average price of certain leading articles of speculation for a series of years. While engaged in preparing such a Table, I discovered that it had already been done by DAVID M. BALFOUR, Esq., of Boston, and published in *Hunt's Merchant's Magazine*, January, 1858. His statement gives the wholesale prices on the first day of January in each year, for *forty years.* I condense from it the following—

TABLE OF THE PRICES OF ELEVEN LEADING ARTICLES OF SPECULATION FOR THIRTY YEARS, FROM JANUARY 1, 1828, TO JANUARY 1, 1858, INCLUSIVE.

In all cases where the articles are dutiable, short prices are indicated. Coffee and tea have been admitted free of duty since 1833.

Year.	Mess Beef, per bbl.	Mess Pork per bbl.	Codfish per quin.	Balto. H. S. Flour per bbl.	Rice per 100 lbs.	St. Dom. Coffee, per lb.	Young Hyson Tea per lb.	Musco-vado Sugar per 100 lbs.	B. A. dry salted Hides. per lb.	N. O mid. fair Cotton, per lb.	Smyr. wash-ed Wool, per lb.
	$	$	$	$	$	cts.	cts.	$	cts.	cts.	cts.
1828	9 87	14 12	2 87	6 12	3 19	8	47	9 62	16¾	12¾	12
1829	10 25	13 25	2 25	9 00	3 75	7	49	7 05	12⅛	12⅜	7
1830	9 12	11 75	2 05	5 37	2 87	6½	42	7 80	14¾	13⅛	12
1831	8 50	12 25	2 37	5 75	2 62	7½	43	5 25	16¼	13	24
1832	10 25	13 75	2 75	6 87	3 12	11	68	5 15	15	10¾	25
1833	10 62	14 37	2 56	6 25	3 50	12	68	7 25	13¾	12½	17
1834	10 50	12 00	2 25	5 75	3 00	12⅛	60	5 00	13⅝	15¼	23
1835	10 75	15 50	2 12	5 25	3 25	10	37	6 37	14½	19¼	30
1836	10 75	19 00	2 57	7 75	3 25	11⅛	47	6 95	13¼	18¼	17
1837	14 50	26 75	3 12	11 25	3 12	11½	42	7 07	12	19½	21
1838	14 25	20 50	3 19	9 50	4 12	8½	45	7 25	14	12	20
1839	16 00	23 50	3 30	8 69	4 12	9⅝	38	5 56	15¾	16	20
1840	12 58	14 73	2 37	6 18	3 62	10	57	6 05	14¾	11¾	20
1841	10 18	13 21	2 62	5 50	3 62	9¾	67	5 87	16¼	10½	20
1842	8 25	9 97	2 00	6 37	3 25	8⅛	56	3 75	14⅛	10	20
1843	6 78	9 41	1 75	4 50	2 87	5¾	47	3 90	12¼	7½	20
1844	7 00	10 25	2 50	4 75	2 50	5⅝	47	3 95	12⅛	9⅝	21
1845	7 25	9 25	2 37	4 75	3 25	5⅝	55	4 75	11¾	6¼	17
1846	8 40	13 25	2 62	5 75	4 75	6⅝	62	6 40	12	8⅛	17
1847	9 00	10 31	3 12	5 50	4 00	6⅝	58	7 30	11	11¼	14
1848	8 62	11 75	3 56	6 50	3 87	6¼	58	4 50	10½	9¼	16
1849	11 00	13 75	2 12	5 50	3 25	5½	55	4 00	9	7⅛	13
1850	10 00	10 37	2 37	5 25	3 25	10⅛	55	5 05	10¾	12⅝	14
1851	10 00	12 25	2 62	5 25	3 62	10⅜	38	5 15	14	15	19
1852	10 00	14 75	2 62	4 75	3 50	8⅜	38	4 55	11½	9⅞	18
1853	13 25	20 50	3 50	6 25	4 62	8¼	38	4 75	14½	11⅜	21
1854	14 25	16 25	3 00	7 62	4 50	11¼	38	4 50	21	11⅝	23
1855	16 25	16 00	2 75	9 62	5 62	9¼	35	5 35	19	10⅜	20
1856	14 25	18 75	3 75	9 50	5 37	10¾	35	7 50	26	11⅛	20
1857	15 25	20 50	3 25	7 37	4 50	10¾	35	9 75	31	14⅜	21
1858	14 50	15 62	3 25	5 50	3 75	9½	37	5 87	19	10	26
Av'r.	11 36	14 76	2 70	6 58	3 66½	8¾	48⅓	5 91	14¾	12	19

CHANCES DI. TO M.—TO MAKE MONEY IN MANUFACTURES, INVENTIONS, ETC.—Passing to another division of the civil arts—MANUFACTURES—which, however, in the progress or growth of society comes next after Agriculture, we enter upon a region whose metes and bounds are co-extensive with the wants, fancies, and ingenuity of mankind. The combinations of which an infinity of numbers is susceptible, may be calculated with more certainty than to foretell the limits beyond which manufacturing cannot go. Any pre-existing material, mineral, vegetable, or animal, that man may desire modified in form or constitution, may give rise to a manufacture. And again, whatever of such modification man may desire remodified, may destroy a manufacture. Hence we might infer, theoretically, that a characteristic of Manufactures must be mobility and instability; and so in practice it has been found that, while Manufactures, as a branch of material industry, are destined to be as fixed and as permanent as the solid globe, the individual manufacturer is often the victim of mutations which he cannot provide for—that to a greater or less extent, he is in a hazardous position—subject to the caprices of legislation, the fluctuations of prices in food, wages, and raw material, the fickleness of fancy and fashions; besides being liable to be undermined by some new invention in mechanics, or discovery in chemistry. Great profits are not, as a general rule, obtained by a manufacturer, unless he possess some special advantage; as, for instance, a large working capital, or a monopoly of an article in demand, or an unusally favorable locality, or a superior mode or process of manufacture. One branch of manufacturing, however, though political economists deny its right to this classification, can generally be entered upon with safety, and that is the establishment of *agricultural mills in localities where they are actually needed.* Mills of this description are essential to progressive settlement, and in a growing country are always in demand. Any one who will advertise in a journal circulating largely through the Western and Southern States, that he is prepared to put up a grist-mill in a large unsupplied grain-growing district, or a saw-mill in a well-situated lumber region, will soon ascertain that many additional mills of both descriptions are much needed. Steam and water, it is hardly necessary to remark, will be found in general the most economical motive-power; but within a few years, very great improvements have been made in *wind-mills;* and in some localities they will be preferable, as for instance, in the vicinity of Cape Hatteras, where the water is too salt for steam, and the wind is never still for twelve hours at a time. Again, let any one take up a recent topographical account of South America, and he will ascertain that improved steam and water mills are much needed in many fertile districts—especially in Brazil, Uraguay, and Venezuela. The profits of a purely local business cannot, of course, be dazzling, but the per-centage upon the capital invested will be large.

In the Southern States, and in California and Australia, *Paper Mills* could be established in many localities, with great profit to the projectors. The raw material is abundant and cheap—and this is a principal item—the manual labor required being less in proportion than in most other branches of manufacturing industry.* The

* A Cincinnati newspaper recently made the following calculation with regard to the supply of cotton fibre at the command of paper-makers :—

author of "Australia Visited and Revisited," remarks:—"It seems surprising, even as it is, that writing and printing papers should be imported, when such abundant materials for their manufacture have been running to waste among the calico-clothed population of these colonies; or, that a *wine-glass* or *tumbler* should be imported, when such a pure element for the composition of crystal is to be found in the snow-white sands of Sidney and

---

"Assuming the value of this to be the same as the cheapest rags in the market, we have—

Total refuse..lbs.	3,733,000,000
Fibre, forty per cent............................	1,493,200,000
Value, at one per cent..........................	$14,932,000

"Now, allowing twenty per cent. for wastage in manufacture, the usual allowance of paper-makers, and the quantity of paper made annually from this refuse, would be as follows:

Fibre..lbs.	1,493,200,000
Waste, twenty per cent.........................	298,640,000
Paper..	1,194,560,000

"The Fibre.—Estimating this as common wrapping paper, at the average price of wrapping paper per pound, and we have—
1,194,560,000 lbs. paper, at five cents..................$59,728,000
And when it is considered that at least two-thirds of this material is suitable for the manufacture of fine printing paper, worth from eleven to fourteen cents per pound, this will be found to be a low estimate.

"A large portion of the profits of this manufacture would accrue to the cotton-growing States, as the labor necessary to be bestowed on paper making is comparatively little.

"To paper makers, and those connected with the press, who know the commercial want of such a material, we need say nothing of the value of such a supply at the present moment. The most careless observer cannot fail to perceive the important bearing which such a saving annually would have on this portion of our agricultural, manufacturing, and publishing interests."

New Castle. Although much has been done, considering the age of these colonies, there is ample scope for capital and labor in this important field."

In Siam, improved *Sugar Mills* are much wanted, and could probably be introduced with profit. The mode of extracting juice from the cane in that country is said to be as follows. The motive power consists of buffaloes; the cane is crushed between two cylinders of hard wood—large fires are applied to the enormous vessels in which the juice is subjected to evaporation; and when it has reached the required consistency, it is poured into cones made of clay. Quick-lime is employed for the purification of the saccharine matter. A single building generally serves not only for the manufacture of the sugar, but for the abode of all the laborers employed. The soil of Siam is admirably adapted to the cultivation of sugar, and it will probably become the most important of all the exports.

But I will not attempt to consider this subject with reference to localities. So rapid is the progress of improvement, that no sooner is a want ascertained than some one sets about supplying it; and during the time that information is passing to us that a manufactory is desired in a given place, one may assume that its foundations have been laid. Besides, so little attention has been paid, especially in the United States, to the collection of the statistics of manufacturing industry, that it is difficult to know whether a given article is made here or not—and still more difficult to tell what are the amount and value of the product; while it is quite impossible in general to ascertain the average profits of the pursuit. The manufacture of Lead Pipe and Sheet Lead is said to be the most profitable branch of manufacturing industry in this country, but even this is a matter of conjecture. On reflection, therefore, I have concluded to limit my researches and observations to the single point of directing your attention to certain inventions and improvements which, if you succeed in making, will insure a monopoly of a manufacture and a fortune as a result. Judging from the numerous patents that are issued for churns, washing-machines, and the like, the knowledge of what novelty is really wanted is rarer than the ability to invent it.

And *first*, as Iron is the most important of metals, I would recommend you to *discover some improved economical process of producing Iron and Steel.* JOSEPH DIXON, Esq., in a letter to the writer, states, that notwithstanding the numerous improvements which have been made of late years, there is a loss in the production of crude or pig Iron from the ores, by the methods in use, amounting to about ten per cent. of the metal they contain, which is carried off by the cinder in the form of unreduced oxide.

"This cinder, although so rich in metal, is thrown away as useless, no attempt ever being made to reduce or separate the large amount of Iron which it contains; and in some of the processes employed for the production of wrought Iron direct from the ore, the loss amounts to as much as thirty-three and one third per cent. If we assume the annual production of Iron in this country and in Europe to be four million tons, which is below the truth, and set down the average loss ensuing from imperfect reduction at ten per cent., the aggregate will be four hundred thousand tons, which, at the moderate price of $35 per ton, amounts to $14,000,000 per annum.

"In the manufacture of *Steel*, as at present conducted, the process is so uncertain that the most experienced workman is unable to predict with any degree of certainty the quality of the article which a given specimen of Iron will exhibit, after passing regularly through the cementing furnace; and even if, when examined after conversion, its appearance prove satisfactory, he is not entirely certain, if he continue his operations upon it, that he will find it to possess, when in the form of *Cast-steel,* all the good qualities which he expected.

"If the processes could be so far improved as to render it practicable, in the ordinary course of manufacture, first to obtain the whole of the metal from the ore, and next to reduce them to such degree of order or system, that the manufacturer could proceed with confidence, and specified results could be calculated upon, if certain courses of operation were pursued, great benefit would result from the discoveries."*

---

* The Hindoos have long been celebrated for their success in making steel. Sword-blades, and other cutting instruments, are made in India, of a quality as yet unequaled by any in Europe. And iron is converted into cast-steel in the short space of *two hours and a half.* Professor Royle, in a lecture read before the Society of Arts, refers to this subject, and perhaps has unvailed the secret. He says: "Mr. Heath describes the ore used by the Hindoos as the magnetic oxide of iron, consisting of seventy-two per cent. of iron with twenty-eight of oxygen, combined with quartz, in the proportion of fifty-two of oxide to forty-eight of quartz. It is prepared by stamping, and then separating the quartz by washing or winnowing. The furnace is built of clay alone, from three to five feet high, and pear-shaped. The bellows is formed of two goat-skins, with a bamboo nozzle, ending in a clay pipe. The fuel is charcoal, upon which the ore is laid without flux; the bellows are applied for four hours, when the ore will be found to be reduced; is taken out, and while yet red-hot it is cut through with a hatchet and sold to the blacksmiths, who forge it into bars and convert it into steel." In an old account which I possess, written on the spot, apparently in Mysore, it is said that one pound and a half

In the United States, minerals are so abundant, that vast beds of very rich Iron ores must necessarily remain comparatively valueless for many years. But it is remarkable, that in a locality adjacent to the great markets for this metal, there is a bed of ore of extraordinary value, as yet in a great degree undeveloped. It is known as the *Franklinite*, in Sussex County, New Jersey. This ore is so rich and pure, and so combined with zinc oxide and manganese, that Iron of surpassing strength may be readily procured from it; while at the same time an oxide of zinc very suitable for paint is obtained. A. A. HAYES,

---

of iron is heated lower than red heat, and then beaten for about three minutes with a *stone hammer* on a *stone* anvil, experience having taught them, they say, that instruments of iron ruin the process. Mr. Heath says, that the iron is forged by repeated hammering, until it forms an apparently unpromising bar of iron, from which an English manufacturer of steel would turn with contempt, but which the Hindoo converts into cast steel of the very best quality. To effect this, he cuts it into small pieces, of which he puts a pound, more or less, into a crucible, with dried wood of the *Cassia auriculata*, and a few green leaves of *Asclepias gigantea;* or where that is not to be had, of the *Convolvulus laurifolia.* The object of this is to furnish carbon to the iron. As soon as the clay used to stop the mouths of the crucibles is dry, they are built up in the form of an arch in a small furnace, charcoal is heaped over them, and the blast kept up without intermission for about two hours and a half, when it is stopped, and the process considered complete. The furnace contains from twenty to twenty-four crucibles; the crucibles are next removed from the furnace and allowed to cool; they are then broken and the steel taken out. The crucibles are formed of a red loam, which is very refractory, mixed with a large quantity of charred husks of rice.

"Mr. Heath, after observing the astonishing fact that the Hindoos had discovered the way of making steel at such early periods, refers to Mr. Mushet's discovery of converting iron into cast-steel by fusing it in a close vessel, in contact with any substance yielding

the eminent Chemist, of Boston, analyzed this ore, and says: "The mechanical and chemical constitution of this iron, point to great ease in working it into malleable iron. Both the manganese and carbon are readily oxydized by the puddling, while the pure iron will take the form of tough or malleable iron very readily. It is also the kind of metal required for manufacturing steel, by fusion with oxide of manganese, losing in the operation a portion of carbon and all its metallic manganese."

---

carbonaceous matter; and then to that of Mr. Mackintosh, of converting iron into steel by exposing it to the action of carburetted-hydrogen gas, in a close vessel at a very high temperature, by which means the process of conversion is completed in a few hours; while by the old method, it was the work of from fourteen to twenty days.

"Mr. Heath observes:—'Now it appears to me that the Indian process combines the principle of both the above-described methods. On elevating the temperature of the crucible containing pure iron, dry wood, and green leaves, an abundant evolution of carburetted-hydrogen gas would take place from the vegetable matter; and as its escape would be prevented by the luting at the mouth of the crucible, it would be retained in contact with the iron; which, at a high temperature, appears from Mr. Mackintosh's process to have a much greater affinity for gaseous than for concrete carbon. This would greatly shorten the operation, and probably at a much lower temperature than even the iron in contact with charcoal powder.'

"In no other way can I account for the fact that iron is converted into cast-steel by the natives of India *in two hours and a half*, with an application of heat which, in this country, would be considered quite inadequate to produce such an effect; while at Sheffield, it requires at least four hours to melt blistered steel in wind furnaces of the best construction, although the crucibles in which the steel is melted are at a white heat when the metal is put into them, and in the Indian process the crucibles are put into the furnace quite cold."

It would be superfluous labor for me to consider in any detail the improvements that have been made, or that are desired in the manufacture of Iron. The theme is one that occupies a prominent place in all works on the Arts and Manufactures. [For Bessemer's, and other recent inventions in the Iron Manufacture, see *Mining Magazine;* and for a description of the various Iron and other Mineral deposits of the United States, see Article on *Mineral and Mining Substances* in "*Progress of Science and Mechanism*," published by Putnam & Co.; and for best methods of extracting metals of all kinds from their ores, see Booth & Morfit's pamphlet on *Recent Improvements in the Chemical Arts*, published by the Smithsonian Institution.] But there is one possibility in the accessories of the Iron Manufacture, which has not received, I think, from scientific or practical men, the attention it deserves; and that is, the fabrication of a compound having the valuable qualities of *Meteoric Iron.* In various parts of the world there have been found, from time to time, metallic masses which are supposed to have fallen from the atmosphere, and which possess, as their distinguishing characteristics, great strength and durability, and apparent freedom from injury by the oxydizing influences of air and moisture. One was discovered in Brazil, some years ago, that weighed 14,000 pounds. Wherever these masses have been found, their composition consists chiefly of iron and nickel, the latter varying from two to ten per cent., with small quantities of cobalt, and (it is said) chromium. A mixture, however, of ninety-eight parts of iron and two of nickel possesses, we are informed, all the peculiarities of the best Meteoric Iron, and is especially adapted for making iron tools and instruments that will possess great strength, and little tendency to rust or oxydization.

In *Newton's London Journal*, for 1856, the following remarks are made in relation to this subject:—

"In all quarters of the world, as if resolved to multiply the lesson, Nature has placed certain metallic masses, to which the name 'Meteoric Iron' has been given, on the supposition that these masses have fallen from the atmosphere. Many of them are known to have lain for ages where they now are; but yet they retain their original metallic character, and seem to suffer little or nothing from the oxydizing influences of air and moisture. The composition of Meteoric Iron is singularly uniform; and whether near the poles or the equator, consists chiefly of iron and nickel, the latter varying from two to ten per cent., with small quantities of cobalt and (it is said) chromium. The remarkable fact that the first three metals, iron, nickel, and cobalt, are the only ones which obey the magnet, seems to establish a connection between these masses and the name they bear, which may one day lead to interesting discoveries; but at present we wish to direct attention wholly to their apparent indestructibility, and to the great strength and ductility of the metal which composes them. To close our eyes upon a lesson of this kind is absolute folly; and as science has demonstrated to us the actual composition of Meteoric Iron, it follows that, if Meteoric Iron possesses any valuable qualities, we ought by art to enjoy those advantages thus providentially placed before us. In other words, the manufacture of Meteoric Iron ought to become a branch of the national industry. So far as science is concerned, this important question has not been lost sight of. Artificial Meteoric Iron has been made; and it has been tested, so as to prove that its qualities are identical with those of the native compound; that, in short, it is more ductile, and has more tenacity than pure Iron, and is not so liable to rust or oxydize."

The difficulty which has hitherto embarrassed all attempts to manufacture Meteoric Iron, is said to be inability to procure nickel exempt from arsenic. In Scotland, however, a mine of pure nickel ore has been discovered on the estate of the Duke of Argyle; and in

Missouri, and some other States, it is said, sulphuret of nickel, free from arsenic, has been found. It is probable, therefore, that a compound possessing the valuable qualities of Meteoric Iron, will ere long be fabricated.

II. Direct your attention to such Mineral and Mining Products as *have been comparatively neglected, with the view of discovering some one that may be made the basis of a profitable manufacture.*

By reference to works that treat of the products of the Mineral kingdom, you will perceive that the number of those which are esteemed of great economical importance is, in comparison with the aggregate that have been found, very limited. Some of these have never been tested, and little or nothing is known respecting their useful qualities; whilst others, though well known to be available for a great variety of purposes, have been neglected in consequence, perhaps, of the superior attractiveness of what may be called the leading minerals. The subject, of course, is too comprehensive to permit, in this place, more than a suggestion that it may prove a profitable study to those mineralogically inclined, and I would indicate in particular *Asbestus, Steatite, Slate, Aluminum,* and *Plumbago* or *Graphite.*

1. Asbestus. This is a mineral of the hornblende family, remarkable for its structure, which is that of parallel fibres, like thread woven closely together, and which are so flexible that they can be picked out and woven into cloth. The finer variety, which has the lustre of white satin, is called *Amianthus.* Cloth made of these minerals is not affected by any ordinary degree of heat, and may be thrown into the fire with no other

effect than cleaning it. The earliest use to which it was applied was wicks for lamps, which *were bright but never consumed.* Napkins have been made of it, which, when dirty, are washed by being thrown into the fire. Bugnon, a French author, mentions that persons traveling in caravans through Asia, in order to be protected from the heat, spun Amianthus and "*made stockings, socks, and drawers*" from it, which fitted closely, and over these they wore other garments. A learned bishop has intimated that the *three children cast into the fiery furnace without being hurt,* were clothed in garments made from Asbestus.

The *New American Cyclopedia* furnishes the following interesting particulars with regard to this remarkable material:—

"The material was long since applied in Milan to the making of firemen's dresses. The fibres are softened by steam, and the cloth made very coarse. We have the following interesting particulars of trials recently made with it for the same purpose in Paris; which it is the more desirable to record, from the fact that the mineral is abundant in this country, and, on Staten Island, in New York Harbor, is found in bundles of fibres resembling slips of dry wood: some specimens furnishing these fibres of several feet in length. These trials commenced by three firemen, with their hands protected by Amianthus gloves, carrying a bar of iron heated to whiteness some distance, and without losing their hold of it, for more than three minutes. A fire of straw and small wood was lighted around a casting boiler, and when it was very hot, a fireman, having his head protected by an Amianthus hood and a metallic tissue, and bearing a wide shield on his right arm, was placed in it, the fire being kept intensely hot while he remained. For a moment his head was surrounded by the flame, but the shield served to keep it off. He remained in this position ninety seconds, when the heat became unendurable. His pulse rose from seventy-five to one hundred and fifty-two. Another fireman repeated the same experiment, protected by Amianthus cotton, and remained exposed to the direct action of the flames upon his head for three minutes and forty-seven seconds. In another experiment, two long and high piles of wood and straw were erected, with side openings, through which the firemen could escape if compelled to do so. The four men who were to enter the enclosure were covered with a new metallic texture; two wore an Amianthus garment over a dress of cloth, made incombustible by borax, alum, and phosphorate of ammonia; the other two had a double garment of prepared cloth; and each of them had Amianthus boots, with a double sole of the same substance. Finally, one of them carried a basket upon his shoulder, covered with metallic tissue, in which was placed a child ten years old, dressed likewise in Amianthus. This metallic tissue dress consisted of a hood, the edges of which covered the shoulder and left sleeve, the right arm being protected by a shield, and of pantaloons fastened by hooks. Clothed with this armor and the habit of which we have spoken, the fireman can run or stoop easily, and can turn readily by placing one knee upon the ground. The four firemen, thus attired, penetrated to the centre of the flaming hedges, and walking leisurely, went over it several times. In one minute, however, the child in the basket raised a cry, which caused the firemen to retreat precipitately. But it was found that he had suffered no harm; his skin was fresh, and his pulse, eighty-four when he entered, had reached only ninety-six. He could undoubtedly have remained much longer had he not been frightened, from the fact that one of the straps to the man's shoulder having slipped a little, he saw the flames, and was afraid of falling. In a few minutes after, he was as playful as ever, and experienced no inconvenience whatever. The pulse of the fireman who carried the child rose from ninety-two to one hundred and sixteen. The other three men were in the fire two minutes and forty-four seconds, and came out without having experienced any further inconvenience than great warmth. Their pulses rose from eighty-eight, eighty-four, and seventy-two, to one hundred and fifty-two, one hundred and thirty-eight, and one hundred and twenty-four, respectively. The fire was very hot during the entire time. Asbestus has also been used for the lining of fire-proof safes, and as a filter for chemical purposes. It is, however, in very little demand, though it is by no means a rare mineral in regions of primary rocks. Many localities in the United States furnish more beautiful specimens than are found at Staten Island, but nowhere is it perhaps so abundant, or of as good a quality for weaving. The

Island of Corsica is noted for the excellent quality and abundance of this mineral.

2. STEATITE. — Steatite, or Soapstone, possesses the useful quality of being readily wrought, bored, turned, and planed by the ordinary tools of the carpenter; and it may be screwed together with nearly the facility of hard wood. It is especially valuable for baths, and sizing-rollers used in cotton-mills, not being affected by acids nor by changes of temperature; and is also an admirable material for fire-stone, kitchen sinks, wash-tubs, bath-tubs, etc. In India, Steatite is largely used for household utensils. A German has lately manufactured *Gas Burners* from this material; and it is said to be superior to iron or brass for this purpose. Heat, which expands iron, causing some waste of gas, has no effect upon the Soapstone; and besides, it is not liable to corrode. Leibig, in his "Annals of Chemistry and Pharmacy," recommends Soapstone Gas Burners highly, and advises all chemists to employ them in their laboratories. The very best material, however, is required; and the process of preparing it for this purpose is peculiar. Soapstone, ground in oil, is said to make a very good paint for common uses. A quarry of Soapstone is now being worked near Baltimore by the MARYLAND SOAPSTONE COMPANY; and another, where Asbestus is also found, about two miles above Manayunk, by SAMUEL F. PRINCE of Philadelphia.

3. SLATE.—Slate, though a material long in use, and familiar to every one, has until lately been limited in its application to roofing and school purposes. Recently, however, it has been made the basis of various imitations of costlier substances; for instance of marble, by the pro-

cess of enameling. Its great strength, exceeding ordinary stone at least four times, and the facility with which it may be decorated—grooves, mouldings &c., being run in it with great dispatch by steam power—peculiarly fit it for household and decorative purposes. It is also suitable as a lining for walls, where it may be placed without even plastering. It is preferable in this respect to any kind of cement.

At the London Exhibition, in 1851, Mr. Sterling exhibited specimens showing the use of Slate for steps, balconies, larders, wine-cellars, dairies, skirtings, linings for damp walls, wine-coolers; bread, pickling, and pig-feeding troughs; urinals; head-stones and foot-stones for graves, tombs and monuments, clocks and sun-dials, sinks cut out of the solid block, floors of conservatories, warehouse floors, railway-stations, paving stables, etc. For billiard tables, it is said to be superior to any other material.

In Lehigh County, Pennsylvania, there are some thirty Slate quarries, in which about three hundred men are employed, and from which the best school-slates are obtained.

New machines have been invented for cutting, splitting and quarrying slates, and which it is supposed will facilitate and increase the production. (See *Ann. Sci. Dis.*, 1856.)

4. Aluminum.—This is a recently-discovered shining white metal, of a shade between that of silver and platinum. It is light, weighing less than glass, and is distinguished for its malleability and sonorousness. Many alloys with other metals, as copper, iron, silicon, gold, etc., have been made with it; and the properties it imparts in these combinations are such that it will probably be used extensively in this way.

It has been compounded of clay, the soluble chloride of aluminum and sodium, which is prepared by passing chlorine gas over a mixture of sea-salt, alumina and charcoal, and a metallic sodium known as cryolite, which is imported from Greenland. With reference to the cost, the *New American Encyclopedia*, Art. ALUMINUM, to which we are indebted for this information, states that it has been made in this country by Mr. Monier, of Camden, New Jersey, at a cost of twenty-five cents per pound; and estimates are given, that by the use of carbonate of soda, costing four cents per pound, it may be prepared for even fourteen cents. (See article by W. J. Taylor, in the "American Journal of Pharmacy," March 1857, Vol. V., No. 2.) The cheapness of the materials would thus seem to render it probable that the metal itself will be eventually obtained at a very cheap rate; but the processes employed are not yet so perfected that this can be definitely known. Not long since the metal sold for its weight in gold. A recent publication states that its present worth is about ten dollars per pound. M. Dumas, some time ago, gave notice to the Academy that it would probably be reduced to one-hundredth of that of gold. In the article above referred to, the following estimate is given of the cost of one pound of metal:

16 lbs. of the double chloride of aluminum and sodium, at 8 cents per lb	$1.28
2¾ lbs. of metallic sodium, at about 26 cents per lb	70
Flux and cost of reduction	2.02
	$4.00

By the use of less quantities of material, and these furnished at much less rates, the author estimates that one dollar will eventually cover all expenses.

5. PLUMBAGO.—Plumbago is employed in the manufacture of lead pencils, melting-pots of a refractory nature, and as a polish for stoves. It has also been used successfully as a substitute for oil in the lubrication of chronometers and fine machinery, and more lately, for the axles of railway carriages. Its dust is also employed in electrotyping. The chief source of supply has hitherto been the mines at Borrowdale, in Cumberland, England, but the difficulty of procuring it, and the consequent high price, have been obstacles that limited its use. Very little of the best Plumbago is now used even in black-lead pencils, as any one may discover by experimenting with india-rubber, a material that will readily and thoroughly erase the marks of a Plumbago pencil, while it will not readily remove the marks of a pencil made from an inferior material. In the United States, Plumbago has been discovered at various localities—in New Hampshire; at Ticonderoga, New York; at Wells' River, in Pennsylvania; and it has been discovered that fine dust can be consolidated by heat and pressure in iron moulds into any desired form.* The field is open for extending its economical value.

---

* Mr. Brockedon received a Council medal at the London Exhibition, in 1851, for making blocks of Plumbago from the dust, suitable for lead pencils. His process is as follows: After having compacted the graphite powder by moderate pressure, and thus reduced it to a certain size, he inclosed it in a very thin paper, glued over the whole surface. He then pierced it in one place with a small round hole, permitting the escape of the air from within, when the block thus prepared was placed under an exhausted receiver; and the air having been removed, the orifice was closed with a small piece of paper, and in this state it was found that it might be left for twenty-four hours without injury. Being submitted then to a regulated pressure once more, the different particles became agglo-

In 1852, the London Society of Arts offered a premium for the discovery in England, or the importation from any of the British possessions, of Plumbago, or of some other substance which may be used in lieu thereof, equal in quality to that now obtained from Cumberland. They remarked: "The use of Plumbago is greatly on the increase, while the supply appears rather to diminish."

III. Discover and manufacture *an artificial substitute for such natural objects as are rare and costly.*

Dr. Daubeny, in an address read before the British Association, at Cheltenham, in 1856, reviewed the recent progress of natural science, and made some suggestive remarks on the probability of forming by art those compounds which it had been supposed were only producible by natural processes.* Besides the articles referred to in

---

merated, and a block of artificial graphite was produced by simple pressure, as solid as the specimens obtained from the mine. From such blocks the exhibiter was enabled easily to obtain small prisms for use, which have yielded pencils equal in quality to those manufactured from the purest specimens from Borrowdale.

* The following is an extract from Daubeny's address: "The last two years have added materially to the catalogue of bodies artificially produced, as in the formation of several species of alcohol from coal gas, by Berthelot; that of oil of mustard, by the same chemist; and the generation of taurine, a principle elaborated in the liver, by Strecker. And if the above discoveries should strike you at first sight rather as curious than practically useful, I would remark that they afford reasonable ground for hope, that the production of some of those principles of high medicinal or economical value which Nature has sparingly provided, or at least limited to certain districts or climates, may lie within the compass of the chemist's skill. If quinine, for instance, to which the Peruvian bark owes its efficacy, be, as would appear from recent researches, a modified condition of ammonia, why may not a Hofmann be able to produce it for us from

that address, it may not be amiss to state what has been done relative to some others, thereby possibly suggesting to you a manufacture that may make your fortune.

1. ARTIFICIAL GEMS.—The manufacture of Imitation Precious Stones and Artificial Gems has become an es-

---

its elements, as he has already done so many other alkaloids of similar constitution? And thus, whilst the progress of civilization and the development of the chemical arts are accelerating the consumption of those articles, which kind Nature has either been storing up for the uses of man during a vast succession of antecedent ages, or else is at present elaborating for us in that limited area, within which alone the conditions would seem to be such as to admit of their production, we are encouraged to hope that Science may make good the loss she has contributed to create, by herself inventing artificial modes of obtaining these necessary materials. In this case, we need not so much regard the exhaustion of our collieries, although Nature appears to have provided no means for replenishing them; nor even be concerned at the rapid destruction of the trees which yield the Peruvian bark, limited though they may be to a very narrow zone, and to a certain definite elevation on either side of the equator. Already, indeed, chemistry has given token of her powers, by threatening to alter the course of commerce and to reverse the tide of human industry. Thus she has discovered, it is said, a substitute for the cochineal insect, in a beautiful dye producible from guano. She has shown that our supply of animal food might be obtained at a cheaper rate from the antipodes, by simply boiling down the juices of the flesh of cattle now wasted and thrown aside in those countries, and importing the extract in a state of concentration. She has pointed out, that one of the earths which constitute the principal material of our globe contains a metal as light as glass, as malleable and ductile as copper, and as little liable to rust as silver; thus possessing properties so valuable, that when means have been found of separating it economically from its ore, it will be capable of superceding the metals in common use, and thus rendering metallurgy an employment, not of certain districts only, but of every part of the earth to which science and civilization have penetrated."

tablished business, particularly in Paris. To make Rubies and Emeralds, Prof. Booth states that Ebelman avails himself of the two properties of boracic acid, of dissolving metallic oxides by fusion and volatilizing at a higher heat. His process resembles the solution of substances in water, and the evaporation of that water to obtain crystals. Having made a mixture of alumina and magnesia, in the same proportion as they exist in spinell, and added ½ to 1 per cent. bichromate of potash, he added to two parts of this mixture, one part fused boracic acid, and exposed it in platinum resting in porcelain to the heat of the porcelain furnace of Sèvres. The product contained cavities lined with minute, rose-red, octahedral crystals, harder than quartz and infusible before the blowpipe. They had all the characters of *ruby*. The constituents of Emerald, treated in the same way, yielded small hexagonal crystals, harder than quartz, and therefore agreeing with true *emerald*.

To make *Sapphires.*—A common Paris crucible is coated in the interior with lampblack, and equal parts of calcined alum and sulphate of potash reduced to powder are introduced into it. The crucible is then closed, and exposed for about a quarter of an hour to an intense heat in the fire of a blast-furnace, when it is taken out and cooled. On breaking the crucible, the lampblack coating is found covered with numerous small and brilliant crystals, composed of the sulphate of potassium enveloping crystals of alumina, which are of the same composition as *Sapphires*, and are transparent and almost colorless. The size of these crystals is in proportion to the mass of material operated upon—the greater the quantity the larger the crystals. It is also stated that they are so hard as to have been found preferable to

Rubies for chronometers by some of the French watchmakers.

Artificial Pearls are made of thin Glass bulbs, and with a degree of perfection that is astonishing. The brilliancy and reflection of natural Pearls are given by means of a liquid termed Essence of Pearl, which is prepared by throwing into liquid ammonia the brilliant particles which are separated by friction and washing from the scales of a small river fish named the Bleak. These pearly particles, thus suspended in ammonia, can be applied to the whole interior of the glass bulbs, by blowing it into them; after which the ammonia is volatilized by gently heating them. It is said that some manufacturers do not employ ammonia, but instead, suspend the pearly particles in a solution of isinglass, well clarified, and which they drop into the bulbs, and then turn them in all directions, in order to spread it equally over their interior surfaces. By this mode of applying the pearly mixture, the same success is obtained as in the before-mentioned process, and it affords a layer of the same thinness and brilliancy.

It is important, to succeed in the perfect imitation of Pearls, that the glass bulbs, or pears employed, should be of a slightly bluish tint, opalized, and be also very thin; and likewise that the glass should contain but little potash, or oxide of lead. In each manufactory of these Artificial Pearls, there are workmen exclusively employed in the blowing of these glass bulbs—an art that requires skill and dexterity, which can only be acquired by long practice.

Gold may be imitated in various ways. Professor Hermstadt has lately made known the composition of a fictitious Gold, which is much used by the German jew elers. To sixteen parts of pure platina add seven parts of brass, and one part of zinc; place them in a crucible, cover the whole over with pulverized charcoal, and keep it over the fire until the composition is in a liquid state, and reduced to one uniform mass. This alloy has not merely the color of Gold, but possesses its ductility and specific gravity.

A chemist of Washington has published the following receipt for a preparation which, if applied to Iron, will make it look like Gold: "Take of linseed oil, 3 oz.; tartar, 2 oz.; yelk of egg, boiled hard and beaten, 2 oz.; aloes, half an ounce; saffron, 5 grains; turmeric, 2 grains. Boil all these ingredients in an earthen vessel, and with it wash the iron, and it will look like Gold. If there be not linseed oil enough, you may put in more."

In the United States, the business of manufacturing Imitation Jewelry is already a large one, particularly in Attleborough, Mass., and Providence, R. I. Some of the compounds used in this manufacture are said to be these: *Manheim's Gold,* an alloy of three parts copper, one part zinc, and a little tin; if the metals are pure, the alloy bears a very close resemblance to Gold; *Pinchbeck,* five parts pure copper, one part zinc; *Princess Metal,* three parts copper, one part common brass, and a little zinc; *Artificial Gold,* sixteen parts platina, seven parts copper, one part zinc, melted together. *Fahlum Brilliants* are made of twenty-nine parts tin and nineteen parts lead, a very fusible and briliant alloy. *Queen's Metal,* imitating Silver, has a fine lustre; it is made of nine parts tin, one part lead, one part antimony, and one part bismuth. *Or-molu,* or *Mosaic Gold,* is made of equal parts of copper and zinc. A common composition for trinkets is seventy-five parts gold, twenty-five parts copper, and a little silver.

2. Essential Oils.—Essential Oils, which constitute a leading ingredient in the manufacture of Perfumery, were formerly derived almost exclusively from the distillation of odorous plants, or parts of plants, and were necessarily very costly. But now, some of the most esteemed modern scents are made, by chemical means, from materials which are generally considered any thing but pleasant. The perfume of flowers often consists of oils and ethers which the chemist makes in his laboratory from the most unpromising articles.

"The *Oil of Wintergreen*, much used in perfumery, and originally obtained from the *Gualtheria procumbens*, is now made from *salicylic acid*, obtained from the willow, and *piroxylic* spirit, produced in the distillation of wood. In the rectification of brandy, whisky, and crude spirits, there comes over with the last portions, an Oil of a burning taste and pungent odor, called *Fusel oil*, or *Amylicalcohol;* this oil, distilled with sulphuric acid and acetate of potash, forms a spirituous solution of acetate of oxyde of amyl, which, when sufficiently diluted with spirit, forms the artificial *Oil of Pear* used in perfumery, and in the so-called Jargonelle-pear drops. The *Oil of Apples* is obtained by distilling the same fusel oil with sulphuric acid and bichromate of potash. The *Oil of Pine-apples* is obtained by boiling *butyric acid* (the product of the fermentation of sugar with putrid cheese, or the making of soap with fresh butter and potash) with strong spirit, and a small quantity of concentrated sulphuric acid. *Oil of Cognac*, used to impart the flavor of cognac to common brandy, is only fusel oil diluted with alcohol; thus, a substance carefully removed from brandy, on account of its offensive flavor, is reintroduced in another form to produce an agreeable flavor. The *Oil of Bitter Almonds* is made by the action of nitric acid on fetid oil of gas-tar.

"Deville (*Comptes Rendus*, 1849), from the action of hydrochloric acid, or oil of turpentine, produces a species of camphor, which, treated with potassium, yields an essential oil, identical in odor, boiling point, density, and composition with *Oil of Lemon*. According to Wagner, *Oil of Rue* is evolved by cod liver oil when acted on by sulphuric acid, and the resulting purplish mass saturated with an alkali or alkaline earth.

"According to Wohler, the odor of *Castor* is due to corbolic acid, which may also be obtained among the products of coal-tar."—*Progress of Science and Mechanism.*

3. ARTIFICIAL INDIA RUBBER AND GUTTA PERCHA.—Chevalier De Claussen, in a paper read before the British Association, in 1855, gave the following account of his experiments in producing Artificial India Rubber: "In the course of my travels as botanist in South America, I had occasion to examine the different trees which produce the India Rubber, and of which the *Hancornia speciosa* is one. It grows on the high plateaux of South America, between the tenth and twentieth degrees of latitude south, at a height from three to five thousand feet above the level of the sea. It is of the family of the *Sapotaceæ*, the same to which belongs the tree which produces Gutta Percha. It bears a fruit in form not unlike a Bergamot pear, and full of a milky juice, which is liquid India Rubber. To be eatable, this fruit must be kept two or three weeks after being gathered, in which time all the India Rubber disappears, or is converted into sugar; and it is then in taste one of the most delicious fruits known, and is regarded by the Brazilians (who call it Mangava) as superior to all other fruits of their country. The change of India Rubber into sugar led me to suppose that Gutta Percha, India Rubber, and similar compounds, contained starch. I have therefore tried to mix it with resinous or oily substances in combination with tannin, and have succeeded in making

compounds which can be mixed in all proportions with Gutta Percha or India Rubber, without altering their characters. By the foregoing, it will be understood that a great number of compounds of the Gutta Percha and India Rubber class may be formed by mixing starch, gluten or flour, with tannin and resinous or oily substances. By mixing some of these compounds with Gutta Percha or India Rubber, I can so increase its hardness, that it will be like horn, and may be used as shields to protect the soldiers from the effect of the Minie balls; and I have also no doubt that some of these compounds, in combination with iron, may be useful in floating batteries and many other purposes, such as covering the electric telegraph wires, imitation of wood, ship-building, &c., &c."

4. ARTIFICIAL MILK.—At the Great Exhibition in 1851, Septimus Piesse, of London, exhibited a compound consisting of the yelk of eggs, gum acacia, honey, and salad oil, which, it is represented, was a perfect Artificial Milk. It contained all the elements of natural milk from the cow: caseine, albumen, gum, grape sugar, and fatty matter. On gradually mixing it with water, it formed either cream or milk, according to the rate of its dilution. Chemically, it resembled milk in its action toward reagents; and, as in milk, yielded butter in water, without the intervention of any alkali. It will keep well, it is said, for two years. "On being mixed with water, it forms Artificial Milk for the use of sailors on a long voyage. With coffee, tea, and chocolate, it acts like ordinary milk, from which it can scarcely be distinguished."

Another Artificial Milk is described in *Sill. Journal,* Vol. XXIII., 2d. Series, 123.

5. Artificial Fuels.—In England, attention has been largely directed to saving the refuse slack or coal dust of the mines. Several patents have been taken out for this purpose; and a Company, having a large capital, has been organized, and has erected works in Wales for manufacturing a *Patent Fuel*, which is especially recommended for marine and steam purposes, it being readily transported in blocks, and is not so liable as ordinary fuel to spontaneous combustion in tropical climates. One of these patents proposes mixing dried and ground spent tan with resin oil, or melted resin, and compressing into blocks. Another patent uses also refuse tan and peat with coal-tar, &c.—(*Lond. Jour.*, 1850.)

A cheap substitute for coal has been prepared as follows: One-third clay, one-third chopped straw, one-third coal-dust, mixed together to a proper consistency, and made in blocks of the size of bricks, and dried in the sun, or by other heat. It is hard, and suitable for burning in stoves, ovens, &c.

6. Artificial Ice.—The economical importance of Ice, at this day, cannot admit of question. It is estimated that the capital invested in the Ice business in the United States amounts to not less than *six* or *seven millions of dollars;* and that from eight thousand to ten thousand men are employed by it, there being from two thousand to three thousand persons who are furnished employment in the vicinity of Boston alone, in gathering Ice for at least part of every winter. Vast storehouses have been erected to hold Ice, the largest being probably that at Athens, New York, which will contain 58,000 tons; and the next largest being those of the Knickerbocker Company, which are capable of holding 40 000 tons each.

In the Southern cities, New Orleans, Mobile, there are ice-houses constructed in the most substantial manner; and at Calcutta, in India, a gentleman from Cambridge, Mass., has put up an ice-house of brick, one hundred and ninety-eight feet long, one hundred and seventy-eight feet wide, and forty feet high, covering more than three-fourths of an acre of ground, and capable of holding 30,000 tons of Ice. Hence it is obvious, that if the artificial manufacture of Ice can be successfully accomplished on a large scale, so as to compete with the natural product in price in warm climates, a new and very important industrial pursuit will be opened up. It is also especially important for inland localities in warm climates.

In France, Ice is made quite extensively by the use of frigorific mixtures, of which a correspondent of *Silliman's Journal*, Vol. VII., 2d. Series, 280, recommends as the best, a solution of nitre and sal ammoniac. He says:

"The solution of nitre and sal ammoniac is liable to none of the objections—the salts are not costly, and the evaporation can be conducted with very little loss. A committee of the Society for Encouragement of the Arts, at Paris, reported favorably upon the apparatus of M. Goubaud. The salts are not named, but undoubtedly are those above-mentioned. To make one pound of Ice, about five pounds of salt, with five pints of water, were required—the duration of the process, fifteen to eighteen minutes. The loss of the salts amounted to not quite one per cent., cost 1.7 cents; the fuel for evaporation, charcoal at Paris prices, four cents. The chief part of the expense being for fuel, it is manifest that Ice may be made most cheaply where wood and coal cost least. A part of the fuel may be saved by evaporating, as far as possible, by the heat of the sun: hence, the hotter and drier the atmosphere, *cæteris paribus*, the less the cost of the Ice.

"In the report quoted above, the committee admit that by these and other expedients, the cost may be greatly reduced from that named, which, it must be remembered, is for the city of Paris, where fuel is very dear. In most of the Southern and Southwestern States, the price of fuel is such as to reduce the cost of evaporation to less than one cent for one pound of ice, being in all two and a half or three cents per pound. The loss in the salts could easily be avoided, wholly or in part; and this would reduce the price to less than two cents. But this is not all. The cold liquor resulting from the solution of the salts may be advantageously employed in cooling provisions, &c.; and in the contrivances for this purpose are found the chief difference between the French freezers and those in common use. It is hardly necessary to state, that the widely-circulated story, that Ice can be produced artificially for one dollar per ton, must be an utter absurdity. The naturally-formed Ice costs at least as much as this by the time it is housed; and that formed artificially must require as much if not more handling.

"Sulphate of soda may be added to the mixture of sal ammoniac and nitre; but we know of no experiments upon its use on the large scale."

A few years ago a machine was invented for making Ice; and though successful in producing it, the cost was probably too great to render it profitable.

7. Artificial Marble.—A Frenchman, resident at Naples, recently discovered a process of rendering Plaster of Paris equal to marble in hardness and susceptibility of polish. He places the plaster in a drum turning horizontally on its axis, and admits steam from a steam boiler; by this means, the plaster is made to absorb in a short space of time the desired quantity of moisture, which can be regulated with the greatest precision.

With plaster thus prepared, and which always preserves its pulverulent state, he fills suitable moulds, and submits the whole for a short time to the action of a hydraulic press; the articles, when taken out of the moulds, being ready for use. The process is simple and economical—the cost very little exceeding that of the material. The plaster thus prepared is perfectly hard and compact, taking the polish of marble; and an experience of three years has shown that productions obtained by this process resist the most unfavorable atmospheric influences; and if so, it can be employed as well for works in the open air as for the interior of buildings.

Objects in plaster may also be rendered like marble, by coating them one or more times, as may be necessary, with a liquid prepared as follows: two parts of stearine and two parts of Venetian soap are mixed with twenty to thirty parts of cold solution of caustic potassa; and after a half hour's ebullition one part of pearlash is added, and the heat continued for a few minutes. Cold ley in sufficient quantity to produce perfect fluidity is then stirred in, and the liquid set aside for several days under cover. (*Archiv. der Pharm.* lvi.)

A prize medal was awarded at the London Exhibition, for an ingenious and cheap imitation of Marble in soft and hard cement. The effect is produced by the waste materials of silk works, or the short cuttings from piled fabrics, as cloth and velvet, mixed with the cement; the whole thus forming a mass having either a uniform color, or a mixture of colors throughout, while the veins are formed by silk threads drawn out to imitate such appearances as may be fancied. A great advantage in point of cheapness is thus obtained, and in some cases a polish can be produced during the laying on of the cement. The material seems adapted for halls, stair-cases, and other internal work in houses, churches, etc., and can be furnished, where polish is not required, for seven cents per square foot in stucco, and nine cents in hard cement. For polished work an extra price would be charged.

A *marble facing* has been given to buildings by the

application of a wash, consisting of hydrate of lime, which, by combination with carbonic acid in the atmosphere, forms a natural Marble paint. The surfaces to which it is applied acquire the brilliancy and polish of Marble almost immediately, and the hardness of Marble in from two to three months. The cost of the application is quite trifling. [See *London Building News*, quoted in *Merchant's Magazine*, 37, 112.] In India a marble facing has long been made from a mortar of shell lime or of limestone, and brought to a lustre by a process similar to burnishing.

8. ARTIFICIAL STONES, CEMENTS, ETC. — During the last twenty years some remarkable specimens of Artificial Stones have been made in Europe, which, besides being cheaper than the natural products, are said to possess qualities that adapt them better for certain purposes. Since 1838, a Mr. Furse has manufactured a material of this description that can be cast in slabs of considerable size, up to eight feet by five, peculiarly applicable for flooring damp places; for cisterns and drains, both pipe-drains and inverts for sewers of large dimensions. It has also been used for fortification works; as a cement for bricks, for lining prisons, casements, etc., and for many minor uses. It is non-absorbent, and is said to stand exposure well. "The price of this material in slabs is 6*d.* per square foot, up to two feet square; and for other works it is cheap in proportion. It was first invented in Hamburg, and is said by the manufacturer to be used on the Continent, in many extensive works for drainage and fortification."

Another firm exhibited at the London Crystal Palace an Artificial Stone compounded of grains of sand, pebbles, portions of limestone, marble or granite, clay or any similar material, cemented together by a true glass, obtained by dissolving flint in caustic alkali in a boiler at a high temperature. The materials are mixed with this solution into a paste of the consistence of putty, which is capable of being moulded into any required form; and after slow air-drying, the articles thus manufactured are burnt in a kiln, at a bright red heat, maintained for some time.

The details of manufacture in this case are thus given in the Reports of the Juries:—

"The flints are used in the rough state in which they are found in the chalk, and of large size. They are suspended in wire baskets in a high-pressure boiler, the pressure being from sixty to one hundred pounds on the square inch. For about a ton, or a ton and a half of flints about a quarter of a ton of caustic soda is required, (about fifty-six per cent. of alkali). The resulting substance, a fluid silicate of soda, is drawn off every forty-eight or fifty-six hours, the quantity being about two hundred gallons, and is afterward evaporated down to a specific gravity of 1.165, when it is fit for use. The further progress is sufficiently described above.

"Although this kind of Artificial Stone appears to offer many advantages, it is right to mention one objection to its use which has not yet been obviated, consisting of an efflorescence of some of the salts of soda, greatly disfiguring the appearance of the work.

"Besides Artificial Stone, adapted for all kinds of garden work, for paving, and for architectural decorations, it has been found easy to manufacture a porous variety for filter stones, which may be made of any size, admirably answer the purposes for which they are intended, and are supplied at extremely small cost. They are cleaned with perfect ease, and may be contrived so as to be applied without a reservoir to filter water, delivered to houses by the system of constant supply. The cost of a filter passing three hundred gallons per day would be 50*s.*; and small filters are prepared with the same materials, the price of which is only 5*s.* Besides these slabs, permanent ascending filters are prepared with the same material, the price of which, complete, varies from 15*s*. to £4, supplying daily from five to sixty gallons; these are especially adapted for ships and for domestic purposes. Other very useful articles have been manufactured from the same kind of material, among which scythe-stones, and other grindstones may be mentioned."

In Pennsylvania, a gentleman informs me that he has discovered a material possessing properties superior to any in use for building purposes, inasmuch as it can be moulded to any shape or form, into columns, entablatures, door facings, etc., and also supersedes the necessity for plastering, as the inside surface is as smooth as polished marble. This material, he assures me, can be compounded, dried, and placed in the building within twelve hours.

At the London Crystal Palace there was exhibited a gigantic slab of *Portland Cement*, measuring twenty feet by twelve and ten inches thick, weighing fifteen tons. This cement is made from carbonate of lime, mixed in definite proportions with the argillaceous deposit of some rivers running over clay and chalk, pounded together under water, and afterward dried and burnt. The strength of this combination is very remarkable, being nearly four times as great as that of any natural kind. Portland Cement makes an admirable and most powerful concrete, the portion of cement required being only a tenth or twelfth part.

Prechtel gives the following simple mode of making *Hydraulic Cement*. Common burned lime is slacked with a solution of copperas, instead of with water, and then mixed with sand. (It may also be used without sand.) It hardens readily in the air or under water, and becomes very hard. Experiments made with it on a large scale proved very satisfactory. When freshly prepared it has a greenish color, from the segregation of protoxide of iron, passing into peroxide, when its color is yellowish; and to this oxydation Prechtel ascribes its hardening property. Sulphate of lime is also formed at the same time.

There are numerous other Cements, some of which, if applied to metals or stone, become harder than the material which they unite.* Of all the Cements, known as

---

* The following Receipt for a Marble Cement, is said to have been repeatedly sold for $20:—

"Take plaster of Paris and soak it in a saturated solution of alum; then bake the two in an oven the same as gypsum is baked to make it plaster of Paris, after which they are ground to powder. It is then used as wanted, being mixed up with water like plaster, and applied. It sets into very hard composition, capable of taking a very high polish. It may be mixed with various coloring minerals to produce a cement of any color, capable of imitating marble. This is a very rare receipt."

Dr. Ure gives the following Receipts for various Cements:—

"The *Diamond Cement*, for uniting broken pieces of china, glass, etc., which is sold as a secret at an absurdly dear price, is composed of isinglass soaked in water till it becomes soft, and then dissolved in proof spirit, to which a little gum resin, ammoniac, or galbanum, and resin mastic are added, each previously dissolved in a minimum of alcohol. When to be applied, it must be gently heated to liquefy it, and it should be kept for use in a well-corked vial. A glass stopper would be apt to fix, so as not to be removable. This is the cement employed by the Armenian jewelers, in Turkey, for glueing the ornamental stones to trinkets of various kinds. When well made it resists moisture.

"Shellac dissolved in alcohol, or in a solution of borax, forms a pretty good Cement. White of egg alone, or mixed with finely sifted quicklime, will answer for uniting objects which are not exposed to moisture. The latter combination is very strong, and is much employed for joining pieces of spar and marble ornaments. A similar composition is used by coppersmiths to secure the edges

Keene's, *Martin's*, *Parian*, and some others, sulphate of lime is the basis; but in these the plaster is thrown, in the state of fine powder, into a vessel containing a saturated solution of alum, sulphate of potash, or borax.

---

and rivets of boilers; only bullock's blood is the albuminous matter used instead of white of eggs. Another Cement, in which an analogous substance, the curd or caseum of milk is employed, is made by boiling slices of skim-milk cheeses into a gluey consistence in a great quantity of water, and then incorporating it with quick-lime on a slab with a muller, or in a marble mortar. When this compound is applied warm to broken edges of stoneware, it unites them very firmly after it is cold.

A Cement, which gradually indurates to a stony consistence, may be made by mixing twenty parts of clean river sand, two of litharge, and one of quicklime, into a thin putty with linseed oil. The quicklime may be replaced with litharge. When this Cement is applied to mend broken pieces of stone, as steps of stairs, it acquires, after some time, a stony hardness. A similar composition has been applied to coat over brick walls, under the name of mastic.

"The *Iron-rust Cement* is made from fifty to one hundred parts of iron borings, pounded and sifted, mixed with one part of sal ammoniac; and when it is to be applied, moistened with as much water as will give it a pasty consistency. Formerly, flowers of sulphur were used, and much more sal ammoniac in making this cement, but with decided disadvantage, as the union is effected by the oxydizement, consequent expansion, and solidification of the iron powder, and any heterogenous matter obstructs the effect. The best proportion of sal ammoniac is, I believe, one per cent. of the iron borings. Another composition of the same kind is made by mixing four parts of fine borings or filings of iron, two parts of potter's clay, and one part of powdered potsherds, and making them into a paste with salt and water. When this cement is allowed to concrete slowly on iron joints it becomes very hard.

"An excellent Cement, for *resisting moisture*, is made by incorporating thoroughly eight parts of melted glue, of the consistence used by carpenters, with four parts of linseed oil, boiled into varnish with litharge. This cement hardens in about forty-eight hours, and

After soaking for some hours it is removed and air dried, subsequently rebaked at a brownish-red heat. When taken out of the oven, it is once more reduced to a fine powder, and carefully sifted, after which it is fit for use; but when slacked, a solution of alum is employed instead of pure water. When borax is used, the plaster is called Parian, but in the other case it forms Keene's Cement. The kind called Martin's Cement is made with pearlash as well as alum, and is baked at a much higher heat than the rest.

The following are said to be excellent Receipts:—

A Great Cement Wash.—A patent has been obtained by a Mr. Daines, of London, for a cement solution for coating the surfaces of stone and plaster, and which appears to be excellent for this purpose. It consists of eight parts by weight of linseed or other oil, in which one part by the weight of flour of sulphur is dissolved. The oil and sulphur are placed in a stoneware or iron vessel, and heated to about 270° in a sand bath, when the sulphur dissolves. It is laid on with a brush, and is stated to be a protective against damp. If it effects the object of

---

renders the joints of wooden cisterns and casks air and water tight. A compound of glue, with one-fourth its weight of Venice turpentine, made as above, serves to cement glass, metal, and wood, to one another. Fresh-made cheese curd, and old skim-milk cheese, boiled in water to a slimy consistence, dissolved in a solution of bicarbonate of potash, are said to form a good cement for glass and porcelain. The gluten of wheat, well prepared, is also a good cement. White of eggs, with flour and water well mixed, and smeared over linen cloth, forms a ready lute for steam joints in small apparatuses. White lead, ground upon a slab with linseed oil varnish, and kept out of contact of air, affords a cement capable of repairing fractured bodies of all kinds. It requires a few weeks to harden. When stone or iron are to be cemented together, a compound of equal parts of sulphur, with pitch, answers very well."

protecting stone and plaster surfaces from damp, it is a most useful discovery.

Cement (glue).—Herberger recommends the following as an excellent cement to join metal with glass or porcelain. To two ounces glue, dissolved in water and boiled down to a thick solution, are added one ounce oil varnish, or three fourths of an ounce Venice turpentine, and the whole heated to ebullition to incorporate them thoroughly. The articles cemented should remain forty-eight to sixty hours before use.

A good *Cement for glass,* porcelain, and pottery, which is not to be exposed to water, is to mix equal parts dry quick-lime and gum Arabic, in fine powder, and to moisten the whole with water or white of egg, to make a thick paste. (*Elsner.*) Quick-lime and white of egg alone make an excellent cement of this kind; but the diamond cement, a dilute alcoholic solution of fish glue and resin, is far superior, although more costly, and will withstand a considerable exposure to moisture.

Soldering Wrought and Cast-iron.—Filings of soft cast-iron are melted with calcined borax, the mass pulverized and sprinkled on the parts to be united. They are then separately heated and welded together on an anvil by gentle blows.

Welding Powder.—To melt borax one tenth sal ammoniac is added, the mixture poured on an iron plate, and an equal weight of quick-lime ground up with it. Iron or steel to be welded is first heated to redness, the mixture laid on the welding surfaces, and the metal again heated, but far below the usual welding heat. The pieces unite firmly by hammering. (*Lond. Builder.*)

9. Imitation Woods. — Various processes have long

been in use to stain the softer woods in imitation of the more costly, and some of them are very successful. The naturally light colors of woods are rendered darker by being covered with oil or varnish, though the latter somewhat checks the change into the deepest hues; the yellowish color of most varnishes seriously interferes with the colors of light and delicate woods, for which the whitest kinds should alone be used. In many cases, the colors of the woods are modified by applying coloring matters, either before or with the varnish; in this way, handsome birch-wood may be made to assume the appearance of mahogany so exactly as often to escape detection.

A *Yellow* color may be given to wood by boiling-hot solutions of turmeric, Persian berries, fustic, etc.; the color is very fugitive; a more permanent color results from nitric acid; and best of all, by the successive introduction of acetate of lead and chromate of potash. Sulphate of iron also stains timber of a yellowish color, when used as a preservative agent; so much so, that it is recommended to use corrosive sublimate for this purpose, when it is desirable to preserve the white color.

A *Red* color may be obtained by immersion in a boiling-hot infusion of Brazil-wood, and afterward washing with alum-water; also by a tincture of Dragon's-blood. An *Orange-red* color may be obtained by the successive action of bichloride of mercury and iodide of potash, madder, and ammoniacal solutions of carmine.

Blue is obtained by hot solutions of Indigo, of sulphate of copper, and by the successive introduction of pyrolignite of iron and prussiate of potash.

Green is the result of the successive formation, in the pores of the wood, of a blue and yellow, as above indicated, and by a hot solution of acetate of copper in water. A *Yellowish-green* may be obtained by the action of copper salts on the red prussiate of potash.

Purple is generally obtained by immersion in a boiling solution of logwood and Brazil-wood: one pound of the former and one quarter of a pound of the latter to a gallon of water.

Dark brown is the result of the action of copper salts on the yellow prussiate of potash. The sulphate of copper, in soft woods, gives a pretty reddish-brown color, in streaks and shades, which is rich after varnishing, and said to be permanent. A *Mahogany* color is obtained by different proportions of madder, logwood, and Brazil-wood.

Black is obtained by immersion in a hot decoction of logwood, and afterward in a solution of galls; this will take a fine polish; and by a solution of copper in nitric acid, and afterward in a decoction of logwood.

But probably the most remarkable mode of coloring woods is that by absorption, adopted since Dr. Boucherie's discovery of the aspirative power of trees; or in other words, that the force which circulates the sap in the living tree may be used to impregnate trees, with various solutions, for some days after they are felled. In this way, a black tint may be produced by introducing "successively solutions of sulphuret of sodium and acetate of lead, whereby the black sulphuret of lead is formed; a similar color may be formed by an infusion of galls and the pyrolignite of iron. A green (Scheele's green) may be produced by acetate of copper and arsenious acid; a solution of sulphate of copper, with a slight excess of ammonia, penetrates wood easily, producing an agreeable blueish tint. As the coloring does not affect equally all parts of the wood, the tints are in waves and veins, which are very beautiful when the wood is polished.

"According to Mr. Hyett, different solutions penetrate with different degrees of facility; in applying, for instance, acetate of copper and prussiate of potash to larch, the sap-wood is colored most when the acetate is introduced first; but when the prussiate is first introduced, the heart-wood is the most deeply colored. Pyrolignite of iron causes a dark-gray color in beech, from the action of tannin in the wood on the oxide of iron; while in larch it merely darkens the natural color. Most of the tints, especially those caused by the prussiates of iron and copper, are improved by the exposure to light, and the richest colors are produced when the process is carried on rapidly.

"Vegetable coloring matters do not penetrate easily by the aspirative process, probably on account of the affinity of the woody fibre for the coloring matter, whereby the whole of the latter is taken up by the parts of the wood with which it first comes into contact.

"Different intermediate shades, in a great variety, may be obtained by combinations of coloring matters, according to the tint desired and the different ideas of the dyer.

"When it is desired to give to wood recently worked the appearance of that which has become dark from age, as is often the case in repairing antique furniture, it is generally effected by washing it with lime-water, or by putting on the lime as water-color, and allowing it to remain a few minutes, hours, or days, according to circumstances." (*Progress of Science and Mechanism.*)

10. Substitutes for Coffee.—Several articles have

been mentioned from time to time, each of which, it is said will answer as a good substitute for the coffee-berry. Liebig states that "Asparagus contains, in common with tea and coffee, a principle which he calls 'taurine,' and which he considers essential to the health of those who do not take strong exercise." Taking the hint from Baron Liebig, a writer in the London *Gardener's Chronicle* was led to test *Asparagus* as a substitute for coffee. He says:—"The young shoots I first prepared were not agreeable, having an alkaline taste. I then tried the ripe seeds, and these, roasted and ground, make a full-flavored coffee, not easily distinguished from fine Mochà. The seeds are easily freed from the berries by drying them in a coal oven, and then rubbing them on a sieve."

In Berlin, Prussia, there is a large establishment for the manufacture of Coffee from Acorns and Chicory, the articles being made separately from each other. The chicory is mixed with an equal weight of turnips to render it sweeter. The acorn coffee, which is made from roasted and ground acorns, is sold in large quantities; and frequently with rather a medicinal than an economical view, as it is thought to have a wholesome effect upon the blood, particularly of scrofulous persons. Acorn coffee is, however, made and used in many parts of Germany, for the sole purpose of adulterating genuine coffee.

Mr. Huchvale, of Oxfordshire, England, has recently taken out a patent for making a drink out of Mangel-wurtzel, designed as a substitute for coffee and for tea. For coffee, he cuts the roots into small pieces about the size of coffee-beans, and then roasts them, after which they are ground in the usual way. For tea, the leaves alone are used. These are denuded of their stems, and heated on plates, when they curl up, and after being perfectly dried are fit for keeping. They are used exactly as tea is.

Dr. Harrison, of Edinburgh, prefers coffee made from the *Dandelion* to that of Mecca; and states that many persons, all over the Continent, prefer a mixture of succory and coffee to coffee alone. Dig up the roots of the Dandelion, wash them well, but do not scrape them; dry them; cut them into the size of peas, and then roast in an earthen pot, or coffee-roaster of any kind. The secret of good coffee is to have it fresh roasted and fresh ground.

It has been stated that *Wheat* makes an excellent coffee, separately or mixed, one-half wheat. It should be well dried and roasted, or it will boil thick, like starch.

The ripe seeds of the *Okra*, burned, is said to make a very good and wholesome substitute for coffee.

IV. *Apply Science and modern discoveries to the utilization of what are now the waste products of Mines.*

It has been remarked, that in no country is less attention paid to the economy of Manufactures, in saving effete and waste products of various processes, than in the United States. This is especially true of Mining. The abundance of mineral wealth has rendered us utterly indifferent to economies that are a source of great wealth in other countries. This may not be a serious fault, as yet; but the point to which I desire to direct attention is, whether, in some instances, it would not pay better to be a gleaner after miners than to mine. With proper apparatus and chemical appliances, I am disposed to think that more gold could be obtained, in a shorter time, by reworking the refuse of the gold washings in California, than to dig in ordinary placers in the usual way; or, that it would be more profitable to compress the fine dust of Coal Mines into blocks, and render it marketable, than to mine coal.

Within a few years, several important improvements and discoveries have been made, which in Europe are greatly facilitating the utilization of what were once waste products. For instance, a Mr. Pattinson has discovered a process for extracting silver from galena, or the sulphuret of lead, which is so economical, that it can be applied with profit when the lead contains only three ounces of silver (instead of twenty ounces, as before) to the ton. The method is founded on the property which bodies possess, of separating from each other during crystallization, and thus become, to a certain extent, purer by its application. It consists in fusing the argentiferous lead in a large vessel, and, when the fusion is complete, arranging the temperature to the point at which the crystallization of pure lead commences. The crystals of pure lead are then removed, as soon as they are formed, by a large iron ladle pierced with holes, and the silver is concentrated in a smaller portion of lead; becoming gradually more and more rich, until it is by successive operations brought to such a state that its separation can be made with greatest advantage by cupellation.—(*Report of Juries*, I., 8.) This process has been adopted in various Lead Works in England, France, Spain, and Prussia; and its application has rendered some Lead Mines profitable which otherwise must have been abandoned.

Again. In the Lead Mines of Missouri, Iowa, and Wisconsin, Dr. Owen states that there are vast stores of *Calamine*, or the carbonate and silicate of *Zinc*, which are treated by the miners as refuse. By mixing this calamine with lime to retain the silica, and with carbon to reduce the oxide, and distilling the mixture in earthen ware retorts, a product, which is every day becoming more valuable, may be obtained.

For separating Gold from the waste of arsenical ores Professor Plattner has discovered a very important process, inasmuch as the Mines of Reichenstein in Silesia, that contain only about two hundred grains of Gold in the ton, have been made profitable by adopting it, after having been abandoned for five centuries on account of their poverty. The ores are roasted in a reverberatory furnace, surmounted by a large condensing chamber, on which the arsenic is deposited as it rises in fumes. Oxide of iron, a certain quantity of arsenic, and the gold in the ore, remain beneath. These are placed in a vessel, so that a current of chlorine gas can be transmitted through them. The gold and iron are attacked, and afterward separated from the residue by the aid of water; and the gold is then precipitated by sulphuretted hydrogen. This simple method may readily be applied to the refuse of old works.

Count Dembinski claims as his discovery the extraction of Gold from quartz, by means of carbonate of soda. As the soda can be recovered after each operation, the cost of extraction is quite inconsiderable; while, in addition, a valuable product is obtained, known as *Silicic acid.* The merits of silicic acid are set forth in the following extract from a scientific journal:

"Wood having been, by means of hydraulic pressure, saturated by silicic acid, is thus protected from rot, and from being worm-eaten or destroyed by ants. This would be of importance for wood used in building, but particularly for sleepers used in the construction of railways. Wood simply wetted with dissolved silicic acid, is penetrated by it to the depth of about one-eighth of an inch, and will now take a fine polish of marble or rather agate, giving it a most elegant appearance. Mixed with lime, the dissolved silicic acid forms an extremely hard, insoluble, hydraulic cement, forming silicate of lime.

"If added to soap, in certain proportions it increases considerably its detergent qualities, giving it, at the same time, a very beautiful, marble-like appearance. The silicic acid having, by the precipitation process already described, been liberated from all extraneous metallic oxides, metals, and other substances, can be made use of in the manufacture of the finest looking-glasses and crystal glass. In this state of solution, the silicic acid is in the most proper state to be, by means of a simple chemical process, reduced to silicium—a metal perfectly similar to silver in color, brightness, malleability, and other qualities. It is, however, nobler than silver, because, except by fluorhydric acid, it is, like gold, not attacked by acids. One ton of pure quartz contains about six hundred and ninety pounds of metallic silicium, the price of which is at present five times that of silver.

"These statements refer only to its properties in its liquid state. When calcined and used as a powder, it is said to form, when mixed with oil, a perfectly white and opaque varnish; and, from the mathematical formation of its particles, and extreme hardness, it is adapted for grinding, and capable of entirely superseding emery for the purpose."

In working *Collieries*—and the process is applicable to shafts generally in Mines—a Mr. Rogers, in England, has adopted a novel and very important method. By employing electricity in blasting, he is enabled to explode three or more holes, inclined to each other in the depth, simultaneously; and thus lifts a large mass at once from the centre of the sinking, other large masses being in like manner afterward detached from the surrounding portions toward the sides. By thus calling in the aid of electricity, and by employing gutta-percha tubes of great size in connection with the pumps, and so avoiding the destruction of the usual arrangements, which frequently takes place during blasts while sinking a pit, better work is accomplished, with greater rapidity, and at less cost, than by the ordinary methods. This successful application of science and of modern knowledge is deserving of all attention by miners. (*De La Beche.*)

V. *In the Manufacture of Leather, more expeditious processes are desired, such as do not deteriorate the product; and new kinds of Leather are wanted—particularly one that will combine the durability of Calf-skin, the waterproof qualities of India-rubber, and the appearance of Patent Leather.*

During the last twenty years, a great number of experiments have been made, designed to expedite the processes in the production of leather, and some considerable progress has been made, as may be seen by reference to *Progress of Science and Mechanism*, Class. xvi. The hair is now removed from hides and skins by immersion, for a few hours, in lime-water, having an addition of red orpiment; and by means of sumach, light skins may be completely tanned in twenty-four hours; and with the aid of alum, it is said, even in one hour. But, unfortunately, leather made by these short processes is too porous, and not so durable as by the old methods; and though *Catechu*, *Cutch*, *Terra japonica*, and *Divi-divi*, (see BARKS FOR TANNING, *ante*,) will produce the effect in half the time required by oak bark, the latter is still preferred. It is stated, as an ascertained fact, that by leaving hides in the vats two years instead of one, the increase of weight and quality thereby compensates for the loss of time, by paying a fair interest on the capital invested. Further experiments, however, should be made in order to attain, if possible, the desideratum of shortening the time in tanning without losing in quality.

With reference to a new kind of leather, we notice that a Mr. Jeune, of London, has invented a process for producing an elastic material having the appearance of patent leather, but having the advantage of not being liable to crack or peel on the surface. He prepares an elastic compound composed of masticated india-rubber, or india-rubber combined with gutta-percha, and mixed with the sulphuret of antimony and woolen dust or waste. This compound, which forms the base of the fabric, he spreads upon thin cotton cloth, and then subjects the same to heat, in order to effect what is called the "change" in the india-rubber compound. The fabric is then ready to receive japan varnish, which is laid on in the usual manner, and subjected to a dry heat; when the first coat is properly set, a second is applied, and submitted in like manner to dry heat; and so on until the required finish or smoothness is imparted.

This is a step in the right direction; but I do not understand from the description that he has invented a leather combining the durability of Calf-skin, the water-proof qualities of Caoutchouc, and the brilliancy of Patent leather.

Among the novelties exhibited at the Crystal Palace, in New York, there was Leather manufactured from the skin of the *Porpoise* and of the *Alligator*. With regard to the former, it was said "the texture is more porous than that of ordinary uppers; but it gives evidence of having all other requisites of shoe-leather. In pleasantness of pressure, it would be quite equal to buckskin for dry weather, while it would probably be more durable." As the Porpoise is quite abundant, the manufacture of Porpoise-leather may become of commercial importance.

Of the *Alligator's* hide a leather has been made as pliant as calf-skin, and beautifully mottled, like tortoise-shell.*

---

* I am inclined to think that the day is not distant when the Alligator will be called upon to discharge his obligations to society, and

VI. *A perfect substitute for Alcoholic Burning Fluids is much needed; and if discovered, would become a very extensive manufacture.*

The Burning Fluid now in use, and of which the value annually produced amounts to some millions of dollars, was first brought into public notice about 1830. It is composed of say nine parts of highly-rectified alcohol and one of camphene. Its advantages are, that it is cheap and cleanly, and may be burned in common lamps; its

---

that the business of catching him will afford another chance for profitable industry. Oil of a very fine quality can be obtained from Alligators, and it is considered most valuable for scalds, burns, and rheumatism. The skin has been tanned, as above stated, and excellent saddles, and beautiful boots and shoes, have been made out of it. The teeth are very hard, white, and polished, and might be used for a variety of purposes. Under the fore-fins, there is an odoriferous substance which resembles musk, and, it is supposed, could be used as a substitute for the expensive secretion of the deer of Thibet or Siberia.

In Siam, there are professional crocodile charmers, in case it may be necessary to import a few. Their mode of charming is represented to be, that they spring upon the crocodile's back and gouge his eyes with their fingers, while the attendants jump into the water, some fastening ropes round his throat, others round his legs, till the exhausted monster is dragged to the shore and deposited in the presence of the authorities. Father Pallegoix affirms that the Annamite Christians of his communion are eminently adroit in these dangerous adventures, and that he has himself seen as many as fifty crocodiles in a single village so taken, and bound to the uprights of the houses. But his account of the Cambodian mode of capture is still more remarkable. He says that the Cambodian river-boats carry hooks, which by being kept in motion, catch hold of the crocodile; that during the struggle a knot is thrown over the animal's tail; that the extremity of the tail is cut off, and a sharp bamboo passed through the vertebræ of the spine into the brain, when the animal expires.

disadvantage is, that when mixed with the atmospheric gases it is highly explosive, and has so repeatedly been the instrument of fearful accidents, that a safer substitute is urgently demanded.

The substitutes that have been suggested by scientifi men, are oil of rosin, or other distilled oils, and oil from Petroleum. With respect to the latter, it is observed, that Petroleum is used in the East in lamps; and the city of Genoa, in Italy, is illuminated by gas made from this material. The drawback to its extensive use in illumination, has been some disagreeable features of smell, etc., but I notice that recently a patent has been taken out by S. White, of Liverpool, for purifying Petroleum, and fitting it for use in lamps; and in California, within a year or two, it has been manufactured into a Burning Fluid, and also applied to cooking and warming.

Petroleum wells, or "tar springs," are quite abundant in the United States; at Hinsdale, New York; Oil Creek, Pennsylvania; Liverpool, Ohio; Kanawha, Virginia; and in California; and it is probable that the day is near at hand, when this material will form the basis of a very important and profitable business.

Prof. Booth remarks: "Let us not abandon the idea of finding a liquid which shall possess the requisite qualities of cleanliness, cheapness, illumination, and freedom from danger. Sperm oil possesses the last two qualities; burning fluids the first three; lard oil is cheap and free from danger, but is not cleanly—is too liable to congeal in winter, and is apt to clog the wick. Naphtha is very little, if at all, liable to explosion; but it contains an excess of carbon, and is too apt to smoke when burned in an ordinary lamp. Since sperm oil has a high illuminating power, and is free from danger, we may yet hope to discover a liquid which shall possess these properties, together with cleanliness and cheapness combined. May not such a liquid be found among the products from the distillation of coal, to be used either by itself, or in conjunction with other substances?"

VII. *Adapt machinery and apply science to the further purification of the Products from Coal—particularly Oil from Coal.*

The discoveries that have been made of the useful products which may be obtained from Coal, are among the most remarkable of the present century. New dyes, medicines, illuminators, and lubricators, have been extracted from this black mineral; and new and very extensive manufactories have been erected to furnish these products.* In Great Britain, capital has been in-

* For the double purpose of illustrating this point, and of suggesting whether a similar manufactory could not be profitably established in the United States, I would refer to Messrs. Spence & Dixon's Chemical Works, near Manchester, England, where, according to Calvert, F.R.S., eight hundred thousand gallons of ammoniacal liquor are annually consumed in the manufacture of ammoniacal alum—the ammoniacal liquor being obtained from the extensive gas works belonging to the corporation of Manchester. He says: "The manufacture of this substance, which was so valuable as an astringent, and also to the dyer and calico printer, furnished such a remarkable illustration of the value of chemistry in aiding manufactures and commerce, that he would explain briefly the method of producing it. To obtain this substance, called ammoniacal alum, a a refuse product of coal-pits, known as aluminous shale, was heaped into small mounds and slowly burned. Shale was generally found in hard masses, which fell from the roofs of the coal mines; and the object of burning it was to render it porous and friable. The calcined friable mass was then placed in large leaden vessels with sulphuric acid, having a specific gravity of 1.65, being the strength in

vested very largely in this business, particularly in the distillation of Oil from coal. About two years ago, a Mr. Young, proprietor of the Paraffine Oil Works, at Bathgate, Scotland, testified before Court that he had made in one year four hundred thousand gallons of lubricating Oil from cannel coal, and sold it at five shillings sterling per gallon; and when asked what portion of it was profit, answered, "the principal portion."

In the United States, one or more companies have been formed for the manufacture of Coal Oil, but the business has not as yet attained an important development, notwithstanding the abundance of raw material suitable for the purpose in Pennsylvania, Ohio, Kentucky, and perhaps other States. When, however, the difficulties which now retard the extensive use of Coal Oil in illumination are removed, viz., its liability to turn red on exposure to the atmosphere, its disagreeable smell, its thickness and viscidness, the business of manufacturing it will probably assume gigantic proportions. [For an article on the Manufacture and Application of the Products from Coal, (Coal-gas excepted,) see *Franklin Institute Journal*, 59, 227, 332.]

---

which it was obtained from the leaden chambers. It was a curious fact, that this sulphuric acid could be produced from another refuse found in coal mines namely, pyrites. The calcined shale and sulphuric acid were heated in these leaden chambers for about forty-eight hours; the liquor was then drawn off, and put into another vessel, into which the ammonia—generated from another refuse of coal, namely, the gas liquor—was introduced in a gaseous state. Thus these three substances—the alumina from the shale, the sulphuric acid obtained from the pyrites, and the ammonia from the gas liquor, combined to produce ammoniacal alum, which then only required purifying by successive processes of crystallization, to give it that remarkable purity in which it was furnished to the commercial world by Messrs. Spence & Dixon, and other manufacturers."

VIII. *Discover, in some innocuous herb, a substitute for Tobacco, or compound one artificially.*

It is no exaggeration to say, that there are thousands of persons whose trembling nerves are anxiously awaiting the announcement of the discovery of a substitute for Tobacco, which shall possess its agreeable properties with none of its injurious effects. A patent has been issued at Washington for making Tobacco, by infusing the leaves of Maize in a decoction of quassia and capsicum; but this is only a very good imitation of the genuine weed. The leaf of the Sun-flower has been mentioned as a possible substitute for Tobacco; and a physician in New York has prepared a compound, to which he has given a hard name, but which, it is said, tastes more like moistened sawdust than Tobacco.

In the meantime, however, until a real substitute is discovered, there are a hundred chances to make money in putting up the genuine article in new shapes, with new colors, in new packages, with new names. HENRY WURTZ, Chemist, has recommended the manufacture of *Glycerin Tobacco*, using Glycerin as a substitute for both tin-foil and molasses. He says:—

"I have repeatedly prepared small quantities of chewing Tobacco, (the variety called 'fine cut') for persons addicted to its use, by admixture with a little glycerin, and always very much to their satisfaction. In the preparation of this drug, the manufacturer must also please the palate of the consumer by introducing some *dulcifying* ingredient. Common sugar, or molasses, however, will not answer the purpose, because they render the mass liable to ferment and turn sour. An infusion of the root, or extract of *liquorice*, is therefore usually resorted to. This does not, however, keep the Tobacco moist, as molasses would do; and to attain this, it is necessary to press into solid compact masses, and pack into very tight cases, or in the case of the finer qualities, to enclose in wrappers of tin-foil. In view of these facts, glycerin will be seen to supply every requirement of the tobacconist, as it will not only keep his product moist for an indefinite time, even when exposed to the air, but will also *sweeten* it. He may look upon glycerin as made especially for his use."

The application of machinery to the manufacture of *Cigars* remains to be successfully accomplished.

IX. *Compound a new Drink, pleasant, wholesome, and exhilarating, without being intoxicating.*

It is a suggestive fact, that the second American patent right, of which there is any record, was granted in February, 1803, for "a method of making Brandy out of all kinds of grain or fruit, equal in flavor, taste, and color, to the best imported French Brandy;" that the third patent right was for an "improved still;" and the fourth for "an improvement in the mode of impregnating Spirits of all kinds—making and improving Wines and impregnating liquids with grass, including the preservation of Milk." But notwithstanding the fact, that inventive genius was directed into this channel at an early period, I am not aware that an American has ever succeeded in producing an original, popular, and innocent beverage. Unfortunately, it has hitherto been more profitable to imitate than to originate, and by means of chemical compounds, to fabricate for a trifle what can only be produced at a considerable cost. Adulteration by poisonous admixture, however, has been carried to such an extent that it has alarmed even inebriates, and never was there a time more favorable than the present for originating a drink that, possessing the proper elements, might attain a wide-spread popularity, making a fortune for its originator.*

In prosecuting experiments for this purpose, if you should see proper to experiment, I do not know that I can aid you, except perhaps in two ways; first, by giv-

* Pure Brandy cannot be sold for less than $2.50 per gallon while an imitation can be made out of common Whisky, by chemical compounds, for 30 cents a gallon, so disguised that no one can tell the difference. The temptation to adulterate is illustrated in the following incident: A dealer in spurious Brandy recently imported enough compounds to manufacture eight hundred hogsheads of the forged Brandy. He sold it for pure, and at $2.50 the gallon; making a clear profit, as he confessed, of $100,000 on the speculation, the fabricated article costing him only about 30 cents a gallon. The fabricator having used up his compound to his samples, took these to a Chemist in Massachusetts to analyze, and for the purpose of having them made in this country if possible. The Chemist made the examination, and found one of the samples a deadly poison. He could not be tempted to have a hand in producing the mixture; whether the fabricator found a Chemist less honest, or had to wait for a new importation, will not probably be known until the Day of Judgment, when all such secrets will be made manifest. Who can begin to estimate the results of the use of these eight hundred casks on those who, before this time, have probably drunk them. Another man, who had either imported or purchased the same kinds of compounds, is now in California with them; and he boasted to a gentleman who mentioned it to the writer, that he should make $100,000 out of the operation. A quantity of French Brandy was imported into New York, and advertised for sale at auction. On a given day it was landed on the wharf. A Brandy fabricator purchased the whole lot of the importer, on the condition that the sale should take place as advertised on his account; during the night it was all removed to his Brandy Brewery, underwent the process of adulteration, was carted back, and sold next day pure as imported. (For Adulterations see APPENDIX.)

ing you the receipts of the principal fermented and distilled beverages now in use, (see APPENDIX), and suggesting to you that it is highly probable some very superior drinks may be produced from the ordinary American, and particularly from the West India fruits.

Cider from the apple, and Perry from the pear, have never been produced in that degree of perfection of which they are susceptible. A German Baron, having large estates on the Rhine, where Hock and other celebrated wines are produced, has said that many sorts of the Herefordshire apples may be made to produce as valuable and desirable a beverage as the Hock grapes, if a different process of making the liquor were adopted. [For a description of his process, see *London Society of Arts*, Vol. II., p. 9.]

For *making a good Cider*, the authorities generally concur in the following points: That the apples should be well ripened, but not in the least decayed. Every apple with the least speck of rot in it should be removed, if you wish a first-rate beverage. The decayed and inferior apples may be reserved for making vinegar. Perfect cleanliness should be observed in the grinding process, which should be performed two days before pressing, and the pomace be permitted to stand and mellow in the vat until it assumes a deep color. Hair-cloth is far preferable to straw to place between the layers of pomace; but if straw be used, care should be taken that it is clean and dry, for if at all musty the flavor will be communicated to the juice; and if water be added, it will make it hard and unpleasant to the taste. The Cider, as it runs from the press, should pass through a hair sieve into a large open vessel, that will hold as much juice as can be expressed in one day. In twenty-four hours, or sometimes less, the pomace will rise to the top, and in a short time grow very thick; and when little white bubbles break through, the liquor is ready to be drawn off. The casks in which it is put for fermentation should be thoroughly cleansed, and finished off with a fumigation of brimstone. This is done by burning a few strips of canvas inside the barrel, dipped in melted brimstone. The fumes will penetrate all the pores, and destroy the must and correct the sourness. After the fermentation is over, the Cider is drawn off into clean barrels and clarified. This can be done by mixing a quart of clean white sand with the whites of half a dozen eggs, and a pint of mustard seed, and pouring it into the barrel. It may stand in the barrel; or, if a nice article is wanted, it should be put into some old quart bottles and corked. Cider made in this manner will readily command an extensive sale and a good price.

Professor HORSFORD, of Cambridge, Mass., recently sent to the Massachusetts Horticultural Society the following receipt for improving Cider, which, he says, has been tested by a number of friends for three or four years, and with great satisfaction.

"*Receipt for Improving Cider.*—Let the new Cider from sour apples (sound and selected fruit is to be preferred) ferment from one week to three weeks, as the weather is warm or cool. When it has attained to lively fermentation, add to each gallon, according to its acidity, from half a pound to two pounds of white crushed sugar, and let the whole ferment until it possesses precisely the taste which it is desired should be permanent.

"In this condition pour out a quart of the Cider, and add for each gallon one quarter of an ounce of sulphate of lime, known as an article of manufacture under the name of *anti-chloride of lime*. Stir the powder and Cider until intimately mixed, and return the emulsion to the fermenting liquid. Agitate briskly and thoroughly for a few moments, and then let the Cider settle. The fermentation will cease at once.

"When, after a few days, the Cider has become clear, draw off and bottle carefully, or remove the sediment and return to the original vessel. If loosely corked, or kept in a barrel on draft, it will retain its taste as a still Cider. If preserved in bottles carefully corked, which is better, it will become a sparkling Cider, and may be kept indefinitely long."

Cider is said to possess medicinal properties of considerable value. It is especially beneficial as a drink for dyspeptic persons; and the *Medical Reformer* recommends it highly as a remedial agent in acute rheumatism.

Perry is the beverage made from the fruit of the pear tree, of the orchard kind. The pears are ground and pressed in exactly the same manner as those of apples in the manufacture of Cider; but it is not usual for the reduced pulp to be kept any length of time without being pressed. Mr. Knight states, that it has never been the practice in Herefordshire, or in the counties in the vicinity of it, to blend the juices of the different varieties of the pear in order to correct the defects of one kind by the opposite properties of the other; but as it is more easy to find the required portion of sugar and of astringency, as well as of flavor, in three or four varieties than in one, he supposes a judicious mixture of fruits affords a prospect of great benefit.

The pear tree supplies a less popular liquor than the apple, but it is more productive, furnishing in the proportion of six hundred gallons of liquor to the acre, when the trees are full grown, and in good bearing, the product of a single tree will often be twenty gallons of Perry; which, when made of the best fruits and bottled, may be produced quite equal to cider.

Mr. Booth, in his work on Wine-making, thus describes a sort of Wine in which pears were employed. "In the North of France, having heated fifty-five pounds of the juice of wild pears to 180°, I added about a tenth of that weight of raisins, and bunged up the whole in a cask. In a short time the heat of the liquor had fallen to 77°, when I drained out the raisins, bruised them, returned them into the must, and closed the cask so as to allow the fermentation to take place. A fortnight after, the Wine, or Perry, was racked into stone jars; and after standing three months in the cellar, it was reckoned, by good judges, to be the best white Wine from grapes."

With respect to the source from which such a beverage as is desired may be obtained, perhaps a hint may be derived from the enumeration of articles that are used as a substitute for grapes, in the manufacture of Wines. A writer mentions the damson and *Black bullace*, from either of which, alone, or with the infusion of claret leaves, a red Wine could certainly be made superior to much of the doctored trash vended under the name of Port. He says: "The Orleans plum has also been highly spoken of. The juice of cider apples, fermented with that of the damson, would form an agreeable, dry red Wine. The lists of available substitutes for the grape might be considerably enlarged; but it will suffice to mention the expressed juice of the *giant rhubarb*, which would yield Wine in excess, so prodigious is the growth and rapid increase of the plant. It naturally contains the Bin or super oxalate of potash, (often termed 'salt, or sorrel'), and malic acid in combination with lime. The addition of argor (tartar of wine), would promote the vinous fermentation. The flavor of the Wine, when completed and perfected by age, is somewhat peculiar, and may be thought somewhat like that of the cocoa-nut."

Ligon, the early historian of Barbadoes, speaks in raptures of a beverage obtained by fermentation from the juice of the pine-apple. He says, that "the last and best sort of drink that this island or the world affords is the incomparable Wine of Pines, and is certainly the Nectar which the gods drink, for on earth there is none like it; and that is made of the pine-juice of the fruit itself, without commixture of water or any other creature, having in itself a natural compound of all excellent tastes that the world can yield. This drink (he adds), is too pure to keep long; in three or four days it will be fine; 'tis made by pressing the fruit and straining the liquor, and it is kept in bottles."

The fruits of the West Indies certainly seem to contain all the elements essential to numerous incomparable beverages.

X. *The discovery of a means of producing Alcohol from substances not used as food, by substituting chemically-formed glucose for starch and sugar, is a desideratum.*

Alcohol is obtained in the United States principally from the redistillation of the juices of Indian corn, potatoes, apples, and molasses—much the greater portion probably being made from corn. Horse chestnuts, it is stated by Dr. Ure, are very prolific in Alcohol; but since the introduction of the *Chinese sugar-cane*, it has been ascertained that this possesses an undoubted advantage over most other articles, rendering the spirit distilled from it of the first quality, and fit for immediate use. M. Vilmorin of Paris, states that the Sorgho Alcohol, distilled but once, and that imperfectly, which he obtained with very incomplete laboratory apparatus, was absolutely deprived of all foreign flavors; and the liquors, when pure, were infinitely less disagreeable than that of rum; after becoming old, he supposed they would be very superior. The method adopted for distilling the sorgho is very simple, and the cost of the apparatus quite moderate. The expense attending the purchase and erection of an improved agricultural distilling apparatus, capable of working up five hundred gallons of sorgho juice in twenty-four hours, is set down by a French chemist at $290.

The amount of profit to be realized from the conversion of sorgho juice into Alcohol, of course, mainly depends upon the market price of the latter. It is evident that when Alcohol commands $1 per gallon, the profit is considerable, especially if it be true, as Mr. Olcott states, that eight cents per gallon is an over-estimate of the cost of converting sorgho syrup into spirit.

One of the most interesting chemical experiments that has yet been made in the production of Alcohol, is that by which M. Bertholet succeeded in obtaining Alcohol from bicarburetted hydrogen, in the following manner:

"Having prepared about thirty quarts of bicarburetted hydrogen, he placed them in a close retort with nine hundred grammes of pure and highly concentrated sulphuric acid. To this was added five or six volumes of water. The whole was then submitted to successive distillations, carbonate of potash being used to retain the water. In the last condenser, M. Bertholet found fifty-two grammes of an alcholic liquid corresponding to forty-five grammes of absolute Alcohol, and three fourths of the gas employed; the remainder was lost in the manipulations. This Alcohol possessed all the properties of ordinary Alcohol; the same taste and odor, the same point of ebullition, and the same colored flame; it had, too, the same dissolving power and the same reaction on all bodies; it was, indeed, regenerated alcohol. The bicarburetted hydrogen used by M. Bertholet was obtained from the decomposition of Alcohol; he made also other experiments with bicarburetted hydrogen found in common illuminating gas, and obtained the same result." (See *Ann. Sci. Dis.*, 1856.)

XI. *An efficient Apparatus for extinguishing Fires is much needed, and will yield a fortune to its inventor.*

The amount of property that is annually destroyed by fire, in the United States alone, exceeds the money value of some considerable cities. The announcement made a few years ago, that a Mr. Phillips, of London, had discovered an annihilator for fires, was therefore received with no little satisfaction throughout this country. His apparatus has been described as follows:—It consists of an iron cylinder, two feet by eight inches, having at its bottom a shallow chamber filled with water. There is also a smaller cylinder, connecting at the side, and enclosing a brick, composed of nitre, charcoal powder, and sawdust. In the brick is a vial with two compartments—the upper containing oil of vitriol, and the lower a mixture of chlorate of potassa and sugar. A plug is fitted into the cover of the apparatus, in such a position that a sudden blow may cause it to crush the vial, and thus ignite the contents. An instantaneous and forcible issue of carbonic acid and oxide, steam, and nitrogen follows; and this stream of vapor, directed upon the blazing fire, smothers and extinguishes it. This result however, unfortunately, would only follow in confined places, such as the hold of a vessel—and in so far it was valuable; but the apparatus was not effective where the current of air was strong.

A writer in the *Révue Scientifique* argues that steam is a far better extinguisher than water; and the following composition, if added to the water of a fire-engine, is said, from experiment, to do five times as much execution as water alone, viz.: a mixture of one part powdered sulphur, one part red ochre, and six parts copperas. Messrs. Booth and Morfit state that this operates doubtless from the evolution of sulphurous acid—but it is probable that anhydrous sulphuric would also be evolved.

To prevent combustion, a chemist (*Amer. Jour.*, 2d. Series, VIII., 118) proposes impregnating wood, &c., with a solution of *sulphate of ammonia*, which, if heated, is resolved into sulphurous acid, nitrogen, &c.; this would tend to extinguish commencing combustion.

XII. *The invention of a Musquito Exterminator, or a cheap substance that will effectually expel Musquitoes from rooms, would be well rewarded.*

Successful war has been made against Bugs, Roaches, Ants, Rats, and Mice; and the manufacture of ammunition for carrying on this war by those who choose to employ it, is an established and, I believe, successful business.* But the Musquito, unmolested by any one,

* The following are said to be effectual in driving away or destroying certain vermin:

To Destroy Bed Bugs.—Spirits of wine, half a pint; spirits of turpentine, half a pint; crude sal ammoniac, one ounce; corrosive sublimate, one ounce; camphor, one ounce. This mixture should be inserted into the joints of bedsteads with a syringe, and with a sponge fastened to a stick; every other part of the wood-work must be washed with it. The weed, well known as the "water pepper," or "smart-weed," (*Polygonum hydropiper*), which may now be found in abundance along ditches, roads, lanes, and barn-yards, is a destroyer of the bed-bug. A strong decoction is made of the herb, and the places infected with the insect well washed with it. The plant may also with much advantage be stuffed in the cracks and corners of the room.

To Destroy Red Ants.—The *American Agriculturist* says: "The best remedy we have found is to sprinkle sugar over a dry sponge which the Ants gather into, when they may be killed in hot water, and the sponge 'set' again."

To get rid of Cock-Roaches.—Strew the floor of that part of the

is fulfilling his appointed destiny of keeping the people in warm climates from idleness, and is also becoming a serious summer pest in northern cities. No remedy that I have heard of is successful in even disgusting him. Pennyroyal, which is recommended by some druggists, is a failure. But in China, according to Fortune (*Residence among the Chinese,* 1853–1856), a substance known as the Musquito Tobacco is in common use, and succeeds admirably. On being lighted, the fumes rise up, and the air is soon filled with odors, not at all disagreeable, though no luxury to the Musquito, for in two or three minutes after it is ignited, not a buzz is heard nor a Musquito to be seen. He took especial pains to discover what are the ingredients of this curious substance, and was informed by a manufacturer that the following articles were used, viz.: the sawings of juniper or pine trees, artemisia or wormwood leaves reduced to powder,

---

house infested by them with *green cucumber peelings cut not very thin.* The juice which they extract from it, and of which they are very fond, is said to be poisonous to them. A repetition of fresh peel for a few nights will effectually clear the house. This receipt *Appleton's Mechanics' Magazine* considers worth the price of a year's subscription.

To rid Animals and Plants of Vermin.—M. Raspail recommends to make a solution of aloes, one gramme of that gum to a little water, and, by means of a long brush, wash over the trunks and branches of trees with this solution, which will speedily destroy all the vermin on them, and effectually prevent others approaching. In order to clean sheep and animals with long hair, they must be either bathed with this solution, or be well washed in it.

To drive away Rats, Mice, and Flies.—Common mullen, and also garlic bulbs, sprinkled in stacks, or put where they frequent, will, it is said, drive away rats and mice. And elder leaves and walnut leaves, in their natural state, or in a decoction, will prevent the attack of flies both on animals and meat, and drive them away.

tobacco leaves, a small portion of arsenic, and a mineral called *nu wang*. With regard to the proportions of each, it appeared that to thirty pounds of the pine or juniper sawings about twenty of artemisia, five of tobacco, and a small quantity of arsenic were added, and each article was well beaten up with water, then the whole mixed together in the form of a thick paste rolled on a slip of bamboo.

Another substance, much cheaper than the former, is made as follows:

"Long, narrow bags of paper, say half an inch in diameter, and two feet long, are filled with the following substances, namely, the sawings of pine or juniper, mixed with a small portion of nu wang and arsenic. The proportions are thirty pounds of sawings, two ounces of nu wang, and one ounce of arsenic. This mixture is not made up in the form of a paste, like the former, but simply well mixed, and then run into the bags in a dry state. Each bag, being filled, is closed at the mouth, and then coiled up like a rope, and fastened in this position with a bit of thread. Many hundreds of these coils, neatly done up and placed one above another, may be seen exposed for sale in the shops during the hot season, when Musquitoes are numerous. When about to be used, the thread which keeps the coil together is cut; then the coil is slightly loosened, so that its sides do not touch each other, for if this happened it would ignite at various parts, and soon be consumed. The outer end is then lighted, and the whole is laid carefully down upon a bit of board, when it goes on burning for the greater part of the night. One hundred of these little coils may be bought for a sum equivalent to three pence of our money; and two of them will suffice for a night in an ordinary-sized room.

"A third substance, cheaper than either of the above, is made of a species of artemisia or wormwood (*A. indica*), which grows wild on every hill in this part of China. It is the same kind I have already noticed as forming one of the ingredients in the genuine Musquito Tobacco, and is that which was used in taking the honey from the bees in the temple of Tein-tung. It is gathered and thoroughly dried, then twisted or plaited into ropes; in which condition it is fit for use. Although cheaper, and consequently more in use amongst the poorer classes than the other kinds, it is not so efficient, and gives out more smoke than is agreeable to a European.

"I may be questioned whether the small quantity of arsenic used in making the Musquito Tobacco is entirely harmless. I am not sufficiently acquainted with the chemical action which goes on during combustion, to answer this in the negative. But it must be borne in mind, that the quantity of this poisonous mineral is exceedingly small; and the fact that Musquito Tobacco is used by probably one hundred millions of human beings, would seem to prove that it could not have any bad effects upon their health."

A physician states that a compound of the following substances is a certain preventive to the attacks of Musquitoes, Black Flies, etc., viz.: Glycerin, four ounces; oil of peppermint, two and a half drachms; oil of turpentine, four drachms—the mixture to be rubbed on the face, neck, and all exposed parts of the body

XIII. Passing on more rapidly in our enumeration of wants, we would say the world wants a *new smokeless Fuel,* which shall occupy less space, and be of less weight than any now in use, *without diminution in the amount of heating power, or liability to injure metals in contact with it.*

It is objected to the two principal fuels—Wood and Coal—that they are uncertain in value and, especially, bulky and weighty. The former objection, however, has been partially, at least, obviated by the various experiments which have been undertaken for the purpose of testing the relative and comparative value of the different kinds of Wood and Coal. [For results, see *Transactions of American Institute,* 1853, and *Overman on the Manufacture of Iron.*] It is ascertained that if a cord of Hickory Wood be worth one dollar, White Oak is worth seventy seven cents, Beach sixty-five cents, Sugar Maple sixty cents, Pine fifty-four cents, etc.; and that a ton of Coal, at $5.25, equals best Wood at $2.28, or Coal at $7, equals best Wood at $3.06. But the other objection, that Wood and Coal are bulky and weighty, is insuperable, and constitutes a serious obstacle, in particular, to the extension of marine navigation. The quantity of Coal which a steamer must carry, even on short voyages, is considerable; while on long voyages, the necessity of calling at various stations to take in fuel—the Coal often having been sent out from the port of departure at a vast expense—causes great delay, and serious inconvenience especially to mail steamers. It is therefore probable that before many years Coal and Wood, for purposes of light and heat, will be among the things that were; and a great fortune will be the reward of the discoverer of an efficient substitute. Chemists have already made considerable progress in abstracting the gases of combustion from many natural substances; and experiments in this direction will never be abandoned until what is equivalent to a ton of Coal or a cord of Wood can be carried in the vest pocket.

XIV. Again, the world wants *new articles of food*, especially a *new plant combining the strengthening qualities of animal flesh with the healthfulness of vegetables.*

It is a favorite argument of vegetarians—and the assertion is supported by the testimony of many chemists and physicians—that all the animal food artificially bred by farmers or others is, with little exception, unwholesome. It is contended that consumption, measles, dropsy, liver complaint, abound in the animals we eat, and that these diseases may thus be reproduced in our own bodies. Be

30*

this as it may, it is certain that if a plant could be discovered which would combine the chemical ingredients of flesh and vegetables, or if a compound of this description could be manufactured, it would be a very desirable addition to the substances used as food. An able writer, in alluding to this point, does not consider the discovery of such a plant by any means an impossibility. He says: "In examining the qualities of vegetables, we find that some are oily, some sugary, some glutinous; as the olive, the sugar cane, and many plants and trees yielding gum. There is yet another variety, seeming to constitute the midway mixture of the animal and vegetable—the mushroom. These vegetables seem to point out to us our course. Could we produce a new vegetable, or cross some old vegetable, so as to unite the three qualities of wheat, olives, and sugar-cane, we should have attained a species of vegetable flesh, no doubt of highly nutritious quality."

XV. In Machinery, the wants of the world are too manifold for enumeration; but there is one which, if invented, would produce such important consequences, that it must be made an exception, viz.: *a machine that will combine, in one operation, the fabrication of Clothing with the manufacture of the Cloth.*

A Westminster Reviewer, in an able article some years ago, remarked: "There is one way, and one only, to uproot the distresses of seamsters and seamstresses. It is to prohibit seams—not by an Act of Parliament, but by rendering them worthless and useless. Take away the stitches, and there would no longer be a mass of people brought up to make them. They are a remnant of our imperfect condition—of the patchwork contrivances which began with the skins of beasts as a necessity, and which we have perpetuated in particular forms till we have grown to believe it ornamental artistry. The Sussex peasant covers his unsightly smock-frock with superfluous stitching, as a rude embroidery; and gent and gentleman do the same by the fronts of their shirts. They go about God's earth, walking reproaches on the inhumanity of man, who, not satisfied with exacting drudgery from his fellow-men and from women, seeks to increase that drudgery by studious contrivance.

"The garment of Christ—without a seam--was the type of that which was to come, when another leaf in man's brain shall have been unfolded. In after years, people will wonder at the ancestral processes which constructed large flat webs of machine-made cloth, and then cut them into fragments to be joined together again by hand-drudgery. The time is coming when shirts will be made perfect in the loom by machine labor. The succinct garments of industry will be produced at prices lower than even '*Moses*' has dreamed of; and the flowing drapery of the man of leisure, or of study, will mark his status better than the cramped, unwholesome clothing that has made a jest of the distinction between standing-up and sitting-down apparel. It is a question for the mechanician to solve, how the powers of nature shall produce human garments by machinery wholly, and not in part. The problem will not be difficult to solve; and he who first solves it, shall be famous amongst men, as the chemist who shall first discover the mystery of the aromas. Then may men and women indulge in artistical decoration of their persons, when it shall cease to be the result of painful handicrafty." The invention of Sewing and Stitching Machines is a step in the right direction, but does not satisfy the want.

In 1852, the Society of Arts, in London, offered premiums for the supply of over a hundred wants (see Vol. I., pp. 47–60) among which the following perhaps were the most important:

1. For the invention of good cheap Candles, requiring no snuffing, and not liable to gutter or drip when carried about.

2. For improvements in the machinery and processes connected with the production of Coffee—both for treating the pulpy fruit and curing the bean.

3. For an improved method of Bleaching Linen safely and rapidly, and without the necessity of any after exposure "on the Green."

4. For a simple mechanical means of refining Vegetable Oils, by a quick and cheap process, so as to render them fit for burning in lamps, and for lubricating machinery.

5. For the discovery, and production to the Society, of any new substance which can be successfully used as a substitute for Gutta Percha.

6. For the production of a perfectly colorless Copal Varnish, not liable to injure the colors over which it is applied.

7. For the best form of *Street Goods' Wagon;* the improvements required are a lower centre of gravity, and a ready means of discharging heavy packages.

8. For an elastic material for Tubing suited to the conveyance of gas, and not liable to be affected by alterations in temperature, or to be acted upon by the gas itself.

9. For the production of a lustrous Wool, to be used in lieu of silk in the manufacture of fringes, carriage laces, etc.

10. For the successful application of some new means (as Electricity or Photography, for instance), for producing ornamental designs in Woven fabrics, which shall be cheaper and easier of application than those at present employed.

11. For an efficient means of removing the fatty matters from Skins, so as to render them capable of receiving mordants by the ordinary printing process.

12. For the best mode of dressing Kid for the upper leather of boots; the improvements required are strength of the grain and a good firm black dye.

13. For the best specimens of Cisterns, suitable for household or other purposes, made of glass in one piece.

14. For a Chair or Couch, affording the greatest possible amount of support to persons of weak physical powers, while writing.

To these we might add many others; a substitute for *Pen and Ink*, combining both in one instrument—a means of preventing *Gas Lights* from flickering—a machine for cleansing *New Zealand Flax*, (see *New Zealand as It Is, the Britain of the South*)—a *Cooler*, for keeping parlors or rooms cool in warm weather; and when you have succeeded in all these, and your genius is unwearied, restore the Arts which Wendell Phillips of Boston will tell you are lost.

MISCELLANEOUS CHANCES.

CHANCE 1001.—Money can be made by the *cultivation of the Osier* or the *Basket Willow*.

The business of Basket-making, extensively carried on in Europe, is yet in its infancy in this country; but that it is a sufficiently important manufacture to justify the extensive cultivation of the Osier, is evidenced by the large importations which are made of this material. Nearly the whole, however, of the more ornamental and costly varieties of Basket and Wicker work continues to be imported. The trouble and expense of peeling the twigs, heretofore almost entirely a manual operation, has been assigned as an objection to the growth of the Basket Willow; but this has recently been obviated by the invention of a machine for the purpose, by which two men, with one horse, peel from one to two tons per day, an amount of work previously requiring from thirty to forty men and boys. Another circumstance that has retarded both the manufacturing and the cultivation, is, that sufficient capital has not been employed in it. The Willow-growers are generally Basket-makers, who have simply aimed at supplying material for their own limited operations, while the mass of manufacturers depend upon the imported twigs. If, however, it be true as stated, that the imported Willow costs from $100 to $250 per ton, while a better article can be produced for $50 a ton; and that five million dollars worth have been imported in one year, the business would well reward the investment of capital.

Dr. J. L. BISHOP, who has given this subject some attention, informs me—

There are not less than one hundred and eighty species of the *Salix*, or Willow, most of them natives of Europe, and the northern and temperate parts of America. Only a few of these are much cultivated. Favorite varieties, grown in Europe, are the common Osier, (*Salix viminalis*); the red (*S. rubra*); Forby's Willow, or fine basket Osier, (*S. Forbyana*); the white Welch Willow, (*S. stipularis*); and a few others. But a practical willow-grower informs me these do not all succeed here. Of some sixty varieties he has cultivated, he finds the best are the *S. Lambertiana, S. pentandria,*

S. Cordata, (native), and the Bedford or Russell Willow, (*S. Russelliana*). The last, a native of Britain, is most cultivated, and produces all the sizes required for different kinds of work. These require a deep sandy loam, well-drained and thoroughly prepared; and a low, level, moist situation, is best. On a dry soil the growth is slower, and the shoots smaller but harder, tougher and more compact and durable. The care during the first year is similar to that for Indian corn, afterward they merely require the long grass to be kept from around the roots. If the soil is poor, it requires manuring; lime injures the twigs. All Willows may be propagated by cuttings. These should be one year's growth, twelve to sixteen inches in length, and planted perpendicularly in the soil. They may be set in rows, from eighteen inches one way by twelve the other, to four feet by two feet apart. The last is the method in this vicinity, particularly for the Bedford Willow. An acre, planted eighteen inches by twelve, will require 29,040 cuttings.

The best season for planting is late in Autumn; the season for clearing and thinning the sticks is March or April, and that for cutting is in Autumn, directly after the falling of the leaf. The shrub reaches a size sufficient for use the first year, but yields a better product if left till second year. It continues to yield for fifteen years. [For further particulars as to the propagation and management of the Willow, see Patent Office Report, 1853.—AGRICULTURAL.]

In addition to Basket-work, the Willow is adapted as a wicker-covering for demijohns, and other glassware; and the common white Willow, (*S. alba*), in Europe, is planted as a timber tree, growing to the height of thirty feet in ten or twelve years. Hundreds of miles of roadside in Russia are planted with it, and its bark is used in northern Europe in tanning and dyeing. Its wood is used for handles of instruments of all sorts—in turning, mill-work, for hoops, weatherboards, etc. Willow hats and bonnets are made of its shavings; and its bark, as well as that of the *S. caprea*, and other varieties, possess valuable febrifuge properties, for which it is much used in medicine. The former is also much cultivated as an ornamental tree in Europe, and the second as a hedge tree. The small and fine shoots of the Willow are very useful as bands for tying-up stalks, flax, grain, shrubs, and vegetables for the market; and for training trees and shrubs in gardens, and numerous other like uses.

CHANCE 1002.—Money can be made by *adding to the stock of Domestic Animals such as are capable of domestication, and possess valuable qualities for burden or draught, or for food, or for providing materials of value in the useful Arts.*

During the last few years, some noteworthy progress has been made in increasing the stock of domestic animals,—the Camel having been introduced as a beast of burden, the Cashmere Goat having been tested, and the Llama imported. A word or two in relation to these may not be amiss, as the inducements for private enterprise to extend the initiatory efforts are very considerable.

The CAMEL, which has so long been regarded as an exclusively oriental appendage, was introduced under a Government appropriation, passed in March, 1853, and has been found well-adapted for traversing the plains of Texas and the far West. As a beast of burden it is distinguished for its great strength and powers of endurance. Camels have been known to rise up with a load of sixteen hundred pounds, which they always kneel to receive. They are affectionate and tractable, and Lieut. Beale, whoh as them in charge, reports it is easier to manage a train of twenty Camels than of five mules, and that every unshod animal reached El Paso lame, except the Camels. Economical to keep, they will go a long time without water, and live upon food on which other animals would starve; requiring, in fact, little but bushes, which they prefer to grass. One Camel, it is said, will do the work of four mules, and bear the burden of three horses.

There are two kinds of Camel employed in Asia—one is the swift Dromedary of the plains, and ship of the desert of the Arabs. It is the more light and fleet of the Camel tribe, and is used exclusively by couriers and express-riders, traveling at the rate of one hundred to one hundred and thirty miles in a day. It is not adapted for carrying burdens or for mountain passes, or wet and clayey soils, on which they slip with fatal injury; but they are admirably adapted, it is believed, to the sands of our great basin and the western plains. The other tribe is the Northern or Bactrian camel, which is stouter-limbed and heavier-bodied than the former, and of great strength; but on account of his two enormous humps, and their intolerance of pressure, it is little used for burden. Its chief use is for rearing the "Booghdee," a cross between the male Bactrian and the female Dromedary. This hybrid has, like the female parent, a single hump, but in other respects is like the male parent. It is short-limbed, stout and muscular, and is the animal it is believed precisely suited to this country. Like the Bactrian original, it has a stout claw on each toe, which the Dromedary has not, by which it is enabled to climb mountains, and sustain itself on slippery ground. It is adapted to colder regions than the fleeter Dromedary, but is not so swift, and therefore well-suited to the cold regions of Western America. They are ready for full service at four years of age.

But another great advantage and profit anticipated from the "Booghdee" and Bactrian camel, in America, is from the value of the long wool of the head, neck, breast, hump, and shoulders, forming a fleece, shorn annually, which is equal to that of three or four sheep, and is employed in forming tissues surpassing in fineness and softness the most delicate flannels. The proceeds of this, it is believed, will repay the cost of maintaining the animal, especially in the far West. The Dromedary does not yield this fleece.

It is deemed necessary for the domestication of the Camel, that a supply of the two original varieties should be imported, as the mixed breed loses its qualities by breeding "in and in," as it is called.

General Harlan states that the Bactrian Camel is worth, in Central Asia, $50; a Dromedary of the plains for breeding may be had in India for $30; but superior courier Dromedaries in Beloochistan are $125 to $350; a "Booghdee" of superior quality, on the borders of Persia, $50. Females of all kinds much less. Mr. Collins states there is no impediment to the transportation of Camels in India, which can be bought for thirty rubles ($22½), and brought down the Amoor on rafts, and then taken to De Castries Bay, can be shipped direct to Puget's Sound in twenty or thirty days, and at much less cost than those imported from Egypt by Lieut. Beale.

THE CASHMERE ANGORA GOAT.—In 1849, Dr. J. B. Davis of Columbia, S. C., imported into the United States, from Central Asia, a number of these animals, which he regards as identical in species with the Persian, Angora, and Circassian Goats; and are the eating, milking, cheese and butter, and clothes-making animal of that whole country. After eight years trial they were made the subject of investigation, detailed in the Patent Office Report for 1857, in which the success of the enterprise is considered eminently favorable for their more complete domestication, and that the Angora is the most valuable species of goat for our country at present known. The following are a few of the recommendatory points: The *fleece* is very white and beautiful, yielding from four to five pounds of long fine wool or curly hair. In fineness and softness it is equal to that of the finest Saxony or Merino wool, as microscopic examination will attest. It is adapted to the fabrication of velvets, equal in all appearance to silk velvet, and of remarkable strength and firmness, as well as of camlets and worsted goods; and ladies' wear, as shallies, mouslin-de-laines, gentlemen's summer cloths, hosiery, etc., promising a beauty, strength, durability, lustre, and permanency of color, superior to the wool of the sheep or alpaca. As an article of food, the *flesh* of this goat is said to be superior to that of the sheep. Like all the goat tribe, it prefers weeds, briars, and leaves, to grass, and is even useful in destroying these in grass lands. It is, moreover, an extremely hardy animal, endures our winters well, and is found to have improved in the climate of Carolina. It is well adapted to the uncultivated mountain districts of our country, as the sides of the Alleghanies and Rocky Mountains, and to worn-out plantations and poor lands generally. It is less liable than the sheep to be destroyed by dogs, which the herd, as a body, successfully resist when attacked. When crossed with the common goat, the mixed breed tends rather to improve than deteriorate as ordinarily happens; and these half-breed females produce two kids at a birth, while the pure produce but one.

The *milk* of the animal is also a valuable article for food; and in the opinion of Irish laborers generally, the *smell* is decidedly wholesome. A goat or two placed in a sheep-cote or stable, will, they say, greatly promote the health of sheep and horses.

THE LLAMA AND ALPACA.—The Llama is to the inhabitants of the mountainous regions of Chili and Peru, what the Camel is to the Arab. When the Spaniards conquered Peru, Gregory de Bolivar states, that at least three hundred thousand Llamas were employed in carrying the produce of the mines to Potosi, and that four million annually were killed for food. Three varieties of this animal—the Llama, the "Paco" or Alpaca, and the Vicuna, inhabit the lofty Cordilleras of the Andes, from Chili nearly to the Equator. The wool of the Vicuna is very fine, resembling silk, or the fur of the beaver; that of the Llama, long, of a texture between silk and wool; and that of the Alpaca, which is a larger animal than the Llama, is very long, often from eight to twelve inches, and resembles hair. Of this, an old animal will sometimes yield, it is said, twenty to thirty pounds. Great quantities of Alpaca silk wool is imported into Great Britain, and woven into exquisite fabrics, chiefly at Paisley and Glasgow.

Several attempts have been made to naturalize the animal in Europe and the United States. The subject was agitated here forty years ago; but from insufficient attention to the natural habits of the animal and climate, the first importations did not succeed. The elevated plains on the eastern side of the Rocky Mountains, north of Texas, it is believed, will be found more congenial to them than the Atlantic States. If these animals can any where be acclimated, they will prove of great value. The Llama, like its congener, the Camel, is hardy, subsisting on the coarsest of green and succulent herbage, and even moss and lichens; and if these are supplied, they seldom seek for water. The abundance of "buffalo" grass on the "Great Plains" alluded to, where wild cattle, horses, sheep, buffaloes, antelopes, elk, and deer abound, would supply abundant forage. But their domestication in many of our inhabited cold mountain districts may be practicable, and once achieved would afford a rich return. They are very docile and manageable, and are put to work at the age of three years. Their flesh is esteemed by the Peruvians before that of the sheep, and their skins are also valuable.

To these animals a large addition might be made, especially from the Deer family. The *Reindeer* of the Laplanders is evidently a very valuable animal, and should be imported and domesticated in the United States, as may be done easily, and with great advantage. Their utility consist in their fleetness in travel, capacity for draught, and for carrying burdens; while their flesh is also valuable as food, and the skin, hair, horns, and hoofs, are of use in the Arts. The *Moose Deer*, which is not only the largest of its class, but of all the tenants of the American forests, might also be made a very valuable animal. The objection to this animal for domestic use has been its enormous antlers, which sometimes weigh seventy pounds, and spread many feet. But this can be remedied by castration, which, besides preventing their growth, and arresting it if begun, also increases its size and docility. Its gait is a long trot; they never gallop; and its speed and strength are remarkable, thus combining the qualities of the horse and the ox. None of the deer, not even the reindeer, are more easily domesticated. The Moose has been frequently used in Canada to draw sleds and carts; and in Europe it has been used by couriers, traveling two hundred and thirty-four miles in a day; and even eight hundred miles, on one occasion, were traveled in forty-eight hours, but with fatal effect to the animal.

The *Carriboo*, or *Barren ground Reindeer*, which supplies the Pemmican of the Arctic regions, is a desirable animal; and even the common Deer might be domesticated with advantage for the excellence of its flesh, and the value of its hide. The *American Bison*, or *Buffalo*, is capable of domestication; a gentleman near Lexington, Kentucky, having had for several years a herd of tame Buffaloes, which feed with the farm cattle, and are not more wild than they. They were broken to the yoke, and for drawing wagons, carts, or other heavy-laden vehicles on long journeys, the owner believes they would be preferable to the common ox. He has cows twenty years old which are still healthy and vigorous. The domesticated Buffalo, he says, will feed or fatten on whatever suits the tame cow, and requires about the same amount of food. Parts of the Buffalo are superior to common Beef. [For an able paper on this subject, see "Ruminants," by Prof. Baird, in Patent Office Report, 1855.]

It is also suggested that it would prove a good speculation to introduce the *Canadian Pony*, or to breed a small horse from Canadian mares, and short, compact, blood stallions. The ponies peculiar to the upper province of Canada are believed to be the very best for teaching boys to ride; and by proper efforts a large demand for them, at good prices, could be stimulated among the wealthy classes in cities.

CHANCE 1003.—Money can be made by the *purchase of lands on the line of progressive settlement, or contiguous to those which have been settled and improved.*

In general, speculation in wild lands has by no means proved a lucrative business. It is stated, that in nearly every instance in which large tracts of land were purchased remote from settlements, and held for a rise in value, the speculation has been a losing one.* It is how-

* Carey, in his *Social Science*, Vol. I., 167, remarks: "The owners of unoccupied lands in the United States have found, to their cost, that the 'natural agent' had no value. Led away in the same manner with William Penn, the Duke of York, the grantees of Swan River Settlement, and many others, they supposed that land must become very valuable; and many men of great acuteness were induced to invest large sums therein. Robert Morris, the able financier of the Revolution, was the one who pushed this speculation to the greatest extent, taking up immense quantities at low prices—often as low as ten cents an acre; but experience has shown his

ever equally true, that large fortunes have been made by the purchase of unimproved lands; but this has generally been by purchasing at a time when the speculation was ripe, and the former holder had not appreciated the fact, or had become wearied and disgusted by hope deferred. The secret of success seems to be in keeping within the

---

error. His property, although much of it was excellent, has never paid the charges upon it; and such has been the result of every operation of the kind. Numerous persons, owners of thousands and tens of thousands of acres, who have been paying county and road taxes, and have been thus impoverishing themselves, would now gladly receive the amount of their expenses and interest—losing altogether the original cost. Their difficulty has not resulted from any absence of fertility, but from the fact that the cost of reproduction being a steadily diminishing one, better farms are obtainable in return to a smaller amount of labor.

"The Holland Land Company purchased large quantities at exceedingly low prices, and their property was well managed; but the proprietors sunk a vast amount of capital. No portion of the United States has improved more rapidly than that part of the State of New York in which it was chiefly situated; none has derived greater advantage from the construction of the Erie Canal; and yet the whole of the original purchase-money was sunk. Had they given away the land, and employed otherwise the same amount of capital that was expended on it, the result would have been thrice more advantageous.

"It would be easy to multiply cases in proof of the position, that property in land obeys the same law with that of all other descriptions; and that this applies to towns and cities as well as land. With all their advantages of situation, London and Liverpool, Paris and Bordeaux, New York and New Orleans, would exchange for but small portion of the labor that would be required to reproduce them, were their sites again reduced to the state in which they were found by the people by whom they were first commenced. Throughout the Union there is not a county, township, town or city, that would sell for cost; or one whose rents are equal to the interest upon the labor and capital expended on their improvement."

circle of progressive settlement, and being observant of the subtle laws which regulate it; but, nevertheless, the business cannot be denominated a safe one.

A very extensive trade has been conducted of late years, in purchasing and locating *military land warrants.* Since the late enormous issue of these warrants, their price in the market has greatly depreciated, and they may now be purchased for seventy-five or eighty cents per acre, and located on land worth, at Government valuation, $1.25 per acre; and which in five years may be worth from $3 to $5 per acre. The taxes during this period are not heavy; and, in general, settlers can be induced to move on the land, pay the taxes, and improve it, upon condition that, at the expiration of three or four years, they shall have the privilege of purchasing it, at a fixed price. In States to which emigration is setting strongly, as in Kansas for instance, a hundred-and-sixty-acre warrant has frequently been sold at $2.50 or more per acre, payable in twelve months, secured by deed of trust of the land entered with the warrant. A good business has been done by judicious management in purchasing warrants, and reselling them in this way.

When you undertake the favorite American speculation of building a city, I would recommend you to try the plan of regulating its temperature by artificial means. The idea has been suggested of founding a city with streets warmed from below; so that the snow shall melt as soon as it touches the soil; and the rain evaporate—and the inhabitants always enjoy a mild temperature. The method to be employed consists in carrying the smoke of all the chimneys into drains, from which it will pass to a great hollow pyramid, erected without the city, and its motion upward to be excited by a powerful steam engine. What, think you, would be the price of lots in such a city?

CHANCE 1004.—*Purchase a tract of land favorably situated for the purpose, and convert it into an Artificial Meadow.*

In England, waste lands have been converted into meadows by artificial irrigation, and have proved one of the most profitable of speculations. Mr. Pusey, an eminent agricultural writer, refers to one of these, when he says: "I have known Mr. Roal's farm for many years. It stands alone on the wild Exmoor range of mountain land. If any one had asserted that, for a trifling outlay, he could enable heath-covered steeps to rival in produce and value the old grazing ground of Northamptonshire, he would be regarded as a dreamer. But if any owner of moors will visit Somerset, or North Devon, he will ascertain the literal truth of the statement, as I did five years ago. All that is required is a streamlet trickling down the mountain side, or a torrent descending rapidly along the bottom of the glen. *The profit of under-draining old arable land appears trifling when compared with the profit of thus forming Water Meadows,* which, according to Mr. Roals, is more than one pound [sterling] interest for two pounds invested.

"The two pages of this report, which state no more than Mr. Roals himself has done, contain a talisman by which a mantle of luxuriant verdure might be spread over the mountain moors of Wales and Scotland, of Kerry and Connemara;" and we may add, New England and other of the United States. In the former especially there are numerous sites, where the expenses of labor and leveling the land, bringing the water into a body and placing it under control, would be repaid many times out of the profits. All water, not naturally bad, will stimulate vegetation, and in many instances increase the value of grass ten times; but the fertilizing effect is greatly accelerated and augmented by using those liquids that flow from barn-yards, or by impregnating the water with manures and offal. Patzig recommends for the purpose a mixture of sheep-dung and lime; and says, if placed in the coffer-dam, it will produce the most astonishing results. In Scotland, the sewerage water of Edinburgh is appropriated to grass lands in the neighborhood with such effect, that land which before let for $500 a-year, now yields an annual rent of from $3,000 to $4,000; and in case the Government should abolish the practice, it was estimated that the proprietors would be entitled to a compensation of $750,000, as damages for the relinquishment.

CHANCE 1005.—*In California, thousands may acquire fortunes by extracting gold from the Quartz rock.*

Quartz Mining, I think, is destined to be the most permanently profitable pursuit in California. It is yet in its infancy; but you can form some judgment of the business and its prospects, by the following synopsis of the operations in progress some two years ago, as published in the *Alta Californian:*

"From Placer County we have the following:—Near Ophir are three Quartz mills, viz.:

"Empire (steam) Mill—cost $7,000; works ten hands; crushes twenty tons per diem, and yields $1,000 per diem.

"Union (water) Mill—cost $6,000; works fourteen men; crushes sixteen tons per diem, and yields $800 per week.

"Naylor (water) Mill—cost $1,000; works four men; crushes six tons per diem; value of yield not stated.

"From Yankee Jim's (Placer County) we learn that the only Quartz mill in that vicinity is that of H. H. Watson, established in July, 1855, on a capital not exceeding $5,000. Works fourteen to twenty men; steam-power; expenses, $400 to $550 per week; yields net $500 to $2,000 per week. Rate per ton not stated.

"From Nevada we have the following:

"'I know of but two Quartz mills in operation above this, viz.:—The National, at Eureka South, driven by water, and thus far not very successful, although the gold that is taken out is said to be the very best in the country, selling at $18.25 per ounce. No further particulars stated. The other mill is said to be of little importance.'

"From Vallecito we hear as follows:—

"'There are three Quartz mills in this vicinity, which have met with moderate success, having paid from four to five dollars per day to the hand. They are on a moderate scale, and work by horse-power, the capital not exceeding $300 each.'

"From Sacramento County we hear as follows:

"'Several rich Quartz Leads have been opened in the vicinity of Prairie City, Walls Diggings, and Carson's Creek, two of which are now being worked with inferior arastras, and produce from twenty to thirty dollars to the ton. Arrangements are now in progress for erecting steam mills, and working them upon an extensive scale.'

"The most extensive operations in Quartz are conducted in Grass Valley, where also is to be found the Allison Ranch Lead, supposed to be the richest in the world, yielding from $250 to $500 per ton. It is the property of six men only, who purchased the ground for a comparatively small sum, and are now reaping unheard-of profits. Since their mill started, on the first of October, they have taken out from $30,000 to $50,000 per week; and there is no apparent falling off in the richness of the ore.'

"There are altogether eleven steam and two water-power Quartz mills in Grass Valley, exclusive of the one of the Allison Ranch, which yields at the lowest, five dollars, and at the highest, two hundred dollars per ton. The whole country around contains Quartz rock; and we are assured that capital, experience, and judicious management are alone necessary to make all these mineral riches of tangible value."

[For a description of the processes of extracting Gold from Quartz, see *M'Elrath's Mining Magazine, October*, 1858.]

Another branch of business in California, which has generally paid a large interest upon the capital invested, is the *construction of ditches and canals* for the purpose of conveying water from creeks and streams to the scene of the miners' operations. These are usually constructed by Companies; and the following extract from a pamphlet on *California and its Resources* explains the *modus operandi*, and gives a glimpse of the profits of the investment.

"The *modus operandi* of the Ditch Companies, for realizing the value of their water, is as follows:

"The main ditch is constructed of a certain size, and conducts the water to the scene of operations, where it generally terminates in a reservoir. From this reservoir branches are constructed, running to the gulches, tunnels, or placers, with sub-branches to the different claims. The latter are from six to nine or twelve inches wide, and have a certain depth of water, and a certain inclination. From the width and depth of the thread of water, *combined with its rapidity*, the amount is reckoned in *inches*. The price of the inch ranges from a half to one dollar per day, according to the distance and richness of the claim. A company of four miners, realizing perhaps from thirty to one hundred dollars per day, use, we will say, from twelve to twenty inches of water, at a cost of about ten dollars per day.

"A ditch capable of supplying one thousand inches per diem would therefore realize from eight hundred to one thousand dollars per day, which, on a capital of outlay of about three hundred and sixty thousand dollars, would pay a dividend of from five to seven per cent. per month, after deducting all expenses for taxes, repairs, management, &c. This estimate is merely given to show the theory of the matter. Of all the ditches enumerated, there is not one that pays, after deducting all expenses of repairs, management, &c., a dividend of less than one and a half per cent. per month; the majority pay much more; and we know of several that yield from five to eight per cent per month clear profit, although many of these ditches were constructed at a time when labor, material, lumber, &c., were five times as dear as they are now.

"The following are reported as accurate statements of the profits of some of the Californian water companies:—

Columbian Water Company	4	per cent.	per month.
Canal on Rich Gulch	12	"	"
Ditch on the head of Rich Gulch	6	"	"
Two Flumes in Butte County	5	"	"
Prairie City Canal Company	3	"	"
Coon Hollow Canal	10	"	"
Two Ditches at Coloma	5	"	"
Rock Creek Ditch (near Georgetown)	5	"	"
Natoma Water-works (Mormon Island)	12	"	"
Gold Hill Ditch	40	"	"
Auburn and Bear River	20	"	per annum.

All these are works made by capital borrowed at extravagant rates of interest.

"A small Ditch at Jackson, which cost $1,700, pays $100 a day.

"The Sutter County Canal Company pays largely; exact revenue not known.

"The south fork of the American Canal cost between $600,000 and $700,000, and yields a profit of $2,500 per week. Constructed with borrowed capital, at five per cent. per month.

"The water companies in Nevada County pay from six to thirty per cent. per month.

"Those counties possessing as yet no ditches, require some; and those already possessing some, require more; and this would afford perhaps fifty times the employment afforded by those now in operation.

"These facts and data justify the assertion, that water or canal enterprises, so indispensable to the elements of wealth possessed by California, are, by intrinsic merit and pecuniary value, entitled to the most favorable consideration of capitalists, and are of the first importance to the commercial world. In extent and certainty of revenue, from their origin to the present time, they have been unequaled by any investments in the State; and finally, from the controlling power they necessarily exercise over the mining interest,

32

coupled with the undoubted prominence of these interests, they must be more reliable, for longer, regular, and permanent dividends, than any class of legitimate enterprises, either in Europe or America."

CHANCE 1006.—The taking and preparation of *Sardines*, though a small business in comparison with Quartz Mining and Ditch Building, is well worthy of attention. The whole Southern coast is said to abound in that small but valuable fish, of which we import from Europe thousands of cases annually, and for which we pay extravagant prices.

CHANCE 1007.—Money can be made by the *purchase of a well-selected Silver Mine in Central or South America, and especially by Associations that have capital sufficient to open up roads and work the Mines in the most effective manner.*

In Central America, it is no exaggeration to say that there are hundreds, and in South America thousands of Mines, now abandoned, that could be worked profitably by the application of proper machinery. At intervals, during the present century, attempts have been made to render available the riches concealed in these Mines; but generally they were abortive, though in some instances remarkably successful. Some thirty years ago, a Spanish empresario purchased one of the abandoned Mines near San Miguel, in San Salvador; and, after investing his own property, borrowed $100,000 to get the Mine in order. In less than six months thereafter, he was able to pay his obligations; and, although he died before the end of the year, he left $70,000 in gold and silver, the produce of the Mine. After his death, the ownership was disputed, and the Mine is now, as before, filled with water.

The Mines in Tobanco, when worked, we are told, yielded upward of one million dollars annually — the principal one alone yielding one-fifth of this amount—although the operations were conducted in a most primitive manner, and without machinery. The want of proper machinery has been the principal cause of the failure which has attended various attempts to work these Mines; and this non-application of the necessary machines has been occasioned principally by the want of roads. In one instance, at least, very fine machinery was sent out from England to work a Mine; but it was made so heavy that it could not be transported from the coast. Hence, an essential preliminary to working these Mines would seem to be the construction of roads; but a Company established with capital sufficient for this purpose, besides purchasing all the principal rich Mines in a given district, and applying the proper machinery, would very probably realize the profits anticipated from the famous speculation of John Law—the Mississippi Scheme.

In the new Territory of Arizona, there are said to be very rich Mines. [For an article on the Gold and Silver Mines of the World, see *De Bow's Rev.*, July, 1856.]

CHANCE 1008.—An extensive and profitable business may also be done by *manufacturing Salt along the Atlantic coast by Solar evaporation, according to the most approved methods of modern discovery.*

The consumption of Salt in the United States amounts to an average of a bushel to each inhabitant—being twice as much as the average in Europe; and of this quantity about one-half, say 15,000,000 of bushels, costing $3,000,000, are imported. Professor Thomassey, during the last two or three years, has been doing good service in calling attention to the importance of increasing the manufacture of Solar Salt, and especially by recommending the adoption of processes by which a superior quality may be made for less than the cost of the inferior. He remarks, referring to the Salt Works at Syracuse, where 6,000,000 bushels are made annually—5,000,000 by boiling, and 1,000,000 by Solar evaporation,—

"When I went, near the close of 1854, to visit this splendid laboratory of human skill, I asked the producing price of the article.' 'It varies in some places ten or twelve cents a bushel, in others seven or eight.' 'Very well, I will take as your standard the minimum price, seven cents. Now, as it would take too long to give you my secret, I prefer to reason with your official reports. In report of 1854 (page 14), Professor Cook, appointed by Syracuse itself, tells you that almost three-fourths of the evaporating power is lost in the actual process of making Salt. Then you will understand that by controlling all the evaporating force of the sun and winds, you could have, as we in the south of France, three times more Salt than is now made in your wooden vats; or the same quality, three times cheaper. Indeed, for the last twenty years, the French Sea Salt per one hundred kilogrammes of two hundred and thirty-two pounds (four bushels) costs eight or nine cents, or about two cents a bushel. This fact is of public notoriety. By some new improvement in Salt Works which I introduced in Italy, in 1848, I have produced the bushel, for one and a-half cents, from the brine of the Adriatic Sea, which is six times weaker than yours; for it has only two-and-a-half per cent. of Salt, while yours has sixteen or eighteen per cent. Thus, in Syracuse, in spite of the richness of the brine, the cost of the manufacture per bushel is seven cents, when in France and Italy it is only two cents. Why so incredible a difference? Read once more the report of Professor Cook: They lose three-fourths of their solar evaporation." [For a description of the modes by which the best Salt is made by Solar evaporation in France and Southern Germany, and the processes deemed most available in this country, see *De Bow's Review* for *August* and for *October*, 1857.]

In France, M. Balard has succeeded in extracting from sea-water a number of important Salts—the Chloride of Potassium, Sulphate of Soda, and Sulphate of Magnesia—for which a Council Medal was awarded at the London Exhibition in 1851. [See *Reports of Juries*, Vol. I., 93.] This may be the germ of a new and important manufacture.

CHANCE 1009.—A fine field for increasing the profits of industry is presented in *the substitution of less valuable raw materials in various manufactures; for instance, Horse Chestnuts and unsound Potatoes in the manufacture of Starch.*

I have already alluded to the importance of discovering a process by which glucose and grape sugar may be converted into the sugar of commerce, and of making alcohol from substances not used as food. Recently a Frenchman has discovered that Horse Chestnuts are a valuable material from which to make Starch; and the *Mark Lane Express* (quoted in *Mer. Mag.*, 38, 505) describes a machine, which any machinist is competent to fit up, by which unsound potatoes may be rasped to a pulp, and made into Starch. It says:

"No grower of potatoes to any considerable extent ought to be without this addition to his agricultural implements of machinery, especially in those parts of the country where it is difficult to dispose of a crop of unsound potatoes, and it may not be convenient to consume them by cattle or pigs. In such cases, the diseased tubers are scarcely worth the raising; and we have this season heard of one instance in which the growers will not go to the expense of raising them. The money produce of manufacturing the potatoes may be stated as follows:

	£	s.	d.
One ton of potatoes, or 2240 lbs., produces, at 17 per cent., 3 cwt. 1 qr. 16 lbs. of Starch, at £22 per ton..........	3	15	0
One cwt. of residue..................................	0	11	0
	£4	6	0

Against this must be charged the expense of manufacture, and the wear and tear of machinery, neither of which is at all costly, as they require neither skilled labor nor complicated machineries. Were it not for the Excise, the Starch, when extracted, might easily be converted into sugar by a chemical process, every hundred-weight of Starch (one hundred and twelve pounds) producing one hundred pounds of sugar."

CHANCE 1010.—The adaptation of *Steam or Hot Air for the propulsion of vehicles on plank or common roads*, is well worthy of attention.

For about one hundred years the notion has been abroad, that vehicles could be propelled on common roads by the agency of Steam. As early as 1758, Dr. Robinson, while a student of Glasgow, is said to have suggested the idea to Watt, who commenced the construction of a model contrivance for that purpose; but, for some reason, abandoned it before completion. It appears, however, that he never lost sight of the project; for, in 1784, in his patent, he describes a "Steam Carriage." But previous to this latter date, in 1782, a Mr. Murdick, a Cornish Engineer, it is generally admitted, constructed a Steam Carriage, though little or nothing is known of its performance. In 1786, Oliver Evans, of Philadelphia, applied to the Legislature of Pennsylvania for an exclusive right to use Steam Wagons in that State; but, as he was considered insane on the subject, no notice was taken of the application. In 1804, however, he constructed a dredging machine, at his works, and moved it on temporary wheels by the steam-engine, a mile and a-half, to the river. From that day to this, at intervals, Steam Carriages for traversing common roads have been constructed; but though sufficiently successful to manifest the entire practicability of the idea, they have not come into general use

Recently, however, several machines, on different models, have been constructed simultaneously at different places; and one was run, for months, along the most crowded thoroughfare in New York city. Hence it is probable that, at an early period, this long-nursed idea will be developed into practical utility, and carriages, propelled by Steam or Hot Air, will constitute a regular mode of conveyance on long lines of level road, both plank and gravel, and will be found especially useful in the West.

Balloons, or Flying Machines, for conveying passengers through the air—appliances for transmitting packages letters, etc., long distances almost instantaneously, and Steam Carriages for common roads, will be established realities before the close of the present century.

CHANCE 1011.—The manufacture of various articles from *Clay—as Pottery and Porcelain—can be profitably extended in the United States, by selecting the best locality, and adopting the processes which have been successful in other countries.*

The progress which has been made in England, and on the Continent of Europe generally, in the Art of Semivitrification, may be learned by reference to the Report of the Juries of the Great Exhibition in London, in 1851, and to a work on Pottery and Porcelain, by Joseph Marryat.

Prof. Booth, of Philadelphia, prefaces an article on the recent improvements in painting Glass and Clay-ware, with the following observations on the progress of the Art in the United States :—

"The materials for all these wares, except brick, are ground fine, made into a slip with water, partially dried to a plastic state, in which state they are formed, by pressing, throwing and moulding, into the endless varieties of forms which we daily witness. A glaze is given to the surface by covering it with red lead, for common ware; with a fusible flux or glass containing lead, for the better wares; and with a glaze chiefly composed of feldspar, for porcelain. A very high heat is given to common earthenware, and a much higher to porcelain, sufficient to cause the ware to undergo incipient fusion. The subject presents a wide field for improvement by the application of chemical principles, although at the present time we need more of sound practice in the United States, especially in the finer kinds of clay-ware. Our common and fire-bricks, and common earthenware and stone-ware, are already of excellent quality, and our black-lead crucibles are superior to the German, the best being made at Taunton, Mass., and Jersey City, opposite New York. We employ pots from both establishments at the United States Mint, and melt in them about twenty-five hundred ounces gold at once. Although the quality is not uniform, they are generally excellent.

"Some attempts have been made to produce fine pottery (*faience*, Liverpool ware), but few have met with success; and among the latter we may mention the Pottery Company at Jersey City, and the Spring Garden Pottery, Philadelphia. Porcelain was made at Jersey City in 1816, and a successful establishment was conducted at Philadelphia for some years, but closed in 1836. Stone-ware of good quality is made in many places, especially in New York, Philadelphia, and Baltimore, but is not yet equal in quality to the Lambeth ware of London. We believe the location is yet to be found, where many potteries can gain a permanent foothold; the first essential being bituminous coal; the next, good clays in some abundance; and the third, facility of communication by water or railroad. The finer qualities of clay and feldspar will bear transportation, and may even be obtained on our seaboard, from Devonshire, etc., England, at about the same cost as they are in the Staffordshire potteries. The most likely position for a potting district is in Western Pennsylvania, or on a few points on the Ohio or Missouri Rivers, where the first and greatest essential, fuel, is abundant."

CHANCE 1012.—*Manufacture Novelties that will pay good profits, and admit of extensive advertising to bring them into public notice.*

In Europe there are several very extensive establishments engaged exclusively in producing fancy articles, called *small-wares*. The firm of Monch & Co., in Germany, employ five hundred persons, and an engine of twelve-horse power, in manufacturing notions *in Leather*. A firm in London make and sell over a half million of *Canes* annually, and maintain their reputation by originating novelties—the latest that I have heard of being Canes ornamented with lithographic impressions on paper, and varnished. The manufacture of *Fans* is a great business in India and China, and it is believed it would pay to import some workmen from India, and establish the manufacture of the rarer varieties in this country. Umbrellas and Parasols are favorite objects with Frenchmen to exercise their genius upon; although something has been done in this way in this country, as may be seen by reference to a work entitled, "Philadelphia and its Manufactures," page 392. One of the French novelties is a great-coat, which, upon occasion, may also serve as an Umbrella. It is made of an impervious material, and has, running along the lower edge, an air-proof tube; while, under the collar, is a little blow-hole communicating with this tube. The wearer applies his mouth to this hole, and with a few vigorous exhalations he inflates it with air. The tube takes the consistency of a hoop, the great-coat takes the form of a diving-bell, and the drops fall a long way outside the wearer's feet. This has suggested the invention of a *Lady's Fan*, which may also be capable of expanding into a Parasol or Umbrella—an idea that, in view of the wonderful applications of Gutta Percha and Caoutchouc, can scarcely be called impracticable. The success of Patent Medicine men shows, that one single good article, if properly and extensively advertised, is sufficient to yield a fortune.

Chances 1013–1017.—The development of the resources now existing for the supply of fibrous materials for Fabrics, Cordage, Paper,* and Papier-Mache; the utilization of the fertilizers now wasted in cities; the condensation and preparation of all *waste animal matter*, so that, as manure, it may become the sustenance of plants and crops; the adoption of scientific processes in *deodorizing* places infected with noxious smells, and *disinfecting drains and sewers*, are all available opportunities for profitable industry to the proper persons.

In the foregoing enumeration of Chances, I have generally selected such as, while also useful and novel, could principally be recommended as lucrative or money-making to the individuals who would undertake and prosecute them in the right way. I might extend the list greatly, by referring to such as could principally be recommended for their benefit to society in general. The following, however, are not unworthy the attention of practical men.

I. The establishment of *Schools for the education of persons, especially young women, in the Arts of Housewifery, and, in particular, scientific Cookery.*

In 1855, a proposition was made in London to open a "College of Domestic Economy," where every thing necessary to a perfect knowledge of the Culinary Art, and other domestic matters, should be taught by persons of experience and ability. The students for practice it was

* Chevalier De Claussen experimented on a great variety of substances as materials for Paper-making, and concluded that the *papyrus* of the ancients, and that our *common Rushes, (Juncus effusus)*, containing forty per cent. of fibre, are a perfect substitute for Rags.—(See *Ann. Sci. Dis.*, 1856.

proposed to divide into classes of four or five each, with a servant student to attend on each class to assist them in their operations. Each class was required to provide what was necessary for their practice, to be arranged by the student managing the class for the week; and the articles prepared, to be consumed at their meals. Without knowing the fate of this proposition, I doubt not that the time will come, when not only such colleges will be established, but teachers of Cookery will be as numerous in the cities, as teachers of French, Music, and Italian now are.

Prof. CHARLES U. SHEPARD, of Charleston, S. C., in a letter to me, states, that he has heard the opinion expressed by eminent physicians, that *if the Art of Cookery, as understood and practiced in France, could be introduced into our country, it would elongate life ten years,* besides diminishing no inconsiderable amount of distressing illness, and consequent incapacity for business. He says:—

The inference may be slightly exaggerated; but having had some opportunity of observing the mode of living in nearly every State of the Union, I am disposed to look upon it as a pretty near approximation of the truth. When you add to our unskilled cookery, the rapid manner in which the food is eaten, and the general non-observance of those precautions of partial rest after the principal meals of the day; of proper exercise in the open air after digestion is nearly completed; and of living, (and particularly of sleeping), in sufficiently ample and thoroughly ventilated rooms, with a judicious regulation of the temperature during the cold season of the year;—when all these considerations are embraced, I think no one can for an instant doubt, that as a nation, we have before us, in the department of Dietetics, a most fertile field for improvement. The evil is, no doubt, appreciated to some extent, and great improvements have been introduced during the past ten years in our principal cities. But good bread and palatable soups, and properly cooked meats, are still rarities among the people at large. Can nothing be done to render their prevalence more common? Could not each State found a Professorship of Dietetics in one of its Colleges, where, by means of a Text-book and Lectures, the young men who are publicly educated might obtain the much needed information? Might not also less extended, but elementary instructions on this branch be afforded and required from competent teachers in all the academies and larger schools, especially in those where girls and young ladies receive their education? Should not our daughters have the opportunity of spending some of their precious hours before the table in the kitchen, as well as around that in the parlor? before the kitchen range, as well as the piano?

If he would be pronounced a great public benefactor, who should teach the farmer to raise two blades of corn where he before could obtain but one, ought not a system of educational measures that would, in a single generation, result in elongating the span of human life one fifth its present dimensions, and greatly augmenting its enjoyment and usefulness, not merely for the space of this prolongation, but for its entire length, be regarded as worthy of our most strenuous care and attention? I communicate this as a mere hint, hoping it may strike you as deserving of a more careful elimination.

In connection therewith, I have sometimes reflected upon the enormous waste that attends every thing connected with the food-crops in the United States. From the time that the harvesting commences, up to their final preparation for the table, the losses are vastly beyond what accrues in the countries of Europe. In making this comparison, I have been led to estimate this waste equal to the support of a population one tenth greater than we now possess; while that which is actually consumed from a defective preparation, and other connected causes, (above hinted at), suffers an unknown loss in the work of nutrition. In the improvement to which I call your attention, is a mine well worthy of the political economist, the educator, and the philanthropist.

II. *The opening of a Museum for the exhibition of all objects bearing upon physical comfort and domestic economy.*

In Paris, a Society exists for this object under the name

of the *Societé d'Economie Charitable;* and we notice, it was recently proposed to establish a similar institution in London. These Museums contain specimens of the most approved and cheapest kinds of furniture, household utensils, clothing, fuel, and other stores; besides models and plans of the external and internal arrangements of buildings of every description—workshops as well as dwelling-houses. Such an institution would be eminently useful, and in a large city could perhaps be made a remunerative investment.

III. *Establish a Universal Natural History depot, for the collection and sale (in scientifically-arranged cabinets) of objects in all the departments of Natural History.*

No one will appreciate the importance of this suggestion so well as scientific men. Prof. SHEPARD, its author, who is eminent alike in practical suggestions and scientific investigations, enters into some detail with regard to it, in a letter to the writer, and says:—

It should be presided over by an eminent naturalist. A body of ten or fifteen well-qualified collectors, in the different departments, should be kept constantly in the field; and an equal number at home arranging and preparing the materials. It should be less the object to sell single specimens, in any department, than to furnish systematically-arranged collections. By such an institution, all our schools, academies, and colleges could be provided, at a cheap rate, with standard cabinets capable of affording the most correct information—far beyond the meagre stock at present acquired from books and teachers without such aid.

If the right persons would engage in the enterprise, and it should come to have something of a national character, I have no doubt it would defray all its expenses, and exert a most favorable influence upon the intelligence and prosperity of the country.

I have thus endeavored to answer, imperfectly as I am

well aware, but carefully as a very limited leisure would permit, your inquiry, *What chances there are to Make Money;* and to revive your courage, by showing how abundant are the opportunities for a man, blessed with a sound mind in a sound body, to acquire an independence, and even a moderate fortune. I could easily duplicate the number of opportunities, especially by entering within the precincts of Machinery, but I fear you may be—I will not say, like the ass between two bundles of hay—already more perplexed than benefitted. Like Franklin, and all my predecessors, you perceive I have not been able to discover any royal road to wealth; and am compelled to express the conviction, that the law is as operative now as in the days of Marcus Tullius—*Nullum bonum sine opere,* no excellence without labor. The fields are golden with the ripened harvest, but we must reap, and thresh, and grind, and bake, before we can eat bread; fuel exists in abundance, but it is overlapped by layers of clay, and shale, and sandstone; or stands in forests, with fibres toughened by a thousand storms. Work, discouragement, anxiety, are inevitable incidents in all pursuits and conditions of life; and so designed, doubtless, to teach us, that even though we make this earth a new Eden, it is not our permanent habitation—that Money is not the one thing needful—and that pecuniary success is not the best nor the final success.

> "And may you better reck the rede
> Than ever did th' adviser!"

APPENDIX.

VALUABLE SECRETS AND RECEIPTS.

The following Secrets and Receipts, appended by request, are selected from reliable sources and high authorities; and include some that, it is said, have been sold for large sums.

ALLOYS. A Good Chance for Fortune in Discovering a New.—It is a curious, but nevertheless an undeniable fact, that no kind of manufacture has received less benefit from the recent progress of chemical knowledge in this country, than the fabrication of alloys. This is all the more surprising, when we consider the enormous field open to inquiry, and the richness of the harvest to be there gathered. A new alloy is really a new metal given to society; and although the apathy of scientific men with respect to the subject has hitherto led to the production of very few such metals, yet more than one example may be cited, where a large fortune has followed upon an invention of this kind.

The following are some of the most important alloys which have yet been discovered. *Brass* of good quality, consists of about thirty-four zinc, and sixty-six copper, in one hundred parts. A *malleable Brass* has been prepared by Elsner, by fusing together sixty parts copper and forty parts zinc. Great care is requisite in the treating, lest too much loss of zinc ensue, and thus render the process unsuccessful. To obviate this difficulty, he advises, as a better plan, substituting a proportional mixture of Brass for the zinc, and supplying the deficiency of copper. *Type-metal* consists of about six parts of lead, and one of antimony. *Bell-metal* is composed of four parts of copper to one part of tin. *Speculum-metal* contains about equal quantities of copper and tin, with small and variable proportions of arsenic; it may consequently be looked upon as composed of two atoms of copper, and one of tin. *Pewter* and *Britannia-metal* are triple compounds of tin, antimony, and lead, in which the proportions approach, for the first, an atom of each ingredient; and for the second, three atoms of tin, two of antimony, and one of lead. *Solder* is more variable than any of the others; but the best kind is made with three parts of lead, and one of tin, which corresponds to about two atoms of lead, and one of tin. An improved *German Silver* is made by melting ten parts copper, two parts nickel, and six parts of iron-zinc alloy; or, eight parts copper, two parts nickel, and four parts iron-zinc alloy. A much larger proportion of the iron-zinc renders the metal too hard for rolling, but good for some casting. The nickel and copper are first melted, and the zinc alloy then introduced under cover of a reducing flux.

Alloys for Bearings of Axles of Locomotives.—An alloy of eighty-five lead and fifteen antimony is recommended to be cast in a box, and then greased in the usual way with soda, tallow, and palm-oil. The part does not become warm, and the alloy prevents the lateral vibrations.

Alloys for Bearings of Rollers, Turning-lathes, Wagon-boxes, &c.—For heavy works, Tapp recommends one pound copper, three and a half ounces tin, and four and a half ounces lead. The copper is first fused, the tin next added, and lastly, the lead; and, before casting, the whole is well mixed. For smaller machinery with hand-power, the best alloy is seventy-three parts tin, eighteen parts antimony, and nine parts copper.

Fenton recommends the following Alloy as having proved serviceable for bearings on English railroads: Eighty parts zinc, five and a half parts copper, and fourteen and a half parts tin. It is forty per cent. cheaper than brass; may be fused in iron pots, and is a good alloy for cocks.

See a tabulated view of many alloys, employed in the arts in different proportions, in the *Polytech. Notizblatt*, 1847, &c.

BEER. Root.—Take of molasses three gallons; add to this ten gallons of water at sixty degrees. Let this stand for two hours, then pour into a barrel, and add powdered or bruised sassafras bark, half pound; bruised wintergreen half pound; bruised sarsaparilla-root, hal.

pound; yeast, fresh and good, one pint. Water sufficient to fill the barrel, which is estimated to hold from thirty-three to thirty-five gallons, is then put in. Let this ferment for twelve hours, when it can be bottled if desired.

Spruce Beer.—Take oil of spruce, forty drops; oil of sassafras, forty drops; oil of wintergreen, forty drops. Pour one gallon of boiling water on the oils, then add four gallons of cold water, three pints of molasses, one pint of yeast. Let stand for two hours, then bottle it for use.

Another receipt for a *transparent Spruce Beer* is as follows: Cream of tartar, four ounces; sugar, ten pounds; essence of pipsissewway, one ounce; yeast, six gills; water twenty gallons. These are all put into a cask and allowed to ferment, when the beer is ready for use.

To make excellent Table Beer.—Take two gallons (eight quarts) of boiling water, put a pound of sugar, a quarter of an ounce of ginger, and two bay leaves; let this boil for a quarter of an hour, then let it cool to the heat of warm new milk; then add yeast, and work it the same as other beer.

BLACKING. BOOT AND SHOE.—The ingredients in Blacking are the same in most cases, and consist of bone-black, sugar or molasses, sperm oil, sulphuric acid (oil of vitriol), and strong vinegar. Each maker has, of course, proportions and methods of mixing these peculiar to himself. Paste Blacking is now made in precisely the same way as liquid Blacking, excepting that the last portion of vinegar is not added.

According to Baron Liebig, Blacking is made in Germany in the following manner: Powdered bone-black is mixed with half its weight of molasses, and one-eighth of its weight of olive oil; to which are afterward added one-eighth of its weight of hydrochloric acid, or nitric acid, and one-eleventh of its weight of strong sulphuric acid. The whole is then mixed up with water to a sort of unctuous paste.

Blacking for Harness.—Melt two ounces of mutton suet with six ounces of beeswax; add six ounces of sugar-candy, two ounces of soft soap, dissolved in water, and one ounce of indigo, finely powdered; when melted and well mixed, add a gill of turpentine. Lay it on the harness with a sponge, and polish off with a brush. Three sticks of black sealing-wax dissolved in a half pint of alcohol, will make a quick-drying varnish, liable, however, to crack the leather.

BOILS. A REMEDY FOR.—A correspondent of the London *Family Herald* states, that when Glycerin is applied to boils in an incipient stage, it soon brings them to a favorable condition, and heals them.

BOOTS AND SHOES. HOW TO PRESERVE.—F. Maceroni, in a communication to the London *Mechanics' Magazine*, says: "I have only had three pairs of boots for the last six years (no shoes), and I think that I shall not require any for the next six years to come! The reason is, that I treat them in the following manner: I put a pound of tallow and half a pound of rosin, in a pot on the fire; when melted and mixed, I warm the boots, and apply the hot stuff with a painter's brush, until neither the soles or upper leathers will suck in any more. If it is desired that the boots should immediately take a good polish, dissolve an ounce of beeswax in an ounce of spirits of turpentine, to which add a teaspoonful of lamp-black. A few days after the boots have been treated with the tallow and rosin, rub over them the wax and turpentine, but not before the fire. Thus the exterior will have a coat of wax alone, and shine like a mirror.

Tallow, or any other grease, becomes rancid, and rots the stitching as well as the leather; but the rosin gives it an antiseptic quality which preserves the whole.

CANDLES. IMPROVED MOULD AND DIPPED.—The ordinary tallow candle is a nuisance, and in no house, whose occupant makes pretensions to thrift, should one be seen. Some very important improvements have been effected in this manufacture within a few years, but they are adapted principally for extensive, not domestic, manufacturing operations. It is possible, however, for those who make their own candles to obtain a much superior article, by attention to the following processes for the purification of tallow: Three and a half ounces of *alum* to each pound of suet, dissolved in a pint of hot water, will stiffen and clarify the tallow. *Cream of tartar* produces even a better result than alum. Morfit, in his "Chemistry applied to the Manufacture of Soap and Candles," gives a German process for preparing tallow so that it will not run or gutter, while it will last longer than ordinary.

"Take twenty-four pounds of mixed suets, coarsely minced, and place in a caldron of boiling water; proportionally as the water evaporates, supply the deficiency. Strain the contents of the kettle through a clean cloth; after which, heat the suet for half an hour with two pints of pure water, in which one ounce and a half of alum, two ounces of potash, and eight ounces of common salt, have been dissolved. The whole being again strained, the same quantity of water is added; and moreover, to every eight pounds of tallow add half an ounce of saltpetre, half an ounce of sal-ammoniac, and one ounce of alum, all finely powdered, and thoroughly mixed together. The mixture being heated, or rather gently boiled until bubbles cease to form, the surface becomes smooth, and a small transparent place is perceptible in the centre; the fire is then withdrawn, and the whole left to cool. As taken from the caldron, the lower surface of the blocks is covered with the precipitated impurities; to separate which, and give a final cleansing to the tallow, it must be melted anew with two drachms of fine saltpetre; and after skimming off the scum that arises to the surface, the clear tallow is run into proper vessels. It is said that candles made of suet thus rectified, endure two hours longer than ordinary candles; and when furnished with wicks half cotton and half hemp, soaked in alcoholic solution of camphor, last still longer, and without running or guttering.'

Directions for making Good Candles from Lard.—For twelve pounds of lard take one pound of saltpetre, and one pound of alum; mix and pulverize them; dissolve the saltpetre and alum in a gill of boiling water; pour the compound into the lard before it is quite all melted; stir the whole till it boils, and skim off what rises; let it simmer till the water is all boiled out, or until it ceases to throw off steam; pour off the lard as soon as it is done, and clean the boiler while it is hot. If the Candles are to be run, you commence immediately; if to be dipped, let the lard be cooled first to a cake, and then treat it as you would tallow.

CHOCOLATE. HOW TO MAKE.—The following is a formula given by a late writer: To six pounds of nut (cocoa) add three and a half pounds of sugar, seven pods of vanilla, one and a half pounds of corn meal (maize, ground), half a pound of cinnamon, six cloves, one drachm of capsicum (bird pepper), and as much of the racono, or arnotto, as is sufficient to color it, together with ambergris, or musk, to enforce (as he says) the flavor, but in reality to stimulate the system.

Hofmann, in his Monographia, entitled *Potus Chocolati*, recommends Chocolate in all diseases of general weakness, macies, *low spirits*, and in hypochondrial complaints, and what, since his time, have been termed *nervous diseases.* As one example of the good effects of Cocoa, he adduces the case of Cardinal Richelieu, who was cured of marasmus, or a general wasting away of the body, by drinking Chocolate. And Edwards informs us that Colonel Montague James—the first white person born in Jamaica, after the occupation of the Island by the English—lived to the great age of one hundred and four; and for the last years thirty years of his life, took scarcely any other food than Chocolate. He remarks: "It is also certain that those who indulge in excesses find their vigor more speedily restored by the alternate use of Chocolate and coffee than by any other ingesta; and pigs, goats, and horses, which are fed even on the spoiled berries, are observed to become very speedily fat, and in good condition."

Chocolate is an economical drink, both in price and amount of nutrition; and its use should be extended among artisans, laborers, and the poor generally.

CORDIALS. MEDICINAL. *Anise Seed Cordial.*—Put into a still one pound of bruised Anise Seeds; proof spirit, six gallons; water, half a gallon; draw off five gallons, with a moderate fire. By infusion, add three-quarters of an ounce of the Oil of Anise Seed, and four pounds of refined sugar to eight gallons of rectified spirits; fine with an ounce of alum.

Caraway Cordial, by distillation, is made as the last; some add orange peel. Or mix together three-quarters of an ounce of oil of caraway and four pounds of sugar; add ten drops of oil of cinnamon; two drops of the essential oil of orange, and as much of that of lemon; fine with alum.

Cinnamon Cordial.—Dissolve one pennyweight of oil of cinnamon with sugar as above; add to this three-quarters of a pound of rectified spirits, half an ounce of orange peel, and as much lemon peel, with the same quantity of cardamom seed; put one gallon of water to this; fine with alum, and, if you wish it colored, add some burnt sugar.

Citron Cordial.—Beat up half an ounce of essence of lemon, and as much of that of oranges, with three or four pounds of refined sugar; add to this a quarter of a pound each of dried lemon and orange peel; infuse this in six gallons of rectified spirits that has stood upon seven pounds of figs for a week; if required, add some water.

Blackberry Diarrhœa Cordial.—To half a bushel of Blackberries, well-mashed, add one quarter pound of allspice, two ounces cinnamon, three ounces cloves; pulverize well, mix, and boil slowly until properly done; then strain, or squeeze the juice through homespun or flannel, and add to each pint of the juice one pound of loaf-sugar. Boil again for some time; take it off, and, while cooling, add half a gallon of best Cognac brandy. Dose for an adult, half a gill; for a child, a teaspoonful, or more, according to age. Also a pleasant beverage.

COSMETICS; OR SKIN BEAUTIFIERS.—Of these, the most universally employed, are soap and water. In Paris, aromatic vinegar is substituted by some ladies for water; and some in all countries use neither soap, water, nor vinegar. To give an artificial bloom to the complexion, *Rouge* is the best Cosmetic that can be employed, and, according to Dr. Ure, the only one that can be used without injury. Many of the liquid preparations, with fanciful names, as Milk of Roses, Cream of Roses, etc., contain sugar of lead, and are extremely injurious.

To *remove freckles* and eruptions, the most valuable Cosmetic is said to be GOWLAND'S LOTION, which is prepared as follows:

Blanched bitter almonds, one ounce; blanched sweet almonds, a half ounce; beat to a paste; add pure water one pint; mix well; strain through a piece of coarse muslin; put into a bottle; add corrosive sublimate, in powder, ten or twelve grains dissolved in a teaspoonful or two of spirits of wine, and shake well. As a beautifier of the complexion, it is employed by wetting the skin with it, either by the means of the corner of a napkin, or the fingers dipped into it, and it is then gently wiped off with a dry cloth

A simple and cheap Cosmetic is made as follows:—Soft soap, a half pound; melt over a slow fire with a gill of sweet oil; add half a teacupful of fine sand, and stir the mixture together until cold. The shelly sea-sand, sifted from the shells, has been found better than that which has no shells.

Piesse, in his Art of Perfumery, recommends Milk of Wax as one of the best Cosmetics. It is simple in its composition, all the ingredients being perfectly harmless, or non-medicinal; therefore its daily use will not produce any future injurious effects. Take virgin wax, oil of sweet almonds, spermaceti, and any fine white soap—of each a quarter of an ounce; of rose water, or elder-flower water, three-quarters of a pint; essence of lavender, or of real *Eau-de-Cologne,* three ounces. Cut up the soap into very small pieces, and place them with about a wine-glassful of water in a jug; put the jug in a saucepan, containing boiling water, at the side of the fire; in a few minutes all the soap will dissolve in the water; when this is done, put into the jug the oil, the spermaceti, and the wax, stirring the whole well together as the wax liquefies. Now very gradually, little by little, pour into these ingredients the remainder of the water; then allow the whole to cool, and add the scented spirit;

when perfume is not desired, plain spirit of wine will answer just as well as that which is called essence of lavender, &c. This operation done, the milk has only to be strained through book muslin to be ready for use.

"Yellow soap, and many of the common soaps, although very good for household cleansing purposes, are far too alkaline for use on "the human face divine;" hence many ladies reject the use of soap for the face on account of its irritating qualities; those who do so, will be much pleased with the emollient properties of the Milk of Wax."

COTTON IN LINEN. How to Detect.—One of the best methods is microscopic examination; for when flax is magnified three hundred times, it appears like long, compact tubes, with a narrow channel in the centre; while cotton appears to be flattened, ribbon-like cylinders, with a wide channel, and mostly in spiral windings.

The test with oil of vitriol is reliable in an experienced hand, but every trace of weaver's gum must have been previously removed by boiling with water. The fibres are laid on a plate of glass, and oil of vitriol dropped on it. A single lens is sufficient to observe the effect. In a short time the cotton fibre is dissolved, the flax unaltered, or only the finest fibres attacked.

The oil test is also a good one, and convenient in execution. When flaxen fibres are rubbed up with olive-oil, they appear transparent, like oiled paper, while cotton, under similar circumstances, remains white and opake. Dyed goods exhibit the same, if previously bleached by chloride of lime.

Elsner's method consists in putting the fibres for a few minutes into a tincture of various red dyes, of which cochineal and madder give the most striking results. The tincture is made by putting one pint of madder, &c., into twenty pints of common alcohol for twenty-four hours. In the cochineal tincture, cotton is colored bright-red; flax, violet;—in madder, cotton becomes light-yellow; pure flax, yellowish-red.

It is better to employ several of these tests, the microscopic, oil, sulphuric acid, and combustion, rather than to rely upon a single test.

DRUNKENNESS. A Cure for.—Dr. Kain recommends *Tartar emetic* for the cure of habitual drunkenness. He says:

"My method of prescribing it has varied according to the habit, age, and constitution of the patient. I give it only in alterative and slightly-nauseating doses. A convenient preparation of the medicine is eight grains dissolved in four ounces of boiling water; half an ounce of the solution to be put into a half pint or quart of the patient's favorite liquor, and to be taken daily in divided portions. If severe vomiting and purging ensue, I should direct laudanum, to allay the irritation, and diminish the dose. In every patient it should be varied according to its effects. In one instance, in a patient who lived ten miles from me, severe vomiting was produced; more, I think, from excessive drinking than the use of the remedy. He recovered from it, however, without any bad effects."

The following singular means of curing habitual drunkenness is employed by a Russian physician, Dr. Schreiber, of Brzese Litewski; it consists in confining the drunkard in a room, and furnishing him at discretion with his favorite spirit diluted with water; as much wine, beer, and coffee, as he desires, but containing one-third spirit; all the food, the bread, meat, and *legumes* are steeped in spirit and water. The poor devil is continually drunk and *dort.* On the fifth day of this regime, he has an extreme disgust for spirit; he earnestly requests other diet, but his desire must not be yielded to; until the poor wretch no longer desires to eat or drink; he is then certainly cured of his *penchant* for drunkenness. He acquires such a disgust for brandy, or other spirits, that he is ready to vomit at the first sight of it.—(*Bulletin de Therapeutic.*)

To cure *Delirium Tremens*, the jail physician of Chicago, Illinois, employs ipecacuanha, and says: "Ipecacuanha, which I have tried in thirty-six cases, I found most remarkably successful, quieting the nervous system, exciting the appetite, acting on secretions, and uniformly producing sleep. When a case is not of too long standing, I give it as an emetic, the first dose; and afterward I give from fifteen to eighteen grains every other hour. Connected with this remedy, I use shower-baths, and let the patient frequently drink strong beef tea, without any alcoholic stimulants."

EDGED TOOLS. How to Sharpen without Whetting.—It has long been known that the simplest method of sharpening a razor is to put it for half an hour in water, to which has been added one twentieth of its weight of muriatic or sulphuric acid, then lightly wipe it off, and after a few hours set it on a hone. The acid here supplies the place of a whetstone, by corroding the whole surface uniformly, so that nothing further but a smooth polish is necessary

The process never injures good blades, while badly hardened ones are frequently improved by it, although the cause of such improvement remains unexplained. Of late, this process has been applied to many other cutting implements. The workman, at the beginning of his noon-spell, or when he leaves off in the evening, moistens the blades of his tools with water acidified as above, the cost of which is almost nothing. This saves the consumption of time and labor in whetting, which, moreover, speedily wears out the blades. The mode of sharpening here indicated would be found especially advantageous for sickles and scythes.

ENGRAVINGS, BOOKS, ETC. HOW TO WHITEN.—They may be whitened by being first subjected to the action of weak chloride of lime water, next to water soured with sulphuric acid, and, lastly, to pure water, to remove any adhering acid or chlorine.

FIGS. HOME-MADE.—Peaches to be pealed, cut in two, the pit taken out: make a thin syrup of sugar and water, put the peaches in while the syrup is warm or hot, and nearly boil for a few minutes; then take them out and place in a slow oven till dry. Said to be better than true figs.

FIRE KINDLER. A CHEAP.—Melt three pounds of rosin in a quart of tar, and stir in as much sawdust and pulverized charcoal as you can, and then spread the mass upon a board till cool, and then break it into lumps as big as your thumb. You can light it with a match, and it will light a fire, for it burns with a strong blaze. It is economical of time and money, It may cost three shillings, and save ten shillings' worth of wood.

FIRE-PROOF DRESSES. HOW TO MAKE.—Many ladies have been burnt to death, by their light gauze and cambric dresses taking fire and blazing up before there was time to extinguish the flames. Actresses and danseuses are most liable to this; and the talented Clara Webster and others lost their lives this way. It ought, therefore, to be generally known that, by steeping the dress, or material composing it, in a diluted solution of chloride of zinc, it will be rendered perfectly fire-proof. Our manufacturers should take the hint.—(*Scientific Am.*)

GINGER POP.—This is an article which has long been in use; but, owing to some cause, the proper mode of making it has been only understood by persons who manufactured it on a very large scale, and endeavored to blind the public by saying that there was great secresy in making the genuine article. But be that as it may, if there is any great secret about it, or has been heretofore, it is all at an end now; for here is the process of making as good an article of "ginger pop," as any of them can make that are keeping the streets in a perfect uproar with their wagons, supplying the grocers and others. Their reason for trying to keep the information from the public on this point is, that they fear too many will be in the business, and the profits, of course, greatly reduced. It is made thus:—

Take crushed (white) sugar, twenty-eight pounds; water, one barrel; yeast, one pint; powdered ginger (fine), one pound; essence of lemon, half an ounce; essence of cloves, a quarter of an ounce. To the ginger pour half a gallon of boiling water; let stand for fifteen or twenty minutes; dissolve the sugar in two gallons of warm water. Pour each of these into a barrel half filled with cold water; then add the essences of lemon and cloves, and the yeast. Let stand for half an hour, when the barrel should be filled with cold water. When sufficiently fermented, it is poured into bottles and corked tightly, until wanted for use. It will generally be sufficiently fermented in the course of a few hours.—(*Practical Brewer.*)

[For a description of the process of making Cider or Beer according to the Bavarian method, from the *Chinese Sugar-cane*, see *Olcott's Sorgho.*]

GLASS STOPPLES. How to Extract.—When the glass stopple will not come out, pass a strip of woolen cloth around the neck of the decanter, etc., and then "see-saw" backward and forward, so that the friction may heat it; this will cause expansion, and the neck becoming larger than the stopple, the latter will drop out, or may be easily withdrawn. A tight screw may be easily loosened from a metal socket, by heating the latter by means of a cloth wet with boiling water, or in any other way, on the simple principle of expansion by heat.

GUNS. Secrets of Loading and Shooting.—Mr. Maceroni instructs us that the jargon about one maker's gun shooting further, another "closer," another "sharper," another "wider," is all invented by the sellers. A twenty-five shilling gun, with a straight barrel and correct, smooth cylinder, will shoot as well as a twenty-five pounder, if equally well pointed. But the greenhorns are made to believe that Mr. A., B., or C., can sell them a costly gun that *must kill*, whether they load or aim properly or not! An important point in the use of bird-shot, in gunning, is the due proportion of it to the gun and powder. Most shooters overload their piece with shot. The rule is, that the shot should be equal to the weight of the ball that would fit the gun. If ever a gun gets so foul (in dry weather) that the wads descend with difficulty, put half a charge, or less, of powder into it, and then a turnip-leaf or wet grass, and working it about with the ramrod, fire it off, so as to clean a great portion of the barrel.

The charge of shot used by most sportsmen is about double what it ought to be; whilst the windage excited by their improper wadding, deprives it of a great portion of the powder's blast, besides causing it to be unduly dispersed. Less than the weight of the ball that fits the gun is better than more. And the wad is all-important. Over the shot a bit of paper or oakum, sufficient to retain it, will be enough. Two drachms of powder, one ounce of shot, *a cork*, or *two metallic* wads, will do good service at sixty to eighty yards; so will one hundred duck-shot kill well at one hundred yards.

HAIR. Lotions for. — Erasmus Wilson, in his "Treatise on Cutaneous Diseases," furnishes the following two receipts for hair preparations:

Take eau de cologne, two ounces; tincture of cantharides, half an ounce; and add twenty drops of the oil of lavender.

Take vinegar of cantharides, half an ounce; eau de cologne and rose-water, each half an ounce.

The following are said to be receipts of those who make these articles for sale:

Take an ounce of castor oil, mix it thoroughly with a pint of alcohol, and add half an ounce of the tincture of cantharides.

Sulphuric ether, one ounce; tincture of cantharides, one ounce; olive oil, one ounce; alcohol, one pint.

HAIR. Dyes for the.—All dyes only color to the root of the hair; they must therefore be applied as often as the natural hair grows out and shows itself. The cheapest hair dyes are powders, principally composed of lime and an oxide of lead. The following, from the *Scientific American*, is one of these:

Take two ounces of powdered litharge, half an ounce of calcined magnesia, and half an ounce of powdered slacked lime. They are mixed intimately together, and are ready to be applied by reducing them to a cream-like consistency with soft water. When thus made into a paste, it is laid on the hair in a good coating, and then covered up with a silk handkerchief. The best time to apply it is before going to bed. In the morning it has to be rubbed off with a hard brush, for it sticks like mortar, and is a disagreeable, although an effectual dye. The hair is rendered harsh by it, and has to be softened with grease or oil. It is too troublesome for coloring the hair on the head, but may answer for dyeing the whiskers. This is the white powder sold for dyeing hair.

Another receipt, of the same kind, is as follows:—Take one ounce of litharge, two ounces of carbonate or white lead, and three ounces of powdered quick-lime. It is applied in the same manner as the former. Litharge and lime alone will also color the hair.

The hair dyes, principally composed of nitrate of silver, are the most convenient and best. This salt of silver, when applied in solution to the hair, and exposed to light, converts it either into a dark brown or black, according to the strength of the solution; but it possesses the defect of staining the skin while it colors the hair. This result, however, can be avoided if moderate care is exercised, as we shall describe:—

Take twenty grains of gallic acid, and dissolve them in an ounce of water in an ounce vial; then take twenty grains nitrate of silver, and dissolve them in half an ounce of soft water, to which should be added a weak solution of gum Arabic or starch, and forty drops of ammonia, so as to fill an ounce vial. The gallic acid is now applied to the hair with a sponge, and allowed to dry; the nitrate of silver solution is then applied in the same manner, and allowed to dry under exposure to bright light. In about ten minutes let the hair be washed, and it is found to be colored from gray to a dark brown. This is a good dye; and although it colors the finger nails and the hair, it scarcely stains the skin—the gum Arabic and gallic acid preventing it from doing this. Considerable of the coloring matter is washed off loosely, but enough is taken up by the capillary tubes to dye the hair. The ammonia may be omitted, and a weak solution of the hydro-sulphuret used as a wash upon the top of the silver, after the latter has been on about five minutes. This is called the "Magic Hair Dye," because it is so rapid in its action. Either ammonia, or hydro-sulphuret of ammonia, is necessary to color gray hair black; a strong solution of galls or sumac may be substituted for the gallic acid. The sulphuret of potassium (in solution) may be substituted for the gallic acid, the ammonia, and sulphuret of ammonia, by applying it to the hair first, and then allowing it to dry before the silver solution is put on. It has a disagreeable odor, however; but this may be counteracted by a perfume, such as oil of bergamot, lavender, or rose-water. In applying any nitrate of silver solution to the hair, some care should be exercised to prevent it touching the skin.

To remove superfluous Hair.—The following is said to be an effectual depilatory:—

Delacroix's Poudre Subtile.—Orpiment, one part; finely powdered quick-lime and starch, of each eleven parts; mix. It should be kept from the air. For use, make it into a paste with a little warm water, and apply it to the part, previously shaved close. As soon as it has become thoroughly dry, it may be washed off with a little warm water.

HORSES. RAREY'S METHOD OF TAMING.—In all countries there have been persons who possess a peculiar power in taming animals.

This has generally been effected by means of scents—of the Oil of Rhodium, in particular, most animals are very fond. The following receipt is said to be very efficacious for taming horses :—

Procure some horse castor, and grate it fine. Also, get some oil of rhodium and oil of cumin, and keep the three separate, in air-tight bottles. Rub a little oil of cumin upon your hand, and approach the horse in the field, on the windward side, so that he can smell the cumin. The horse will let you come up to him then without any trouble. Immediately rub your hand gently on the horse's nose, getting a little of the oil upon it. You can then lead him any where you please. Give him a little of the castor on a piece of loaf sugar, apple, or potato. Put eight drops of oil of rhodium into a lady's silver thimble. Take the thimble between the thumb and middle finger of your right hand, with the forefinger stopping the mouth of the thimble, to prevent the oil from running out whilst you are opening the mouth of the horse. As soon as you have opened the horse's mouth, tip the thimble over upon his tongue. He is your servant. He will follow you like a pet dog.

During the last two or three years, a Mr. Rarey has made a fortune by teaching the wealthy men of England how to tame horses, and the following is his secret, as given in the *Tribune*:—

Choking a horse is the first process in taming, and is but the beginning of his education. By its operation a horse becomes docile, and will thereafter receive any instruction which he can be made to understand. Teaching the animal to lie down at our bidding, tends to keep him permanently cured, as it is perpetual reminder of his subdued condition.

It requires a good deal of practice to tame a horse successfully ; also a nice judgment to know when he is choked sufficiently, as there is a bare possibility that he might get more than would be good for him. We advise persons not perfectly familiar with a horse to resort rather to the strapping and throwing down process (unless he is very vicious) described below ; this, in ordinary cases, will prove successful. It is the fault of most people, who have owned a horse, to imagine that they are experts in his management ; while, on the contrary, many professional horsemen are the very worst parties to attempt his subjugation. Unless a man have a good disposition, he need not attempt horse-taming.

Retire with the animal to be operated on to a stable having plenty of litter upon the floor (tan-bark or sawdust is preferable). In the first place, fasten up the left fore-leg with the arm strap, in such a manner that it will be permanently secured. Then take a broad strap and buckle, and pass it around the neck just back of the jaw bone. Draw the strap as tight as possible, so tight as to almost arrest the horse's breathing. The strap must not be buckled, but held in this position to prevent slipping back. The animal will struggle for a few minutes, when he will become perfectly quiet, overpowered by a sense of suffocation; the veins in his head will swell; his eyes lose their fire; his knees totter and become weak; a slight vertigo will ensue, and growing gradually exhausted, by backing him around the stable, he will come down on his knees, in which position it is an easy matter to push him on his side, when his throat should be released. Now pat and rub him gently for about twenty minutes, when, in most instances, he will be subdued. It is only in extreme cases necessary to repeat the operation of choking. The next lesson is to teach him to lie down, which is described below in the account of the second method of taming. No horse can effectually resist the terrible effects of being choked.

It must be constantly borne in mind that the operator must not be boisterous or violent, and that the greatest possible degree of kindness is absolutely essential. When the horse is prostrate, he should be soothed until his eyes show that he has become perfectly tranquil.

Another method.—Buckle or draw a strap tight around the neck, lift a fore-leg and fasten around it the opposite end of the strap; the shorter the better. It will be seen that in this plan the horse is made the instrument by which the punishment is inflicted. When he attempts to put his foot down his head goes with it, and he thus chokes himself; care should be taken that he does not pitch on his head, and thus endanger his neck.

Taming a Horse without resort to Straps.—Secure the horse with a stout halter to the manger. If extremely unruly, muzzle him. Soothe him with the hands for a few minutes until he becomes somewhat pacified. Then seize him by the throat, close to the jaw-bone, with the right hand, and by the mane with the left. Now forcibly compress his windpipe until he becomes so exhausted that, by lightly kicking him on the fore-legs, he will lie down, after which he should be treated as previously described. This process requires courage in the operator, and also great muscular strength.

Another method of taming a Horse; also, to teach him to lie down.—The horse to be operated upon should be led into a close stable. The operator should be previously provided with a stout leather halter; a looped strap to slip over the animal's knee; a strong surcingle, and a long and short strap—the first to fasten round the fore-foot which is at liberty, and the second to permanently secure the leg which is looped up.

In the first place, if the horse be a biter, muzzle him; then lift and bend his left fore-leg, and slip a loop over it. The leg which is looped up must be secured by applying the short strap, buckling it around the pastern joint and fore-arm; next put on the surcingle, and fasten the long strap around the right fore-foot, and pass the end through a loop attached to the surcingle; after which fasten on a couple of thick leather knee-pads—these can be put on in the first place, if convenient. The pads are necessary, as some horses in their struggles come violently on their knees, abrading them badly. Now take a short hold of the long strap with your right hand; stand on the left side of the horse, grasp the bit in your left hand; while in this position back him gently about the stable until he becomes so exhausted as to exhibit a desire to lie down, which desire should be gratified with as little violence as possible; bear your weight firmly against the shoulder of the horse, and pull steadily on the strap with your right hand; this will force him to raise his foot, which should be immediately pulled from under him. This is the critical moment; cling to the horse, and after a few struggles he will lie down. In bearing against the animal do not desist from pulling and pushing until you have him on his side. Prevent him from attempting to rise by pulling his head toward his shoulder. As soon as he has done struggling, caress his face and neck; also, handle every part of his body, and render yourself as familiar as possible. After he has lain quietly for twenty minutes let him rise, and immediately repeat the operation, removing the straps as soon as he is down; and if his head is pulled toward his shoulder it is impossible for him to get up. After throwing him from two to five times, the animal will become as submissive and abject as a well-trained dog, and you need not be afraid to indulge in any liberties with him. A young horse is subdued much quicker than an old one, as his habits are not confirmed. An incorrigible horse should have two lessons a day; about the fourth lesson he will be permanently conquered.

How to break a Colt.—Before putting a halter upon a colt, he must be rendered familiar with it by caressing him and permitting him to examine the article with his nose. Then place a portion of it over his head, occasionally giving it a slight pull, and in a few minutes he will be accustomed to these liberties, and then the halter may be fastened on properly. To teach him to lead is another difficulty. Stand a little on one side, rub his nose and forehead, take hold of the strap and pull gently, and at the same time touch him very lightly with the end of a long whip across his hind legs. This will make him start and advance a few steps. Repeat the operation several times, and he will soon learn to follow you by simply pulling the halter. The process of saddling and bridling is similar. The mouth of the colt should be frequently handled, after which introduce a plain snaffle between his teeth, and hold it there with one hand and caress him with the other. After a time, he will allow the bridle to be placed upon him. The saddle can now be brought in and rubbed against his nose, his neck and his legs; next hang the stirrup strap across his back, and gradually insinuate the saddle into its place. The girth should not be fastened until he becomes thoroughly acquainted with the saddle. The first time the girth is buckled, it should be done so loosely as not to attract his attention; subsequently it can be tightened without inspiring him with fear, which if fastened immediately it would most certainly do. In this manner the wildest colt can be effectually subjugated by such imperceptible degrees that he gives tacit obedience before he is aware of his altered condition.

How to tell a Kicking Horse.—When you go to harness a horse that you know nothing about, if you want to find out whether he is a kicking horse or not, you can ascertain that fact by stroking him in the flank where the hair lies upward, which you can discover easily on any horse; just stroke him down with the ends of your fingers, and if he does not switch his tail, and shake his head, and lay back his ears, or some of these, you need not fear his kicking; if he does any or all of these, set him down for a kicking horse, and watch him closely.

How to subdue a Kicking Horse.—When you harness a kicking horse have a strap about three feet long, with a buckle on one end; have several holes punched in the strap; wrap it once around his leg just above the hoof; lift up his foot touching his body; put the strap around the arm of his leg, and buckle it ; then you can go behind him, and pull back on the traces ; you must not fear his kicking while his foot is up, for it is impossible for him to do it. Practice him in this way a while, and he will soon learn to walk on three legs. You should not hitch him up until you have practiced him with his leg up two or three times, pulling on the traces, and walking him along. After you have practiced him a few times in this way, take up his foot as directed ; hitch him to something, and cause him to pull it a short distance ; then take him out ; caress him every time you work with him. You will find it more convenient to fasten up his left fore-foot, because that is the side you are on. After you have had him hitched up once or twice, you should get a long strap ; put it around his foot as before directed (above the hoof and below the pastern-joint) ; put it through a ring in your harness ; take hold of it in your hand ; hitch him up gently, and if he makes a motion to kick, you can pull up his foot and prevent it. You should use this strap until you have him broken from kicking, which will not take very long. You should hitch a kicking horse by himself ; you can manage him better in this way than to hitch him by the side of another horse.

To break a Horse from Scaring.—He says, let the animal see the object and touch it with his nose. Try him with an umbrella. *To teach a horse to follow you.*—Take him into a large stable or shed, with the bridle or halter in your left hand, and a long switch or whip in your right ; after caressing him a little, put your right hand over his shoulder, with the whip extending back, so that you can touch him up with it gently around his hind legs. Start him up a little, saying, "*Come along, boy,*" and take him around the stable a few times, holding him by the bridle. In a short time he will follow you without the bridle ; then take him into a lot, and continue practicing in the same way, and he will soon like to follow you. *To teach him to stand without hitching,* practice him first in the centre of the stable. Begin fondling him gently at the head, working gradually backward ; and if he move, give him a cut with the whip, and put him back in the same spot from which he started. If he stand, caress him. Do not practice him longer than a half an hour at a time.

HYDROPHOBIA, A CURE FOR.—A man was cured of Hydrophobia in Italy, lately, by swallowing vinegar in mistake for a medicinal potion. A physician at Padria heard of this and tried the remedy on a patient; he gave him a pint of vinegar in the morning, another at noon, and a third at sunset, which cured him.

In Bohemia, there is a man by the name of Schweida, living at Bey, who notoriously cures this terrible disorder.

Prince Joseph de Schwarzenberg, from motives of humanity, bought his secret, to give it to the profession. After many happy cures by it, the prince gave a house and lands to Schweida for life. The remedy is a powder and bathing. It had been known many years before in the vicinity of Frauenberg, by the name of *Powder of Bubutsky*, and that all cases of Hydrophobia were cured by it. Persons bitten by mad dogs, and having the malady, were cured thirty-five years ago, and no symptoms have ever been felt since. The powder is made of *Italian Poplar leaves*, Pennyroyal, and Savory.

Poplar leaves, ...2 ounces.
Pennyroyal, ...4 "
Savory, ...4 "

The whole must be reduced to a powder, well mixed, kept in a vial well corked. A dose of it is given in good sweet oil, mixed with it until its consistence is somewhat soft. Put as much as lies on the point of a knife into a *pint of beer*, warmed, and drink it three times a day. For a mad dog, mix the powder in half a pint of milk; for horses, spread it on a piece of bread; for other domestic animals, mix it with their ordinary drink. After giving the remedy, give no food whatever for many hours. The bath is prepared by putting the same constituents in it. Let the bath be tepid, that is, lukewarm.

ICE-CREAM. How to Make.—The richest quality of Ice-cream is made from cream in the following manner:—To one quart of cream use the yelks of three eggs. Put the cream over the fire till it boils, during which time the eggs are beaten up with half a pound of white sugar, powdered fine; and when the cream boils, stir it upon the eggs and sugar, then let it stand till quite cold; then add the juice of three or four lemons. It is then ready to be put into the freezer. The heat of the cream partially cooks the eggs, and the stirring must be continued to prevent their cooking too much. A somewhat simpler receipt, given by the confectioners, is the following: To half a pound of powdered sugar add the juice of three lemons. Mix the sugar and lemons together, and then add one quart of cream. This is less rich and delicate than the preceding one, but is quite rich enough for common use, and some trouble is saved.

The following receipt makes a very good Ice-cream :—

Two quarts of good *rich* milk, four fresh eggs, three quarters of a pound of white sugar, six teaspoonsful of Bermuda arrow root. Rub the arrow root smooth in a little cold milk, beat the eggs and sugar together, bring the milk to the boiling point, and then stir in the arrow root; remove it then from the fire, and immediately add the eggs and sugar, stirring briskly to keep the eggs from cooking; then set aside to cool. If flavored with extracts, let it be done *just before* putting it in the freezer. If the Vanilla bean is used, it must be boiled in the milk. The preparation must be *thoroughly cooled* before the freezing is proceeded with. The Ice-cream, by this receipt, may be produced at a cost not exceeding twenty-five cents a quart—calling the milk five cents a quart, and the eggs a cent a piece, and including the cost of labor. It is quite equal to that commonly furnished by the confectioners at seventy-five cents a quart. The arrow root may be dispensed with. The freezer is a cheap and simple machine.

After the Cream has frozen in the machine it should stand one hour or two to harden, before it is used. (*C. L. Flint.*)

INKS.—Dr. Stark, a Scotch Chemist, has experimented with more than two hundred different kinds of Inks, and his conclusion is, that no preparation equals the common sulphate of iron, or commercial copperas for ink-making. His receipt for a persistent Black Ink is six parts of the best blue galls to four parts of copperas.

A beautiful Blue-black Ink, that will *not corrode steel pens*, may be made by boiling one hundred and twenty-five parts rasped logwood with so much water that it will yield one thousand pints of decoction, and when cold, stir in one part yellow chromate of potassa.

Red Ink.—Ground Brazil wood, eight ounces; vinegar, ten pints; macerate for four or five days; boiled in a tinned copper vessel to one half; then add roach alum, eight ounces, and gum, three ounces; dissolve. Water or beer may be used instead of vinegar.

Inks of various colors may be made from a strong decoction of the ingredients used in dyeing, mixed with a little alum and gum Arabic. Any of the water-color cakes employed in drawing, diffused through water, may be used for colored Inks.

Indelible Ink.—Nitrate of silver, quarter of an ounce; hot distilled water, three-quarters of an ounce; when cooled a little, add mucilage, quarter of an ounce; and sap green or syrup of buckthorn to color; mix well. The linen must be first moistened with "*liquid pounce*," or "*the preparation*," as it is commonly called, dried, and then written on with a clean quill pen. This Ink will bear dilution, if not wanted very black.

The Pounce, or "Preparation."—Carbonate of soda, one ounce to one and a half ounces; water, one pint; color with a little sap-green or syrup of buckthorn.

Without Preparation.—Nitrate of silver, one to two drachms; water, three quarters of an ounce; dissolve; add as much of the strongest ammonia water as will dissolve the precipitate formed on its first addition; then further add mucilage one or two drachms, and a little sap-green to color. Writing, executed with this ink, turns black on being passed over a hot Italian iron.

To remove Spots of Indelible Ink.—T. and H. Smith propose moistening the spots for a few moments with moist chloride of lime, which forms chloride of silver, and then dissolving the latter by caustic ammonia. It may be sometimes necessary to repeat the operation. Cyanide of potassium may also be employed.

Ink stains may be readily removed from white articles by means of a little salt of lemons, dilute muriatic acid, oxalic acid, or tartaric acid and hot water; or by means of a little solution of chlorine, or chloride of lime. The spots should be *thoroughly* rinsed in warm water before touching them with soap. *Marking Ink* may be removed by ammonia water, solution of chloride of lime, liquid chlorine or iodine.

Invisible Ink.—Rice-water and iodine. The plan of writing with rice-water, to be rendered visible by the application of iodine, was practiced with great success in the correspondence with Jellalabad. The first letter of this kind received from thence was concealed in a quill. On opening it a small paper was unfolded, on which appeared a single word, "Iodine." The magic liquor was applied, and an interesting dispatch from Sir Robert Sale stood forth.—*Major Smith's United Service Magazine.*

JUJUBE PASTE.—The Jujube plant has been recently introduced into this country. The following receipt for making Jujube Paste, is furnished by the United States Patent Office :—

Take jujubes one pound, and water two quarts ; boil half an hour, strain with expression, settle, decant the clear, and clarify with white of eggs ; add a strained solution of gum Arabic, six pounds in four quarts of water ; add to the mixture six pounds of white sugar ; gently evaporate, at first constantly stirring, and afterward without stirring, till reduced to the consistence of soft extract; add orange-flower water six ounces, and place the pan in a vessel of boiling water. In twelve hours carefully remove the scum ; pour the matter into slightly oiled tin moulds.

LEPROSY.—Count de Segur, in his travels, states, that in South America, a lizard cut into small pieces, and administered perseveringly for about three weeks, is considered a remedy for the Leprosy. It is supposed to operate by causing very strong sweats, and a desire to discharge saliva, whereby the blood becomes more pure. Hydrophobia, it is said, has also been cured in the same way.

OILS AND TALLOW. How to Bleach by Chromic Acid.—Mr. C. Watt, Sen., uses the following method for bleaching dark oils or tallow. To every half ton of oil take ten pounds bichromate of potassa. Powder the salt, dissolve it in four pints of hot water, stir, and carefully add fifteen pounds sulphuric acid, and continue the stirring until complete solution. This mixture is then thoroughly incorporated with the melted fat, previously separated from foreign matters by repose and decantation. The containing vessels should be of wood, and the temperature about 135° F. When, after much agitation, the liquid fat assumes a light-green color, the bleaching is completed, and four buckets of boiling water are then to be added, the whole stirred for five minutes and then left to repose for several hours, when it will be white and ready for use.

Mr. Watts, Jr., proposes to recover the chromic acid *ad infinitum*, and thus render the process very economical, in manner as follows. Transfer the green chrome liquor, after the separation of the fat, to a tub, dilute it with water, and then add thick milk of lime until the sulphuric acid is nearly saturated ; leave to repose, decant the liquor from the sulphate of lime, and carefully add to it another portion of cream of lime, until the precipitation of all the green oxide, and the supernatant liquor is clear and colorless. Drain off this liquor, add fresh water, and, after settling, again decant. Repeat this washing, then transfer the precipitate to a red-hot iron slab, and keep it constantly stirred until it changes to a yellow powder.

The chromate of lime, thus formed, if decomposed by sulphuric acid in slight excess, yields chromic acid as well suited for bleaching purposes as that from bichromate of potassa.

OIL-FILTER—A good oil filter is said to be made of fine sand, charcoal, and gypsum; the sand to retain substances suspended in the oil, charcoal to decolorize it, and plaster to remove water.

PASTE FOR ENVELOPES.—Mix, in equal quantities, gum (substitute, dextrine) and water in a vial; place it near a stove, or on a furnace register, and stir or shake it well; it will soon dissolve, and is then fit for use. A little alcohol added after it is well mixed, will prevent it from becoming sour, and keep it any length of time. This is better and much cheaper than any of the gums used for labels and envelopes, and does not crack.

POISONS, AND THEIR ANTIDOTES.—Oxalic acid, or salt of lemons, is often mistaken for Epsom Salts, and causes death in a short time; a safe antidote for this, and all other acids, is magnesia made into a paste with water, or a solution of common soap. In the case of prussic acid, however, laurel-water, or chloride of lime, and bichloride of iron, are effectual remedies. Tartar emetic is another poison, often taken designedly or in mistake; large quantities of warm water should be given to induce vomiting, and also powdered Peruvian bark.

For arsenic, the hydrated oxide of iron is the only cure, in a dose thirty times greater than that of the poison; while for poisoning by lead, in any form, sulphate of magnesia, potash, and soda are good, and phosphate of soda is a safe antidote. Mercury, or corrosive sublimate, is counteracted by the white of eggs, or milk; and for sulphate of zinc, or white vitriol, cream, butter, and chalk, will act as preventives. For poisoning by copper, the whites of eggs; iron filings, prussiate of potash will stay its action; and for sulphuretted hydrogen and carbonic acid, free exposure to the air, and a leech or two applied on the head, have proved successful. For all other poisons, such as fungi, poisonous mushrooms, laudanum, strychnine, nux vomica, and vegetables generally, it is always safe to administer an emetic.

SERPENT BITES.—Perry, in his "Japan Expedition," p. 119, refers to a remedy for venomous bites, for which, he says, popular opinion in the East claims considerable efficacy. This is a paste made by moistening the powder of ipecacuhana with water, and applying it to the external injury. "Some wonderful effects have been reported from the use of this simple means in various cases of not only bites from venomous Serpents, but of stings by the Scorpion, and various poisonous fish."

In South America, the most popular remedy is the leaves of *Guaco*, or Snake-plant, a species of willow which flourishes along the banks of streams in the sultry regions shaded by other trees. It is said to be both a preventive and a cure.

SCROFULA.—N. Longworth, of Cincinnati, says he has done wonders in curing Scrofula, and old sores, with the following Receipt: Put one ounce of aquafortis in a bowl, or saucer; drop into it two copper cents—it will effervesce—leave the cents in; when the effervescence ceases, add two ounces of strong vinegar. The fluid will be of a dark-green color. It should and will smart. If too severe, put in a little rain-water. Apply it to the sore, morning and evening, by a soft brush or a rag. Before applying it, wash the sore with water.

SOUPS. CHEAP.—SOYER, the celebrated Cook, in his "Culinary Campaign," furnishes a number of valuable receipts for Soups, etc., of which the following are particularly recommended for the poor, and to those who have charge of charitable associations:—No. 1. *For two gallons of Soup, costing about one cent a quart*, viz.: Take two ounces of drippings; quarter of a pound of solid meat, at four pence per pound, cut into pieces one inch square; quarter pound of onions, sliced thin; quarter pound of turnips; (the peel will do, or one whole one cut into small slices); two ounces of leeks—the green tops will do—sliced thin; three ounces of celery; three quarters of a pound of common flour; half a pound of pearl barley, or one pound of Scotch; three ounces of salt; quarter of an ounce of brown sugar; two gallons of water. I first put two ounces of dripping into a saucepan, capable of holding two gallons of water, with a quarter of a pound of leg-beef without bones, cut into square pieces of about an inch; and two middling-sized onions, peeled and sliced; I then set the saucepan over a coal fire, and stirred the contents around for a few minutes with a wooden (or iron) spoon until fried lightly brown. I had then, ready-washed, the peelings of two turnips, fifteen green leaves or tops of celery, and the green part of two leeks (the whole of which, I must observe, are always thrown away). Having cut the above vegetables into small pieces, I threw them into a saucepan with the other ingredients, stirring them occasionally over the fire for another ten minutes; then added one quart of cold water, and three-quarters of a pound of common flour, and half a pound of pearl barley, mixing all well together; I then added seven quarts of hot water, seasoned with three ounces of salt, and a quarter of an ounce of brown sugar, stirred occasionally until boiling, and allowed it to simmer very gently for three hours; at the end of which time I found the barley perfectly tender. The above Soup has been tasted by numerous noblemen, Members of Parliament, and several ladies, who have lately visited my kitchen department, and who have considered it very good and nourishing.

The Soup will keep several days when made as above described; but I must observe, not to keep it in a deep pan, but within a flat vessel, where the air could act freely upon it. Stir it now and then until nearly cold, or, otherwise, the next day it will be in a state of fermentation. This does not denote the weakness of the Soup, because the same evil exists with the strongest of stock, or sauce, if not stirred, or confined in a warm place (a fact known to every first-rate cook). The expenses may come to three farthings per quart in London; but as almost every thing can be had at less cost in the country, the price of the Soup will be still more reduced. In that case, a little additional meat might be used. By giving away a small portion of bread or biscuit, better support would be given to the poor at a trifling cost; and no one, it is to be hoped, hereafter would hear of the dreadful calamity of starvation.

No. 2. *Same Cost.*—Quarter of a pound of beef, cut into pieces one inch square; two ounces of dripping, or melted suet; quarter of a pound of turnips, or carrots, cut into fragments half an inch square; four drops of essence; one and a half pounds of maize flour; three ounces of salt; quarter ounce of brown sugar; one teaspoonful of black pepper, ground fine. Take two ounces of either dripping, American lard, or suet, to which add the turnips or carrots; fry for ten minutes; add one quart of cold water, and the meal, well mixing, and moisten by degrees with seven quarts of hot water; boil five hours, and season with three ounces of salt, one quarter ounce of brown sugar, one teaspoonful of black pepper, *two drops* of essence of garlic, *one drop* of essence of mint, a little celery, stir quickly, and serve directly.

No. 3. *Same as No.* 2—and add one pound of potatoes.

Having promised to make my receipts public for the benefit of the laborious classes of society, as well as for the poor, I think that if a man could treat his family, once a week, with a food called potato soup, each member of it, who had previously fed on that root, and who are *now* nearly deprived of that food, would worship the day of the week when such a luxury should be displayed on their humble table.

Jenny Lind's famous Soup, and which is supposed to be beneficial to the voice, was prepared as follows: "Wash quarter of a pound of the best pearl sago, until the water poured from it is clear; then stew it quite tender in water or thick broth (it will require nearly or quite a quart of liquid, which should be poured on it cold, and heated very slowly;) then mix gradually with it a pint of good boiling cream, and the yelks of four eggs, and mingle the whole carefully with two quarts of strong veal or beef stock, which should always be kept ready boiling. This Soup, it should be noticed, is not a soup whose virtues are bounded by the adaptation to the mere nourishing of our earthly tabernacles; they extend to the improvement of our vocal powers, and of our capacity to giving delight to our fellow-creatures; for to the influence of this soup it appears that part of the fascination of Jenny Lind's voice is owing. 'We were informed by Miss Bremer,' says Miss Acton, 'that Mademoiselle Lind was in the habit of taking this soup *before she sang*, as she found the sago and eggs soothing to the chest, and *beneficial* to the voice.'"

TIMBER. For Preserving.—The cheapest solution for preserving timber is sulphate of copper and alum. Steep the timber in this in a cask—one pound of each for twenty cubic feet of water—for a few days, then take it out and dry it well. It would be well to coat with tar, before you drive in your spiles; if boards, paint them with white lead. (*Scientific American.*)

TOOTHACHE.—"Silliman's Journal," 2d Ser., Vol. VII., 304, recommends gun-cotton for Toothache. It says gun-cotton, dissolved in ether, constituting what is called *collodion*, has become an important material for dressing incised wounds. It has been also ascertained, that it may be successfully used for the Toothache. The cavity of the tooth being cleaned out, a little asbestus saturated with collodion, to which a little morphia is added, is placed in it. All soon becomes solid; and thus an excellent stopping and a powerful anodyne are applied at the same time.

TOOTH-POWDERS.—The following is a safe and excellent receipt for tooth-powder : Fine chalk, two ounces ; powdered cuttle-fish, two ounces ; and powdered orris-root, one ounce ; mix all together. 1. Red bark and Armenian bole, of each one ounce ; powdered cinnamon, and bicarbonate of soda, of each half an ounce ; oil of cinnamon, two or three drops ; all in fine powder ; mix. 2. Substitute cassia for cinnamon ; and cream of tartar, carbonate of magnesia, or prepared chalk, for bicarbonate of soda. 3. (*Grosvenor's.*) Rose pink, three pounds ; orris-powder, half a pound ; oyster-shells, two and a half pounds ; oil of rhodium, twenty-five drops ; as above.

WATER, HARD. How to Soften.—Half an ounce of quick-lime put in nine quarts of water, and the clear solution put into a barrel of hard water, will make it soft when clear. A correspondent of the *Maine Farmer* states, that a teaspoonful of sal-soda will soften from three to four pails of hard water. This is a valuable receipt for housekeepers, and one which may be easily tested. Perinet has found that binoxide of manganese will preserve the sweetness of water for years. Sixty gallons of water, containing three pounds of the powdered binoxide, remained perfectly sweet and clear for seven years in a wooden vessel.

WINES, DOMESTIC. From other Fruits than the Grape.—The principles applied to making Wine from the grape are in general applicable to other fruits, yet certain peculiar circumstances require peculiar attention. Dr. Macculloch has given this subject a large share of attention, and is probably the best authority in the manufacture of Domestic Wines. He recommends the addition of tartar in preparing the *must*—say from two to six per cent., in proportion to the sweetness of the fruit and the quantity of added sugar —the sweetest *must* requiring most tartar.

The malic acid, which derives its name from its abundance in apples, is the predominant acid in our fruits, and, indeed, constitutes the chief difference between cider and wine. It might be a question for chemists, whether some means might not be contrived for getting rid of a portion of the malic acid, which is so detrimental to our Domestic Wines. Dr. Macculloch observes, that perhaps a hint might be taken from the manufacture of Sherry in Spain, in which lime is added to the grapes, which probably acts in neutralizing what portion of malic acid they may contain, or a part of the tartaric acid.

In proportioning the sugar according to the desired strength of the Wine, Dr. Macculloch gives the following rules: Two pounds of sugar added to a gallon of compound containing all the other ingredients requisite to a perfect fermentation, produce a liquor equal in strength to the lightest class of Bordeaux White Wines. Three pounds' produce are equal in strength to the Wine known by the name of White Hermitage; and from four, if fermented till dry, a Wine resembling in strength the strong Sicilian Wines—that of Massala, for example, or the Cape Madeira is produced.

One of the faults frequently occurring in our Domestic Wines is excessive sweetness, arising from too large a proportion of sugar having been employed, compared with that of the fruit juice—or from the imperfect fermentation which the fluid has undergone. But it is generally prudent to have the full quantity of sugar; for it is said that there is seldom such a balance of the two fermenting substances—the saccharine matter and the yeast—that both are perfectly neutralized; and it is not possible always to determine if this has been the case; for the palate is unable to detect a very small portion of sugar, as its taste is masked by that of the Wine: and the fermenting principle is still less ascertainable by the taste. If the Wine be sweet after the fermentation, it is evident that some sugar remains undecomposed, and that all the ferment has been expended. In this case the Wine will not turn sour immediately, particularly if it be strong, because there is no ferment to carry it on to the acetous stage. But if the Wine be light, that is, not strong, and the fermentation should have been carried on so far that the Wine is *dry*, that is not sweet, it is a proof that all the sugar has been expended; there is then great danger of its passing into the acetous state, and becoming vinegar. In this case, the addition of sugar *immediately* will prevent the change, as it will serve for the ferment to act upon; but should the acetous change have already begun, sugar will only accelerate instead of retarding it.

The proportion of water to be used in the prepared *must* is of great consequence; and Dr. Macculloch reprobates the current practice of using too great a quantity, and too little juice of the fruit—a custom apparently originating in a misplaced economy. In the practice of making wine from grapes in the wine countries, no water is used, but the whole fluid is composed of the juice of the fruit itself; but in the common practice, as recommended in the English domestic receipts, the juice of fruit rarely forms more than one-third of the whole liquor, and often much less; this proportion being also fixed without regard to the ripeness of the fruit. The artificial *must*, thus compounded of water, sugar and juice, contains in general too small a quantity of the fermenting principle so essential to a perfect fermentation; the fermentation is too slow, and only a small quantity of alcohol can be the result; hence the liquor is so weak that it soon changes into vinegar. When green fruit is used, in which little exists but acid and ferment, of which the former in this case exceeds, bulk for bulk, the quantity in ripe fruits, the acid would generally be too abundant, and would require a dilution with water.

Wines may be manufactured from all saccharine fruits, but we shall only give the receipt for Gooseberry Wine in *extenso*.

Gooseberry Wine, properly made, is perfectly durable; as much so as Champagne of corresponding strength, provided an equal care be taken in the bottling, cellarage, and other management, all of these being circumstances in which our domestic fabricators are too apt to fail.

The following

Dr. Macculloch's Receipt for Making Gooseberry Wine.—The fruit must be selected before it has shown the least tendency to ripen, but about the time when it has nearly attained its full growth. The particular variety of gooseberry is perhaps indifferent; but it will be advisable to avoid the use of those which in their ripe state have the highest flavor. The *Green Bath* is perhaps among the best. The smallest should be separated by a sieve properly adapted to this purpose, and any unsound or bruised fruit rejected: while the remains of the blossoms and fruit-stalks should be removed by friction or other means. Forty pounds of such fruit are then to be introduced into a tub carefully cleaned, and of the capacity of fifteen or twenty gallons, in which it is to be bruised in successive proportions, by a pressure sufficient to burst the berries without breaking the seed, or materially compressing the skins; four gallons of water are then to be poured into the vessel, and the contents are to be carefully stirred and squeezed in the hand, until the whole of the juice and pulp are separated from the solid matter. The materials are then to remain at rest from six to twenty-four hours, when they are to be strained through a coarse bag by as much force as can conveniently be applied to them. One gallon of fresh water may afterward be passed through the *marc*, for the purpose of removing any soluble matter which may have remained behind. Thirty or twenty-five pounds of white sugar are now to be dissolved in the juice thus procured, and the total bulk of the fluid made up with water to the amount of ten gallons and a half. If I name two quantities, it is because the fruit itself varies in quality, and it depends on the operator to distinguish. The old receipts allow forty pounds, of which the consequence is invariably a sweet Wine, while it fails of being brisk in nine out of ten cases. And the smaller proportion here given will most frequently insure a brisk wine, if the operator will but attend to the progress of fermentation, and the treatment as formerly described. The liquor thus obtained is the artificial *must*, which is equivalent to the juice of the grape—that is, made to resemble it as nearly as possible. It is now to be introduced into a tub of sufficient capacity, over which a blanket or similar substance, covered by a board, is to be thrown, the vessel being placed in a temperature varying from 55° to 60° Fah. Here it may remain for twelve or twenty-four hours, according to the symptoms of fermentation which it may show; and from this tub it is to be drawn off into a cask in which it is to ferment. When in the cask, it must be filled nearly to the bung-hole, that the scum which arises may be thrown out. As the fermentation proceeds, and the bulk of liquor in the cask diminishes, the superfluous portion of *must* which was made for this express purpose must be poured in, so as to keep the liquor still near the bung-hole. When the fermentation becomes a little more languid, as may be known by a diminution of the hissing noise, the bung is to be driven in, and a hole bored by its side, into which a wooden peg, called the *spile*, is to be fitted. After a few days this peg is to be loosened, that, if any material quantity of air has been generated it may have vent. The same trial must be made after successive intervals; and when there appears no longer any danger of extensive expansion, the spile may be permanently tightened.

"The Wine thus made must remain over the winter in a cool cellar, as it is no longer necessary to provoke the fermenting process. If the operator is not inclined to bestow any further labor or expense on it, it may be examined in some clear and cold day on toward the end of February, or beginning of March, when, if fine, as it will sometimes be, it may be bottled without further precautions. To insure its fineness, however, it is a better practice to decant it, toward the end of December, into a fresh cask, so as to clear it from the first lees. At this time also, the operator will be able to determine whether it is not too sweet for his views. In this case, instead of decanting it, he will stir up the lees, so as to renew the fermenting process; taking care also to increase the temperature at the same time. At whatever time the Wine has been decanted, it is to be fined the usual way with isinglass. Sometimes it is found expedient to decant it a second time into a fresh cask, and again to repeat the operation of fining. All these removals should be made in clear, dry, and if possible, cold weather. In any case, it must be bottled during the month of March. The Wines thus produced will generally be brisk, and similar in their qualities (flavor excepted) to the Wines of Champagne, with the strength of the best Sillery, if large portions of sugar have been used; but resembling the inferior kinds with the smaller allowance. Inattention, or circumstances which cannot be controlled, will cause it to be sweet, and still at other times to be dry. In the former case, it may be manufactured the following season, by adding to it that proportion of juice from fresh fruit which the operator's judgment may dictate, and renewing the fermentation and subsequent treatment as before. In the latter case, as its briskness can never be restored, it must be treated as dry Wine by decanting it into a sulphured cask, when it must be fined and bottled in the usual manner. Such dry Wines are occasionally disagreeable to the taste in the first or second year, but are much improved by keeping; nor ought they to be drank under five or six years."

Cooley gives the following receipt for making Wine from all ripe saccharine fruits: Ripe fruit, four pounds; clear soft water, one gallon; sugar, three pounds; cream of tartar, dissolved in boiling water, one and a quarter ounces; brandy two to three per cent. Flavoring as required; makes a good family wine. Using one pound more each of fruit and sugar makes a superior Wine. These receipts are adapted for making *Gooseberry Wine, Currant Wine, Cherry Wine, Elder Wine, Strawberry Wine, Mulberry Wine, Whortleberry Wine, Blackberry Wine, etc.*

www.ingramcontent.com/pod-product-compliance
Lightning Source LLC
LaVergne TN
LVHW011152110826
845150LV00006B/1219

9781425545826